Atlas of American Politics, 1960–2000

Atlas of American Politics, 1960–2000

J. Clark Archer, Stephen J. Lavin,

Kenneth C. Martis, and Fred M. Shelley

CQ PRESS

A Division of Congressional Quarterly Inc.
Washington, D.C.

CQ Press
A Division of Congressional Quarterly Inc.
1255 22nd Street, N.W., Suite 400
Washington, D.C. 20037

(202) 822-1475; (800) 638-1710

www.cqpress.com

⊖ The paper used in this publication meets the minimum requirements of the American National Standard for Information Sciences—Permanence of Paper for Printed Library Materials, ANSI
Z39.48-1992.

Printed and bound in the United States of America

05 04 03 02 01   5 4 3 2 1

Library of Congress Cataloging-in-Publication Data

[in process]

ISBN 1-56802-665-X

To our life partners with love

Jill A. Archer

Ruth Schmidle Lavin

Myra N. Lowe

Arlene Shelley

Contents

Maps, Tables, Figures, and Boxes

Preface

Because American politics is a complex and multifaceted undertaking, the best explanations of political phenomena usually do not come from a narrow political science or history perspective; rather, they are multidisciplinary. Moreover, in a nation as large as the United States, political phenomena may vary widely from place to place as well as change over time. The purpose of the *Atlas of American Politics, 1960–2000* is to examine government and the affairs of state from a combined historical, geographical, and political perspective. In fact, this atlas is the first work to map in one volume the myriad aspects of the political geography of the United States for a specific period of time.

The more than 200 maps, illustrating a wide variety of phenomena involving spatial aspects of U.S. government and politics, are the centerpiece of the atlas. The maps bring together thousands of pieces of information in an illustrative format, often at the county level. The geographical patterns revealed are striking and, in many instances, are presented here for the first time. Many of the maps display geographical patterns at the federal level, such as the conduct and outcomes of presidential or congressional elections and data on federal revenues and expenditures. Maps depicting public policy matters at state or local levels illustrate the effects of political culture, which can be traced back to the nation's beginnings. The variations manifest themselves in areas such as gubernatorial powers, term limits, and public spending for items such as prisons or schools. Maps depicting foreign relations show, for example, recent patterns of U.S. defense assistance overseas, defense deployment, and foreign trade, as well as some of the effects of direct foreign investments or of defense contract procurements within the United States.

It should be remembered that any graphical or cartographic display of data is subject to misinterpretation. Where applicable, the text cautions readers about the possibility of misinterpretation, and we advise using the atlas as one of many tools to grasp the nuances of American politics. That said, what we have learned is this: because politics American style occurs in both time *and* space, a consideration of both is important to understanding the past and the present and the hope of making better educated predictions about the future.

The four authors of the atlas have devoted their careers to the research, analysis, cartographic display, and interpretation of American political phenomena. They have known each other and have worked together for twenty years under the auspices of the Political Geography Specialty Group of the Association of American Geographers. At annual and regional meetings, and through numerous books and articles, the authors collaborated, shared, critiqued, and criticized one another's work and then decided to create a comprehensive atlas of American politics. J. Clark Archer is professor of geography at the University of Nebraska and was primarily responsible for the collection of political and social data and the initial map design. Stephen J. Lavin is professor of geography at the University of Nebraska and is the atlas cartographer. The text was written by Kenneth C. Martis, professor of geography at West Virginia University, and Fred M. Shelley, professor of geography at Southwest Texas State University.

We give special recognition to CQ Press for the courage to produce an atlas, a type of book with special needs and considerations. We thank Adrian Forman, Carolyn Goldinger, Jeanne Hickman, and Paul Pressau of the CQ Press staff and designer and compositor Karen Doody for their guidance, understanding, and suggestions, all of which have made this a much more attractive and accurate work.

J. Clark Archer
Stephen J. Lavin
Kenneth C. Martis
Fred M. Shelley

Introduction

The purpose of this atlas is to display in map form the major aspects of American politics and to foster an understanding of the relationship between the geography of the United States and its political life. Topics include presidential elections, Congress, federal administration, the judiciary, state and local government, foreign policy and trade, and the social and economic underpinnings of contemporary American public life.

A Geographical Perspective on Contemporary American Politics

The facts of geography affect many aspects of American political life, including the selection of the president and members of Congress, the administration of public policies, and the territorial organization of the legislative, executive, and judicial branches of government.

Elections of the chief executive and members of the Senate and House of Representatives are perhaps the most important functions of American democracy. It is through the electoral process that, in Lincoln's words, government of the people, by the people, and for the people operates. How does geography affect the election of these officers? First, the Constitution recognized the geographical equality of the states, no matter how large or small their population, by calling for each to elect two members of the U.S. Senate. Second, the seats of the House of Representatives are apportioned by population, which is determined by the decennial census. The Constitution, however, guarantees each state at least one representative, no matter how small its population. In addition, each member of Congress must be a legal resident of the state from which he or she is elected. Although the Constitution does not require that members of the House be elected from territorially defined districts, current law requires states to divide themselves into districts for electoral purposes. Each member of the House, therefore, is elected by and responsible to a geographically defined constituency, and each is expected to represent the interests of that constituency in the course of developing national legislation. Every decade, states redraw district boundaries to equalize district populations. As the maps in Chapter 3 indicate, the number of members afforded each state and the district boundaries may change every decade. Hence, political power is redistributed every ten years.

Third, the procedure by which the president of the United States is elected is inherently geographic. Technically, the president is not elected directly by the voters; rather, the voters select members of the electoral college, who vote for the president. The number of electoral votes in each state equals its congressional delegation—in other words, the number of its representatives in the House plus its two senators. Since before the Civil War, the electors, with a few exceptions, have supported the candidate who wins the popular vote in the state. An American presidential election, therefore, can be thought of as fifty-one simultaneous elections—one in each of the fifty states and the District of Columbia. The successful candidate is the one who wins enough states to ensure an electoral college majority. The system ensures that candidates and their supporters must pay careful attention to geography, and therefore to issues of importance to people in widely separated communities, in waging their campaigns. As maps in Chapter 2 illustrate, these geographic considerations often have considerable influence on the outcomes of elections. Decisions about where to campaign and what issues to emphasize are usually made with an eye toward increasing a candidate's chances of winning critical electoral votes. By the same token, a candidate may opt to save time and money by not campaigning in a state that is considered safe or in a state that the opponent is sure to win.

The organization of executive agencies is also influenced by geography. Many federal agencies divide the country into administrative regions to bring government services to the people in the area. The federal judiciary is also organized along territorial lines. As Chapters 4 and 5 illustrate, the specific territorial divisions vary from one agency to another.

1

Geographical Definitions

Demographers and the U.S. Census Bureau use many different terms to designate areas and geographical features of the United States. Different terms are also used depending on the context. Below are terms found in this atlas and their definitions or the states they encompass.

American Manufacturing Belt. Area with a history of high levels of industrial production. It extends from southern New England south to Philadelphia and Baltimore and westward to the western Great Lakes. It includes the cities of Boston, New York, Philadelphia, Baltimore, Pittsburgh, Cleveland, Detroit, Chicago, and Milwaukee along with many smaller manufacturing cities and towns.

Appalachia. The highland areas of the eastern United States in and near the Appalachian Mountain range. Appalachia extends from central Pennsylvania southwestward to central Alabama. It includes all of West Virginia and parts of Pennsylvania, Maryland, Virginia, Kentucky, Tennessee, North Carolina, Georgia, and Alabama. This region is characterized by a long history of poverty and isolation, but federal initiatives such as the Tennessee Valley Authority and the Appalachian Regional Commission have fostered the region's development.

Border States. Slaveholding states that did not secede from the Union during the Civil War, including Delaware, Maryland, Kentucky, and Missouri. West Virginia, which seceded from Virginia and joined the Union during the Civil War, and Oklahoma, which did not join the Union until 1907, are also often included as Border States.

Central Appalachia. Central Appalachia refers to those parts of Appalachia located in and near the Border States of Maryland, Kentucky, and West Virginia, as well as the Appalachian portion of Virginia.

Continental Divide. Separates the rivers that flow into the Atlantic Ocean and Gulf of Mexico from those that flow into the Pacific Ocean. It enters the United States in Glacier National Park, Montana, forms part of the boundary between Montana and Idaho, and extends through Wyoming, Colorado, and New Mexico.

Core South. South Carolina, Georgia, Florida, Alabama, Mississippi, and Louisiana.

East. Maine, New Hampshire, Vermont, Massachusetts, Rhode Island, Connecticut, New York, New Jersey, and Pennsylvania.

East North Central. (East North Central Census Region) Ohio, Indiana, Illinois, Wisconsin, and Michigan.

East South Central. (East South Central Census Region) Kentucky, Tennessee, Alabama, and Mississippi.

Far West. California, Oregon, and Washington.

Front Range. The major range of the Rocky Mountains near the Continental Divide, primarily in Colorado.

Great Plains. Vast expanse of grassland extending from Canada to Mexico for several hundred miles east of the Rocky Mountains, including most of North Dakota, South Dakota, Nebraska, and Kansas and parts of Oklahoma, Texas, New Mexico, Colorado, Wyoming, and Montana.

Interior West. Western states that do not border the Pacific Ocean, namely, Idaho, Montana, Wyoming, Utah, Colorado, Nevada, New Mexico, and Arizona. These states make up the Mountain Census Region (see below). Sometimes the Great Plains, especially the western part of this region, is included with the Interior West.

Mason-Dixon line. Boundary between Pennsylvania and Maryland. It was surveyed originally by two British surveyors, Charles Mason and Jeremiah Dixon, between 1763 and 1767 to settle a boundary dispute between the two colonies. Because Pennsylvania was a free state and Maryland was a slave state, the Mason-Dixon line came to symbolize the divisions between the North and South before and after the Civil War, and the term is sometimes used to represent the boundary between the North and the South.

Middle Atlantic. (Middle Atlantic Census Region) New York, New Jersey, and Pennsylvania.

Midwest. (Midwest Census Division) Includes the East North Central states (Ohio, Indiana, Illinois, Michigan, and Wisconsin) and West North Central states (Minnesota, Iowa, Missouri, North Dakota, South Dakota, Nebraska, and Kansas).

Mountain. (Mountain Census Region) Idaho, Montana, Wyoming, Utah, Colorado, Nevada, New Mexico, and Arizona.

New England. (New England Census Region) Maine, New Hampshire, Vermont, Massachusetts, Connecticut, and Rhode Island.

Northeast. (Northeast Census Division) it is also sometimes construed to include the eastern Great Lakes states along with Maryland and Delaware, particularly their urban areas.

Northern Plains. North Dakota, South Dakota, Nebraska, and Kansas.

Old South. States that seceded from the Union in 1860 and 1861 to form the Confederacy: Virginia, North Carolina, South Carolina, Georgia, Florida, Tennessee, Alabama, Mississippi, Arkansas, Louisiana, and Texas.

Pacific. (Pacific Census Region) Washington, Oregon, California, Alaska, and Hawaii.

Snow Belt or Frost Belt. Refers to states not included in the Sun Belt, or more generally those states north of approximately the 37th parallel of latitude. In particular this term refers to the Northeast and upper Midwest from the Dakotas and Minnesota eastward to New York and New England.

South. (South Census Region) Delaware, Maryland, West Virginia, Virginia, North Carolina, South Carolina, Georgia, Florida, Kentucky, Tennessee, Alabama, Mississippi, Louisiana, Arkansas, Oklahoma, and Texas.

South Atlantic. (South Atlantic Census Region) Delaware, Maryland, West Virginia, Virginia, North Carolina, South Carolina, Georgia, and Florida.

Sun Belt. States south of the approximately 37th parallel of latitude.

Upper Midwest or Upper Middle West. Wisconsin, Minnesota, Iowa, North Dakota, and South Dakota.

Upper South. Southern states that do not border the Gulf of Mexico or the Atlantic Ocean, namely, Arkansas, Tennessee, Kentucky, and West Virginia.

West. (West Census Division) Idaho, Montana, Wyoming, Utah, Colorado, Nevada, New Mexico, Arizona, Washington, Oregon, California, Alaska, and Hawaii.

West North Central. (West North Central Census Region) Minnesota, Iowa, Missouri, North Dakota, South Dakota, Nebraska, and Kansas.

West South Central. (West South Central Census Region) Louisiana, Arkansas, Oklahoma, and Texas.

Not only is geography a fundamental organizing principle of American government and politics, but also the size and diversity of the United States make familiarity with its geography critical to understanding how Americans govern themselves. The United States is the third largest country in the world in population (after China and India) and in land area (after Russia and Canada).[1] It is characterized by unparalleled physical, environmental, economic, and ethnic diversity, all of which influence aspects of American life from political culture to international trade to the organization of state and local government. Throughout this atlas, relationships between the underlying geographic diversity of the United States and its system of government are evident. Clearly, understanding American politics requires a recognition of the geographical linkages between the political system and the country and people it governs. The intent of this atlas is to illustrate these linkages through maps depicting various aspects of American politics and government and their relationships to population, natural environment, and the U.S. economy.

Almost all of the maps in the atlas are *choropleth* maps. A choropleth map is a map of areal units, in which the shading of each unit is dependent on the value of one or more variables. In most of the maps, the areal units are states or counties. For example, some of the maps in Chapter 2 depict the popular outcomes of presidential elections by county between 1960 and 2000. The shading of each county is determined by whether a Republican, Democrat, or third party candidate won a plurality of popular votes there.

Maps IN-1, IN-2, and IN-3 provide the geographical information necessary to understand the various places and regions discussed in the text. Map IN-1 shows the fifty states, along with their capitals and other major cities. In many states, the capital is considerably smaller in population than other cities within their borders. The capitals of the four largest states are Sacramento, California; Austin, Texas; Albany, New York; and Tallahassee, Florida. None of these cities is anywhere near the size of the largest cities in their states—Los Angeles, Houston, New York, and Miami, respectively. Only in a minority of states (for example, Arizona, Colorado, Georgia, Hawaii, Indiana, Iowa, Massachusetts, and Utah) is the state capital also the largest and most important city. The decision to locate a state capital in a relatively small city resulted from the desire to separate political and economic power geographically.[2] The city of Washington, D.C., was in fact founded and its location was chosen to ensure that the federal capital would not be located in the major financial centers of New York and Philadelphia.[3]

Map IN-2 shows, in broad terms, the major physiographic regions of the United States. Europeans who set-

IN-1 *Major Metropolitan Statistical Areas and State Capitals of the United States*

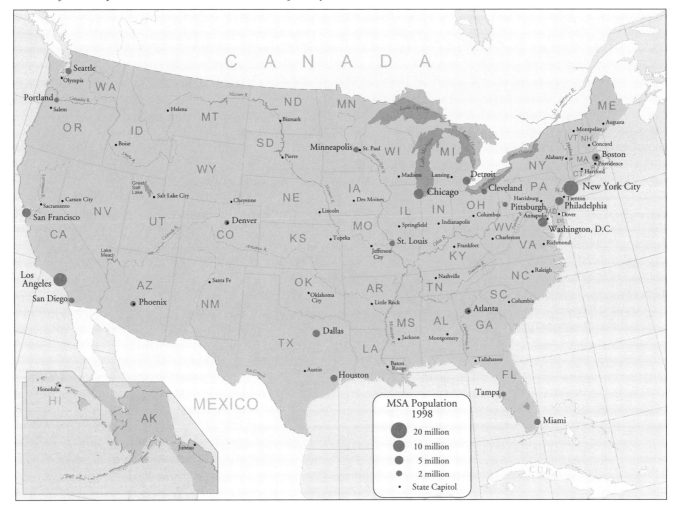

tled the original thirteen colonies in the seventeenth century first encountered the Atlantic Lowlands, a coastal plain that is narrow in the northeast and widens to the south and west. West of the Atlantic coastal plain is the Piedmont (literally, foot of the mountains), which leads to the Appalachian mountain chain. The Ozark Plateau, with rugged hills reminiscent of the Appalachians from which many of its settlers came, is located in Arkansas, Missouri, and Oklahoma. Settlers crossing the Appalachians next encountered the vast Interior Plains, another area of lowlands. These lowlands grade imperceptibly into the Great Plains, which stretch along the eastern side of the Rocky Mountains from Texas northward to the Canadian border, which in turn gradually slope upward to the Rocky Mountains in Montana, Wyoming, Colorado, and New Mexico. The western third of the country is generally arid and mountainous. The major physical regions west of the Rockies are the Western Plateaus and mountains, often referred

to as "basin and range" topography, and the Pacific coastal lowlands, which, unlike those on the Atlantic coast, also contain mountains of considerable height. The Hawaiian Islands, shown here as part of the Pacific coast, are in fact the tops of very large and isolated volcanoes that formed along the floor of the Pacific Ocean. Alaska, located in the northwestern corner of North America, includes a rugged coastline, the Alaska Range, an interior lowland, the Brooks Range, and the North Slope, which is an important and controversial area for oil exploration.

Map IN-3 identifies the major political sections and regions of the United States. The largest-scale divisions are between major political sections, which divide the United States into North, South, and West sections. Historical voting patterns and other significant variations in political behavior, institutions, and culture have tended to differentiate these large sections from one another for more than a century.[4] Smaller-scale, less-striking differences can also be

IN-2 *Landscape Regions*

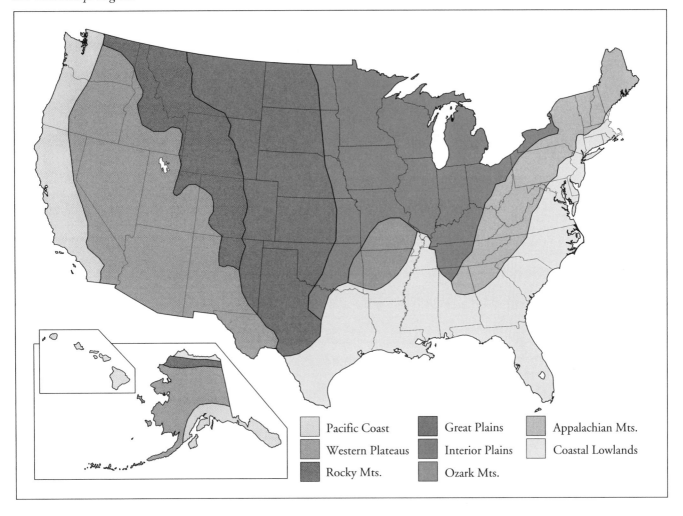

Pacific Coast

Western Plateaus

Rocky Mts.

Great Plains

Interior Plains

Ozark Mts.

Appalachian Mts.

Coastal Lowlands

found within each major section. For example, within the North section, politically important distinctions differentiate the New England, Northeast, and Midwest regions, although they tend to be more similar to one another than they are to regions within either the South or West sections. Although physiographic regions cut across state boundaries, the political sections and regions of the United States generally conform to state boundaries. For example, the physiographic region of the Great Plains includes much of eastern Montana, Wyoming, Colorado, and New Mexico. For political purposes, however, these states are joined with neighboring mountain states, in part because on a statewide basis their economies and their populations are linked more closely with the Mountain West than with their plains neighbors to the east. Regional terms used to refer to various groupings of states in this Atlas often, but not always, follow the divisions shown in Map IN-3. For example, the "Core South" or "Deep South," as discussed in conjunction with various maps throughout the text refers to Alabama, Florida, Georgia, Louisiana, Mississippi, and South Carolina, as shown on the map. Other regional designations can overlap those shown on Map IN-3. For instance, a sometimes geographically vague division between the Sun Belt and the Frost Belt seems to correspond in popular usage to a boundary line drawn at about 37 degrees north latitude, which is roughly the northern border of several states from North Carolina to Arizona, although Virginia, Nevada, and all of California are often also deemed to be Sun Belt in character.

Organization

The atlas is divided into eight chapters. Chapter 1 looks at the geography of the United States as it relates to American politics and government. The first two maps illustrate the

IN-3 *Political Behavior: Sections and Regions*

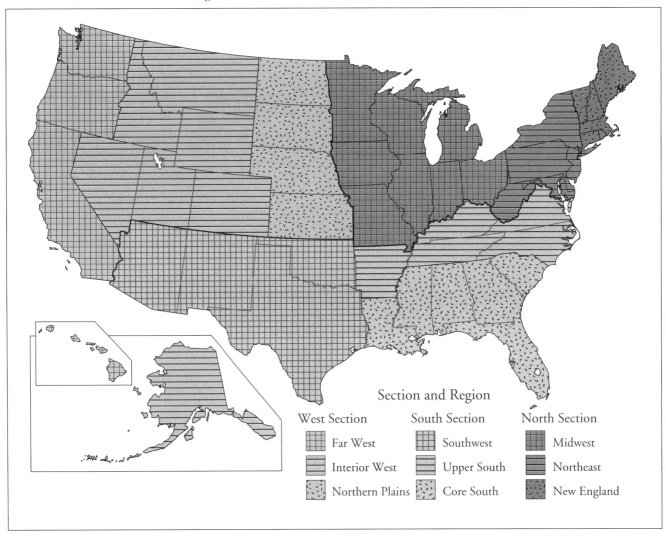

Section and Region

West Section	South Section	North Section
Far West	Southwest	Midwest
Interior West	Upper South	Northeast
Northern Plains	Core South	New England

acquisition of territory by the United States and the date of admission of each state to the Union. These maps are followed by several that illustrate population density and population change. Demographic components of population change, including birth rates, death rates, migration rates, and rates of natural increase, are also shown at a county level.

The next section of Chapter 1 looks at the ethnic background of the U.S. population. It includes county-level maps of the percentages of African American, Hispanic, Asian American, and Native American populations. Religious affiliation, like ethnicity, is often a major factor in political decision making. Maps in Chapter 1 illustrate the percentage of Catholics, Southern Baptists, Mormons, Jews, Evangelical Lutherans, and United Methodists by county, along with the overall percentage of church adherents. The next section includes maps illustrating levels of income and

poverty and is followed by maps illustrating the structure of the American economy, including percentages of people working in various occupational categories.

Chapter 2 focuses on presidential elections. Two maps are provided for each of the eleven elections that occurred between 1960 and 2000: the first shows the percentages of popular votes for president by county, and the second shows electoral votes by state. Next are maps showing how many times Republican and Democratic presidential nominees made campaign appearances in different states in elections from 1988 through 2000. The last three maps in Chapter 2 show voter turnout by state. Voter turnout is often critical to election outcomes because barely half of eligible voters generally participate.

Congress is the subject of Chapter 3. The first sequence of maps deals with reapportionment and shows the gains and losses of seats in the U.S. House of Representatives by decade. The next maps show partisan control of House and Senate seats by state in each decade between 1960 and 2000. Next are maps of legislators' votes, by district, on several critical roll call votes in the House and Senate. Maps of interest group ratings, which broadly measure a senator's or representative's level of support for liberal or conservative positions, are also included.

Chapter 4 looks at the executive branch of the federal government. The first group of maps shows the delineation of administrative areas and districts for several important federal agencies including the Census Bureau, Federal Reserve System, and Environmental Protection Agency. The home states of cabinet officers from 1961 to 2000 are shown. The maps in the final section of Chapter 4 depict patterns of federal tax revenues and expenditures.

Chapter 5 examines the judicial branch of the government. The first map shows the boundaries of federal circuit and district courts. Next are maps identifying the home states of Supreme Court justices and maps of roll call votes in the Senate to confirm controversial Court nominees. The last three maps in this chapter identify the origins of major Supreme Court cases in three issue areas: abortion and reproductive rights, electoral districting and apportionment, and the environment.

Chapter 6 is an analysis of state and local government. Several maps identify and compare the powers of the governor of each state. Then comes a sequence of maps identifying partisan control of the governor's chair and the upper and lower houses of the state legislatures. This chapter also contains maps depicting various aspects of state and local government finance and maps identifying the number of African American elected officials, Hispanic elected officials, and women in state legislatures by state.

Chapter 7 focuses on foreign policy. The first group of maps looks at immigration into the United States, along with movement of refugees. Maps showing American military aid, troop commitments, and nonmilitary economic aid to foreign countries follow. In contrast to maps in earlier chapters, several of the maps in Chapter 7 are choropleth maps of the world, showing country borders. The final section of Chapter 7 is devoted to trade relationships, including imports, exports, and foreign direct investment.

Chapter 8 deals with social and economic policies. The maps portray a variety of indicators of the quality of American social and economic life. Many of these maps, like those in Chapter 7, deal with issues that often have a considerable effect on voters' preferences, candidates' campaign strategies, and election outcomes. The first group of maps in Chapter 8 focuses on Social Security and income maintenance, issues that have been of great importance in the political arena for many years. Next is a sequence of maps involving indicators of health, including death rates from various causes, and maps showing the distribution of Medicare payments and abortion rates.

The next group of maps deals with education, another topic of major political interest. Included are maps on education expenditures, teacher salaries, high school graduation rates, and literacy rates. A series of maps on crime and punishment follows and includes crime rates, capital punishment, and law enforcement expenditures. The chapter concludes with several maps on environmental quality. The issues covered in Chapter 8—income and poverty, health, education, crime, and the environment—continue to be the most significant domestic policy issues in contemporary American politics.

Notes

1. John C. Hudson, ed. *Goode's World Atlas*, 20th ed. (Chicago: Rand McNally, 2000).

2. F. M. Shelley, J. C. Archer, F. M. Davidson, and S. D. Brunn, *The Political Geography of the United States* (New York: Guilford, 1996).

3. Kenneth R. Bowling, *The Creation of Washington, D.C.: The Idea and Location of the American Capital* (Lanham, Md.: George Mason University Press, 1991).

4. Shelley et al., *Political Geography of the United States.*

Chapter 1

Contemporary Government and Politics: Geographical Background

Article I of the U.S. Constitution requires a count of the population every ten years to determine how the seats in the House of Representatives are to be apportioned. When the first census was conducted in 1790, the U.S. population was 3,929,214, and the size of the country was 913,285 square miles.[1] At the 2000 census the United States—that is, the fifty states and the District of Columbia—had a population of 281,421,906. The size of the nation in land and inland water area is 3,717,796 square miles. As illustrated in Map 1-1, the acquisition of various parcels of land took place from 1783 to 1898.

The original area of the United States, which was set in the 1783 Treaty of Paris with Britain following the Revolutionary War, stretched from the thirteen original colonies along the Atlantic Coast west to the Mississippi River, north to the Great Lakes, and south almost to the Gulf of Mexico. The size of the original nation—913,285 square miles, which was larger than the countries of western and central Europe—raised some philosophical questions. What was the ideal size of a republic? Could a democratic system effectively govern regions a great distance from the capital and core area? At the time of the 1783 treaty, Americans were already settling the trans-Appalachian west, and the new nation's delegates at the Treaty of Paris negotiations demanded and received sovereignty over this region. In the 1790s, two smaller areas officially became part of the United States. The disputed area of Vermont became the fourteenth state in 1791, and in 1795 Spain ceded an area that is now part of southern Alabama and Mississippi.

Growth of a Nation

The first large expansion of the United States came with the Louisiana Purchase, which the United States acquired from France in 1803. This vast area of 909,130 square miles nearly doubled the size of the country. The land purchase was not without controversy. Some easterners feared that the expansion would give too much power to the new states and the West, and some northerners feared that it would give too much power to the South. Smaller expansions took place with the purchase of Florida, including parts of present-day Alabama and Mississippi, from Spain in 1819, and adjustments to the northern border with British territory in what is now Minnesota and North Dakota in 1818 and Maine in 1842.

The second major expansion was the 388,687 square mile annexation of Texas in 1845. This area had been under the sovereignty of Mexico, which had won its independence from Spain in 1821. By the 1830s English-speaking residents, or Anglos, constituted a majority of the Texas population. For a variety of reasons, Anglo Texans felt that their rights were not recognized by Mexico, and in 1836 they declared an independent Republic of Texas. Many Texans had emigrated from the United States and wanted Texas to join the Union. Its admission was delayed by northern members of Congress who opposed the expansion of slavery and the subsequent growth of southern power. Texas remained an independent republic until its formal admission.

The idea that the United States of America could stretch from the Atlantic Ocean to the Pacific Ocean goes back to the early 1800s. From 1803 to 1806 Meriwether Lewis and William Clark explored and mapped the area from the Mississippi River to the Pacific and back again. By the mid-1840s expansionist fervor reached its peak and found its expression in the term "Manifest Destiny," the view that it was the right, even the divine right, of the United States to occupy the land between both coasts. Two large areas stood in its way to the Pacific Ocean—the northwestern portion of Mexico and the area called the Oregon Country that Great Britain and the United States both claimed.

The Oregon question was resolved first. American settlement in Oregon substantially increased in the 1840s. The Oregon Trail led settlers to the Willamette Valley, bypassing the less-desirable Great Plains, Rocky Mountains, and the deserts of the Interior West. As in Texas, Americans became the majority nonnative residents in the region. Sentiment for the annexation of Oregon was strong in Con-

Map 1-1 *Acquisition of U.S. Territory, 1783–1898*

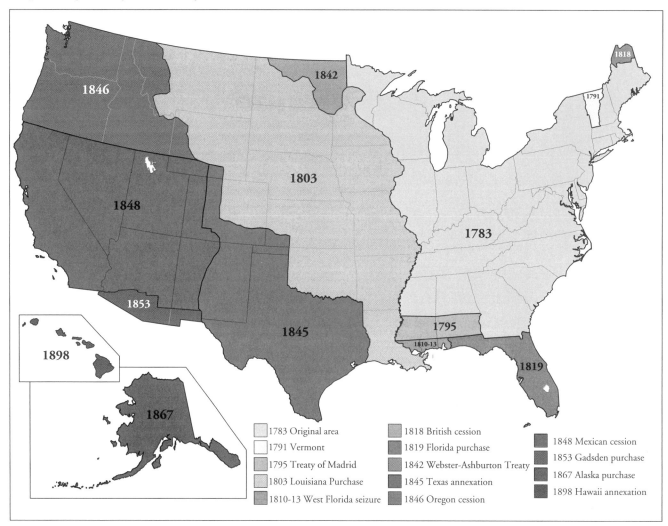

1783 Original area
1791 Vermont
1795 Treaty of Madrid
1803 Louisiana Purchase
1810-13 West Florida seizure
1818 British cession
1819 Florida purchase
1842 Webster-Ashburton Treaty
1845 Texas annexation
1846 Oregon cession
1848 Mexican cession
1853 Gadsden purchase
1867 Alaska purchase
1898 Hawaii annexation

gress, especially among members from northern states. Extreme expansionists wanted the whole of the Pacific Northwest all the way to, in the words of James K. Polk's campaign slogan, the "54° 40' or fight" line of latitude, or the southern boundary of present-day Alaska. Eventually, the British proposed extending the 49th parallel line, the northern border of the Louisiana Purchase and British Cession of 1818, all the way to the Pacific, with the exception of Vancouver Island and other nearby islands, which remained under British control. In June 1846 the Senate ratified the British proposal, which ceded 286,541 square miles and completed the northern boundary of the forty-eight contiguous states, as shown in Map 1-1.

In the meantime, tensions were growing between Mexico and the United States over the southern border of Texas and other issues. Expansionists in the United States were eager to complete the westward extension to the Pacific, and

their desires culminated in the May 1846 declaration of war on Mexico. The war was fought on many fronts: in California, on the Texas-Mexico border, on the east coast of Mexico, and eventually in Mexico City itself, which the United States captured in September 1847. In early 1848 Mexico signed the Treaty of Guadalupe Hidalgo, which ceded 529,189 square miles, or nearly one-third of its territory, to the United States. As Map 1-1 shows, with this acquisition the United States obtained all or part of seven present-day southwestern states. Five years later, the Gadsden Purchase, 29,670 square miles of present-day Arizona and New Mexico, completed what is now the southern boundary of the United States. Just seventy years after the 1783 Treaty of Paris with Britain was signed, the area of the forty-eight contiguous states was complete.

Expansionist desires did not wane after the Oregon and Mexican cessions. Two additional areas were acquired in the latter half of the nineteenth century. In 1867 Secretary of State William Seward negotiated the purchase of Alaska, a territory of 590,066 square miles, from the Russians for $7.2 million. Although at the time it was derided as "Seward's Folly," the purchase turned out to be one of the great land deals in world history. Alaska constitutes approximately one-sixth of the entire land area of the United States, equal to the size of Arizona, Oklahoma, New Mexico, and Texas added together. (Because of space constraints, Alaska's true size cannot be represented in the atlas maps.)

The final acquisition of what is now the United States came with the annexation of Hawaii in 1898. Many now see this annexation as America's first overseas imperialist intervention. In 1893 powerful American planters in Hawaii overthrew the native Hawaiian monarchy. The subsequent turmoil, including intervention by the U.S. marines, led to many years of debate over whether Hawaii should be annexed. Finally, during the Spanish-American War, Con-

gress voted for annexation, in light of Hawaii's strategic value. Alaska and Hawaii were admitted as states in 1959, completing the official legal definition of the United States as fifty states and the District of Columbia.[2]

The U.S. Constitution established a system of government in which power is divided between a central government and the states. According to Article X of the Constitution, "The powers not delegated to the United States by the Constitution, nor prohibited by it to the States, are reserved to the States respectively, or to the people." States thus retain a substantial amount of autonomy, a natural outgrowth of their independence as colonies. The British colonization of the East Coast of North America did not comprise a homogenous unit; rather, the thirteen colonies were established along a considerable stretch of land at different times. Each colony developed its own character, laws, and methods of self-governance. These thirteen units banded together to declare themselves independent of Britain, to

Map 1-2 *Date of Admission, by State, 1789–1959*

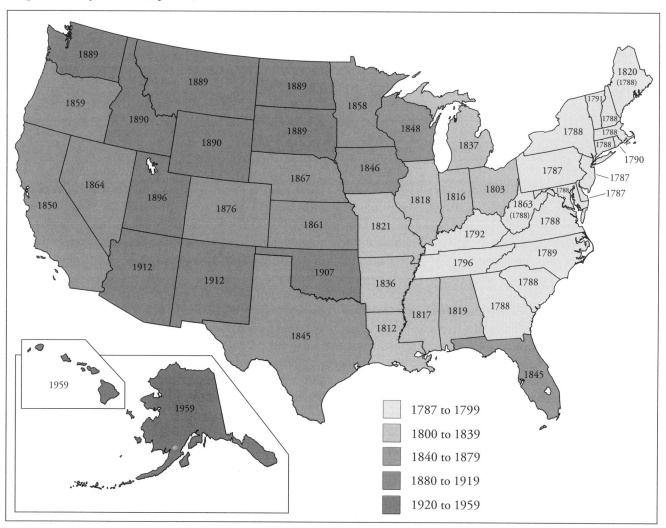

Legend:
- 1787 to 1799
- 1800 to 1839
- 1840 to 1879
- 1880 to 1919
- 1920 to 1959

fight and win the Revolutionary War, and to establish a government under the Articles of Confederation. When it became evident in the 1780s that a stronger central government was needed, the states sent delegates to a convention that, instead of reforming the Articles of Confederation, wrote a new constitution and established the federal system. Once two-thirds of the states had ratified the Constitution, the document was considered binding on all the states. As each new state was admitted into the Union, it acquired the same powers and rights as the original thirteen.

We can divide the admission of states into five eras of settlement and political organization. During the first era, 1787–1799, the thirteen original states voted to approve the Constitution, with Delaware being the first in 1787 and Rhode Island the last in 1790. Parts of Massachusetts and Virginia were later made into two additional states. Maine was part of Massachusetts until it was admitted as a separate state in 1820, and West Virginia was part of Virginia until became a separate state during the Civil War, in 1863. Because both of these areas were politically organized and part of the United States at its origin, they are designated on Map 1-2 as part of the first era. Two dates are shown for these states, the original date of ratification and the date of separate admission. Three other states came into the Union in the 1790s—Vermont in 1791, Kentucky (also once part of Virginia) in 1792, and Tennessee (once part of North Carolina) in 1796.

Map 1-2 shows a clear pattern of admission of nine states from Michigan south to Louisiana during the second era, 1800–1839. This group of states is just west of the original group. Congress imposed certain population and political organization criteria on the admission of new states. As the frontier of American settlement moved west, migrant Americans were anxious to organize territorial governments, apply for admission, and eventually join the Union.

The third era of admission, 1840–1879, brought in Florida in 1845 and a group of six western states. Florida had been fully acquired from Spain in 1819, but did not meet the population requirements until the 1840s. Texas was admitted in 1845, after several years as an independent country. Northern members of Congress, who wanted to halt the expansion of slavery, delayed admitting Texas to the union for several years. During this period, three states in the Far West were admitted. California and Oregon along the Pacific Coast had acquired the requisite population, and Nevada was admitted in 1864 during the Civil War as an important silver-mining state that was friendly to the Unionist Republican cause.

Ten states were admitted during the fourth era, 1880–1919. Most of these states were in the drier areas of the northern Great Plains and Interior West. Six states along the northern tier were admitted in 1889 and 1890. With completion of the second transcontinental railroad, new settlement exploded along its route. Utah was admitted in 1896, after a long battle with the U.S. government over polygamy and other practices of the dominant Mormon Church. Oklahoma was admitted in 1907. The eastern part of the state had been designated as early as the 1820s as Indian Territory—that is, a place where eastern Native American tribes were to be placed after removal from their ancestral homelands (Map 1-15). Settlement restrictions were later removed, however, and Oklahoma soon became a state. Finally, two southwestern states, New Mexico and Arizona, were admitted in 1912, filling out the forty-eight states of the continental United States.

In the final era, 1920–1959, the United States admitted two states that made the country a "fragmented," or noncontiguous, nation, as defined by political geographers. Alaska and Hawaii were admitted in 1959, forty-seven years after the admission of the last continental state. This gap was the longest between admission dates in U.S. history. In addition, these states were the first outside the continental United States to be admitted, and the distances are considerable: Honolulu, the capital of Hawaii, is nearly 5,000 miles from the nation's capital, Washington, D.C., and Juneau, the capital of Alaska, is nearly 3,200 miles from Washington.

Population

Map 1-3 depicts population density by county. Population density is a measurement of the number of individuals living in a certain space, commonly expressed as persons per square mile. Population density figures for any of the more than 3,000 U.S. counties can be calculated by dividing the county's population, as determined by the Census Bureau, by its size in square miles. After the initial settlement period, the number of counties in each state stabilized, and the size of the counties has usually remained the same. Therefore, a gain of population in a county amounts to an increase in population density and a loss of population means a decrease in density.

The population density patterns depicted in Map 1-3 reflect the country's physical geography and the agricultural and urban settlement patterns of U.S. history. The most densely populated region, located in the original settlement zone, stretches from the Boston area southwest to Washington, D.C. The second most densely populated area is the Midwest industrial core, which extends from western Pennsylvania to northern Ohio and southern Michigan and farther west to Chicago and Milwaukee. The South has two extensive areas of dense population, one along the Piedmont

Map 1-3 *Population Density, by County, 2000*

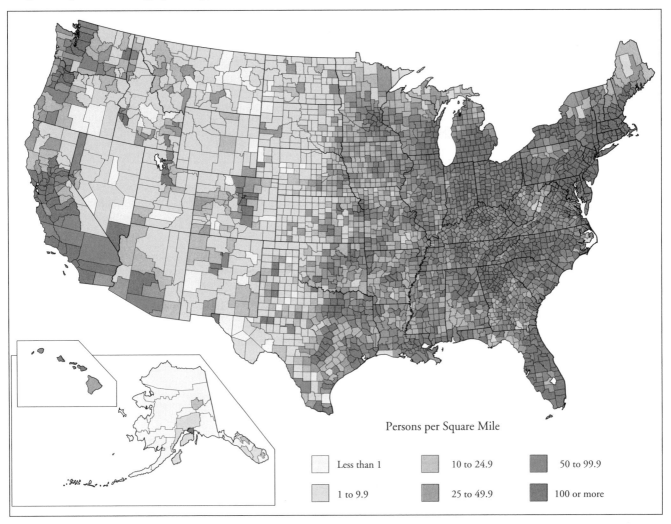

Persons per Square Mile

Less than 1   10 to 24.9   50 to 99.9

1 to 9.9   25 to 49.9   100 or more

industrial area of North Carolina and South Carolina, stretching south to Atlanta, and the other in central and south Florida, especially along the Atlantic coast. In the West the only large area of high population density is in California, along the Pacific coast. In addition, pockets of dense population are found in the Willamette Valley of Oregon, near Portland, and the Puget Sound area of Washington, near Seattle.

Census figures show a great variation in population density across the United States. For example, New York County (Manhattan) has a population density of more than 52,000 persons per square mile. At the other extreme is Eureka County, Nevada, which has a population density of less than one (.4) person per square mile. These figures can be misleading, however. In many western counties, a high percentage of the population may live in one town, usually the county seat, while vast areas have little or no settlement. In some urban counties, hundreds of thousands of individ-

uals live in a small central city, with much lower concentrations in the suburban and rural areas.

Map 1-3 clearly illustrates the vast difference in population density between the eastern half of the United States and the central and Interior West. The map shows that from the Great Plains region west to the Rocky Mountains and the Interior West deserts is a vast region of sparse population, with only a few high-density areas surrounding Denver, Salt Lake City, and other large southwestern cities. The western edge of the densely populated counties of the East and Midwest forms a clearly distinguishable boundary down the center of the nation. The line of the 100th meridian, or 100° west longitude, marks a sharp decrease in rainfall and a corresponding decrease in traditional farm settlement. The topography of the Rocky Mountains and of the deserts of the Interior West further inhibits dense agricultural habitation.

The population density map is important for reading and understanding the political maps in subsequent chapters. For example, maps that display voting patterns in certain counties in the Great Plains and Interior West represent the voting choices of only hundreds or thousands of citizens, whereas the maps showing the same information for the counties where Boston, Chicago, Detroit, New York City, Philadelphia, and other large cities are located represent hundreds of thousands or even millions of citizens. The presidential election of 2000 provides a perfect illustration of the need to compare maps showing voting patterns with the population density map. Map 2-21 shows that the Republican candidate, Gov. George W. Bush of Texas, won a majority of U.S. counties. To be exact, Bush won 2,434 counties, with a total area of 2,427,039 square miles, while the Democratic candidate, Vice President Al Gore, won 677 counties, with a total area of 580,134 square miles. Looking at the presidential election map alone would lead one to believe that Bush had won an overwhelming victory, but in fact Gore won the popular vote by more than half a million. Small counties in the North and East with large cities voted heav-

ily for Gore, and large but sparsely populated counties in the central and western regions reported majorities for Bush. In the 2000 election, as with most in American history, the population density map is a critical tool for understanding and analyzing the geographic patterns of political phenomena.

Map 1-4 is a depiction of the Metropolitan Statistical Areas of the United States, as defined by the Census Bureau. Data from the 1920 census onward show that most of the U.S. population lives in cities. Starting with the first census in 1790, the Census Bureau has defined a city as a place with a population of 2,500 or more. Urban geographers and other social scientists, especially since 1920, have considered this number too small for the modern nation. Just before the 1950 census the Census Bureau designated the term *metropolitan* to better define urban settlement, and, since 1983, it has used, the term *Metropolitan Statistical Area* (MSA).

An MSA, as defined by the Census Bureau, is an area of at least one county that meets certain criteria. The most important is that an MSA must contain at least one city with

Map 1-4 *Metropolitan Statistical Area Counties, 1999*

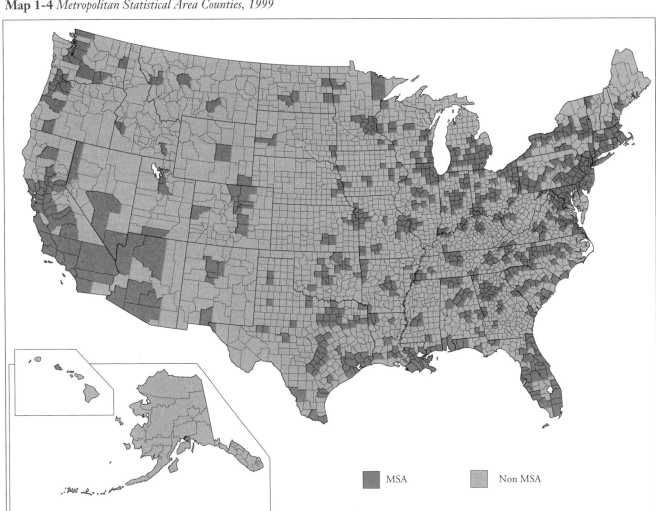

MSA   Non MSA

a population of 50,000 or more. The county in which this city is located is designated the "central county" in the MSA. Adjacent counties also can be designated *metropolitan* if either of two conditions are met: if at least 50 percent of the adjacent counties' population is in the urbanized area surrounding the largest city, or if the adjacent county has a dense population, a high urban population, and is economically connected to the central county. The chief measurement of economic connection is the pattern of daily commuting. In some cases a county or group of counties receives MSA status without having a city with a population of 50,000, if the total urban area has a population of at least 50,000 and the total adjacent area has a population of at least 100,000 (75,000 in New England). The MSA designation is an indicator not just of the political boundaries of a city, but the area surrounding a city that is considered a connected and coherent whole. According to these criteria, 80 percent of the U.S. population is designated metropolitan.

Map 1-4 is similar to Map 1-3, the population density map, but better defines the actual urban and metropolitan character of the United States. Many areas of dense population do not meet the metropolitan threshold. All regions have large metropolitan areas, but, as discussed in connection with Map 1-3, some areas historically have large cities and some areas are rural and agricultural.

MSAs vary greatly in population. The five largest MSAs and their official titles, states, and 1999 populations were as follows:

New York-Northern New Jersey-Long Island; New York, New Jersey, Connecticut, and Pennsylvania; 20,196,649
Los Angeles-Riverside-Orange County; California; 16,036,587
Chicago-Gary-Kenosha; Illinois, Indiana, and Wisconsin; 8,885,919
Washington-Baltimore; District of Columbia, Maryland, Virginia, and West Virginia; 7,359,044
San Francisco-Oakland-San Jose; California; 6,873,645.

The five smallest MSAs were:

Enid; Oklahoma; 56,954
Casper; Wyoming; 63,157
Pocatello; Idaho; 74,881
Corvallis; Oregon; 77,192
Jonesboro; Arkansas; 77,668.[3]

The most metropolitan states are New Jersey (100.0 percent), California (96.7 percent), Massachusetts (96.1 percent), Connecticut (95.6 percent), and Rhode Island (93.8 percent).[4] The least metropolitan states are Maine (35.8 percent), Mississippi (35.3 percent), Montana (33.7 percent),

Wyoming (29.7 percent), and Vermont (27.7 percent). In these states only a few counties are designated metropolitan. Many other states show the same pattern. The land area of Nebraska, for example, is virtually all nonmetropolitan; most of its population is in the Omaha-Lincoln Metropolitan Statistical Area, and the rest of the state is sparsely populated and nonmetropolitan.

The population characteristics of metropolitan areas are similar to those discussed in connection with Map 1-5 on population growth and change. Northern MSAs are generally in decline or growing slowly. Sun Belt MSAs are generally growing at a rate above the national average. The three fastest growing MSAs in the 1990s in terms of population were those that included the southern tier cities of Atlanta, Dallas-Ft. Worth, Houston, Los Angeles, and Phoenix. In terms of percentages, Las Vegas, Nevada, was by far the fastest-growing MSA.

Because Census Bureau statistics about an MSA measure the conditions of the entire region surrounding a city, an MSA with a stagnant inner city and a booming suburban fringe can have an overall positive growth rate. For example, Washington, D.C., lost an estimated 87,900 people between 1990 and 1999 (14.5 percent of its population), yet the Washington MSA boomed. In general, U.S. economic growth and development has taken place in metropolitan areas because they are employment centers with the educated population and urban infrastructure that corporations want. In the 1990s nearly 90 percent of the growth in the United States came in the 317 MSAs.

The largest concentration of metropolitan counties in the United States is the corridor from Boston south to the Washington, D.C., area. The second largest area of metropolitan counties is a band that stretches from upstate New York west along the southern Great Lakes. These two regions make up the old American Manufacturing Belt of northern industrial cities. Other large metropolitan conglomerations east of the Mississippi River are the Piedmont industrial belt of the Carolinas, areas surrounding large southern cities, and most of central and south Florida.

In the West the largest metropolitan concentration is in California, an overwhelmingly metropolitan state, larger in percentage terms than all the northeastern states except New Jersey. California is truly a "postmodern" place, where residents tend to live in large sprawling metropolitan areas spread over several counties and connected by freeways. Other large western cities—Albuquerque, Denver, Phoenix, Portland, Salt Lake City, and Seattle—are also spread out over more than one county. These cities are islands of urban concentration in an otherwise sparsely settled rural region.

Certain political issues tend to be important to metropolitan areas, no matter where they are located. The U.S.

Conference of Mayors publishes a list of these issues at its annual meeting. Although some relate primarily to inner cities, many deal with the problems of a large central political city connected with suburban communities and an even more distant commuting zone. In recent years, some of the top conference issues have been gun control, police support from the federal government, public schools, affordable housing, preservation of open space and parks, and high-speed rail systems.[5] Gun control is a good example of an issue that may evoke different opinions, depending on where one lives. Many metropolitan police departments as well as parents living in cities and suburbs favor strong gun safety regulations, while most rural residents advocate complete freedom to buy and own weapons. In 2000 the National Rifle Association ran an effective campaign against Democratic presidential candidate Al Gore in rural areas in Appalachia, the South, and West, where hunting is popular.

Voting patterns increasingly reflect the metropolitan-rural split. Results of the 2000 presidential election (Map 2-21) show that Bush carried a majority of nonmetropolitan counties, while support for Gore was concentrated in metropolitan areas. Although Gore won the popular vote by more than 500,000, Bush won enough rural and suburban votes to swing the requisite states in the electoral college.

Map 1-5 outlines the rate of population change, in percentages, of all the counties in the United States in the 1990s, as estimated by the Census Bureau. Counties with an increase in population of 10 percent or more are higher than the national average and are labeled high-growth counties. Counties with a rate of population growth of between 1 percent and 9.9 percent are said to be slow-growth counties. Although the national population increased greatly during this period, a number of counties lost population and these are termed decline counties.

The population change of a county, state, or region comes about through four primary demographic factors:

Map 1-5 *Population Change, by County, 1990–2000*

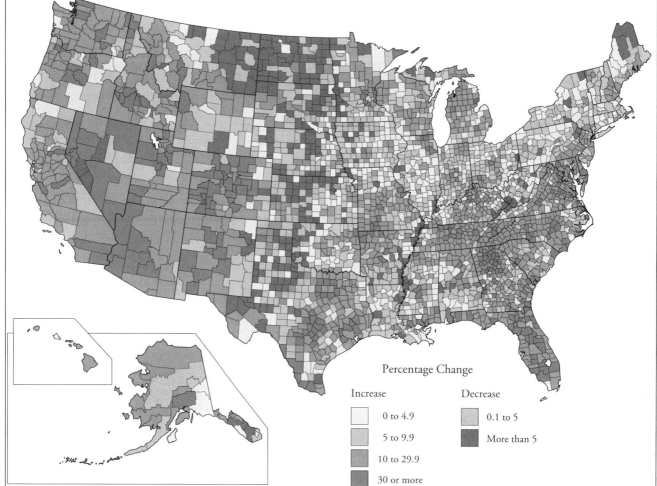

birth rate, death rate, internal immigration, and international migration. From colonial times to the present, the United States has continuously increased in population, but with regional differences in growth. Since 1790 population growth and decline have been measured statistically every ten years by the Census Bureau.

Many factors play a role in population change, but physical geography and the location of natural resources have always influenced patterns of human settlement. New England towns situated on waterpower sites became centers of textile industrialization. The fertile soil of the Midwest and Great Plains lured new immigrants as well as settlers from New England to establish farming communities. The Great Lakes provided perfect sites for steel mills and other heavy industry, and large manufacturing cities sprang up along them. Appalachia provided some of the richest coal seams in the world. Today, all of these regions are in relative decline because of the technological, economic, sociological, and cultural changes in modern society. The South was long a poor rural region, and the West a distant and sparsely settled area. Today, the South is undergoing a multi-decade boom, partly because of the widespread use of air-conditioning technology and partly because of societal changes encouraging in-migration from other regions. The West has been growing by phenomenal percentages because of its tourist attractions, high-tech industries, and the in-migration of retirees. Such cycles of growth and decline have occurred since the first settlement and still occur today.

Although the U.S. population has increased steadily from about 4 million in 1790 to more than 281 million in 2000, the growth rate has varied from decade to decade. In the 1890s a high birth rate, declining death rate, and high rates of immigration resulted in tremendous growth. In the 1930s growth slowed because of the Great Depression and a low birth rate, which reflected economic uncertainly among the population. In spite of fluctuations, the overall population has increased continuously, but not in all counties, states, or regions. The fluctuations have been the story of every census report, and so it is with the 1990s.

From 1990 to 1999 the United States grew an estimated 9.6 percent, from 248,790,925 to 272,690,813, an increase of 23,899,888 people. During this period there were 36,820,132 births and 20,934,303 deaths, and 7,478,078 legal immigrants entered the country. The fastest-growing state was Nevada, which grew at a rate of 50.6 percent. The growth was so rapid in Clark County (Las Vegas) that on average one new school opened every month during the school year.[6] Five other states had growth rates of 20 percent or more: Arizona (30.4 percent), Idaho (24.3 percent), Utah (23.6 percent), Colorado (23.1 percent), and Georgia (20.3 percent). At the opposite end of the spectrum were

three states with negative growth rates: Rhode Island (-1.3 percent), North Dakota (-0.8 percent), and Connecticut (-0.2 percent). Two states reported growth of less than 1 percent: Pennsylvania (0.9 percent) and West Virginia (0.7 percent). In general, the West dominated the list of the fastest growing places in America, and the Northeast, the Great Plains, and Appalachia have been growing slowly.

The largest area of decline counties is in the rural agricultural Great Plains and Midwest. The changing nature of farming and the rural farm economy has spurred a decades-long exodus from this region. In many counties this exodus goes back to the Dust Bowl and agricultural depression of the 1930s or even earlier. Many counties in the Great Plains were at their peak population in the 1890, 1900, or 1910 census and contain fewer people today than they did a century ago. The mechanization of farming in the twentieth century allowed significantly fewer farmers to produce greater yields. The ability of family farms to make enough money each year to support a standard American lifestyle has always been suspect. Some of the great third party movements in American political history, such as the Greenbacks (1880s), Populists (1890s), and Farmer-Labor (1920s–1940s), arose, in part, because of unrest among farmers in the central portion of the nation. From 1990 to 1999 the rural counties of this region continued their sharp decline. New economic opportunities have not come close to compensating for the jobs lost in agriculture. Other characteristics of this region, such as the great distances from the business centers on the East and West Coasts and the severe physical geography, especially topography and climate, also discourage development and growth.

The second largest pocket of decline counties is in the Delta country of the Mississippi River Valley, where Arkansas, Louisiana, and Mississippi come together. The Delta, like the Great Plains region, is also a rural agricultural area where the population has been in decline for many decades. Historically, the Delta was one of the most important cotton growing regions in the United States. Prior to the Civil War and after, a high percentage of the Delta's population was African American. As cotton cultivation was mechanized, the need for agricultural workers declined, and many African Americans left the area. Before the 1960s blacks from the Delta usually migrated north, but since the 1970s they have moved to other Sun Belt locations. The Delta has not been able to lure economic development to replace agriculture, and Mississippi is one of the two southern tier states that lost representation in the U.S. House of Representatives based on the 2000 census.

Appalachia is another area of declining population. This region runs north from Alabama to central New York. In Kentucky, West Virginia, and western Pennsylvania, the population loss has largely been caused by the decline in the coal industry. Although the amount of coal produced has remained steady, mine mechanization and surface production have greatly reduced the need for workers. In some counties, mines are the only alternative to service jobs, and, therefore, the economies of whole counties have been devastated when mines run out of coal, lose their markets, or become inefficient. The topography and soils of the region offer few economic alternatives to mining, and a historically poor infrastructure has not attracted modern high-tech development.

Several regions, in contrast, have experienced tremendous population growth. The largest is in the West, from the Front Range of the Rockies all the way to the coast. The beauty of the physical environment and invigorating climate have contributed to a fast-growing tourist and retirement sector. In addition, a pattern of high-tech and postindustrial expansion has lured not only migrants from other parts of the country but also immigrants from Mexico, Asia, and other parts of the world. Because many western counties are still small in population, an increase of a few thousand people can amount to a significant change in terms of percentages. In certain counties some of the change has come through natural increase because of the high birth rate in the Mormon, Native American, and Hispanic communities (Map 1-6).

Another area of population growth is Florida. In 1920 Florida had less than 1 million people and ranked thirty-second of the forty-eight states in population. The 1999 census estimates put the Florida population at almost 15 million, making it the fourth most populous state. Many migrants left cold, expensive, crowded, high-crime northern cities for Florida's warm climate, beautiful coast, moderately priced housing, and favorable tax structure. In addition to many retirees (Map 1-10), Florida also has lured high-tech economic development. Its population increase, therefore, has included both the elderly and the young.[7]

Another growth area of the Sun Belt is in the upper South, starting in the Washington, D.C., metropolitan area and running south to the Carolina Piedmont, to Atlanta, and to northern Alabama and the major cities of Tennessee. The Sun Belt South is not one continuous growth region. The upper South is separated from Florida by a band of slow-growth counties. Texas is also a part of the Sun Belt growth; in fact, it is the second largest state in population and one of the three great poles of numerical growth along with California and Florida. The Ozark Mountains of Arkansas and Missouri are a region of positive change separated from the rest of the upper South by the counties of the Mississippi River Valley Delta.

Map 1-6 displays the average annual birth rate by county. Nearly 4 million babies are born each year in the United States. The crude birth rate—the average birth rate per 1,000 persons—is approximately 14.5. The U.S. birth rate has decreased steadily for most of the twentieth century. In 1909, for example, the rate was 30.0 births per 1,000 persons. In nondemographic terms, in recent years American women have given birth to an average of two children, compared to an average of four a century ago.

A number of variables, including age, race, and religion, some of which are interactive, help explain the American birth rate map. Although it counts every person born in the United States, the U.S. census reports birth statistics on women aged fifteen to forty-four. In the late 1990s the U.S. average annual fertility rate was 65.6 births per 1,000 women in this age group. Naturally, the age structure of the female population in a state or county affects the number of births and, therefore, the geography of birth rates. In addition, significant differences exist in birth rates among ethnic and racial groups. Hispanic women have the highest fertility rate (101.1 per 1,000 women in the target age group), followed by African Americans (71.0), Native Americans (70.7), whites (64.6), and Asians (64.0). Within the Hispanic group are noticeable differences among nationalities. Mexican Americans had a fertility rate of 112.1; Puerto Ricans, 75.5; and Cubans, 50.1. These Hispanic groups have specific geographic concentrations (see Map 1-13), with consequences for the analysis of the birth rate map. In other words, the geographic concentration of ethnic groups is an important consideration in understanding the national birth rate map.

As Map 1-6 indicates, the birth rate varies significantly from region to region, state to state, and county to county. According to the U.S. Census regional divisions (Map 4-1), New England has the lowest birth rate (56.7 births per 1,000 women, and the Mountain West has the highest (73.0). The state data show that Maine and Vermont have the lowest birth rates (49.5 and 49.6, respectively) and that seven western states, including Alaska, have birth rates over 70.0. Utah has the highest birth rate, with 88.5 births per 1,000 women per year. This birth rate can be attributed to the influence of the Mormon religion, which encourages large families and a traditional role for women (Map 1-19). In addition, many Hispanics in the West come from a Roman Catholic tradition that also favors large families (Map 1-16). The youthful population of Alaska and the high numbers of Native Americans account for the state's high birth rate.

The largest area of lower-than-average birth rate, as shown in Map 1-6, is in the center of the nation, the Great Plains region, an extensive area of decline in farm population and massive out-migration of the young. Hard labor and the lack of economic viability associated with farming make the vocation unappealing to many farm children.

Map 1-6 *Average Annual Birth Rate, by County, 1990–1999*

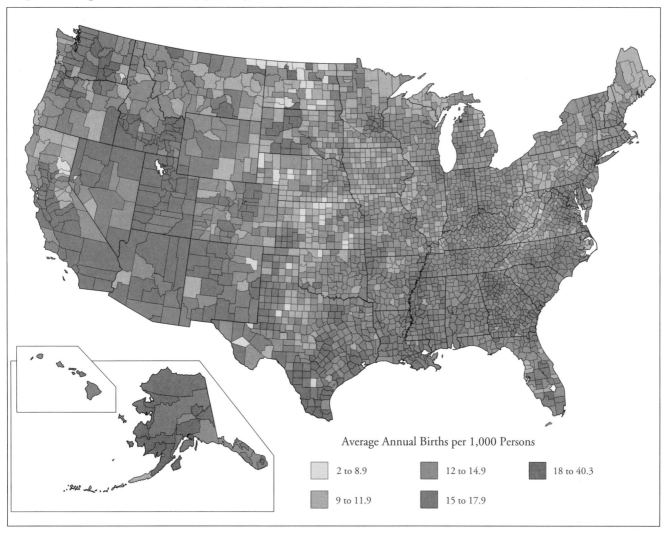

Average Annual Births per 1,000 Persons

- 2 to 8.9
- 9 to 11.9
- 12 to 14.9
- 15 to 17.9
- 18 to 40.3

Improvements in mechanization has increased the size of farms but decreased the number of farms and farmers. In most rural counties in the Great Plains and the western agricultural Midwest, the population is "aging in place," meaning that the average age of a county's population is increasing as young people move away. With fewer women of childbearing age living in these counties, the birth rate drops. The situation is the same in central Appalachia and northern Maine, where average birth rates also are low.

The largest area of high birth rates is the West. In addition to the high percentage of Mormons and Roman Catholics in this region, several counties in northern Arizona and New Mexico are heavily populated by Native Americans, who have a higher-than-average birth rate. Native American concentrations also account for the high birth rate in several counties in the upper Great Plains, in an otherwise low birth rate area (Map 1-15). Other areas with higher-than-average birth rates, including some counties with a high percentage of African Americans are found in the South, especially in the Mississippi River Valley Delta area of northwestern Mississippi (Map 1-12). In general, in the areas that attract young, mobile people who are seeking employment, the average age tends to be lower and the average birth rate tends to be higher, as can be seen in the metropolitan areas of Atlanta, Charlotte, Dallas-Ft. Worth, and Houston.

The age structure of an area's population influences its political agenda in significant ways. Regions with a growing population are concerned with the number and quality of schools, aid to dependent children, day care, and the availability and cost of housing. Conversely, regions with an aging population are concerned with issues such as Social Security, prescription drug coverage for the elderly, nursing home legislation, and medical research on diseases such as

Alzheimer's. As the population of the United States ages, the latter issues may gain more of the national political agenda.

Map 1-7 illustrates the geographic variation in death rates. The crude annual death rate in the United States has averaged around 8.64 per thousand since 1990. Because death is most highly correlated with age, the regional patterns are somewhat similar to the patterns for birth rates, shown in Map 1-6. Rural counties in the central portion of the county have a high percentage of elderly residents and, therefore, high death rates. Areas that are similarly aging in place are found in rural Appalachia and in some areas of the rural South and West. Areas with a higher-than-average number of retirees, such as many counties in Florida, also have high death rates.

In an average year in the United States, approximately 2,333,000 people die. Because there are almost 4,000,000 births a year, the nation's population is increasing naturally. The average life expectancy in the United States is between seventy-six and seventy-seven years, a record high. White females have the greatest life expectancy (80.0 years), followed by African American females (74.8 years). White males live an average of 74.5 years, and African American males live an average of 67.6 years. Life span is highly correlated with lifestyle and health, as measured by statistics on alcoholism, diet, drug abuse, education, and marital status. Class and income levels are correlated with access to quality health care, which in turn affects life spans.[8]

The western states, including Alaska, have clusters of counties with low death rates. In general, the youthful population and healthy environment enhance their statistics. Utah and surrounding counties are a high life expectancy area because of the influence of the Mormon religion, which forbids the use of alcohol and encourages marriage. Clusters of low death-rate counties in the eastern half of the nation are found in urban and suburban areas with youthful populations living near quality health care facilities.[9]

Map 1-7 *Average Annual Death Rate, by County, 1990–1999*

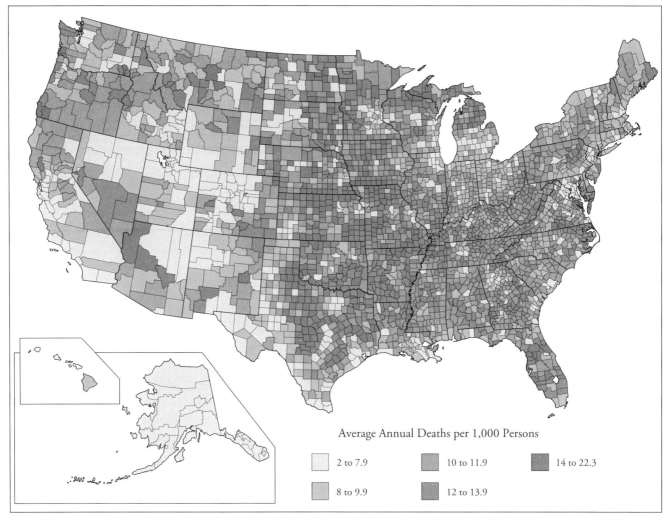

Average Annual Deaths per 1,000 Persons

2 to 7.9   10 to 11.9   14 to 22.3

8 to 9.9   12 to 13.9

The political issues surrounding the death rate map are similar to those discussed in the birth rate map. The age structure of the population is an important variable with respect to the political agenda of an area. Regions with an aging population are more concerned with issues such as Social Security, prescription drug coverage for the elderly, nursing home legislation, and funding for medical research on diseases such as Alzheimer's disease, cancer, diabetes, heart failure, and stroke.

Natural population change is the difference between the total number of births and deaths per year. Natural population change explains much about the demographic makeup of a place, but it is not the only determinant of population growth or decline. Internal migration and international immigration also are important, and all four variables determine total population change. In the United States the population is increasing. Not only do births far outnumber deaths each year, but also the sum total of persons immigrating to the United States far exceeds the sum total of Americans leaving to live in other countries.

Map 1-8 illustrates the average natural population change by county from 1990 to 1999. For the United States as a whole the population increased from 248,790,925 to an estimated 272,690,813, and births outnumbered deaths, for a positive natural population change rate. Counties with an annual natural change rate of 1 percent or higher, as shown in Map 1-8, are well above the national average, and counties with a negative natural change rate are well below the national average of .71 percent.

The state with the lowest natural change rate in 1999 was West Virginia (.09 percent), followed by Maine (.28 percent), Pennsylvania (.26 percent), and Florida (.36 percent). In no state in the 1990s did deaths outnumber births, but that was the situation in numerous counties. Map 1-8 shows that the largest group of contiguous counties in which deaths outnumbered births is in the Great Plains and parts

Map 1-8 *Natural Population Change, by County, 1990–1999*

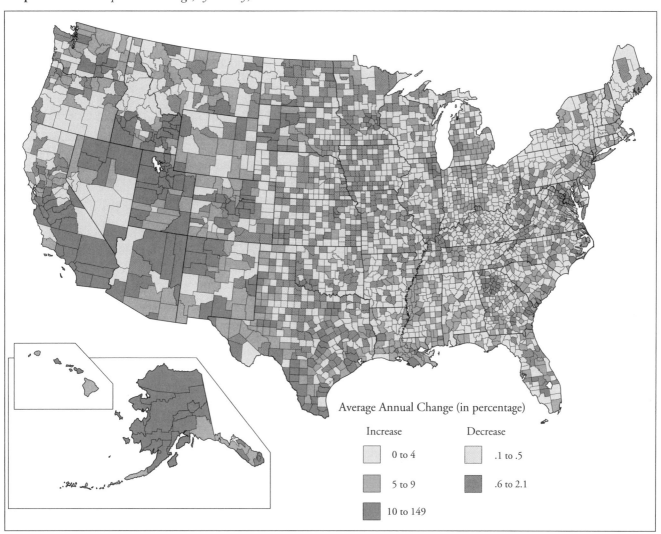

Average Annual Change (in percentage)

Increase
- 0 to 4
- 5 to 9
- 10 to 149

Decrease
- .1 to .5
- .6 to 2.1

of the rural agricultural Midwest. The counties with a negative rate of natural change have elderly populations. Many people of childbearing age leave the region to pursue economic opportunities elsewhere because the dominant rural agricultural economy of the Great Plains is in decline and cannot sustain employment for a growing population. Other pockets of negative natural change have economies that depend on agriculture, ranching, or mining, such as the Upper Peninsula of Michigan, northern Maine, southern Illinois, and a few counties in the Interior West. In central Appalachia the slumping mining economy and mountainous terrain has also prompted negative natural change.

Florida provides one of the most interesting demographic studies in the United States. As Map 1-8 indicates, in the 1990s sixteen counties in central Florida registered more deaths than births, as would be expected in a state with one-fifth of its total population age sixty-five or over (see Map 1-10). Florida also has one of the fastest growing populations of any state. In fact, most of the same sixteen counties have a net population growth far *above* the national average (Map 1-5). The only variable that can account for this phenomenon is the high net migration rate of American citizens and overseas immigrants moving to Florida in general and to these counties in particular (Map 1-11). Even though the elderly are dying at a rate higher than the birth rate in these Florida counties, the number of people moving in is more than enough to produce a high total net population growth.

In the Mississippi River Valley Delta country, located where the states of Arkansas, Louisiana, and Mississippi adjoin, the opposite demographic situation occurs. This region has a positive natural population change, as shown in Map 1-8. It has a high percentage of young people (Map 1-9) and African Americans (Map 1-12), and the birth rate is above the national average. Map 1-5, however, shows that the Delta's overall population is declining because migration out of the area is occurring so rapidly that it outweighs the natural increase (Map 1-11).

Map 1-8 also shows counties with a natural change above the national average. For the latter part of the 1990s, the states with the highest rate of natural increase were Utah (1.74 percent), Alaska (1.54 percent), California (1.19 percent), Texas (1.16 percent), and Hawaii (1.06 percent). The West is increasing in population, not just from in-migration, but from high birth rates relative to death rates, especially among Mormons (Map 1-19). The West and Alaska also have large Native American populations, another group with a high birth rate (Map 1-15). Areas along the Mexico border and California have a large Hispanic population, including many young Mexican immigrants, who have the highest birth rate of any major segment of American society (Map 1-13).

The young and middle-aged who have left the Great Plains, the rural agricultural Midwest, the Mississippi Delta, and Appalachia generally have migrated to job-generating urban areas, giving the metropolitan areas a more youthful demographic profile. In the East other pockets of high natural population change are found in metropolitan areas. In the Midwest similar population growth has occurred in the suburban counties near large cities, for example, Chicago and Minneapolis-St. Paul. The metropolitan areas of Atlanta, Charlotte, Dallas-Ft. Worth, and Washington, D.C., are especially notable on Map 1-8.

Residents of places with a negative natural change are concerned not only about economic development and the future of the state or county but also about health care policies that affect the elderly. People in regions with a high positive increase may be more concerned with controlling growth and providing increased health care facilities and hospitals. Natural growth or decline is an important variable in understanding the total population picture of any county, state, or nation.

Demographers identify two "dependent" age groups when examining age structure—persons over sixty-five and those under fifteen. These groups are dependent in the sense that, for the most part, they are consumers rather than producers of goods and services. The atlas considers the younger group in Map 1-9, which illustrates the age structure of counties in the United States with respect to the percentage of the population under fifteen years of age.

The age makeup of an area reveals much about its demographic, social, and economic composition. The Census Bureau uses two measurements of youth—the percentage of the population under fifteen, which is historically the age before procreation and childbearing, and the percentage of the population under eighteen, which is currently the common age of legal adult status. In the United States a citizen may exercise the right to vote at age eighteen, and most state statutes give eighteen-year-olds adult standing. The state, however, still has certain obligations to individuals under age eighteen, with respect to education and many other aspects of the care of minors. Their numbers, ages, and locations are therefore critical to effective planning for schools and other facilities. Counties with 27 percent of the population under fifteen are considered youthful, and counties with fewer than 18 percent of the population under age fifteen are considered middle aged or elderly.

In 1996 approximately 26.0 percent of the U.S. population was under eighteen. In comparison, 40 percent to 50 percent of the population in most nations in Asia, Africa, and Latin America—where the majority of the world's population lives—is under eighteen. Even the states in the United States with the most youthful populations come nowhere near the

Map 1-9 *Percentage of Population Under Fifteen Years of Age, by County, 1996*

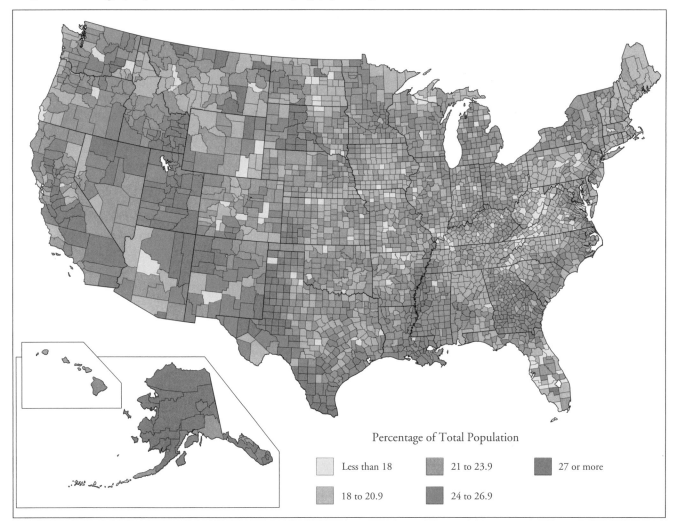

Percentage of Total Population

Less than 18 — 18 to 20.9 — 21 to 23.9 — 24 to 26.9 — 27 or more

world average. The youngest state is Utah, with 33.9 percent of its population under age eighteen. Ranking second through fifth are the western states of Alaska (30.4 percent), Idaho (29.3 percent), New Mexico (29.3 percent), and Texas (28.5 percent). At the opposite end of the spectrum is West Virginia, with 23.1 percent of its population under eighteen, followed by three northeastern states—Massachusetts (23.3 percent), Rhode Island (23.8 percent), and Pennsylvania (24.0 percent)—and Florida (23.8 percent).

In addition to these regional differences, racial differences also affect the population age structure. In 1996 approximately 21.8 percent of the population of the United States was under the age of fifteen. At 20.9 percent, whites are below the national average of young people in the population. Among minority groups the percentages are larger than the national average: Hispanics (29.9 percent), Native Americans (29.2 percent), African Americans (26.7 percent), and Asians (24.3 percent). From these numbers, we can con-

clude that counties and states with large minority populations also tend to have a high percentage of persons under fifteen years of age. Likewise, states and counties with small minority populations usually have a smaller percentage of their population under age fifteen.

One common characteristic of most areas with a low percentage of youth population is that they have a high percentage of whites and a low percentage of minorities (Utah is an obvious exception). West Virginia, where the population is 97 percent white, is a perfect example: in fifty-one of the state's fifty-five counties the percentage of children is below the national average. Appalachia's declining mining economy encourages out-migration of young families and attracts few youthful immigrants. Areas of agricultural decline in the Midwest and Great Plains also show similar clusters of low-youth counties.

Almost all the counties with a high percentage of youths are located in the West. These clusters are strongly correlated with specific demographic groups. The cluster in Utah and southern Idaho is the core of the Mormon cultural region (see Map 1-19). The Latter Day Saints religion encourages large families, and Utah has the largest percentage of young people in the nation, more than all other large segments of the white population. High percentages of youths in Alaska, northeastern Arizona, northwestern New Mexico, and some Great Plains counties reflect concentrations of Native Americans (Map 1-15). The youthful clusters along the U.S.-Mexican border, in west Texas, and in the Central Valley of California correlate with a high Mexican American presence (Map 1-13). In addition, there is a high percentage of youths in the Mississippi River Valley Delta country, an area of high African American population (Map 1-12).

The political implications of the youth population, whether large or small, are similar to those of birth rates, as discussed above. A declining youth population can cause disruptions in the public school system. In West Virginia some schools have closed and others have consolidated because of declining enrollments. Federal education support dollars are also impacted, and the state's higher education system must recruit students from out of state. In California, with its high rates of immigration and above average minority birth rates, the demographics of the school population have radically changed. In recent years more than half of the public high school graduates in the state have been African American, Asian, or Hispanic.

In general, voters in areas with youthful populations are more concerned with schools, school bond levies, child care, children's health insurance, immunizations, public parks, and similar issues. Areas with a declining youth population are more concerned with issues relating to aging or with reversing a declining economy and retaining and attracting young families.

Map 1-10 illustrates the age structure of U.S. counties in terms of the percentage of the population age sixty-five and over. The map of the elderly population of the United States shows some distinct patterns. The largest and by far the most significant concentration of elderly as a percentage of the population is found in the Great Plains and rural Midwest. Here the population is aging in place; that is, the older population remains while a high percentage of the young leave after high school and college. This exodus is motivated by the decline in the farm sector economy and the lack of other economic opportunities in the region. Another region aging in place is Appalachia, the center of which is shown on Map 1-10 by a band of rural counties in West Virginia and western Pennsylvania. The decline in the coal and steel industries and a lack of new economic opportunities in these mostly rural places encourage out-migration of the more

youthful population. Most of the dark-shaded counties on Map 1-10, therefore, are indicators of not only a high proportion of elderly inhabitants but also of a declining economy. Many remaining in these places are retired and living on fixed incomes.

Age sixty-five is the traditional age of retirement in the United States and the rest of the western world. First established in Europe more than a hundred years ago, sixty-five was the age in which state retirement benefits began and was also the average life span at that time. Today, most people still regard age sixty-five as the standard for retirement age. What is interesting is that, although life spans are getting longer, many workers take "early retirement" before age sixty-five. For decades the Census Bureau has reported various demographic statistics using age sixty-five as a benchmark. Professional gerontologists use sixty-five and over to define old age. They even classify groups within the "elderly" category—sixty-five to seventy-four as young-old, seventy-five to eighty-four as middle-old, and above eighty-five as old-old. Because of medical advances, healthier lifestyles, and declining birth rates, the over-eighty-five age group is the fastest growing in the United States in percentages.

In 1996 approximately 12.8 percent of the American population was over age sixty-five. The United States, Canada, and most of the nations of Western Europe have the highest percentage of elderly in the world. In contrast, the poorer developing nations have much lower elderly percentages, many less than 5 percent. The top five, or most elderly states, are Florida (18.5 percent), followed by Pennsylvania (15.9 percent), Rhode Island (15.8 percent), Iowa (15.2 percent), and West Virginia (15.2 percent). Slow-growing states and out-migration areas in the North, Appalachia, Great Plains, and the agricultural Midwest have the highest percentage of elderly. States reporting the smallest percentage of population sixty-five and over are Alaska (5.2 percent), followed by Utah (8.8 percent), Georgia (7.9 percent), Colorado (10.1 percent), and Texas (10.2 percent). The West has the lowest percentage of the elderly, and low percentages are also found in other growing areas in the Sun Belt, such as Georgia and North Carolina.

In addition to regional differences, racial differences can be observed in the population age structure. In 1996, 13.0 percent of the white population was above sixty-five, slightly above the national average. Among minority groups the percentages are smaller: African American (7.3 percent), Asian (6.4 percent), Native American (5.9 percent), and Hispanic (5.2 percent).

Some counties have a high percentage of elderly not because they are aging in place but because they attract more mobile, more affluent retirees. For example, in almost

Map 1-10 *Percentage of Population Age Sixty-Five or Over, by County, 1996*

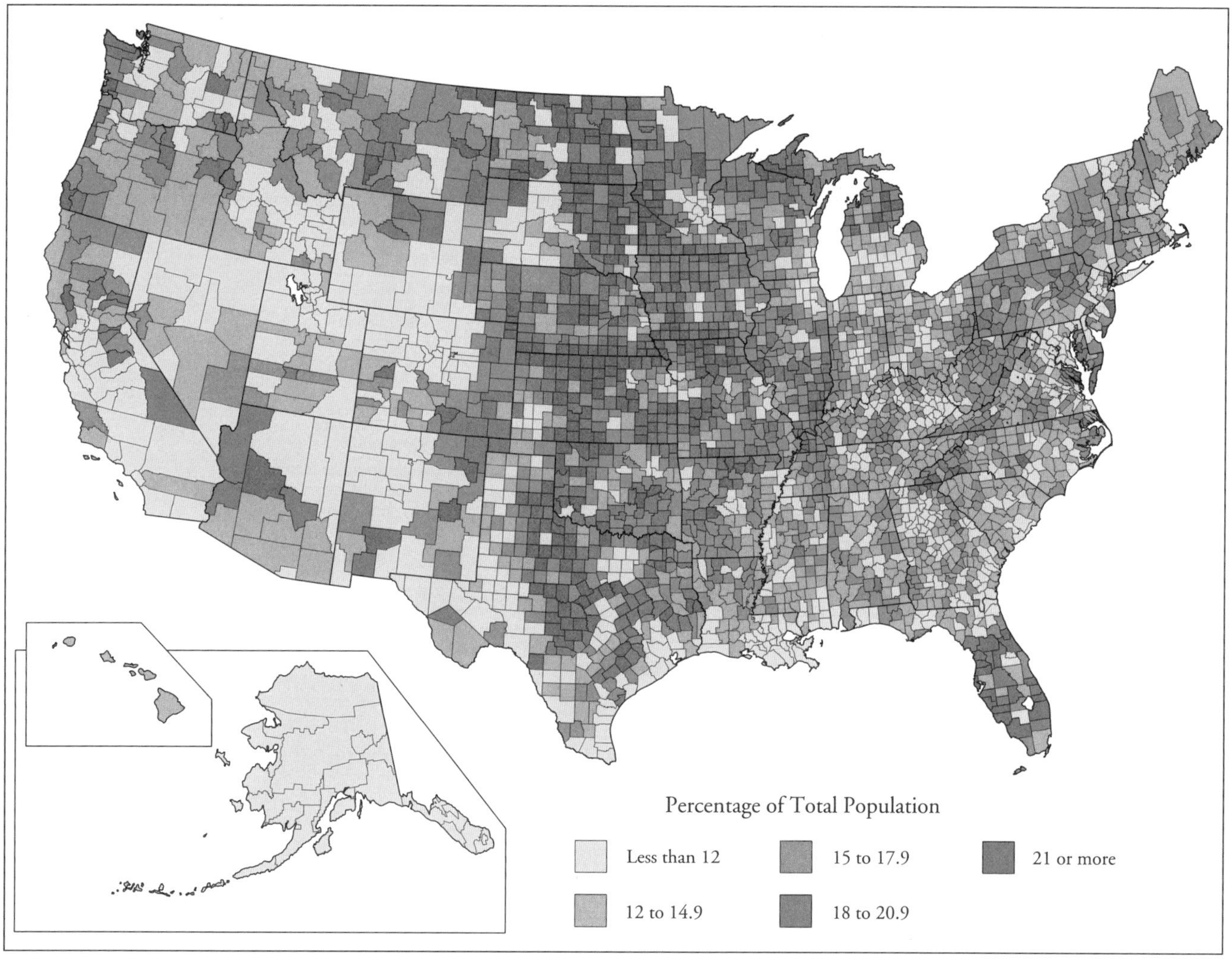

Percentage of Total Population

Less than 12 | 15 to 17.9 | 21 or more

12 to 14.9 | 18 to 20.9

twenty counties of Florida, mostly those along the coast, 20 percent or more of the population is older than sixty-five. Florida has been a magnet for retirees for more than a half century. As private pension plans become the norm in the postindustrial age, the number of retirees who can afford to move south will no doubt increase. In addition to Florida, western retirement centers also attract wealthy and middle class retirees. Some large retirement communities have sprung up in Yavapai County, Arizona (Prescott and Sedona).

As was discussed in connection with Map 1-7, as the average life span increases, the U.S. population ages. AARP, formerly known as the American Association of Retired Persons, is one of the most active lobbying groups in Washington, D.C. AARP's list of important political issues includes Medicare, Social Security, long-term care, private health insurance reform, prescription drug coverage for the elderly, assistance for older people in voting by absentee bal-

lot, health and safety regulation for nursing homes and senior housing facilities, and grandparents' rights.

In 1900, 4 percent of the national population was over sixty-five; in 1996, 12.8 percent was. By 2030, as the baby boom generation ages, about 20 percent will be sixty-five and older. Election data show that the elderly register and vote at a higher rate than any other age group, and it is clear that the issues that concern them will continue to grow in political importance.

Map 1-11 illustrates net migration for the ten-year period from 1990 to 1999. Net migration counts both internal migration from other U.S. counties and international immigration. The more than 3,000 U.S. counties on the map fall into two large categories. The first is counties with net out-migration, that is, counties that have lost population through migration and have a negative number. The second category is counties with net in-migration, counties that have gained population through migration and have a pos-

Map 1-11 *Average Annual Net Migration, by County, 1990–1999*

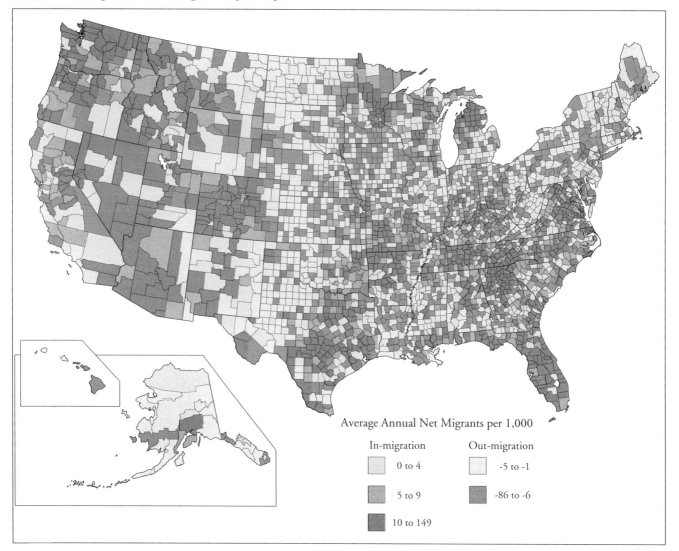

Average Annual Net Migrants per 1,000

In-migration

	0 to 4
	5 to 9
	10 to 149

Out-migration

| | -5 to -1 |
| | -86 to -6 |

itive number. The map also gives the intensity rate for both categories. This type of detail furnishes an in-depth examination far greater than state level data.

Map 1-11 shows that the largest single region of out-migration is the Great Plains agricultural region stretching north and south down the center of the nation. Changes and decline in the rural farm economy encourage such migration. Many counties in the agricultural Midwest, for example along the Ohio-Indiana border and upstate New York, are also in this category. Changes in agriculture also explain the large cluster of counties in the Mississippi River Valley along the Arkansas, Louisiana, and Mississippi border and scattered counties in the rural subtropical South (Map 1-12). A cluster of counties in central Appalachia shows out-migration from declining coal counties (Map 1-26).

The population of a county or state grows or declines based upon four demographic factors: births, deaths, internal migration, and international immigration. California's population changes, for example, illustrate why all four factors must be considered to understand the total population change in an area. In 1999 California experienced negative internal migration because more Americans moved out of the state than moved in. However, California experienced an overall increase in population because of high international migration and a high birth rate.

The United States has a long history of internal migration. Almost from the beginning of settlement on the Atlantic seaboard, migrants moved westward with the frontier. When the country began to industrialize, a large-scale migration from farms to cities also began. After World War II, millions of Americans moved from cities to suburbs, creating metropolitan areas that eventually spread into adjacent counties. The movement of population to cities and suburbs is still evident in recent years, and Map 1-11 captures a number of these trends.

Internal population migration occurs for a number of reasons, including economic opportunities, technological changes, and social conditions. Places that offer employment tend to grow rapidly, while those that lack jobs either grow slowly or decline. Economic opportunities may shift over time. For example, in the early twentieth century the industrial cities of Cleveland and Pittsburgh grew rapidly, but more recently industrial employment has declined, and these cities have stagnated and even declined. Technological changes affected the livability of some places. Before air conditioning came into widespread use after World War II, many people regarded summers in the South and Southwest as intolerable. Today, the ability to be comfortable during the summer and the pleasant winter climates contribute to the regions' population growth. The movement of retirees to Florida, Arizona, and other Sun Belt states (Map 1-10) has greatly increased in recent decades because of the universal availability of Social Security and private pension plans. Internal migrants, therefore, tend to be young people seeking first employment, middle-aged individuals transferring jobs or recently unemployed, or recently retired people changing residence. In any case, the out-migrants are not only a demographic loss to an area but also an economic and social loss, while in-migrants are usually a gain for the community.

The rates of state in-migration and out-migration show vast regional differences. New York, Illinois, and Pennsylvania have annual negative migration numbers in the tens of thousands, while Arizona, Nevada, Florida, and Georgia have positive migration numbers in the tens of thousands. The Sun Belt and the West in general have the largest areas of in-migration, which results from both internal migration and international immigration. The Colorado Rockies, Interior West, and Pacific Northwest all have many growing counties. Even in this region, however, not all counties are growing. In mining areas, Indian reservations, and ranching counties, out-migration exceeds in-migration. In the South, Florida continues its many-decade in-migration pattern. Atlanta's rapid expansion leads the growth of the entire area of North Georgia, while some counties in South Georgia declined. The Ozarks and Hill Country of central Texas are two other Sun Belt areas that gained population.

A close examination of the map also shows the growth of suburban counties adjacent to large cities. Although Cook County, Illinois, has net out-migration, many people are moving to suburbs in adjacent counties. Similar patterns are seen in Cleveland, Dallas-Ft. Worth, and Pittsburgh.

Of the political consequences of internal migration and international immigration, perhaps the most important is the reapportionment of the U.S. House of Representatives. State and regional power in the House depend on numbers of representatives. For several decades Illinois, New York, and Pennsylvania have been losing population and representatives, and Arizona, California, Florida, and Texas have gained population and representatives. In late 2000 the Census Bureau announced that the nation's resident population on Census Day, April 1, 2000, was 281,421,906, a 13.2 percent increase over the 248,709,873 counted in the 1990 census. Based upon the final state counts, seats in the U.S. House of Representatives were reapportioned as follows. Eight states gained representatives: Arizona (+2), California (+1), Colorado (+1), Florida (+2), Georgia (+2), Nevada (+1), North Carolina (+1), and Texas (+2). Nine states lost representatives: Connecticut (-1), Illinois (-1), Indiana (-1), Michigan (-1), Mississippi (-1), New York (-2), Ohio (-1), Oklahoma (-1), Pennsylvania (-2), and Wisconsin (-1).

An internal shift in population in the United States causes a subsequent shift in political power. States and regions gaining population also gain more power in setting the political agenda in Congress and the nation. What is important for Florida and Georgia may not be for New York and Pennsylvania. The larger a state's congressional delegation, the better its chances for gaining seats on powerful committees and for having federal projects directed to it.

Ethnicity

Maps 1-12 through 1-15 display the distribution of African Americans, Hispanic Americans, Asian Americans, and Native Americans in the United States. Map 1-12 shows the percentage of African American population by county. The map also shows one of the most striking spatial patterns in U.S. geography, history, and politics. The pattern is quite similar to the census map on the eve of the Civil War in 1860.

The first Africans were probably brought to the American colonies in 1619. African slavery, legal in the British colonial system, spread with the cultivation of tobacco, rice, and cotton in the coastal areas and slavery continued with the establishment of the United States. In fact, the Constitution permitted the legal importation of slaves until 1808. African slaves were settled in the tobacco-growing areas of southern and eastern shore Maryland and in the tobacco belt along the Virginia-North Carolina border, and these areas have high African American percentages today. The second concentration of African settlement occurred in the rice-growing lowland areas of South Carolina and eventually in the coastal and interior areas of cotton cultivation. The invention of the cotton gin in the 1790s allowed the spread of cotton cultivation, and the continuation of the

Map 1-12 *African American Population, by County, 2000*

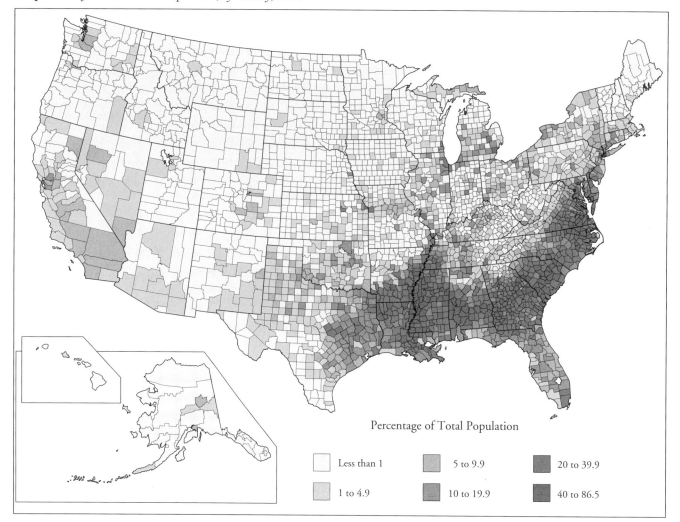

Percentage of Total Population

Less than 1	5 to 9.9	20 to 39.9
1 to 4.9	10 to 19.9	40 to 86.5

slave system, across the subtropical belt of the United States westward through Georgia, Alabama, and Mississippi, into east Texas. One area of extensive cotton cultivation was along the southern portion of the Mississippi River Valley. All these areas today have the highest percentage of African American counties in the United States.

The 1790 census gave the first accurate count of the racial composition of the United States. Nearly one-fifth (19.3 percent) of the population was black, the highest percentage in U.S. history. More than 95 percent of the black population lived in the Middle Atlantic and southern states. Not all blacks were slaves, however, even in 1790. Nearly 8 percent of blacks were free, and this percentage rose to almost 11 percent after the ratification of the Constitution when the northern states began to ban slavery. Many, but not all, free blacks lived in this region. Still, a majority of African Americans were held as slaves until the end of the Civil War in 1865.

In 2000 the census counted the African American popu-

lation at 34,658,190, 12.3 percent of the total population.[10] One aspect of the current African American population, which is not adequately illustrated in Map 1-12, is that millions of blacks reside in the northern states. Black migration to the North increased dramatically with the cessation of European immigrant labor when World War I began in August 1914. This migration north continued until the 1960s, except during the Great Depression years of the 1930s. This flow was almost exclusively to large and medium sized industrial cities rather than rural agricultural areas. At the beginning of the twentieth century, roughly 95 percent of blacks lived in the South. Today, only slightly more than half of all African Americans live in the South. Thirty-eight percent live in the North. States with a large black population are New York (3,222,461), mostly in New York City and other large cities; Illinois (1,854,173), mostly in the Chicago area; Michigan (1,415,201), mostly in the Detroit area; and Ohio (1,304,126), mostly in Cleveland and other large cities. Some black migration to the western states has occurred since World War II, but less than 10 percent of all blacks live in the West. Most western blacks are again concentrated in the cities and most in California (2,487,006).

The general pattern of the black population map is sharp in its divisions. Vast areas of the United States have almost no African American population, notably the northernmost tier, including northern New England, from Wisconsin through to the West Coast, Interior West, and the northern Great Plains. One large area of the East also has almost no blacks. Most of Appalachia, even areas in the South, was not inhabited by blacks in the initial plantation slave regime and did not attract large black population subsequently. For example, the state of West Virginia, the only state wholly within Appalachia, is 97 percent white.

The most striking pattern is the area beginning south of the Mason-Dixon line in Maryland and Delaware and continuing south through the subtropical zone of the United States west to east Texas. Much of this area consists of rural counties in which the African American population is either the majority or a very large minority. The concentration of the African American population in the South has affected American history and politics in significant ways, including the formula for counting slaves for purposes of representation, the abolitionist movement in the North, and the Civil War. Freedom and voting rights won by blacks after the Civil War were gradually lost in the post–Reconstruction Era and the period of Jim Crow laws. In was not until the civil rights movement gained strength and the passage of voting rights laws of the 1960s that African Americans began to register again in large numbers and to be a force in southern and American politics. This force has grown steadily up until and including the presidential election of 2000. Blacks constitute more than 25 percent of the population and electorate in a number of southern states, and have become influential in deciding who is elected U.S. senator, governor, and other statewide officials. The southern and northern black electorate is roughly 90 percent Democratic.[11] Since the 1970s small numbers of blacks have been elected to the U.S. House from the South, but because of the creation of minority-majority congressional districts, the number of African American representatives increased in the 1990s. In addition, more African American mayors, county officials, and other officers have been elected.

The black electorate in the north and California also plays a critical role in local and statewide politics. In the North, most African Americans initially voted Republican, the party of Abraham Lincoln. This pattern held until the 1930s, when Franklin Roosevelt forged a new Democratic coalition. The northern Democratic Party grew more favorably inclined toward civil rights and social legislation important to blacks, which contributed to a split in the party after World War II and eventually pushed conservative southern whites to the Republican Party. Because northern blacks were often concentrated in inner-city ghettoes, they were able to elect city council members, mayors, state legislators, and eventually U.S. representatives. In recent decades, African Americans have been elected to almost every level of government in both black majority and white majority constituencies. In statewide elections blacks again play an important role, especially in close contests. The Democratic Party has counted on roughly 90 percent of this large voting bloc in many gubernatorial, senatorial, and presidential elections.

In addition to electoral strength, the geographical location of African Americans affects a wide variety of legislation. Civil rights, minimum wage, aid to dependent children, welfare reform, equal opportunity, and affirmative action are important issues to this community. In some cases, however, the "reverse" pattern is evident. In many areas of the South, the white population sees these issues as threats to the majority community. Some areas of the North, Minnesota and Wisconsin, for example, show strong support for such issues, even though—or perhaps because—small numbers of blacks live in these places.

Map 1-13 shows the distribution of people of Hispanic origin by county. In 2000 the census counted the Hispanic population in the United States at 35,305,818, 12.5 percent of the nation. Hispanics are officially the largest minority group in the nation. The Hispanic population has different origins, each with a particular geographic concentration in the United States. Mexican Americans are by far the largest group, constituting 58.4 percent of all Hispanics. Mexican Americans are concentrated in the four states bordering Mexico, but in recent decades millions of Mexican Americans have immigrated to northern agricultural areas and cities. Because the Mexican presence in the northern United States is historically concentrated in central cities, Map 1-13 does not fully illustrate their numbers.

Almost 10 percent (9.6) of the Hispanic community is Puerto Rican. As American citizens since 1916, Puerto Ricans have had unrestricted access to residence in the United States for most of the twentieth century. Their migration to the mainland intensified in the 1940s and 1950s and aimed at large northern industrial cities, which were expanding at that time. New York City, Buffalo, Rochester, New Haven, and Chicago have large Puerto Rican communities. Map 1-13 indicates a Hispanic presence in Cook County, Illinois (Chicago) and surrounding counties, and this group is both Mexican and Puerto Rican. In fact, one minority-majority district is a Hispanic district in Chicago linking a Puerto Rican neighborhood with a Mexican neighborhood.

Map 1-13 *Hispanic Population, by County, 2000*

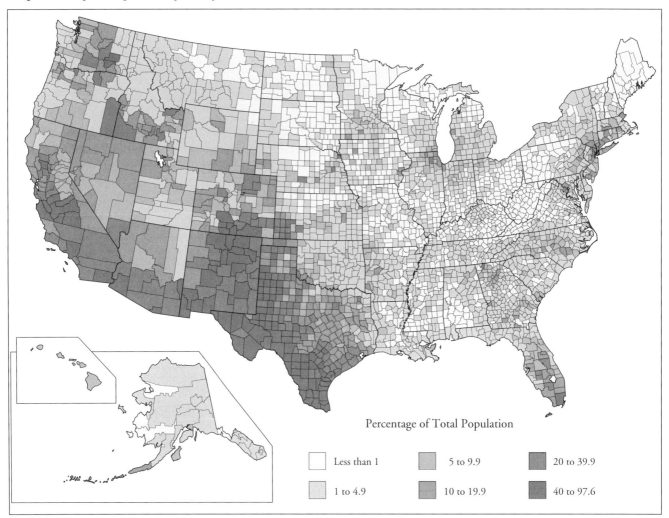

Percentage of Total Population

Less than 1	5 to 9.9	20 to 39.9
1 to 4.9	10 to 19.9	40 to 97.6

Cuban Americans constitute another significant part of the Hispanic population. Although only 3.2 percent of the national Hispanic total, Cubans are concentrated in Florida, especially the southeast portion. Cubans began arriving in great numbers in the 1960s after the Cuban revolution and the establishment of a communist state by Fidel Castro. Preferring to stay close to Cuba in a subtropical climate, most settled in Miami and the surrounding counties.

The remaining one-fourth (28.8 percent) of Hispanics come from many countries, mostly in the Caribbean and Central and South America. Political turmoil and poor economic conditions in El Salvador, Guatemala, and Nicaragua led to increased immigration to the United States. The Dominican Republic also has an immigrant presence in the United States, as do large countries in South America such as Brazil and Colombia.

The influence of Hispanic Americans in U.S. politics is considerable, and, as they are the fastest-growing large ethnic group, their political power is expanding at a significant rate. But in heavily Hispanic areas in the American southwest, Mexican Americans were elected to local offices as early as the nineteenth century. Eventually, Mexican Americans from this region and Puerto Ricans from northern cities were elected to the U.S. House of Representatives. As are most immigrants, Mexicans and Puerto Ricans are predominately Democrats, and, therefore, most Hispanic state legislators, statewide elected officials, and U.S. representatives are Democrats.[12] This voting pattern also holds true in races for governor, senator, and president. Counties with a heavily Hispanic population, as illustrated in Map 1-13, tend to support Democratic candidates for president (Maps 2-1 to 2-22). The growing influence of the Hispanic vote has gained the attention of both national political parties. Indeed, in 2000 the first Spanish speaking modern presidential candidate, Republican governor George W. Bush of Texas, made inroads, especially in his home state, in the normal Hispanic Democratic voting pattern.

One Hispanic community, the Cubans, is heavily Republican, not Democratic.[13] In fact, the Cubans are the only large immigrant group in the twentieth century not to align with the national Democratic Party. Many fleeing communist Cuba in the 1960s were conservative, well-educated, and upper or middle class, unlike earlier immigrant groups. Because of their geographic concentration in Florida, the Cubans' influence in their state's politics is becoming legendary. The Cuban vote can be decisive in races for U.S. representative, U.S. senator, and especially the winner of the large number of Florida's electoral college votes. The Cuban community's staunch support of Bush was one of his strongest electoral bases in Florida, eventually giving him the state and allowing him to capture the presidency in 2000. In addition, Cuban American activism and strong anti-Castro policies give the community a powerful, some say dominant, voice in U.S. foreign policy with respect to Cuba.

Map 1-14 shows the percentage of Asian Americans by county. In the census category Asian and Pacific Islander, the 2000 census counted 10,641,833 people, 3.7 percent of the total U.S. population. The Pacific census region, made up of Alaska, California, Hawaii, Oregon, and Washington, contains approximately half of all Americans of Asian descent. More than a million Asians live in California, by far the largest number in any state. New York is second, with slightly more than 1 million. One state, Hawaii, has an Asian majority of nearly two-thirds (63.3 percent). Hawaii is the only state with a nonwhite majority. Other states with a high percentage of Asians are California (12.2 percent), Washington, (6.0 percent), New Jersey (5.8 percent), New York (5.6 percent), and Nevada (4.9 percent).

Map 1-14 indicates only a few small areas in the United States, with the exception of Hawaii, where Asians make up more than 5 percent of the population. On the mainland, the center of the Asian population is a large cluster of counties

Map 1-14 *Asian American and Pacific Islander Population, by County, 2000*

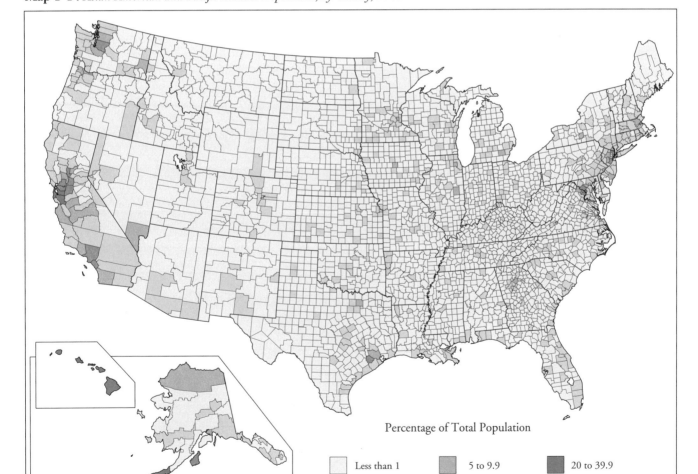

Percentage of Total Population

Less than 1	5 to 9.9	20 to 39.9
1 to 4.9	10 to 19.9	40 to 46.1

surrounding the San Francisco Bay area. This area was the first on the mainland with significant Asian immigration, which began with the need for labor to build the transcontinental railroad in the 1860s. The Asian community in the Bay area continued to grow internally and attract new migrants for more than a century. Other West Coast cities with historic Asian populations are Los Angeles, Portland, and Seattle, and their surrounding counties. The economies of these cities continue to attract new immigrants. Outside of the West two other areas of Asian population are notable. New York City has been a magnet for Chinese immigrants in recent decades, and the population of historic Chinatown has experienced significant growth. The Asian community also has spread to many counties surrounding New York City, including those in northern New Jersey. The other large Asian community is located in the Washington, D.C., region, primarily in the suburban counties in Maryland and Virginia.

Because the Asian community is significantly smaller than the black and Hispanic communities, their impact upon national politics is not on the same level. Where Asian Americans have large numbers, however, their influence is apparent on local and statewide levels. In Hawaii Asians have held virtually all elected state and local offices, including those of U.S. senator and representative. Within the diverse Hawaiian Asian community, those of Japanese descent are by far the largest component, and they have held most of the above offices. Within California, Asians have also made an impact, both around San Francisco Bay and statewide, including a former U.S. senator and a number of representatives. The Asian American community is growing in numbers and influence in the scientific, medical, and business sectors. This influence will make itself felt in the political arena, especially with respect to U.S. relations with China and the rest of Asia.

Map 1-15 shows that most of the United States has little or no Native American population, which is the smallest

Map 1-15 *Native American Population, by County, 2000*

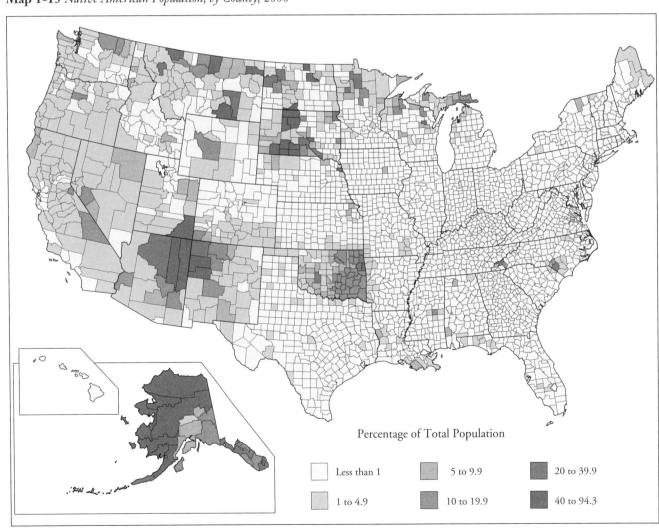

Percentage of Total Population

	Less than 1		5 to 9.9		20 to 39.9
	1 to 4.9		10 to 19.9		40 to 94.3

racial group measured by the U.S. Census. The 2000 census counted 2,475,956 descendants of the original settlers of North America. In census documents the terms *American Indian, Eskimo, and Aleut* and *American Indian and Alaska Native* are used to identify this group. Native Americans comprise a little under 1 percent (0.9) of the population.

The Native American population is concentrated in several areas. Six states have more than 100,000 Native American residents: California (314,000), Oklahoma (263,000), Arizona (261,000), New Mexico (166,000), Washington (105,000), and Alaska (101,000). Although California has the highest number of Native Americans, it ranks sixteenth in percentage of total population (0.9 percent). States with higher percentages are Alaska (16.4 percent), New Mexico (9.5 percent), North Dakota (9.2 percent), Oklahoma (7.8 percent), Montana (6.5 percent), Arizona (5.5 percent), and North Dakota (4.8 percent).

These concentrations reflect the historical policies of both the British colonial and U.S. governments. The conflict over land and resources between Native Americans and European settlers goes back to the earliest colonial days. As the frontier of white settlement moved west, the Native Americans were either exterminated, assimilated with the white population, or driven farther west. The Indian Removal Act of 1830 called for the expulsion of all remaining Native Americans east of the Mississippi River to a reserve in what is now Oklahoma. As a result, the Native American population in the eastern United States is small, and today Oklahoma has the highest number of counties with significant numbers of Native Americans and the second largest Native American population in the United States. These Native Americans are primarily "eastern Indians," that is, members of tribes with origins elsewhere whose ancestors were transported to Oklahoma. For example, the Cherokee are the largest single tribe (19.0 percent of all Native Americans); most live in Oklahoma, but some remain in three ancestral counties in western North Carolina.

The greatest concentration of Native Americans in the United States is in the West. Alaska is nearly one-fifth Eskimo and Aleut. In the forty-eight contiguous states, there are clusters of counties with high Native American populations. These clusters correspond to large Indian reservations. In addition, these "western Indians" live mostly on the remnants of their ancestral lands. The largest reservation and second largest tribe, the Navajos (11.6 percent of all Native Americans), are located in northeastern Arizona, northwestern New Mexico, and part of Utah. Large Indian reservations are also located in the northern Great Plains in South Dakota, North Dakota, and Montana.

More than half of all Native Americans do not live on reservations. Throughout the twentieth century Native Americans have migrated to urban areas seeking employment and economic mobility. Tens of thousands of Indians live in large western cities such as Albuquerque, Denver, Las Vegas, Los Angeles, Phoenix, and Salt Lake City.

The political issues of concern to the Native American population have two major components: participation in civil American society and the policies and governance of Native Americans and their lands. Indians have the right to vote in federal, state, and local elections, and each tribe has its own elections for tribal offices. In addition to Native Americans' serving in state and local offices, four have served in the U.S. Senate, seven in the U.S. House, and Vice President Charles Curtis had a Native American grandparent. The other issues concern reservation and tribal administration, preservation of native culture, reservation gambling and casinos, education, health, natural resource management, and general economic development. The Bureau of Indian Affairs oversees and manages many of these matters, making its budget and effectiveness of interest to the governors, senators, and representatives from the Great Plains and Western states.

Religious Affiliation

The next series of maps shows the distribution of affiliates to religious groups in the United States. Map 1-16 depicts the percentage of Roman Catholics in the United States by county. The map shows that Catholics live in the northern tier of states and in the Southwest. The Catholic descendants of immigrants from Ireland, Italy, and Eastern Europe who began arriving in the nineteenth century still live in the metropolitan areas of the old industrial Northeast and the industrial Great Lakes. Catholics from southern Germany and Ukraine settled in the upper Midwest, Wisconsin, Minnesota, and farther west in mining communities. Along the southern tier, parts of Louisiana stand out as an anomaly in the South. Many people there are the descendants of French, Spanish, and Cajun Catholics. In addition, the heavily Hispanic regions along the Mexican border are also predominately Catholic (Map 1-13).

The areas of little or no Catholic presence are striking. Vast areas of the nation, including the southern Appalachians and the Deep South, have few Catholics. During the period of heavy Catholic immigration in the late nineteenth and early twentieth centuries, these areas were not industrializing. Also, Catholics immigrants tended to avoid settling in the South because a strong anti-Catholic sentiment persisted there.

Map 1-16 *Roman Catholic Adherents, by County, 1990*

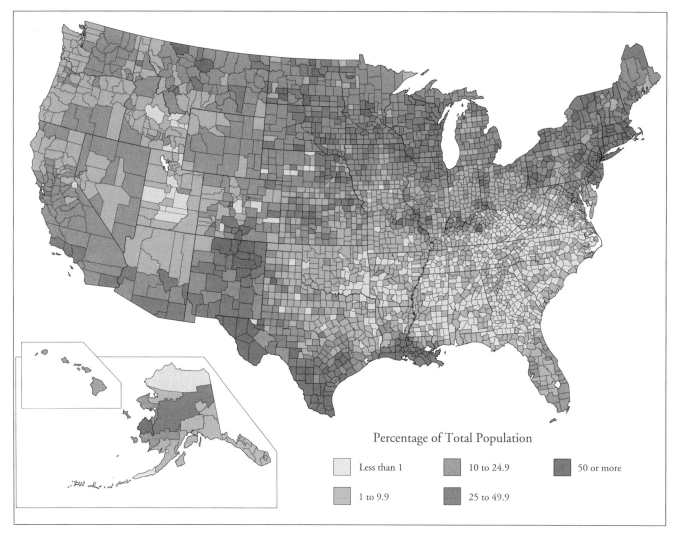

Percentage of Total Population

Less than 1	10 to 24.9	50 or more
1 to 9.9	25 to 49.9	

The Roman Catholic church is the largest single denomination in the United States. There are approximately 72 million Catholics in the United States, about 26 percent of the total population. In thirty-six states Catholics are the largest single denomination. Rhode Island, at 63 percent, is the most Catholic state. The states with the lowest percentage of Catholics are found in the South, as Map 1-16 indicates. As the northern migration to the Sun Belt continues, however, and Hispanic immigration grows, the religious and electoral makeup of this region is changing. The map of Catholics in Florida is perhaps a precursor of the distant southern future.

Catholics first came to America in colonial times. In 1634 Catholic and Protestant settlers landed and established Maryland. At the time of the Revolution, however, Catholics remained a very small percentage of the total population. The admission of Louisiana as a state in 1812 brought the

first large Catholic presence. Catholic France and Spain settled Louisiana, and the number of Catholics was increased by the arrival of French Acadian Catholics expelled in the 1770s by the British from Maritime Canada. French Canadian Catholics from Quebec began to migrate to New England after the textile industry began to grow in the 1820s. The most profound changes, however, resulted from overseas immigration from the Catholic nations of Europe. A huge migration from Ireland began in the 1840s. The Irish settled in New York City, Boston, and in the booming textile towns nearby.

Anti-Irish, anti-Catholic sentiments led, in part, to the founding in the 1840s of the Know-Nothing or Native American Party, one of the largest third party movements in U.S. history. The Know-Nothings elected many state and local officials, and on the national scene elected dozens of members to the U.S. House. In the late 1850s the emerging

Republican Party absorbed many of the northern Know-Nothings. Irish immigrants then solidified their affiliation with the Democratic Party in northern cities and mining areas.

The vast industrialization that occurred from the 1880s to the 1920s further changed the ethnic and religious makeup of the United States. The need for labor in expanding mines, mills, and factories of the industrial North was insatiable and was fed by immigrants from the Catholic countries of eastern and southern Europe. Although immigration slowed from the 1920s through the 1960s, the last great phase of immigration history has also been a Catholic-dominated phase. Immigrants from Cuba, the Dominican Republic, Mexico, Puerto Rico, and the rest of Latin America are predominately Catholic.

Virtually all subsequent immigrant groups followed the same path as the Irish to the Democratic Party. Northern industrial cities with large immigrant populations were bas-

tions of Democrats in a largely Republican North, especially after the political party realignment of 1932. As second and third generation northern Catholics became more suburbanized, middle class, and detached from their immigrant roots, many became less fervent Democrats. Many of the "Reagan Democrats" in the 1980s were northern working class, but socially conservative, Catholic Democrats. The newest groups of immigrants, Mexicans and other Latin Americans, also vote heavily Democratic. As the immigrant Catholics of the past, they find themselves torn between economic issues, where the Democratic Party is strong, and social issues, such as abortion, which the Catholic church opposes, as do many in the Republican Party.

Map 1-17 illustrates the geographic location of the members of the Southern Baptist Convention, the largest Baptist denomination, which represents 7.6 percent of the total population and slightly less than half of all practicing Bap-

Map 1-17 *Southern Baptist Adherents, by County, 1990*

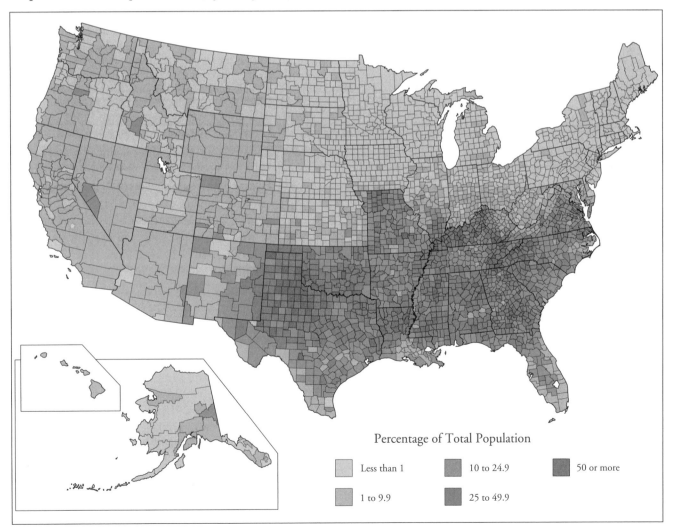

Percentage of Total Population

Less than 1   10 to 24.9   50 or more

1 to 9.9   25 to 49.9

tists. Baptists, who trace their origins to a separatist group from the Church of England, are the largest Protestant denomination in the United States. The establishment of Rhode Island by splinter religious groups led to the first American Baptist congregation in the 1630s. American Baptists were noted for both their evangelical growth and numerous breakaway assemblies and associations. After some unity in the early 1800s, theological schisms continued. The most serious division in the American Baptist Church came over slavery, which caused the northern and southern Baptists to split in 1845. That division continues today. Modern-day religious surveys count as many as 19 percent of Americans claiming a Baptist heritage, although the number of Baptists in full membership and participating in an individual church is somewhat lower. In addition, the Baptist denomination includes more than a dozen major and many more small, separate associations of individual congregations. The largest group is the Southern Baptist Convention, which originated with the split between the northern and southern wings of the American Baptist Convention in 1845.

Southern Baptists are the largest denomination in ten states: Mississippi (the largest with 33 percent of all church attendees), Alabama, Oklahoma, Tennessee, Kentucky, South Carolina, Arkansas, Georgia, North Carolina, and Virginia (12 percent). Map 1-17 reveals strong Southern Baptist areas in these states and in adjacent areas. For example, northern Florida, northern Louisiana, and rural central Texas are heavily Southern Baptist. Missouri is also strongly Southern Baptist, historically staying with this wing of the Baptist church. Even some counties in southern Illinois have high Baptist populations, owing to its original settlement from the South. Some lines of Southern Baptist adherence are very sharp. The Oklahoma-Kansas border is an extremely sharp religious divide. There are many Baptists in Kansas, but a majority are American (northern) Baptists. This is also the case in West Virginia, where the pre–Civil War schism is reflected today in the locations of these types of Baptist churches.

Many political and cultural geographers view the geography of Southern Baptists as a good surrogate for the geography of southern culture. Where exactly is the American South? Where does it begin and end? Some geographers recognize another region of the South—the "Deep South," but the Deep South is cultural rather than geographic. For example, north Florida is in the Deep South, but south Florida is not. Northern Louisiana is in the Deep South, but the area around New Orleans is not. Even east and west Texas may be in the Deep South, but border Texas is not. Tidewater Virginia is in the Deep South, but the Appalachian counties of Virginia are not. There is no doubt that the Southern Baptist tradition is part and parcel of the Deep South culture.

The views of the Southern Baptist church exert a strong influence on American politics. The original split in the defense of slavery in 1845 continued in the form of opposition to civil rights laws through most of the twentieth century. In the 1990s, however, the Southern Baptist Convention began to address its past and present role in race relations. In other areas of politics, many Baptist congregations are aligned with, or help to shape, the American conservative agenda. Among the issues on the conservative political agenda are opposition to abortion and support for prayer in public school, the teaching of creationism, and public vouchers for private Christian schools. Many Southern Baptists disapprove of the sexual mores and premarital sex depicted on American television and in movies, music, the Internet, and other media. Most important, many Southern Baptists see these moral issues as political issues.

Conservative Christians became active in the 1980s and 1990s through the actions of the Christian Coalition. The coalition's goal was to organize political action on many fronts supported by many different Christian fundamentalist groups. In 1988 coalition leader and ordained Southern Baptist minister, Pat Robertson, ran as a candidate for president in the Republican primaries. The coalition continued to play a role, although with somewhat diminished influence, in the Republican primaries through the 2000 campaign.

The geography of Southern Baptists portrayed in Map 1-17 is helpful in deciphering a number of American political patterns. Map 2-5 depicts the vote for Gov. George Wallace of Alabama in the 1968 presidential race. Wallace received almost 14 percent of the national vote and forty-six electoral votes, carrying the states of Alabama, Arkansas, Georgia, Louisiana, and Mississippi. Outside of his home state Wallace received his highest vote percentage in Mississippi (63.5 percent), which is also the state with the highest percentage of Southern Baptists. The area depicted on Map 1-17 is still a politically conservative area, as reflected in presidential voting behavior, roll call voting in Congress, and the political ideological structure of Congress.

The largest non-Christian denomination in the United States is Judaism. Practicing Jews and persons of Jewish heritage make up 2.4 percent of the population. Jewish migration and Jewish concentration is overwhelmingly urban. Map 1-18 shows that the largest concentration of Jews is in the New York City metropolitan area, but Boston, Philadelphia, Baltimore, Washington, D.C., and their surrounding counties also rank high. In fact, the Jewish map in the 1 to 4.9 percent category looks quite similar to Map 1-4, which depicts the metropolitan statistical area counties. In addition to the northeastern cities, Los Angeles and San Francisco also rank high in Jewish population.

Map 1-18 *Jewish Adherents, by County, 1990*

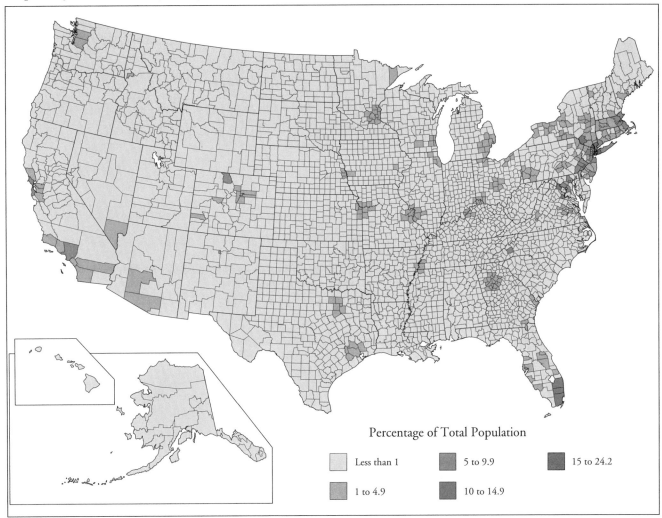

Percentage of Total Population

Less than 1   5 to 9.9   15 to 24.2

1 to 4.9   10 to 14.9

The first Jews in what is now the United States settled in the Dutch colony of New Amsterdam (New York City) in the mid-1600s. Like many dissenting Protestants and Catholics, Jews saw America as a place that would be free from discriminatory European traditions and offer a freer religious life. Colonial Jewish settlement was small and dispersed. The 1763 Touro Synagogue in Newport, Rhode Island, is the oldest surviving synagogue in the United States. The first large Jewish presence came after 1840 by way of immigration from Germany. Jewish immigrants usually settled in urban areas and became laborers, traders, and merchants. During this period the midwestern growth centers of Chicago, Cincinnati, and Minneapolis-St. Paul were especially attractive.

American immigration from Europe hit its peak from the 1890s through 1914 and came primarily from southern and eastern Europe. Hundreds of thousands of Jews came from the regions of what are now Poland and Russia and other East European nations. With the frontier closed in the American West, this immigration was almost entirely to the booming industrial cities of the Northeast and Midwest. New York City and, eventually, all the counties surrounding it, became one of the world's largest centers of Jewish settlement, especially for Jews of east European origin. Unlike their central European counterparts, east European Jews were rural, poorer, and less educated, and most started out as industrial laborers.

One of the great population growth stories in U.S. demographic history is the migration to Florida after 1920, especially after World War II. Retirees from the North and Northeast make up part of this migration, and Jewish migrants from New York, New Jersey, and northern cities are a substantial segment of this population change, especially in three counties in extreme southeast Florida—Broward, Dade, and Palm Beach. Judaism is the single largest religious denomination in Palm Beach County.

Because of unparalleled religious and economic freedom, second-generation immigrants quickly climbed the social-economic latter and began to exert political influence, especially in New York City, the state of New York, and other areas of the Northeast. In the first half of the twentieth century, new Jewish immigrant citizens joined other immigrant groups in the Democratic Party. Radical Jewish labor groups were among the most left wing in the United States. Their history of battling discrimination made Jews sensitive to social struggle and many supported liberal civil rights and social justice issues. Even though the Jewish population prospered and entered mainstream America, most continue to vote Democratic. This strong Democratic support continued through the 2000 presidential election, when the party's vice-presidential nominee was Sen. Joseph Lieberman of Connecticut, the first Jew on the national ticket of a major American political party.

After World War II and the revelation of the extent of the Holocaust, American Jews pushed for the creation of a Jewish state in Palestine. Once Israel was created in 1948, American Jews backed U.S. aid for its maintenance. Because of its activism and affluence, the American Jewish community has political influence far beyond its small percentage of the population. In New York, New Jersey, Connecticut, and Florida, the Jewish vote is important in statewide elections for governor, senator, and president. In many other states, Jewish organizations support candidates who favor liberal causes and the continuation for U.S. support for Israel. Some observers contend that Jewish lobby groups dominate American foreign policy with respect to Israel, and therefore the Middle East and the Arab world, which is one of the most sensitive and geopolitically important regions in the world.

There are approximately 5 million members of the Church of Jesus Christ of Latter-day Saints (LDS), known as Mormons, in the United States, a little more than 1.5 percent of the population. Although Mormons are small in

Map 1-19 *Mormon Adherents, by County, 1990*

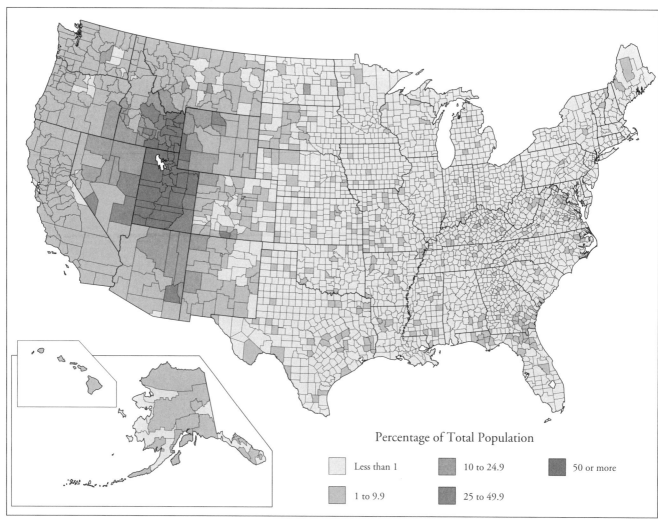

Percentage of Total Population

Less than 1   10 to 24.9   50 or more

1 to 9.9   25 to 49.9

number they are a large factor in the eleven western states and Hawaii. As Map 1-19 illustrates the LDS church is a dominant institution in the Interior West region. In two states Mormons are the largest denomination, Utah (71 percent) and Idaho (27 percent). In eight states—Arizona, California, Idaho, Nevada, Oregon, Utah, Washington, and Wyoming—Mormons have more individual congregations than any other religion. Established in 1830 in western New York by Joseph Smith, the LDS church holds the unique distinction of being the only large international religion to be founded in the United States. Mormons consider themselves neither Catholic nor Protestant, but a restoration of the primitive and only true church.

Many Protestants found LDS beliefs repugnant and sacrilegious. Faced with discrimination and persecution, the Mormons moved west from New York to Ohio, Missouri, and Illinois, where Mormons founded the town of Nauvoo. By 1840 Nauvoo had become the largest city in Illinois, with nearly 20,000 residents. The numbers of Mormons and their beliefs frightened and angered the local population, and in 1844 Smith was jailed, abducted, and murdered by a local mob. The Mormons decided to move west to a point beyond American settlement to a place where they could practice their religion in isolation and freedom. Their new leader, Brigham Young, brought them to Utah, and Salt Lake City was founded in 1847.

Mormons were the first permanent Anglo-American settlers in the Interior West. In subsequent years thousands of Mormon settlers and new converts moved to Utah. Internal growth rate was also high, owing in part to the practice of plural marriage (polygamy) and a high birth rate. As the population grew, the church sent adherents out of the Salt Lake Valley to create new towns and colonize the rest of Utah and the West. The discovery of gold in California and the transcontinental railroad brought some non-Mormons to the Interior West, but Mormons remained the dominant religious, social, and political force in the region. Utah was admitted as a state in 1896, almost fifty years after initial settlement. The practice of polygamy was the reason for the delay, but after the U.S. Congress banned plural marriage, the LDS Church complied and also banned it in 1890.

Mormons dominate Utah politics. More than 98 percent of all the governors, U.S. senators, and members of the U.S. House in Utah history have been Mormons. No other state has experienced this degree of control by one group. Some observers view Utah as a near theocracy, that is, the melding together of the practices and politics of church and state, whereas others view Utah's politics as merely a reflection of the beliefs of the population. Utah's politics is squarely in the moralist tradition that is also found in the upper Midwest and New England. Following this tradition, Utah has one of the highest voter participation rates in the nation (Maps 2-31 to 2-33).

The LDS church teaches the following of scripture, importance of good works, participation in church services and activities, tithing, abstaining from alcohol, the sanctity of marriage, and traditional roles for women. Map 1-6 shows that Mormon counties are in the highest category of annual birth rates. Young Mormon men are expected to perform two years of missionary work in the United States or overseas. This practice partially explains the rapid growth of the religion while many others have stagnated or declined. Because of their strict adherence to scripture Mormons' political beliefs tend to be similar to those of conservative Christian fundamentalists. Utah has the lowest child poverty rate and lowest teen pregnancy rate in the nation. In state politics in Utah and Idaho, the LDS church has a strong influence on, for example, laws and regulations with respect to the sale of alcoholic beverages.

Mormons vote conservative, and the Republican Party has benefited from this voting behavior in recent decades. In presidential elections the Interior West in general, and Utah and Idaho in particular, have been among the highest percentage Republican counties in the nation (Maps 2-1 to 2-22). Utah has voted Republican in every presidential election since 1968. In Congress the Republicans have elected every senator since 1976, and the Utah congressional delegation tends to vote conservative, whether Republican or Democrat. Within Utah the Republicans have controlled the State House since 1976 and State Senate since 1978.

Map 1-20 illustrates the geography of adherents of the Evangelical Lutheran Church in America, the largest Lutheran denomination, which was formed in 1987 by a merger of three Lutheran churches. With more than 5 million members, Evangelical Lutherans make up 2.1 percent of the U.S. population. Map 1-20 indicates that their heaviest concentration today is in Wisconsin, Minnesota, North Dakota, and South Dakota, and adjacent counties. In North Dakota, Evangelical Lutherans are the largest single denomination with 28 percent of the population. Two other significant pockets of Lutherans today are in the historic German settlement areas of eastern Pennsylvania and central Texas.

Lutherans comprise the third largest Protestant denomination in the United States. The church is named for Martin Luther, who founded Protestantism in the early 1500s in Germany. Luther's followers spread throughout northern Germany and the Scandinavian countries, Denmark, Finland, Norway, and Sweden. Lutherans first came to America in large numbers with the settlement of Pennsylvania by Germans in colonial times. Pennsylvania Germans were active, even dominant, in Pennsylvania politics before and after the

Map 1-20 *Evangelical Lutheran Adherents, by County, 1990*

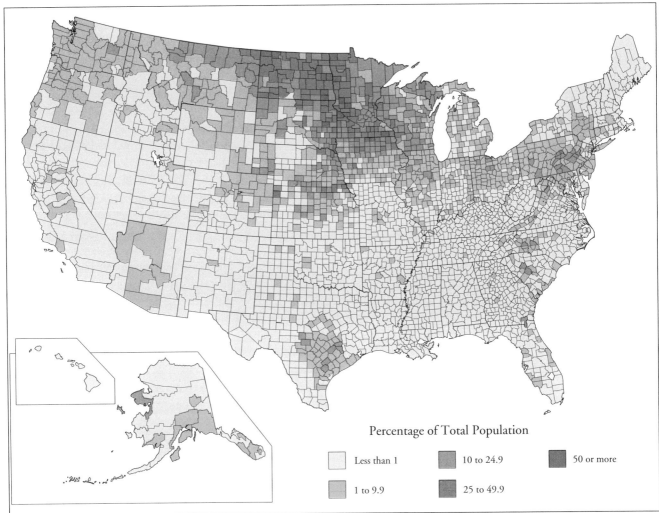

Percentage of Total Population

	Less than 1		10 to 24.9		50 or more
	1 to 9.9		25 to 49.9		

Revolution. Lutheran presence began to dominate the religious geography of a wide area when Scandinavian and German immigrants settled in the upper Midwest in the mid-1800s. Altogether, there are more than 14 million Lutherans in the United States, about 5 percent of the population.

The concentration of Lutherans shown in Map 1-20 is one of the most striking patterns in American religious geography. As do the concentrations of United Methodists (Map 1-21), the Lutheran map shows its greatest strength in areas of stagnant or declining population. In these areas the population is aging in place, and the more elderly the population the more likely it is that they attend church and have kept the religion of their youth. Moreover, these areas are less likely to have new migrants who bring religions different from those of the original settlers.

Lutheran politicians of Scandinavian and German descent hold many of the political offices in the upper Midwest region. For 100 years after the Civil War the upper Midwest

led the progressive reform wing of the national Republican Party. The upper Midwest is also noted in American politics for a high percentage of voter registration and turnout, a moralist political culture, clean and efficient government, and progressive political movements. The Nonpartisan Political League of North Dakota (1910s), Farmer-Labor Party of Minnesota (1920s–1940s), Progressive Party of Wisconsin (1930s–1940s), and even the antislavery movements of the 1850s, are all examples of radical yet democratic political movements arising from the upper Midwest region. The impacts of these regional movements on the nation as a whole are well documented in the American political history.[14] The region also has a long tradition in national politics of supporting progressive or alternative third party candidates for president. The 1980 candidacy of John Anderson and the 1992 and 1996 candidacies of Ross Perot received strong support from this region. The lack of support for segregationist George Wallace in 1968 also is noteworthy.[15]

Map 1-21 *United Methodist Adherents, by County, 1990*

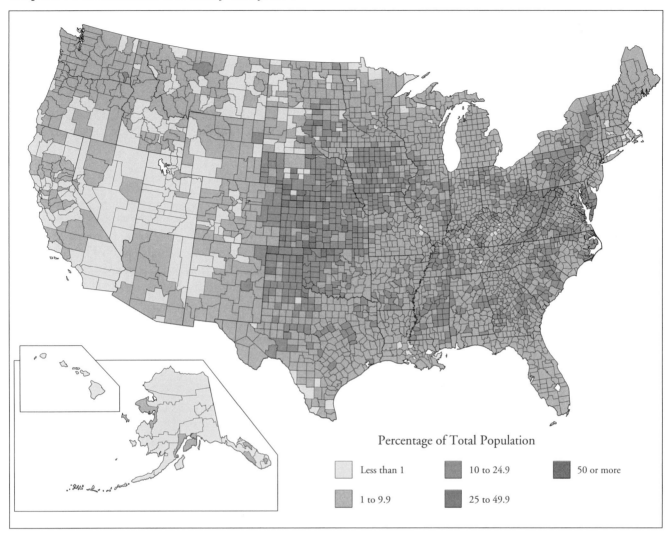

Percentage of Total Population

Less than 1   10 to 24.9   50 or more

1 to 9.9   25 to 49.9

Map 1-21 illustrates the geography of membership in the United Methodist Church, the largest of the Methodist churches in the United States. Methodism was started in 1729 by brothers John and Charles Wesley in England as a movement within the Anglican Church. The religious study and practice of the Wesleys stressed certain habits and methods, and the designation Methodist was eventually accepted as the movement's name. English immigration brought Methodists to North America, but, as late as the 1770s, Methodists in America were still communicants in the Anglican Church. During the Revolution most American Methodists were thought to be loyal to England, as John Wesley dictated.

The Methodist Church has gone through numerous divisions, as have almost all the original major Protestant denominations. The most serious split occurred in 1845 over slavery, and the split resulted in southern and northern branches of the church. Unlike the Baptist Church, the Methodists were reunited, and many mergers and combinations occurred in the twentieth century. These moves made the Methodists a church of national scope. The largest merger occurred in 1968, when the Methodist Church joined with the Evangelical United Brethren Church, forming the United Methodist Church, the second largest Protestant denomination in the United States.

The geography of Methodists highlighted in Map 1-21 has several core areas. The central Great Plains is the largest concentration of counties with high percentages of Methodists. A second concentration is in central and northern Appalachia. These are areas with declining or static population (Map 1-5). The population is aging in place, and the people who remain tend to be elderly and likely to carry on their childhood religion. Pockets of high Methodist population are also found throughout the South. Methodists are least concentrated in the Interior West, a region of growing population.

After recognition of American independence in 1783, Wesley recognized a separate church, and in 1784 the Methodist Episcopal Church in America was organized. Because of discrimination, northern free blacks formed the African Methodist Episcopal Church (AME) in 1816, and today the AME Church remains a separate body with more than 1 million adherents.

The four so-called "mainline" Protestant churches in the United States—Episcopal, Lutheran, Methodist, and Presbyterian—are considered more liberal than the fundamentalist churches, such as the Southern Baptists. For example, the Methodists approved the right of women to be ordained in 1956. As late as 2000 the Southern Baptists were still rejecting the ordination of women. The mainline churches have also taken liberal stances on many social issues such as abortion, AIDS, the environment, human sexuality, peace, and racism. In general, the mainline churches view ecumenism and possible Christian unification in a positive light.

The Methodist Church was the largest Protestant denomination until the 1960s, when it lost that distinction to the Southern Baptists. Like the Baptists, Methodism was strong in the both the North and South and spread west with American migrants. Unlike the Baptists, the northern and southern Methodists were reunited and, therefore, a strict geographical division is not apparent. Religious geographers call the Methodists the most widely dispersed major church in the United States, which gives it adherents cultural and political influence not only in the areas outlined in Map 1-21 but also in most of the United States.

In general religious polling, 86.2 percent of Americans identify themselves as Christian, 7.5 percent as nonreligious, 1.8 percent as Jewish, 0.7 percent as agnostic, 0.5 percent as Islamic, 0.4 percent as Buddhist, 0.3 percent as Unitarian Universalist, and 0.2 percent as Hindu. Even though 88 percent of the population identify as part of the Judeo-Christian heritage, only 55 percent are actually members of a local church or synagogue. Even at these numbers, the United States ranks high in the world with respect to the percentage of the population that regularly attends religious services.[16]

Map 1-22 represents the percentage of the population who are members of one of the more than 250,000 individual parishes or places of worship in the United States. In interpreting Map 1-22, it is important to note that membership is defined differently by the various denominations and even by member congregations. Some denominations count all members of the family if one or more adults attend. Others count only "communicants and confirmed"

as members. In these cases some children are not counted as full members even though they attend. Nevertheless, Map 1-22 is a good indication of the percentage of church membership and attendance by county. Map 1-22, in combination with Maps 1-16 to 1-21, provides a comprehensive overview of the religious geography of the United States.

Total church membership varies with region. Using the Census Regions of the United States (Map 4-1), the rankings are West South Central (65.2 percent of the population are church members), East South Central (65.1 percent), Middle Atlantic (63.4 percent), West North Central (61.1 percent), New England (59.7 percent), East North Central (54.2 percent), South Atlantic (51.0 percent), Mountain (48.2 percent), and Pacific (40.1 percent). Total church adherence also varies vastly by state. The top five states in church attendance are Utah (79.8 percent of the total population), Rhode Island (76.7 percent), North Dakota (75.9 percent), Alabama (71.0 percent), and Louisiana (70.5 percent). The lowest rates of church attendance are found in Hawaii (35.3 percent), Washington (33.1 percent), Oregon (32.2 percent), Alaska (32.2 percent), and Nevada (32.1 percent).

In addition to regional and state cultures, several other factors correlate with church membership. Older people attend religious services at a higher rate than younger people do. People who are established in their community or who have lived in the same house or neighborhood for an extended period attend services at higher rates than those who have recently moved out of their state or region. All of these variables help explain the patterns seen in Map 1-22.

The largest continuous area of high percentage church attendance is in the central portion of the nation, the Great Plains region from North Dakota to Texas. This pattern is perhaps explained more by the population geography of the region than the religious geography. First, the counties depicted are largely rural. Second, the region is aging in place (Map 1-10). Because the population is older, rural, and stable, church attendance is high. Other areas of high adherence are a band of counties in the South, in keeping with its rural and fundamentalist nature. Areas that are high percentage Catholic (Map 1-16)—the Texas-Mexico border, southern Louisiana, Massachusetts, and the New York City area—have a high percentage of church attendance.

The largest area of low church membership is the West, perhaps because the population tends to be young and migrant. One significant exception is the Mormon cultural region of Utah and surrounding counties (Map 1-19), where church attendance is in the highest category. Another area of low percentage of membership is Florida, a significant exception to other areas of the South. Even though Florida has a large retirement population, a large percentage of them have left their established roots and moved there. At

Map 1-22 *Total Church Adherents, 1990*

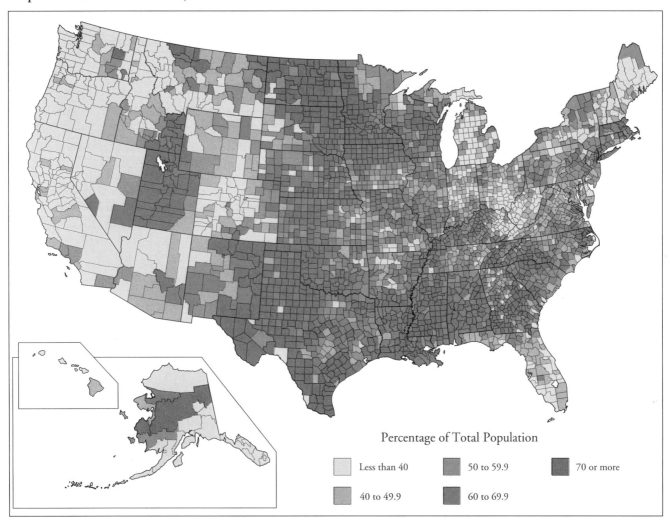

Percentage of Total Population

Less than 40	50 to 59.9	70 or more
40 to 49.9	60 to 69.9	

the other extreme is a large migrant youth segment who have come to Florida for the climate and for employment in the booming Sun Belt economy. Central Appalachia is an area of low attendance. Although it is an elderly rural region, Appalachia is also an area with many "independent holiness" churches that are not affiliated or counted with any denomination. The mountainous topography has always bred isolation and created difficulties in traveling to places of worship. In addition, Appalachian out-migration has led to the closures of many churches and the loss of trained pastoral leadership.

In general, regions with high church affiliation are also regions with conservative voting patterns. The Great Plains, Deep South, and Mormon Interior West were among the strongest supporters of Republican presidential candidates (Maps 2-1 to 2-22). However, almost all of the counties in the Interior West have a Republican voting pattern, even though Map 1-22 indicates a lower-than-national-average church attendance. One explanation is that those who vote at a high rate in the West are the long-time established residents and church adherents. Another exception is the high adherence rate in Massachusetts and the New York City area, two of the most liberal voting areas in the United States. Catholic and Jewish voters (Maps 1-16 and 1-18) historically have liberal Democratic voting records, which partially explains the anomaly.

Income, Poverty, and Wealth

The threshold of poverty as measured by the U.S. Census Bureau varies by the number of people in a household, that is, the "size of family unit." The threshold is adjusted annually based upon the Consumer Price Index. In 1995 the threshold of poverty for one person was an annual income of $7,763. For persons over age sixty-five, this number is

Map 1-23 *Percentage of Persons in Poverty, by County, 1995*

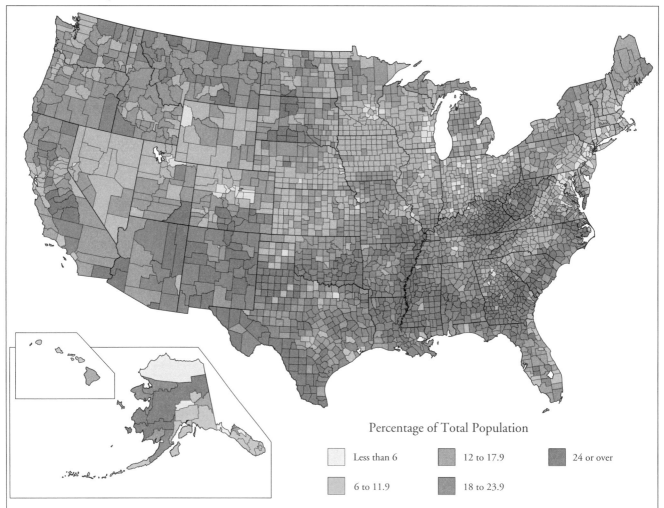

Percentage of Total Population

Less than 6   12 to 17.9   24 or over

6 to 11.9   18 to 23.9

slightly less. The poverty threshold for two adults living together was $9,933. If a two-person family unit was one adult and one child, this amount would be slightly higher. As the size of the family unit increases, the line of where poverty begins also increases. For 1995 the threshold for three people was $12,158; for four, $15,569; and five, $18,408, and so on. Obviously, an income of $18,408 per year would provide little beyond the bare necessities for a family of five in the United States. Moreover, the poverty threshold is a national figure and is not adjusted for geographic variances of cost of living (see Map 1-24). Because the cost of living varies widely from region to region, and from metropolitan areas to rural, the standard figure is a flaw in the poverty measurement system.

Map 1-23 displays the pattern of percentages of persons living in poverty by county for 1995. In general, an overriding North versus South pattern is apparent. Along the southern tier of the United States is a band of contiguous counties

in which the poverty rate is 20 percent to 25 percent or more of the total population, while along the northern tier, poverty rates are much lower. There are four major geographic concentrations of poverty in the United States: Central Appalachia, Deep South, Native American reservations, and the border Southwest. In addition, poverty is prevalent in inner cities, but at a geographical scale that cannot be detected by the national maps in this *Atlas.* Patterns of inner city poverty, however, can be detected even at the national level; for example, Fulton County, Georgia (Atlanta), and Wayne County, Michigan (Detroit), have high rates of poverty surrounded by a sea of relative suburban affluence.

Appalachia has long been one of the poorest regions in the United States. Since the establishment of the Appalachian Regional Commission (ARC) in 1965, parts of Appalachia have joined the American economic mainstream, especially in the northern and southern portions of the region. The ARC, however, still considers many counties in West Virginia and eastern Kentucky "distressed." This rural mountainous area is characterized by a declining coal industry, little economic growth, out-migration of the young, and aging in place. In 1995 West Virginia had a child poverty rate of 25.8 percent, the fourth highest in the nation. Map 1-23 clearly shows Central Appalachia as a large area of relative poverty surrounded by better off areas of the North and upper South.

In the Deep South is another band of poverty counties that begins in southern Virginia and continues across the interior South through Mississippi, Louisiana, and Arkansas, into East Texas. North Florida is generally part of this zone, but Central and South Florida are not. Also, the industrialized area of the South, from the Piedmont of the Carolinas through Atlanta and northern Alabama, is not in the high-poverty category. The area of high-poverty counties correlates with the area of predominately rural African American population (Map 1-12). For example, Mississippi, the state with the highest percentage black population, also had the highest percentage (36.4) of child poverty in 1995. It should be noted, however, that in Mississippi and much of the rest of the South, the poverty rates of rural whites are also above the national average.

Another band of high-poverty counties is along the Mexico-United States border, including much of New Mexico, where there are large numbers of rural agricultural workers, many of whom are recent Mexican immigrants (Map 1-13). Even within the affluent state of California, a pattern has developed correlating with recent Mexican immigration. Away from the coastal counties, in the agricultural Central Valley, poverty rates are above the national average. In Los Angeles County, which has the second largest urban Mexican population in the world, the poverty rate is higher than 20 percent of the population.

In addition to the large Hispanic population, the Southwest also has significant concentrations of Native Americans (Map 1-15). The unemployment and poverty rates on the reservations are among the highest in the United States, and, therefore, areas of northern Arizona, New Mexico, and Oklahoma have higher than average percentages. Because of the combined Mexican American and Native American populations, New Mexico ranked second in child poverty in 1995 at 34.9 percent, and Arizona and Oklahoma tied for sixth at 24.2 percent.

Some U.S. counties and clusters of counties have extremely low rates of poverty, which is explained by suburban affluence. The largest concentrations are counties adjacent to major eastern cities, especially New York, Philadelphia, and Washington, D.C. At 9.5 percent statewide, highly suburban New Jersey has one of the lowest poverty rates in the United States. One or two counties

of affluence can be seen near almost all northern industrial cities. This is especially noticeable around Chicago, Milwaukee, and the ring of prosperous counties surrounding Minneapolis-St. Paul. In the West, counties with extreme wealth, such as those containing Aspen and Vail, Colorado, and Jackson Hole, Wyoming, the cost of living is so high that the poor must seek affordable housing in adjacent counties. In the Salt Lake Valley poverty rates are low because of the booming economy and the private welfare system of the LDS church. Utah's child poverty rate, 8.4 percent, is the third lowest in the nation.

Poverty is a persistent issue in American politics. In the rural America of the past, most people were self-sufficient. As the United States became more urban, city and rural poverty became a more political issue, especially during the Great Depression years and from the 1960s forward. The federal government established regional commissions, such as the ARC, to address geographical wealth and income disparities. In recent decades, however, federal poverty programs have been the subject of ideological and partisan debate. Conservatives argue that personal responsibility, hard work, education, and limited public programs administered by private faith-based institutions will lead to lower poverty. Liberals argue that extensive welfare programs, federal government mandates, affirmative action, and redistribution of wealth are more effective at relieving poverty. In general, members of Congress who represent districts with high elderly, high unemployment, and high child poverty rates generally wish to continue these types of federal aid programs.

Map 1-24 illustrates the median household income for the more than 3,000 counties in the United States. Household income is the total earnings received by all individuals in one family unit. For example, if a family of four has one parent working full time, the other working part time, and some interest income earned by the children, all these funds become the household income for the year. Household income is just part of the equation, however, of relative wealth and poverty. The cost of living is a measurement of wealth flowing out of a family unit. Before household income statistics can be fully appreciated, therefore, the cost of living also must be taken into account. Consider the situation of a high-income individual living in an area with a high cost of living. That person actually can be less well off than a middle-income person living in a place with a low cost of living.

Cost of living statistics generally consider the price of a number of items purchased in the local area. The American Chamber of Commerce Researchers Association (ACCRA) compiles one of the most frequently used U.S. cost of living indexes. The ACCRA index takes into consideration hous-

Map 1-24 *Median Family Income, by County, 1995*

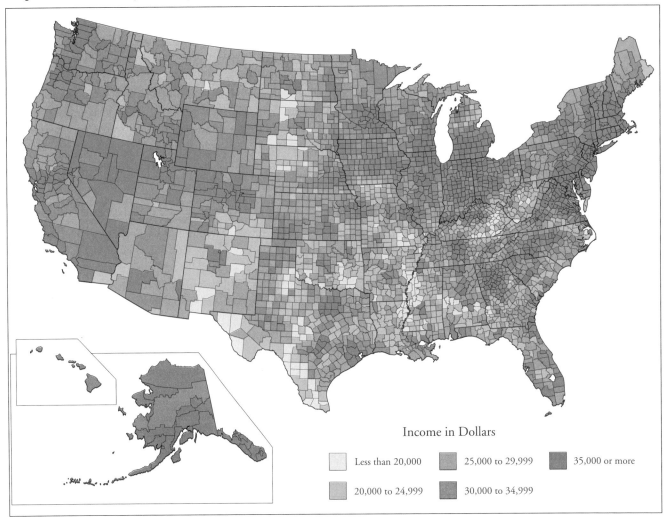

Income in Dollars

Less than 20,000   25,000 to 29,999   35,000 or more

20,000 to 24,999   30,000 to 34,999

ing, food, utilities, transportation, health care, and a variety of goods and services to measure the expense of living in a particular place. The index indicates definite regional differences in cost of living in the United States. In general, it is more expensive to live in a city, in the North, or on the West Coast. The most expensive place to live is New York City. Within the New York City area, Manhattan is the most expensive, with an ACCRA index of 219.7 points. Most cities in the Northeast have high ratings, for example, Boston (138.9) and Washington, D.C. (123.4). Another region with a high cost of living is coastal California and the West Coast, in general. With 172.0 rating, San Francisco is ranked as the most expensive western continental place to live. Anchorage (125.6) and Honolulu (177.4) are also expensive.

The least expensive places to live tend to be in the South and Great Plains, especially in nonmetropolitan areas. For example, the Fort Smith, Arkansas, metropolitan area has

an index of 88.5, and the area around the small town of Douglas, Georgia, has an 89.4. In the Great Plains, Omaha, Nebraska, has an 89.3 index. In the South, even large cities have a modest cost of living, such as Atlanta's rating at 99.2.

Like the cost of living, median household income also varies greatly across the United States. In fact, the two measurements are related. In a free market economy, the cost of living and the rate of wages interact, whether for working class, middle class, or upper level workers. Where the cost of living is high, a high wage rate must be paid to secure good workers, which, in turn, drives up the local cost of doing business.

In 1995 the median household income was $34,076. The states with the highest annual household income were Alaska ($47,954), New Jersey ($43,924), Hawaii ($42,851), Maryland ($41,041), and Wisconsin ($40,955). The states with the lowest household income were Oklahoma ($26,311), Alabama ($25,991), New Mexico ($25,991),

Arkansas ($25,814), and West Virginia ($24,880). In general, the very old and the very young have the lowest household incomes. Middle aged workers, especially those in their late income earning years, generally have the highest income. Households with more education generally earn more than those with little education, and married couples usually have an average income higher than single heads of household. Single male heads of household earn more than single female heads of household. White and Asian households earn considerably more than black and Hispanic households. All of the above demographic variables help explain national regional income variations. Income varies greatly not only over the country but also within most states. In fact, in only one state, Connecticut, is the median income in the highest category in every county.

The largest contiguous area of high-income counties in the United States is in the region stretching from the Boston metropolitan area south to the Washington, D.C., metropolitan area. In general, the average annual salary of any category of job is higher here than almost anywhere in the nation. However, the northeastern cities are among the most expensive places to live in the United States—especially New York City and Boston—and high rates of poverty occur in the inner city of these great metropolitan areas. Another band of high-income counties in the Northeast is in the southern Great Lakes manufacturing zone, where there is a high concentration of union wage industrial workers in, for example, automobile plants, earning well above the average manufacturing worker.

The West has two significant high-income clusters. One is a group of counties in the Rocky Mountains and Interior West. The Salt Lake City metropolitan area is part of this area. In addition, many expensive resorts and second home and retirement retreats are located in prime areas of the Rockies, such as Aspen and Vail, Colorado, and Jackson Hole, Wyoming. Northern Nevada is sparsely populated, but many residents are well-paid miners. The other areas of the West with large median incomes are Southern California and the San Francisco Bay area, areas of dense population. Over the past decade San Jose, California, south of San Francisco and the center of Silicon Valley, has been ranked by the Census Bureau as the city with the highest average income in the United States.

Numerous other clusters of high-income counties are scattered around the nation, and they are almost all major metropolitan areas (Map 1-4) surrounded by a ring of wealthy suburban counties—for example, Atlanta, Charlotte, Dallas-Ft. Worth, Minneapolis-St. Paul, Portland, and Seattle. The concentration of wealth in metropolitan areas is a significant aspect of the social and economic character of the United States.

The median household income map also reveals large areas characterized by low income households. Low income does not necessarily mean poverty because many of these areas are rural counties with a somewhat low cost of living. Although many wealthy people can be found in almost every county in the nation, the low-income areas on Map 1-24 indicate the majority of the people in these counties do not have a high income. Central Appalachia, especially West Virginia and Kentucky, stand out. These are counties with a high percentage of elderly population and marked by rural unemployment and underemployment. Another area of lower than average income is found in a band of counties through the Deep South into Arkansas and Louisiana, a region of high African American and rural poor white populations. Areas along the Texas-Mexico border have a high Mexican American population, many of whom are recent immigrants. Counties with high Native American population in Oklahoma and New Mexico, and other parts of the West, also have low median incomes, as shown in Map 1-24.

Map 1-24 points out, as have several other maps, a clear metropolitan versus rural divide in the United States. Some familiar economic patterns also can be discerned. Income in the North and Northeast, California, and the Pacific Coast is much higher than in the South and Great Plains. These income disparities manifest themselves in several political issues. People living in high-income areas need a higher than average income to survive. Minimum wage earners in New York City or San Jose, California, find it impossible to live on such small incomes. Some economists argue that a national minimum wage is meaningless because of the large regional variations in cost of living.

Economic Sectors

The economy of the United States is usually discussed in terms of sectors. One classic technique of economic analysis is to divide the economy into primary, secondary, tertiary, and quaternary activities. Primary activities are those that involve production from the physical geography of the earth and its natural resources. Agriculture, forestry, and fishing are primary activities. Secondary activities include all types of industrial and manufacturing activities. Tertiary activities include service and government activities, and quaternary activities include information-oriented transactions.

Map 1-25 illustrates the percentage of workers in each county employed in the primary industries of agriculture, forestry, and fisheries. Because the vast majority of Americans live in urban and metropolitan areas and are employed in the service, information, and manufacturing sectors of the economy, it is not surprising that fewer than 3 percent of

Map 1-25 *Percentage of Workers in Agriculture, Forestry, and Fisheries, by County, 1990*

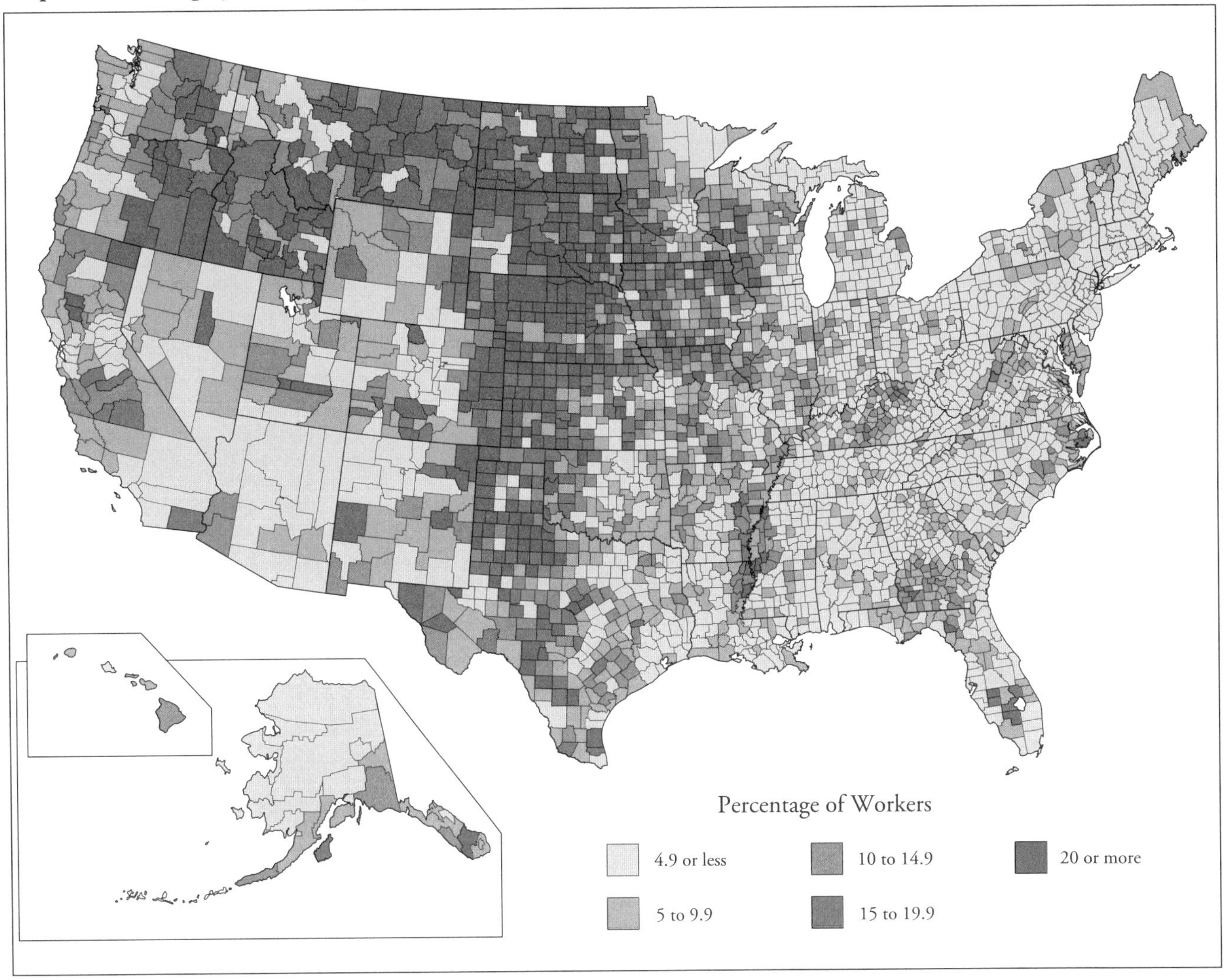

Percentage of Workers

4.9 or less   10 to 14.9   20 or more

5 to 9.9   15 to 19.9

workers in the United States work in primary activity areas. The counties with 10 percent or more of workers in primary activities have two general characteristics. First, they are mostly rural, small population counties with few different kinds of economic activity. Second, the economic activity in question dominates the employment structure and therefore the local economy. Local, state, and federal representatives are obliged to give these activities top priority.

As shown in Map 1-25, the largest geographical extent of high percentage primary activity employment in the United States is in the Great Plains region from west Texas north to North Dakota and Montana. This pattern begins in the rural agricultural Midwest in Iowa and surrounding states. The 20 percent or more worker counties are found toward the western edge of the Great Plains, where farming and ranching form the base of the local economy. On the western edge of the Great Plains, the farms are larger and use

irrigation or dry farming techniques. In some places, such as Montana, the major agricultural activity is ranching.

Another large area of primary activity employment is in the Pacific Northwest in Idaho, eastern Oregon, and eastern Washington. Eastern Oregon and Washington are dry areas where ranching and irrigated farming dominate small population counties. This type of farming is also practiced in Idaho where, in the mountainous areas, forestry contributes to the map's pattern. The map shows major forest, ranching, and agricultural counties in other parts of the West, such as California. The prominence of the fish and forest industries in Alaska is also evident.

In the eastern portion of the United States, only the Mississippi River Valley "Delta" county has a significant number of counties with 20 percent or more workers engaged in primary activity employment. The Delta lies on both sides of the Mississippi River where the states of

Louisiana, Mississippi, and Arkansas meet. It has always been a rich agricultural area. Many of the rural counties in this region have remained agricultural with few other economic activities and have not benefited from the general Sun Belt boom.

For the first 100 years of U.S. independence, the primary sector dominated the national economy. By the 1890s the growing industrial sector made the United States the leading manufacturing nation in the world in many categories of production. The 1920 census signaled an important economic transition: it reported for the first time that more Americans lived in cities than in rural small towns and farms. In the postindustrial age, service and information activities, such as retail, wholesale, financial services, education, tourism, data, Internet, and computers employ more people than all the other sectors combined. Approximately 83 percent of the workforce is employed in the tertiary (service) and quaternary (information) sectors, 15 percent in the secondary (manufacturing) sector, and just 2 percent in the primary (agricultural, forestry, fishery, mining) sector. Although it is the smallest, the primary sector remains important not only in dollar value and employment, but also in many regional economies and the total health and self-sufficiency of the national economy.

Agriculture is one of the mainstays of the American economy. It not only provides Americans with the cheapest and most diversified food products in the world but also is a major component of U.S. exports. In 1990 there were approximately 2 million "farm operators" in the United States, a number that has been falling for many decades. Only about half of the 2 million farmers earned more than $10,000 in farm sales. Many farmers work in jobs off their farms to make an average family farm household income of around $39,000. In 1990 Texas had the largest actual number of farms (186,000), followed by Missouri (108,000) and Iowa (104,000). In value of farmland and buildings, Texas ($65.34 billion) and California ($52.48 billion) were far ahead of other states.

Concentrated in the Midwest, corn and soybeans are the most valuable crops harvested in the United States each year ($13.34 billion and $10.75 billion in 1990). In California oranges and grapes are the most valuable orchard crop ($1.71 billion and $1.67 billion). In livestock, cattle and dairy products ($39.9 billion and $20.14 billion) are the largest. In the 1990s the states that produced the overall greatest dollar value in agriculture were California, Texas, Iowa, Nebraska, and Illinois.

Forestry is another primary sector activity. There are about 740 million acres of forests in the United States of which about 490 million are timberland, that is, capable of yield and harvest. Of the national timberland, 73 percent is in

private hands (both large corporate and small holders), 20 percent is owned by the federal government, and 7 percent is held by states, counties, and municipal governments. Forestry is carried on in the Pacific Northwest and Upper Rocky Mountains (softwood trees producing lumber and building products), in the southern states (softwood trees producing pulp and paper products),and in the Appalachian region (hardwood trees producing furniture and flooring). The top five states in logging workers in the 1990 census mirror this regional breakdown. Oregon was the top state with 9.9 percent of all U.S. workers in this employment category, followed by Washington (8.7 percent), California (6.0 percent), Georgia (5.6 percent), and North Carolina (5.0 percent).

Fisheries play a small but important role in the American economy. The coastal states dominate, but the inland South has a growing fish farm industry. The fish economy can be measured in both weight and value. In 1990 pollack (3.1 billion pounds), harvested off the coast of Alaska, was the largest tonnage caught but ranked fourth in value. Menhaden (1.9 billion pounds), caught mainly off the Gulf Coast, was second in tonnage but ranked ninth in value because it is not consumed by humans but used for meal, oil, and other products. The most valuable fish was salmon ($612 million) caught in Alaska and the Pacific Northwest, followed by shrimp ($491 million), which is caught mostly off the Gulf Coast.

Port of entry is an important geographic consideration for the fish industry. The Alaskan ports of Dutch Harbor ($160 million) and Kodiak ($126.2 million) ranked second and third in value of catch. The Louisiana harbors of Dulac ($52.7 million) and Empire ($46.3 million) ranked fourth and fifth in value of catch. New Bedford ($160.4 million) and Gloucester ($40.5 million), Massachusetts, ranked first and sixth, respectively, because of their high-value cod, flounder, and herring catches.

In any county where more than one-fourth of the workforce is involved in a particular economic activity, the elected officials must be aware of the political issues that impact it. The general health of the agricultural, forestry, and fishing economy is important to all the areas discussed above. In agricultural regions the issues may be farm subsidies or export trade. In forestry areas they may be federal Forest Service regulations or timberland set aside from harvesting. In fishing areas the political issues may be conservation rules set by the Fish and Wildlife Service or foreign trawlers within the 200-mile fishery zone. Almost all members of Congress from states involved in primary activities request membership on agriculture, forestry, or fisheries committees, depending upon the local economic structure of their district or state.

Map 1-26 shows the distribution of workers engaged in

Map 1-26 *Percentage of Workers in Mining, by County, 1990*

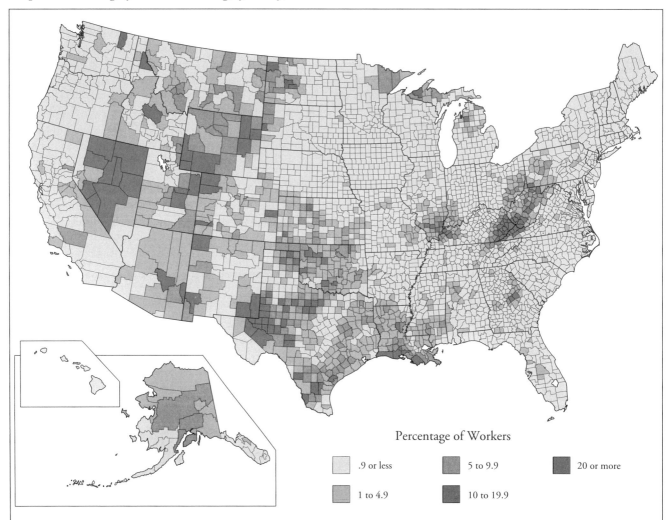

Percentage of Workers

.9 or less   5 to 9.9   20 or more

1 to 4.9   10 to 19.9

the various components of the mining industry in the United States. Mining is defined by the Census Bureau as "the extraction of naturally occurring mineral solids, such as coal and ores; liquid minerals, such as petroleum; and gases, such as natural gas. The term *mining* is used in the broad sense to include quarrying, well operations, beneficiating (for example, crushing, screening, washing, and floatation), and other preparations customarily performed at the mine site or as part of the mining activities." In recent years, approximately 575,000 individuals were employed in the mining sector, generating more than $120 billion in economic activity.

The largest area of mining activity shown in Map 1-26 is the sparsely populated northern portion of Nevada. Here precious metals, gold and silver, and various nonferrous metals make up the bulk of the production. Mining is carried on in other western states, including important copper

production in Utah and southeastern Arizona. The mining of metals makes up 5 percent, and nonmetals' mining makes up 10 percent of the dollar value of mining production.

Coal mining represents more than 10 percent of all mining value in the United States and 16 percent of all mining employment. Map 1-26 shows that the largest number of high employment mining counties is in southern West Virginia and eastern Kentucky, the coal fields of central Appalachia. Coal is also concentrated in north central West Virginia, northeastern Pennsylvania, and southeastern Ohio. Other coal mining areas shown in Map 1-26 are the interior fields of southern Illinois and western Kentucky and the western field, especially the Powder River Basin of northeastern Wyoming and adjacent areas of Montana and western North Dakota.

Kentucky, Pennsylvania, West Virginia, and Wyoming are the largest coal-producing states, and their senators and representatives must be sensitive to coal policy and mining legislation. Mine safety regulation, reclamation, and black lung disease are issues of special concern. The mining community is also interested in environmental legislation, especially laws concerning acid rain, which is caused by burning high-sulfur coal, and global warming treaties, such as the Kyoto Agreement, which deals with the release of carbon dioxide. Regional differences also occur; for example, amendments to the Clean Air Act have hurt high-sulfur coal mining areas such as north central West Virginia, but they have increased the demand for low-sulfur coal mined in Wyoming.

In the West mining was the earliest and often the most important economic activity. Today, the proportion of employment and state revenue from mining is still highest in the West, and members of Congress from this region, as in the coal mining states, remain sensitive to mining concerns. Environmental and reclamation laws dealing with surface and deep mine operations have affected this region, just as they have in coal country. In addition, air pollution laws have impacted smelting operations common near most metals mine sites. Acid mine drainage from old abandoned mines in the Rocky Mountain West is a major problem. Although they are cautious of some environmental legislation, many western lawmakers welcome federal Superfund dollars to clean up the legacy of the unregulated past.

Petroleum and natural gas account for more than three-fourths of the mining gross domestic product and 57 percent of mining employment. Three areas stand out: a cluster of counties in west Texas and eastern New Mexico, counties along the Gulf Coast of Louisiana, and counties in northern Texas and western Oklahoma. The top petroleum producing states are Texas (23 percent of U.S. domestic production), Alaska (20 percent), California (12 percent), and Louisiana (6 percent). The top natural gas producing states are Texas (32 percent of U.S. domestic production), Louisiana (26 percent), Oklahoma (9 percent), and New Mexico (8 percent).

May 1-26 shows that in the vast majority of counties less than 1 percent of the labor force is employed in the mining sector. Most counties, however, have some mining employment, most often quarry and sand and gravel operations important to the local construction industry. The counties that show a significant amount of employment in mining reflect the diversity of the industry. Most of these counties are rural, allowing single-industry domination of the work force.

Map 1-27 illustrates manufacturing by county as the percentage of workers in 1990. Manufacturing in the United States has an eastern bias. The heaviest manufacturing takes place in the old industrial belt of Ohio, southern Michigan, Indiana, northern Illinois, and southeastern Wisconsin, as shown by the continuous stretch of counties along the southern Great Lakes. Manufacturing is also found in the South. For a number of decades, branch plants have moved to the South from the North seeking inexpensive non-union labor and a more pleasant climate. Automobile manufacturing has moved into an area stretching from central Kentucky to central Tennessee and other parts of the South. A large cluster of counties in the Carolina Piedmont represent textile and other manufacturing centers in the first area of the Deep South to industrialize. Indeed, North Carolina ranks eighth in the nation in total manufacturing employment. Many of the counties in the highest category are rural counties in which one textile mill or one auto parts manufacturer is located, but little other employment is available. Of the small number of people employed in the county, a large percentage are in manufacturing. The opposite is true of some large urban industrial counties. For example, Cook County, Illinois (Chicago), has thousands of manufacturing workers, but because the employment mix is so varied and Cook County has so many service workers, the actual manufacturing percentage is low. Because of government employment and services, a similar pattern can be see in the counties surrounding Washington, D.C.

The Census Bureau conducts an economic census every five years. Manufacturing is defined in this census as the "mechanical, physical, or chemical transformation of materials or substances into new products." This transformation takes place "in establishments often described as plants, factories, or mills and typically use power-driven machines and materials-handling equipment." In this very broad definition, traditional types of manufacturing, such as auto assembly or computer fabrication, are included along with all types of natural resource fabrication, such as furniture making, and agricultural processing, such as cigarette production.

The United States is one of the great manufacturing nations in the world, but in recent decades, the U.S. economy has shifted from manufacturing to a postindustrial economy in which services are the more important aspect of the total employment picture. Approximately 15 percent of all employment in the United States is in manufacturing, with about 18,666,000 people, according to the Census Bureau's last Annual Survey of Manufactures. The top five states in manufacturing employment percentage are Indiana (23.4 percent of all nonfarm employment), Wisconsin (22.7 percent), Arkansas (22.6 percent), North Carolina (21.9 percent), and Mississippi (21.6 percent). Only two of these states, Indiana and Wisconsin, are located in the traditional northern American Manufacturing Belt, and two, Mississippi and Arkansas, are poor states that, unlike others in the South, have not attracted large amounts of tertiary and qua-

Map 1-27 *Percentage of Workers in Manufacturing, by County, 1990*

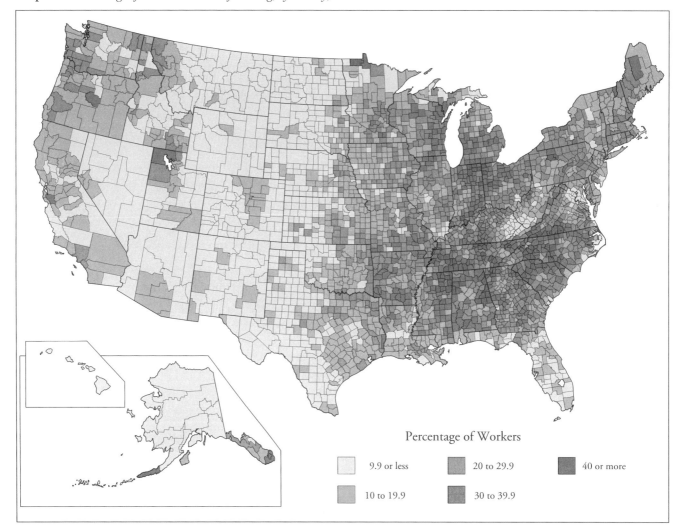

Percentage of Workers

9.9 or less	20 to 29.9	40 or more
10 to 19.9	30 to 39.9	

ternary sector employment. Three western states, Hawaii (3.9 percent), Nevada (4.5 percent), and Wyoming (4.8 percent) rank last in manufacturing employment.

To understand the manufacturing structure of the United States and its related politics, it is helpful to look at the ranking of states in total manufacturing employment. California ranks highest with approximately 1,940,000 workers employed in manufacturing in recent years. Five of the next six states are in the traditional American Manufacturing Belt: Ohio (1,075,000 workers), Texas (1,050,000), Illinois (1,000,000), Michigan (966,000), New York (950,000), and Pennsylvania (925,000).

Map 1-27 shows that manufacturing employment is not a dominant factor in the entire nation from the Great Plains westward, except for a small area of the West Coast. Manufacturing is indeed part of the economy of the West but not a dominant part. Some areas in the East also lack industrial employment—Central Appalachia stands out. Florida is

notable because of its high service employment sector, a pattern shared by virtually all the Gulf and Atlantic coastal counties.

Manufacturing jobs generally have higher wage rates than service jobs. Safeguarding and acquiring industrial jobs has always been a priority for local and states officials. Depending upon the particular component of the wide definition of manufacturing, each county, congressional district, state and region has a particular economic interest of which politicians are keenly aware, and they usually vote accordingly.

The general economic policy of the United States in recent decades has favored open international trade and free markets. Some argue that this trend has benefited the nation as a whole, but it has devastated a large number of old industries, including steel, auto, textile, and television manufacturing. U.S. manufacturing and industrial employment continue to decline as a percentage of the total economy. Trade agreements such as the North American Free Trade Agreement (NAFTA) have further impacted traditional north-eastern American manufacturers and have moved jobs to Mexico. U.S. participation in the World Trade Organization (WTO) has angered industrial workers, their unions, and in some cases their industry trade organizations. Recent political debates have dealt with U.S. laws regulating industrial production. Minimum wage legislation, union rules, union organization, occupational safety, and environmental regulations affect the cost of doing business and the ability to compete with low-wage Mexican, Caribbean, East European, and Asian labor.

The geography of manufacturing public policy is complex. Traditionally, many members of Congress from the North and Northeast have been protectionist with respect to overseas trade and competition, while many members from districts and states of the "new economy"—aerospace, computers, software, and biotech—have encouraged free trade, open American markets, and participation in NAFTA and WTO. Democrats usually defend union workers and the old industrial economy and have closely aligned themselves with the issues and sentiments of leading labor unions. Republicans usually defend entrepreneurial activity and align with the issues and sentiments of the National Association of Manufacturers. In the 2000 presidential election a majority of counties in industrial and manufacturing economic decline tended to vote for Democrat Al Gore, and most counties with economic growth tended to vote for Republican George W. Bush.

Conclusion

The United States is a large country with vast differences in its physical and human geography. Chapter 1 attempts to outline some of the more important regional aspects of the American nation in order to better understand American politics. The U.S. population varies not only in geographic density but also in birth rates, death rates, age, in-migration, and out-migration. America is a multiracial and multicultural society, and Maps 1-12 to 1-15 illustrate the important regional structure in its ethnic makeup. The Judeo-Christian heritage has imbued a particular character to the American nation, and the church adherence maps help explain the religious influence in local, state, and national politics. In the economic geography of the United States, some regions are lagging in development, while others have high annual income. Some areas depend on a particular economic activity, for example, agriculture, mining, or traditional manufacturing. All these factors give character to the congressional district or state and eventually have an impact on the formulation and development of

national legislation and the pattern of elections. The maps in Chapter 1 give a basis for a deeper discussion of the political phenomena in the chapters that follow. The Chapter 1 maps are referred to on numerous occasions to help better explain and understand the political maps under discussion.

Notes

1. Territorial size of the United States as recognized by Great Britain in 1783, including land and water area. Franklin K. Van Zandt, *Boundaries of the United States and the Several States*, Geological Survey Professional Paper 909, United States Geological Survey (Washington, D.C.: Government Printing Office, 1976), 168.

2. In October 1898, during the Spanish-American War, the islands of Puerto Rico and Guam were surrendered by Spain to the United States and eventually ceded to the United States by the treaty. In July 1952 Puerto Rico became a commonwealth. The United States purchased the Virgin Islands from Denmark in 1917 and acquired American Samoa in accordance with an agreement among the United States, Germany, and Great Britain, ratified in 1900. The Northern Mariana Islands, previously under Japanese mandate, were administered by the United States between 1947 and 1986 under the United Nations trusteeship system and became a commonwealth in 1986. Currently, the U.S. Census Bureau collects data on the following possessions and commonwealths: American Samoa, American Virgin Islands, Guam, the Northern Mariana Islands, Palau, and Puerto Rico.

3. "Metropolitan Area Rankings by Population Size and Percent Change for July 1, 1998, to July 1, 1999, and April 1, 1990, to July 1, 1999," Population Estimates Program, Population Division, U.S. Census Bureau. Navigate to: http://www.census.gov/population/estimates/metro-city/ma99-04.txt.

4. "Population Estimates of Metropolitan Areas, Metropolitan Areas Inside Central Cities, Metropolitan Areas Outside Central Cities, and Nonmetropolitan Areas by State for July 1, 1999, and April 1, 1990," Population Estimates Base, Population Estimates Program, Population Division, U.S. Census Bureau. Navigate to: http://www.census.gov/population/estimates/metro-city/ma99-06.txt.

5. United States Conference of Mayors, "Official Policy Resolutions," adopted at the 68th Annual Conference, Seattle, Washington, June 9–13, 2000. Navigate to: http://www.usmayors.org/uscm/resolutions/68th_conference/.

6. Ten new schools were opened during the 2000–2001 school year, and thirteen were planned for 2001–2002. For Clark County School District, navigate to: http://www.ccsd.net/.

7. William J. Serow, "Determinants of Interstate Migration: Differences Between Elderly and Nonelderly Movers," *Journal of Gerontology* 42 (1987): 95–100; Larry Long, *Migration and Residential Mobility in the United States* (New York: Russell Sage Foundation, 1988).

8. Department of Health and Human Services, Centers for Disease Control and Prevention, National Center for Health Statistics, Division of Data Services. Navigate to: http://www.cdc.gov/nchs/about/otheract/hp2000/hp2000.htm.

9. Ibid.

10. When individuals reported more than one race, the African American population reported by the Census Bureau was 36,419,434, or 12.9 percent of the population.

11. Paul R. Abramson, John H. Aldrich, and David W. Rohde, *Change and Continuity in the 1992 Elections* (Washington, D.C.: CQ Press, 1994); Louis Bolce, Gerald De Maio, and Douglas Muzzio, "Blacks and the Republican Party: The 20 Percent Solution," *Political Science Quarterly* 107 (spring 1992): 63–79. In an opinion poll prior to the 2000 presidential election, 4 percent of blacks identified themselves as Republicans, 20 percent as independent, and 74 percent as Democrats. Nine percent planned to vote for George W. Bush. David A. Bositis, "2000 National Opinion Poll-Politics," Joint Center for Political and Economic Studies. Navigate to: www.jointcenter.org.

12. For example, in the 107th Congress, there are twenty-one Hispanic House members—eighteen Democrats and three Republicans. Two of the three Republicans are from Cuban-dominated Florida. The first Hispanic Republican representative from Texas was elected in 1992. See Geoffrey E. Fox, *Hispanic Nation: Culture, Politics, and the Constructing of Identity* (Tucson: University of Arizona Press, 1997); and Louis DeSipio, *Counting on the Latino Vote: Latinos as a New Electorate* (Charlottesville: University Press of Virginia, 1996).

13. Fox, *Hispanic Nation.* Alejandro Portes and Rafael Mozo, "The Political Adaptation Process of Cubans and Other Ethnic Minorities in the United States: A Preliminary Analysis," *International Migration Review* 19 (spring 1985): 35–63. Alejandro Portes and Cynthia Truelove, "Making Sense of Diversity: Recent Research on Hispanic Minorities in the United States," *Annual Review of Sociology* 13 (1987): 359–385.

14. Howard P. Nash Jr., *Third Parties in American Politics* (Washington, D.C.: Public Affairs Press, 1959); Millard L. Gieske, *Minnesota Farmer-Laborism* (Minneapolis: University of Minnesota Press, 1979); and Steven J. Rosenstone, Roy L. Behr, and Edward H. Lazarus, *Third Parties in America* (Princeton: Princeton University Press, 1984).

15. Fred M. Shelley, J. Clark Archer, and Ellen R. White "Rednecks and Quiche Eaters: A Cartographic Analysis of Recent Third-Party Electoral Campaigns" *Journal of Geography* 83 (January-February 1984): 7–12.

16. Jeff Manza and Clem Brooks, "The Religious Factor in U.S. Presidential Elections, 1960–1992," *American Journal of Sociology* 103 (July 1997): 38–81; and H. Paul Chalfant et al., *Religion in Contemporary Society* (Itasca, Ill.: F. E. Peacock, 1994), 441.

Chapter 2

Presidential Elections

On the first Tuesday after the first Monday every fourth year, Americans elect their president, but they do so indirectly. Even though the names of the presidential nominees appear on the ballots, Americans actually vote for a slate of electors known collectively as the electoral college. The electors are charged with formally electing the president and vice president. In nearly all of the states, all of the electoral votes go to electors pledged to support the candidate who receives a plurality, or the largest number of popular votes in the state. The candidate who earns a majority, or more than half, of electoral votes across the United States is then elected president. If no candidate earns a majority of the electoral vote, members of the House of Representatives choose the president. The process of electing the president of the United States, therefore, can be thought of as fifty-one simultaneous elections, one in each state and the District of Columbia, the results are added together to determine the winner.

The first twenty-two maps in this chapter depict the distribution of popular and electoral votes for each presidential election from 1960 to 2000. Some of these elections were closely contested, while others were landslides for one of the two major parties. Indeed, the Republicans won the elections of 1972 and 1984 with forty-nine of the fifty states. Maps of the electoral vote in these and other landslide elections convey the impression that an overwhelming majority of the voters supported the winning candidate. In American presidential politics, however, the popular vote is much more evenly distributed, with losing candidates seldom earning less than forty percent of the major party vote (see Table 2-1). The popular vote maps illustrate that both parties have strong bases of popular support. Because these maps show popular vote by county, they are also useful indicators of Americans' opinions on presidential nominees and on the major issues of the day.

Table 2-1 *Popular Vote for President, 1960–2000*

Year	Democrat	Republican	Other
1960	34,226,731	34,108,157	503,331
1964	43,129,566	27,178,188	336,838
1968	31,275,166	31,785,480	10,151,229
1972	29,170,383	47,169,911	1,378,260
1976	40,830,763	39,147,793	1,577,333
1980	35,483,883	43,904,153	7,127,185
1984	37,577,185	54,455,075	620,582
1988	41,809,074	48,886,097	899,638
1992	44,909,326	39,103,882	20,411,806
1996	47,402,357	39,198,755	9,676,760
2000	50,992,335	50,455,156	3,949,136

SOURCE: Richard M. Scammon, Alice V. McGillivray, and Rhodes Cook, *America Votes 24: A Handbook of Contemporary American Election Statistics* (Washington, D.C.: CQ Press, 2001), 11.

NOTE: The Other column is an aggregate of the votes received by third party and independent candidates.

Election of 1960

The relationship between popular and electoral votes is illustrated in Maps 2-1 and 2-2, which show the popular votes by county and electoral votes by state in the election of 1960, one of the closest in U.S. history. The Democrat, John Kennedy, won a narrow plurality of popular votes and a larger majority in the electoral college by winning strong support in the Northeast, especially in cities, along with much of the traditional Democratic base in the South.

In 1960 Republican president Dwight D. Eisenhower was barred from running for a third term by the Twenty-second Amendment to the Constitution. The Democrats controlled both houses of Congress, however, and the Democratic majority in Congress had made dramatic gains—fifty seats in the House and fifteen seats in the Senate—in the off-year election of 1958. These wins, along with Eisenhower's absence from the head of the ticket, made many Democrats optimistic that they would regain the White House.

Map 2-1 *Popular Vote for President, by County, 1960*

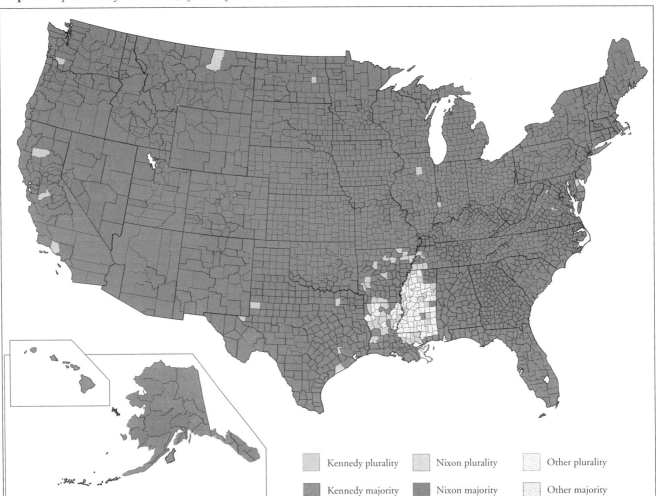

Kennedy plurality   Nixon plurality   Other plurality

Kennedy majority   Nixon majority   Other majority

Vice President Richard Nixon turned back a challenge by Gov. Nelson Rockefeller of New York and won the Republican Party's nomination with only token opposition. He selected Henry Cabot Lodge, a former senator from Massachusetts, as his running mate.

Several prominent Democrats set their sights on their party's nomination. Candidates included Sens. John Kennedy of Massachusetts, Lyndon Johnson of Texas, Hubert Humphrey of Minnesota, and Stuart Symington of Missouri, along with former Illinois governor Adlai Stevenson, who had lost to Eisenhower in 1952 and 1956. Some Democratic voters and party officials saw Kennedy's youth (he was only forty-three) and his Roman Catholic faith as drawbacks, but the wealthy and personable Kennedy defeated Humphrey in primaries in Wisconsin and West Virginia and knocked him out of the race.[1] Senate Majority Leader Johnson stayed out of the primaries, hoping that his extensive contacts in Congress would give him substantial

delegate support. His strategy did not work, however, and Kennedy wrapped up the nomination by defeating Johnson on the first ballot at the Democratic National Convention. In a surprise move, Kennedy selected Johnson as his running mate, expecting that Johnson's roots and popularity in Texas and the South would bolster the Democratic campaign in that region. Kennedy's selection of Johnson typified the long-standing tradition of selecting a running mate who would bring geographic balance to a major party presidential ticket.

Throughout the fall campaign, polls showed Kennedy and Nixon running neck and neck. For the first time, the candidates participated in televised debates—four altogether—and a majority of those who saw the broadcasts thought the telegenic Kennedy came out on top. Accepting the Republican nomination, Nixon promised to campaign in all fifty states—a promise he would soon regret, as it forced him to spend time and campaign resources in

Map 2-2 *Electoral Vote for President, 1960*

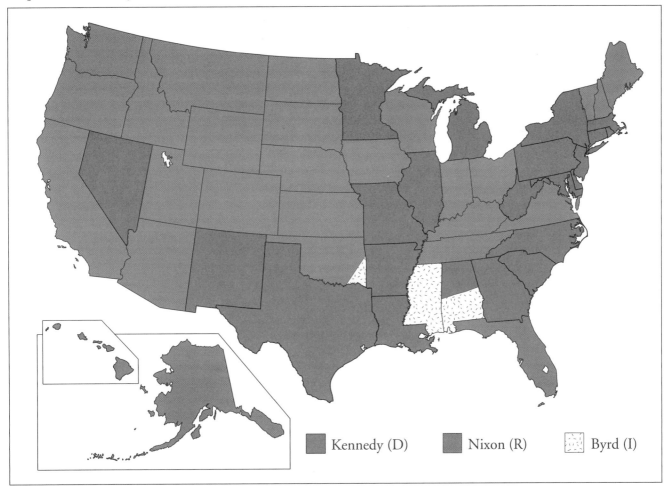

Kennedy (D)   Nixon (R)   Byrd (I)

sparsely populated states. For example, it took three days for Nixon to travel to heavily Republican Alaska, with only three electoral votes that he would have won anyway.

The 1960 election was the closest of the twentieth century, and it was not clear that Kennedy had won an electoral college majority until the morning after. Kennedy's margin in the popular vote was only about 112,000 votes of the nearly 70 million cast. His electoral college victory was more decisive, however, with a margin of 303 to 219. He prevailed by winning large urban states, including Illinois, Massachusetts, Michigan, and New York, as well as several southern states (Map 2-2). In states other than the heavily Catholic Connecticut, Massachusetts, and Rhode Island, where he won decisively (Map 1-16), Kennedy won popular vote pluralities in northeastern industrial states by piling up large margins in urban counties. For example, Kennedy won only 12 of New York's 62 counties and only 9 of the 102 counties of Illinois, but he won very large majorities in the cities of New York and Chicago, which more than offset

Republican strength in suburban and rural areas (Map 2-1).

Following a Democratic Party tradition that dated back to the Civil War, Kennedy held a substantial majority of counties in the South, carrying most of Alabama, Arkansas, Georgia, and North Carolina. In several Deep South states, however, local Democratic Party officials placed slates of unpledged Democratic electors on the ballot, and these slates outpolled the national Democratic ticket in parts of Louisiana and Mississippi. Kennedy won most of the counties in Johnson's native Texas but, significantly, lost the already rapidly growing suburbs of Houston and Dallas.

Nixon won a large majority of midwestern and Great Plains counties. Presaging a trend that would continue in future elections, the Democrat's wins in these areas were for the most part in heavily Catholic counties such as Dubuque, Iowa, and Hays, Kansas, along with counties in which Native Americans (Map 1-15) or other minority populations were found. In California, Kennedy won the Central Valley between Sacramento and Bakersfield—a region populated by large numbers of people who had moved from the South, the Southwest, and the southern Great Plains during the Great Depression of the 1930s. He carried Los Angeles and San Francisco but lost most other coastal counties in the Golden State.

The Democratic coalition linking the urban Northeast and the rural South held together sufficiently to provide Kennedy a narrow margin of victory, but the close election of 1960 marked the beginning of the end of some long-standing trends.

Election of 1964

When President John Kennedy was assassinated on November 22, 1963, Vice President Lyndon Johnson assumed the presidency. Johnson pledged to carry out Kennedy's agenda, including support for a strong civil rights

bill.[2] A white backlash against Johnson's support for civil rights encouraged Gov. George Wallace of Alabama to challenge Johnson's stand-ins in primaries in Maryland, Michigan, and Wisconsin. Wallace ran surprisingly well in these primaries but was defeated. Johnson was nominated by acclamation, and he chose Sen. Hubert Humphrey of Minnesota as his running mate.

Few Republicans expected to defeat the popular Johnson, especially in light of public outpouring of grief for Kennedy. Nevertheless, several Republicans began active efforts to pursue their party's nomination. The most prominent candidates were Sen. Barry Goldwater of Arizona, an ardent conservative, and Gov. Nelson Rockefeller of New York, who came from the liberal wing of the party. Both halves of the 1960 Republican ticket that had been narrowly defeated by Kennedy and Johnson—former vice president Richard Nixon and former senator Henry Cabot Lodge, who was serving as U.S. ambassador to South Vietnam—also attracted

Map 2-3 *Popular Vote for President, by County, 1964*

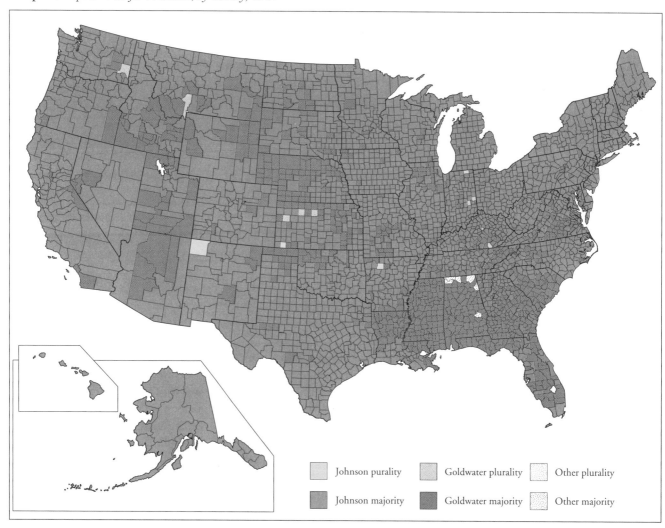

Johnson purality

Johnson majority

Goldwater plurality

Goldwater majority

Other plurality

Other majority

Map 2-4 *Electoral Vote for President, 1964*

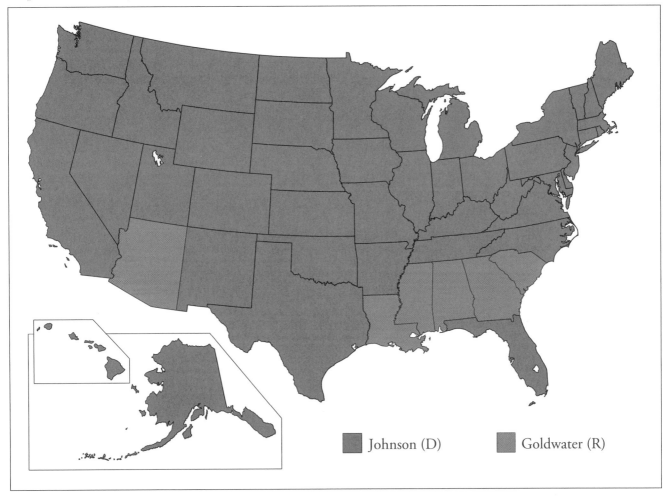

Johnson (D) Goldwater (R)

numerous supporters. The decisive primary occurred in California, where Goldwater narrowly defeated Rockefeller. Goldwater was nominated on the convention's first ballot. He selected William Miller, a U.S. representative from upstate New York, as his running mate.

Johnson maintained a steady lead in the polls throughout the campaign, and the outcome was never in doubt. On election day in November, the voters delivered Johnson a landslide victory. Johnson won a substantial majority in both the popular vote and the electoral college. Goldwater won only his native Arizona and five Deep South states: Alabama, Georgia, Louisiana, Mississippi, and South Carolina (Map 2-4). Johnson won the remaining forty-four states along with the District of Columbia, which was given the opportunity to cast presidential ballots for the first time following ratification of the Twenty-third Amendment in 1961.

Not only did Johnson win a decisive majority in the electoral college, but also he won large popular vote margins in areas that had long been dominated by the Republicans. For

example, he won every county in New England, even though Kennedy, a native of the region, had won less than half of New England's counties four years earlier (Map 2-1). Johnson was the first Democrat to carry Vermont since before the Civil War. He swept rural upstate New York, which Kennedy had lost. He won all but one of the 102 counties of Illinois, losing narrowly only in suburban, conservative Du Page County near Chicago. Johnson piled up large margins in urban, suburban, and rural counties across the northern half of the country from San Francisco and Seattle to New York and Boston. He also won a substantial number of counties in the Middle West and Great Plains states that Nixon had won in 1960.

Johnson did less well in the South, however, than Kennedy had done four years earlier. White southerners, angered at Kennedy and Johnson for supporting strong civil rights legislation, turned out in large numbers for Goldwater. Passage of a voting rights act was still a year away, and African American turnout in the Deep South was minimal. In general, Johnson was more successful at holding Democratic strength in areas on the margins of the South, such as his native Texas, and Kentucky, North Carolina, and Tennessee. Opposition to his civil rights policies was more concentrated in Deep South states, such as Alabama and Mississippi.

Johnson swept many areas throughout the West. He retained counties dominated by Native Americans, mining communities, and other ethnic minority groups while making inroads into normally Republican areas elsewhere, such as in Colorado and Oregon. Johnson dominated the 1964 election by holding the traditional Democratic base and sweeping many normally Republican areas in the North, where voters were dismayed by Goldwater's conservatism and his opposition to civil rights guarantees and numerous other federal programs.

Election of 1968

Early in 1968 Sen. Eugene McCarthy of Minnesota and Sen. Robert Kennedy of Massachusetts challenged incumbent president Lyndon Johnson for the Democratic nomination. McCarthy and Kennedy opposed the Johnson administration's policy of continued escalation of the war in Vietnam.[3] After McCarthy's successes in early primaries persuaded Johnson to announce that he would not run for reelection, Vice President Hubert Humphrey also announced his candidacy. Tensions were heightened by the assassinations of civil rights leader Martin Luther King Jr. in April and of Senator Kennedy in June. At the Democratic National Convention in Chicago, which was marked by violent street protests, Humphrey, who had not entered a single primary contest, won the nomination. He chose Sen. Edmund Muskie of Maine as his running mate.

Map 2-5 *Popular Vote for President, by County, 1968*

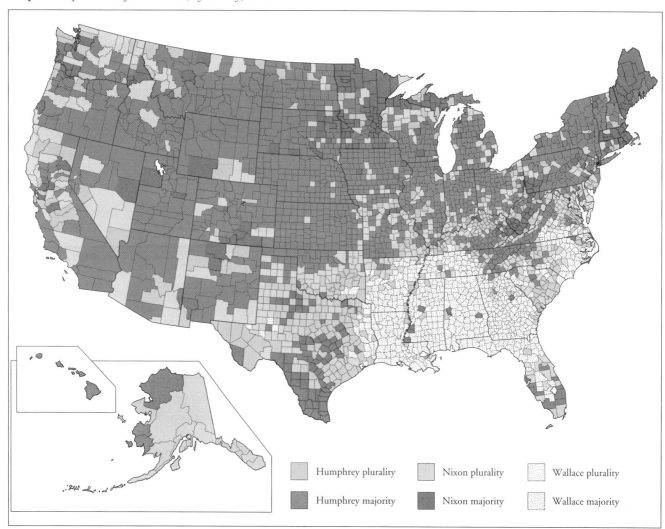

Humphrey plurality   Nixon plurality   Wallace plurality

Humphrey majority   Nixon majority   Wallace majority

Map 2-6 *Electoral Vote for President, 1968*

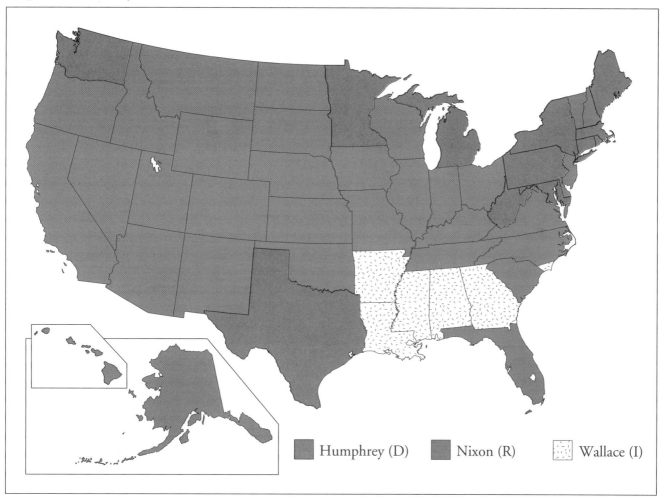

Humphrey (D) Nixon (R) Wallace (I)

Former vice president Richard Nixon became the Republican nominee, fending off challenges from Gov. Nelson Rockefeller of New York and Gov. Ronald Reagan of California. Nixon avoided controversial statements on Vietnam and tried to steer a moderate course between the liberal Rockefeller and the conservative Reagan. Nixon selected Maryland's governor, Spiro Agnew, as his running mate.

Gov. George Wallace of Alabama entered the race as a third party candidate. Known for his efforts to retard the integration of Alabama's public institutions, Wallace claimed that there was not "a dime's worth of difference" between the two major parties. He opposed further federal intrusion into local affairs and argued for states' rights and "law and order."

Nixon began the fall campaign with a substantial lead in public opinion polls. By September, Wallace began to increase his support among working class voters in northern cities as well as with white southerners. A few weeks before the election, Humphrey repudiated Johnson's poli-

cies in Vietnam and announced his opposition to further escalation of the war. Antiwar activists who had opposed Humphrey now began to support him, while Wallace's support began to decline outside the South.

On election day, voter turnout was generally higher in the North and West than in the South, a pattern consistent with previous trends. The 1968 election, however, was the first since the enactment of the Voting Rights Act of 1965, and turnout increased dramatically in those portions of the South with significant African American population. The voters gave Nixon a narrow plurality of the popular vote but a solid majority in the electoral college, with 301 electoral votes to 191 for Humphrey and 46 for Wallace (Map 2-6).

Map 2-5 reveals clear-cut regional divisions in patterns of support for the three major candidates. Nixon won majorities throughout much of the West, Great Plains, and Midwest. In Kansas, for example, he won a majority in 98 of the state's 105 counties. He carried the rural areas of Indiana, Ohio, Pennsylvania, and New York. He ran well in suburbs of major cities such as Atlanta, Chicago, Detroit, and New York. Nixon's showing was weak in most of the South, except for traditionally Republican Appalachia, and in Florida, with its already substantial influx of northerners.

Humphrey won large majorities in counties with large inner cities, including Boston, Chicago, Denver, Detroit, New York, St. Louis, San Francisco, and Washington. He carried many counties in his and Muskie's home states. He won several traditionally Democratic constituencies, including Hispanic South Texas (Map 1-13), northern New Mexico and Colorado, and Native American reservations throughout the West. In the South, his support was strongest among newly enfranchised African Americans. He won many steel- and coal-producing counties of Kentucky, Ohio, Pennsylvania, and West Virginia, where Johnson in 1964 and Kennedy in 1960 had done well. He was successful in traditionally Democratic areas in the southern bor-

derlands, including Kentucky, Oklahoma, Tennessee, and Texas, where voters continued their long-standing habits of voting Democratic. Because so many of his supporters resided in inner city counties with small land areas, the extent of Humphrey's support is less obvious to the casual viewer than might be expected.

Wallace, despite his efforts to campaign nationally, was essentially a regional candidate. He won majorities in counties from Louisiana to Virginia, losing only in counties with large African American populations. Outside the South, he exceeded 20 percent of the popular vote in just a handful of counties.

Overall, Nixon put together an electoral college majority by balancing conservative and liberal opposition, making significant inroads in the South, and holding the Republican areas of the Middle West and West.

Map 2-7 *Popular Vote for President, by County, 1972*

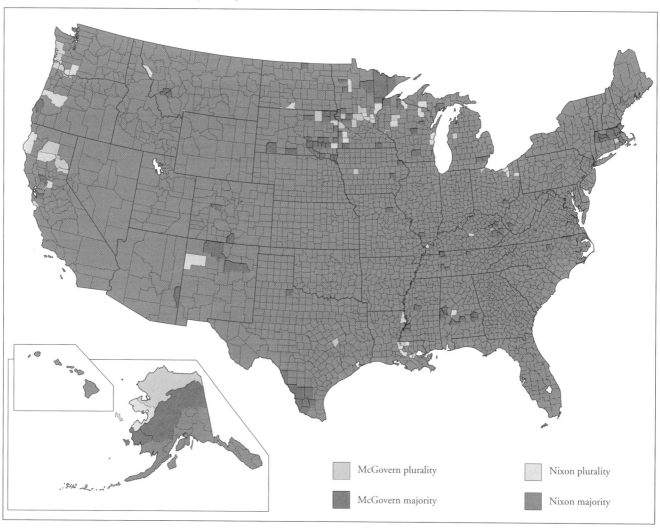

McGovern plurality

McGovern majority

Nixon plurality

Nixon majority

Map 2-8 *Electoral Vote for President, 1972*

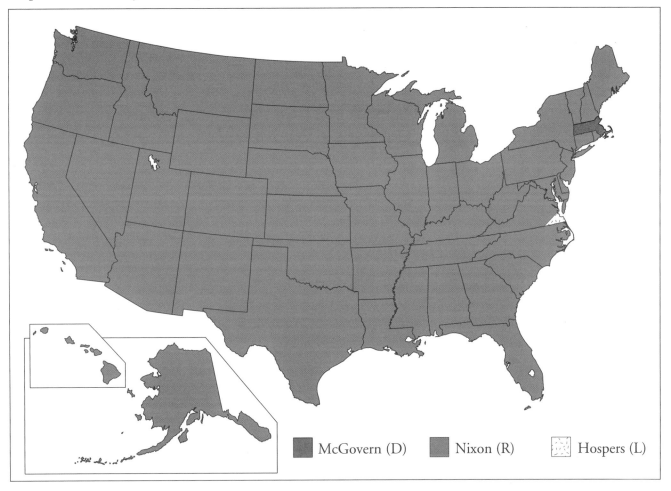

McGovern (D)   Nixon (R)   Hospers (L)

Election of 1972

In 1972 President Richard Nixon was reelected easily, with the largest Republican landslide in nearly fifty years. He won 61 percent of the popular vote; four years earlier, Nixon had taken office with only 43 percent of the popular vote. During his first term, he remained unpopular with liberals and those opposed to continuing the United States' involvement in Vietnam. On the Republican side some conservatives also distrusted Nixon but for different reasons. They argued that he had moved too far to the left by establishing the Environmental Protection Agency, recognizing Communist China, and pursuing détente with the Soviet Union.[4] Nixon's popularity ratings increased as the 1972 election approached, and he and his running mate, Vice President Spiro Agnew, were renominated by acclamation by the Republican Party.

The Democrats hoped to win the presidency by capitalizing on the disapproval many Americans felt for Nixon and the growing opposition to the war in Vietnam. Several promi-

nent Democrats competed in party primaries during the spring of 1972. The early front-runner was Sen. Edmund Muskie of Maine, who had been the party's vice-presidential nominee in 1968. Former vice president Hubert Humphrey, now back in the Senate, was a contender. Sen. George McGovern of South Dakota, a leading liberal and antiwar activist in the Senate, competed for the nomination, as did George Wallace, who had returned to the Democratic Party after running as an independent four years earlier.

McGovern won several early primaries in the Northeast and his native upper Middle West. He was less popular in the South and West, but his rivals were unable to mount a consistent challenge. The conservative Wallace fared well among disaffected conservative Democrats inside and outside the South. While he was campaigning in Maryland, however, Wallace was the victim of an assassination attempt, which left him paralyzed and forced him to withdraw. McGovern was nominated on the first ballot over the objections of delegates supporting Humphrey, Muskie, or Wallace. McGovern selected Sen. Thomas Eagleton of Missouri as his running mate. A few weeks later, Eagleton revealed that he had been given electroshock therapy for depression. Although McGovern at first expressed support for Eagleton, he eventually asked the Missouri senator to leave the ticket and replaced him with R. Sargent Shriver, a brother-in-law of the late president John Kennedy.

The Eagleton incident as well as doubts about McGovern's domestic policy proposals allowed Nixon to maintain a comfortable lead in the polls throughout the campaign. On election day, Nixon won forty-nine of the fifty states (Map 2-8). McGovern won only Massachusetts and the District of Columbia.

The magnitude of Nixon's landslide is evident from Map 2-7, the county-level map. In most of the South, for example, McGovern outpolled Nixon only in those counties where the population was predominately African American, for example, in parts of Alabama and Georgia and in the Delta region of Arkansas, Louisiana, and Mississippi (Map

1-12). Many rural Texas counties that Humphrey had carried in 1968 were solidly for Nixon in 1972. In general, McGovern's popular vote pluralities were limited to highly urbanized counties, counties with large cities, and counties with economies oriented to the primary and secondary sectors (Maps 1-25–1-27). The enactment of the Twenty-sixth Amendment gave eighteen-year-olds the right to vote, and McGovern did well in college communities such as Johnson County, Iowa (Iowa City), and Washtenaw County, Michigan (Ann Arbor). The concentration of Democratic strength in large cities, minority communities, college towns, and farming and manufacturing areas would continue for the rest of the twentieth century. Republican strength, although considerable throughout the country, was especially concentrated in suburban areas, in the traditional Republican heartlands in the Great Plains and Appalachians, and in the West, but it also made gains in the South.

Map 2-9 *Popular Vote for President, by County, 1976*

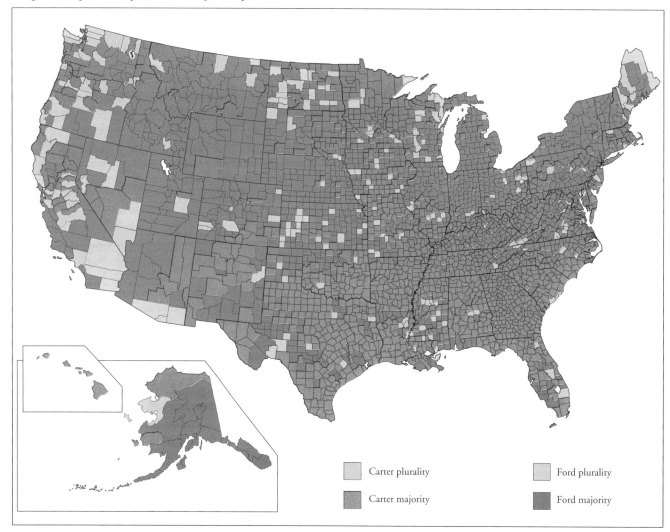

Carter plurality

Carter majority

Ford plurality

Ford majority

Map 2-10 *Electoral Vote for President, 1976*

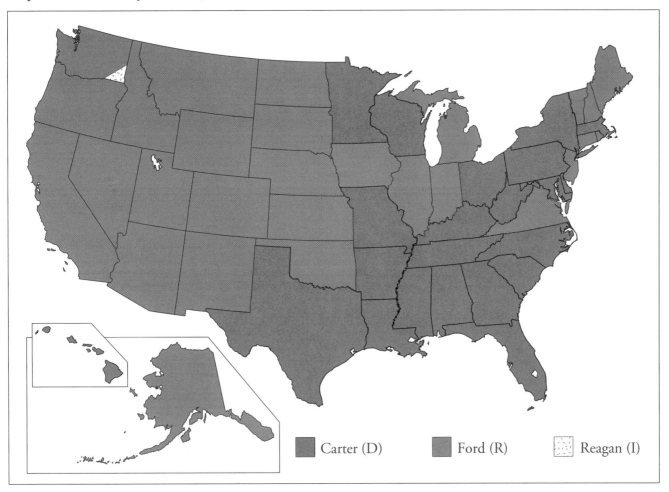

Carter (D)   Ford (R)   Reagan (I)

Election of 1976

In the 1976 election, former governor Jimmy Carter of Georgia narrowly defeated President Gerald Ford of Michigan, the country's first unelected president, to win the presidency. Carter was the first native of the Deep South to win the presidency since the Civil War.

Richard Nixon's second term had been marked by scandals that eventually brought down his administration. In 1973 Vice President Spiro Agnew admitted having taken bribes while serving as governor of Maryland. He pleaded no contest to federal charges of bribery and resigned. In accordance with the Twenty-fifth Amendment, which had been enacted in 1967, the president was empowered to select a new vice president, subject to majority confirmation of both houses of Congress. Nixon selected Ford, minority leader of the House of Representatives, who was easily confirmed by his congressional colleagues.

The most damaging scandal of Nixon's administration is known as Watergate. It started with a break-in at the offices of

the Democratic National Committee in the Watergate office and hotel complex in Washington, D.C. Eventually, links between the burglars and White House staff members came to light and questions arose about the president's knowledge of his aides' activities. Following congressional investigation of charges against Nixon's closest aides, the House Judiciary Committee voted three articles of impeachment against Nixon in July 1974. Facing certain impeachment by the full House and likely conviction by the Senate, Nixon resigned on August 9, and Ford became president. Ford then selected Gov. Nelson Rockefeller of New York to be vice president.

Just a month after he became president, Ford issued Nixon a full pardon. Ford took considerable criticism for this decision but was also respected for his conciliatory demeanor. As the 1976 election neared, Ford announced his intention to run for a full term. He was opposed in the Republican primaries by former governor Ronald Reagan of California, who was strongly supported by conservatives, especially in the Sun Belt. Ford narrowly defeated Reagan to win the nomination. Knowing that conservatives in his party distrusted Vice President Rockefeller, Ford declined to keep him on the ticket and instead selected Sen. Robert Dole of Kansas as his running mate.

The Watergate scandals had created an opening for the Democrats. Many prominent Democrats, including Humphrey, Wallace, Rep. Morris Udall of Arizona, Sen. Frank Church of Idaho, and Gov. Jerry Brown of California, sought their party's nomination. Former governor Jimmy Carter of Georgia defeated Wallace in the South and his more liberal opponents in the North to win the nomination. Carter was the first native of the Deep South to earn a major party presidential nomination since before the Civil War. He selected Sen. Walter Mondale of Minnesota as his running mate.

Early in the general election campaign, Carter enjoyed a substantial lead in public opinion polls, which Ford narrowed as election day approached. Nevertheless, Carter won a plurality in the popular vote along with an electoral college majority of 277 to 251 (Map 2-10). Carter won by sweeping the South and winning substantial support in the Northeast. West of the Mississippi, he carried only Texas and Hawaii.

These results are illustrated by the county-level map (Map 2-9). McGovern had carried only a small percentage of southern counties in 1972, but Carter carried a substantial number, including many white majority as well as African American majority counties. He won the large cities of the Northeast, while Ford prevailed in most suburban counties. Ford also dominated the West, winning nearly all of the counties in the Great Plains and Rocky Mountain states except for those dominated by mining and those where the populations were primarily African American, Hispanic, or Native American. He also won solid majorities in traditional Republican heartlands in the Middle West and Appalachia, as well as along the increasingly Republican Gulf Coast. Although this pattern foreshadowed gains in Republican support in the 1980s and early 1990s, Ford was unable to amass a sufficient number of popular or electoral votes to overcome Carter.

Map 2-11 *Popular Vote for President, by County, 1980*

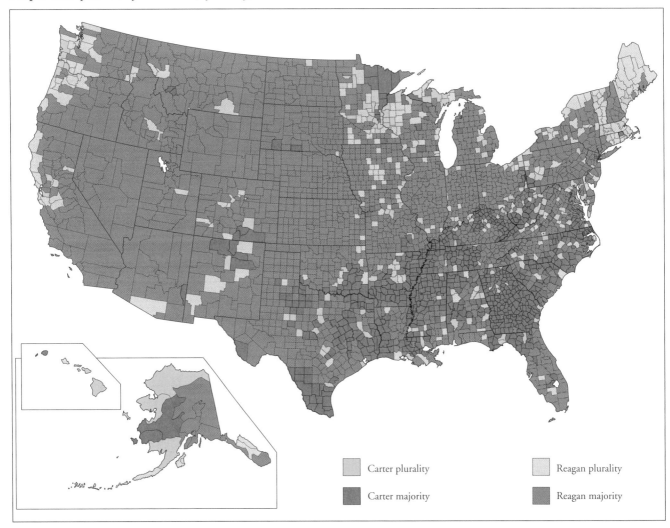

Carter plurality

Carter majority

Reagan plurality

Reagan majority

Map 2-12 *Electoral Vote for President, 1980*

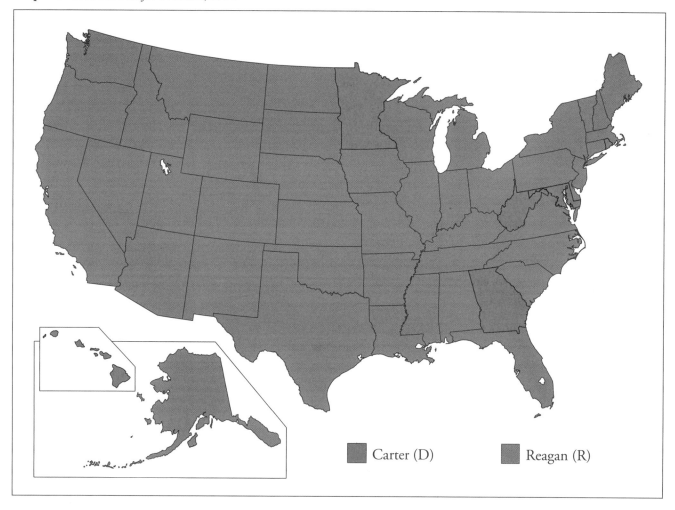

Carter (D)   Reagan (R)

Election of 1980

In the 1980 presidential election the incumbent, Jimmy Carter, was ousted by his Republican challenger, former California governor Ronald Reagan. Carter's administration had been marked by economic problems, including high unemployment and inflation. The administration's problems were compounded by Iran's seizure of fifty-three hostages at the American Embassy in Tehran in fall 1979. The Iranian hostage crisis reinforced for many Americans a belief that Carter was a weak, indecisive leader. Carter faced a challenge for his party's nomination from Sen. Edward Kennedy of Massachusetts. Although he lost some early primaries to Kennedy, Carter eventually won the nomination along with his running mate, Vice President Walter Mondale.

The Republicans also waged a spirited fight for the presidential nomination. Reagan, who had narrowly lost the Republican nomination to Gerald Ford four years ear-lier, was the early front-runner. He was challenged by several other Republicans, however, including former United Nations ambassador George Bush and Rep. John Anderson of Illinois. Reagan won the decisive New Hampshire primary and then several southern primaries. With the nomination secured, Reagan selected Bush as his running mate. Anderson, who had challenged Reagan from the left, decided to run as an independent with a Democrat, former governor Patrick Lucey of Wisconsin, as his running mate.

The fall campaign was closely contested. Public opinion polls showed Carter and Reagan running evenly until shortly before the election, when the Republican pulled away. On election day, Reagan won just over 50 percent of the popular vote, with 43 percent for Carter and 7 percent for Anderson. Reagan's margin in the electoral college was much larger. Carter won only seven states and the District of Columbia, losing the remaining forty-three to Reagan, whose electoral college majority was 489 to 49 (Map 2-12).

Throughout the country, Reagan improved on Gerald Ford's performance of four years earlier. He did particularly well in the South (Map 2-11). Carter had swept the South in 1976, and in 1980 Reagan won all the southern states except Carter's native Georgia. Increased levels of support for Reagan compared to Ford were particularly evident in white majority counties and among evangelical voters, who responded favorably to Reagan's conservative message. Many of the counties in the South that gave pluralities to Carter have substantial minority populations.

Reagan held the Republican base established in previous elections, including the rural Great Plains and Appalachia, outer suburbs, the Interior West, and military base communities that had been trending Republican since the Vietnam War. He ousted Carter by holding his base while cutting into Democratic support in traditionally Democratic places. This trend was evident not only in the South but also in the industrial areas of the Northeast and Midwest where many "Reagan Democrats" abandoned their traditional loyalty to the Democratic Party and supported Reagan.

Election of 1984

In 1984 President Ronald Reagan won reelection with one of the largest popular and electoral vote landslides in American history, defeating his Democratic challenger, former vice president Walter Mondale, with more than 60 percent of the popular vote and carrying the electoral college by a margin of 525 to 13.

Although the U.S. economy had fallen into recession in 1981 and 1982, by 1984 economic conditions had improved. Reagan retained his popularity with the voting public, and his approval ratings remained high. He and his running mate, Vice President George Bush, were renominated without opposition. Mondale defeated Sen. Gary Hart of Col-

Map 2-13 *Popular Vote for President, by County, 1984*

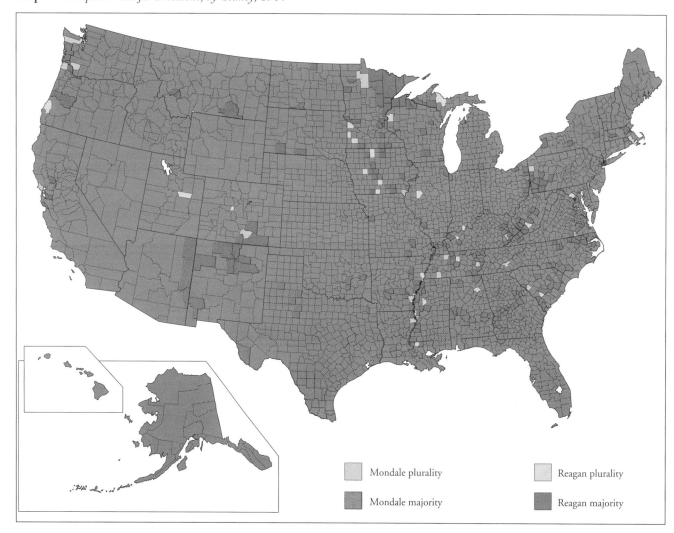

Mondale plurality   Reagan plurality

Mondale majority   Reagan majority

Map 2-14 *Electoral Vote for President, 1984*

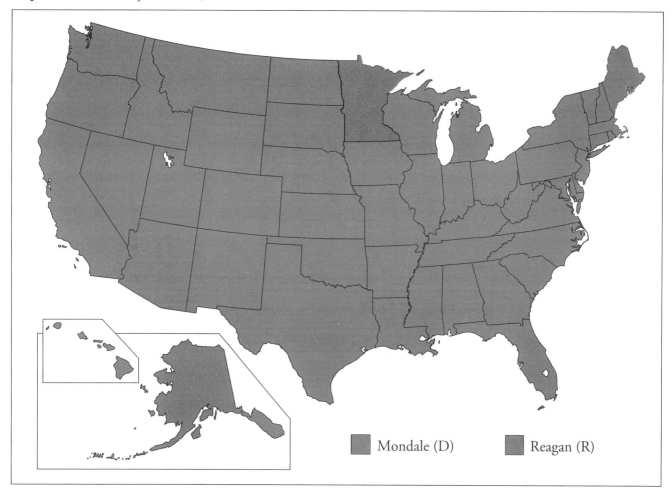

Mondale (D)   Reagan (R)

orado and civil rights activist Rev. Jesse Jackson in the primaries to gain the Democratic nomination. As his running mate, Mondale selected Rep. Geraldine Ferraro of New York, the first woman to be nominated for the vice presidency on a major party ticket.

Reagan held a comfortable lead in public opinion polls throughout the fall campaign. Before election day, pollsters predicted a landslide, which proved to be accurate. Reagan carried forty-nine states, losing only Mondale's native Minnesota and the District of Columbia (Map 2-14).

In the popular vote, Reagan's performance was equally impressive. He carried nearly 90 percent of the country's more than 3,100 counties (Map 2-13). As in 1980, Reagan did especially well in the Interior West, the Great Plains, the Gulf Coast, and the Appalachian region. He also won impressive majorities in suburban areas throughout the country. Differences between central city counties and their surrounding suburbs were particularly pronounced. For example, Mondale won Fulton County, Georgia, but lost all of the suburban counties surrounding the city of Atlanta.

Similar patterns are evident in Chicago, Detroit, New York City, and other urban centers. Mondale won only 320 counties, most of which were counties with large ethnic minorities, central cities, academic communities, or areas in the industrial Midwest and Northeast. Most of the few exceptions were located in Mondale's native Upper Midwest.

The 1984 election represents the high-water mark of Republican support in the late twentieth century. Reagan won his easy reelection victory not only by sweeping the Republican heartland but also, as in 1980, by cutting into traditional Democratic strength in many other areas. Most of the places that Mondale carried have remained in the Democratic column ever since.

Election of 1988

In 1988 Vice President George Bush became the first sitting vice president since Martin Van Buren to win election to the presidency in his own right. He defeated the Democratic

Map 2-15 *Popular Vote for President, by County, 1988*

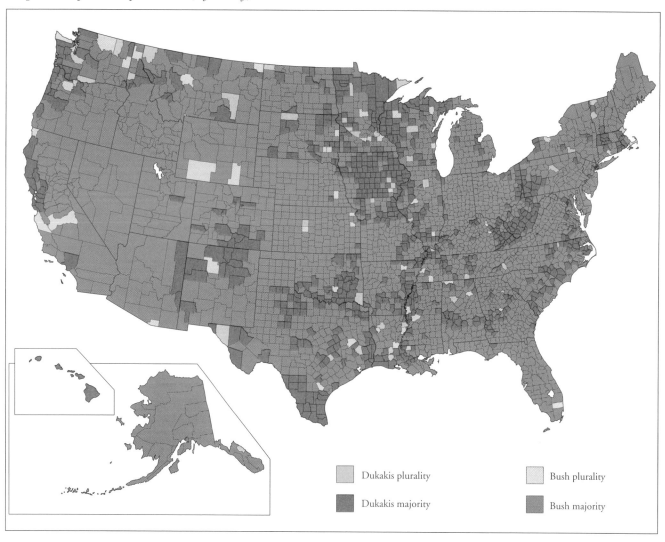

Dukakis plurality

Bush plurality

Dukakis majority

Bush majority

candidate, Gov. Michael Dukakis of Massachusetts. Although Bush had served as vice president for eight years under Ronald Reagan, many conservative Republicans distrusted him as a representative of the northeastern, moderate wing of the party. Several other candidates challenged Bush for the Republican nomination, notably Sen. Robert Dole of Kansas and religious broadcaster Rev. Pat Robertson. Bush won several critical primaries, however, and soon clinched the nomination. He chose Sen. Dan Quayle of Indiana as his running mate.

In addition to Dukakis, several prominent Democrats competed for their party's nomination, including Sen. Paul Simon of Illinois, Sen. Al Gore of Tennessee, and Rev. Jesse Jackson. Each won several primaries, but Dukakis eventually wrapped up the nomination and selected Sen. Lloyd Bentsen of Texas to run for vice president.

Dukakis began the fall campaign with a lead in the public opinion polls, but Bush surged ahead as election day approached. Bush won a solid victory, losing only ten states and the District of Columbia to Dukakis. Bush's electoral college margin was 406 to 132 (Map 2-16).

The geographic pattern of popular votes in 1988 is similar to those of 1980 and 1984, although in most places Bush failed to do as well as Reagan had done in 1984 (Map 2-15). The decline in Republican support was especially evident in traditionally Republican farming areas. Counties in states such as South Dakota and Iowa, which went Democratic for the first time since 1964, gave Bush 20 percent less of the popular vote than Reagan had earned four years earlier. Bush also lost the Pacific Northwest to Dukakis. Throughout Washington, Oregon, and California, however, the Democrats tended

Map 2-16 *Electoral Vote for President, 1988*

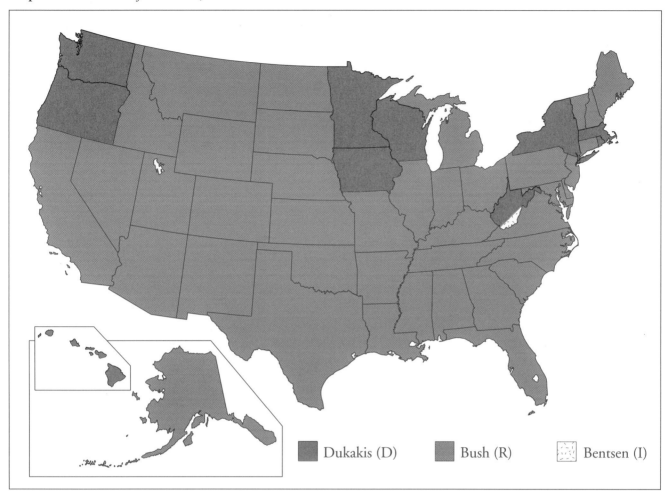

Dukakis (D)   Bush (R)   Bentsen (I)

to do best in areas along the Pacific coast and were less successful in inland areas—a reversal of the pattern of the 1960s (see Map 2-1). Like Reagan in 1980 and 1984, Bush swept the South. In most areas of the South, Dukakis carried only those counties in which African Americans comprised a substantial majority of the population (Map 1-12).

Election of 1992

President George Bush's bid for reelection was derailed by Gov. Bill Clinton of Arkansas, who defeated the Bush-Quayle ticket and business executive H. Ross Perot in a three-way race. Clinton restored Democratic Party control to the White House.

The end of the cold war occurred while Bush was in office. In 1989 the communist governments of Eastern Europe fell, and the communist government of the Soviet Union collapsed in 1991. Bush had presided over the Persian Gulf War, in which the United States joined other members of the United Nations to repel the Iraqi invasion of Kuwait. When the American economy went into a decline, however, the Democrats had an issue they could successfully exploit in the 1992 election.

Bush and his running mate, Vice President Dan Quayle, were renominated without significant opposition. Given Bush's popularity in 1991, several prominent Democrats, including Sen. Bill Bradley of New Jersey and Gov. Mario Cuomo of New York, declined to run for the 1992 nomination. The field included Clinton and several senators—Paul Tsongas of Massachusetts, Tom Harkin of Iowa, and Bob Kerrey of Nebraska. On Super Tuesday, Clinton swept the southern primaries, giving him momentum that carried him to the nomination. He selected Sen. Al Gore of Tennessee, who had run unsuccessfully for the 1988 nomina-

Map 2-17 *Popular Vote for President, by County, 1992*

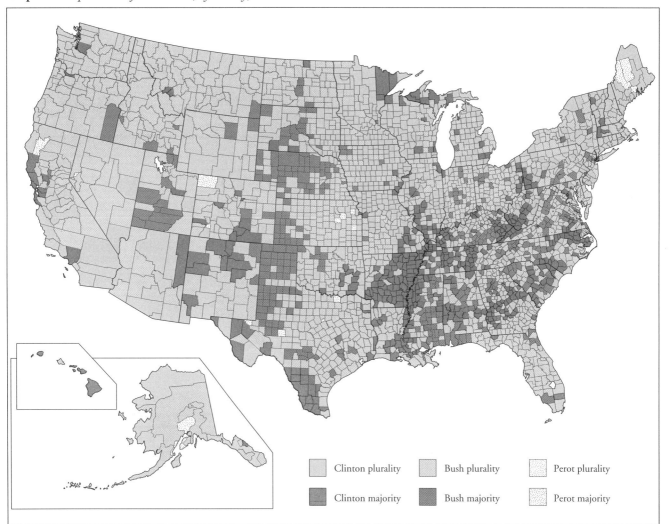

Clinton plurality   Bush plurality   Perot plurality

Clinton majority   Bush majority   Perot majority

tion, as his running mate. In doing so, Clinton broke with the tradition of using geographic balance as a criterion for choosing a vice-presidential nominee.

Meanwhile, Perot announced his intention to run for the presidency as an independent candidate. Promising to "clean up the mess" in Washington, Perot briefly took the lead in a three-way race in spring public opinion polls. He dropped out of the race during the summer but resumed campaigning in the fall and selected James Stockdale, a retired admiral, as his running mate. Perot was unable to regain the lead, which Clinton held throughout the fall campaign.

On election day Clinton won 43 percent of the popular vote, with 38 percent for Bush and 19 percent for Perot. Clinton won a solid majority in the electoral college by sweeping the Northeast, breaking even in the South, and winning several states in the West (Map 2-18). He carried Oregon and Washington, which Dukakis had won in 1988,

and won California, Colorado, Nevada, and Montana, which had not gone Democratic since the Lyndon Johnson landslide of 1964. These results broke the long-standing Republican hold on the West, although Bush carried a large majority of counties in the Interior West and the Great Plains (Map 2-17). Clinton's strongholds in the West included old mining areas and places with large Native American and Mexican American populations that had previously supported Democrats. Clinton did better than his Democratic predecessors in suburban communities, for example, the suburbs of Denver, San Francisco, and Seattle.

Bush was successful in traditionally Republican areas, including the Gulf Coast, much of Appalachia, the Plains states, and the Interior West. The Republicans carried many suburban counties, but by less impressive margins than in the 1980s. Perot, with 19 percent of the vote,

Map 2-18 *Electoral Vote for President, 1992*

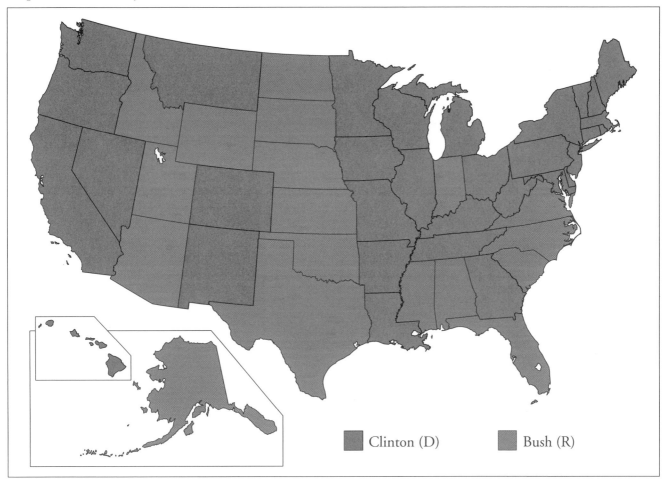

Clinton (D)   Bush (R)

turned in the best showing for a third party nominee since Theodore Roosevelt's 27 percent in 1912. Perot was strongest in his native Texas, in northern New England, and in rural areas of the Great Plains and Rocky Mountain states. In percentage terms, Perot's top five states were Maine (30.8 percent of the popular vote), Alaska (29.0 percent), Utah (28.6 percent), Idaho (27.7 percent), and Kansas (27.0 percent). Whether he took enough votes away from Bush to cost the Republicans a victory is doubtful because most of Perot's strongest areas, including four of his five strongest states, were states that the Republicans carried anyway.[5]

Election of 1996

President Bill Clinton won reelection by a decisive margin in 1996 and became the first Democrat since Franklin Delano Roosevelt to be elected to two full terms. In the con-

gressional elections of 1994, the voters had rebuked Clinton by giving the Republicans solid majorities in both Houses of Congress for the first time since the early 1950s. The Republican majority in the House, led by Speaker Newt Gingrich, promoted a strongly conservative agenda. They blocked the president's policy initiatives and tried to portray Clinton as a free-spending liberal.

As the 1996 election approached, however, Clinton's popularity was on the rise. The economy had begun to boom, and the government deficit was reduced substantially. In early 1996 Clinton and Republican leaders failed to agree on a budget, forcing the shutdown of some government agencies for several weeks. Many voters blamed the Republican Congress, and the antigovernment rhetoric of their party's leadership, for the temporary loss of government services.

Clinton and Vice President Al Gore were renominated without serious opposition, while the Republicans held a spirited contest for their party's nomination. Former sen-

Map 2-19 *Popular Vote for President, by County, 1996*

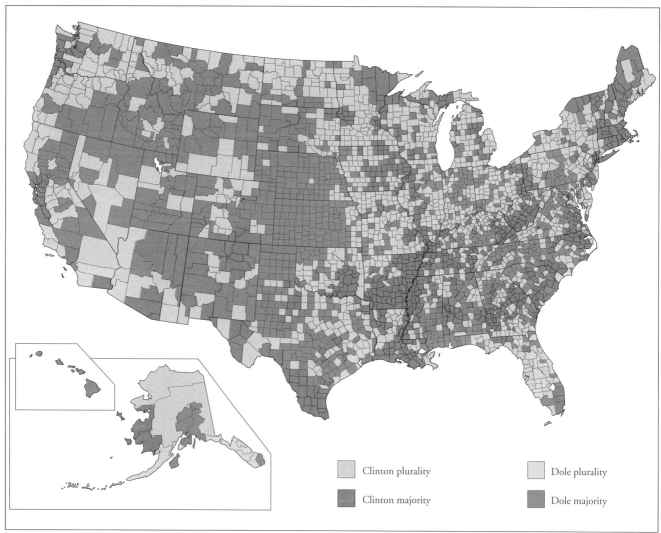

Clinton plurality

Clinton majority

Dole plurality

Dole majority

ator Bob Dole of Kansas, who had been nominated for vice president in 1976, was an early favorite. Other major contenders included conservative broadcaster Pat Buchanan, former Tennessee governor Lamar Alexander, Sen. Richard Lugar of Indiana, and publishing executive Steve Forbes.

Although he lost some early primaries, Dole scored an important victory over Buchanan in South Carolina. A decisive issue was trade policy. In the state with the largest per capita European investment in the country, Dole ran in support of free trade and portrayed Buchanan as an isolationist. Dole ran well in other southern and midwestern states and clinched the nomination well before the Republican National Convention. He selected Jack Kemp, a former representative and secretary of housing and urban development under George Bush, as his running mate. Ross Perot,

now running as the candidate of the Reform Party, made another try for the presidency, but his campaign failed to attract the attention it had four years earlier, in part because of the increasing strength of the national economy. His running mate was economist Pat Choate.

During the fall campaign, Clinton maintained a steady lead over Dole and coasted to victory on election day. Between the 1992 and 1996 elections, only five states shifted between parties in the electoral college. Dole carried Colorado, Georgia, and Montana, all of which had gone for Clinton in 1992. Clinton picked up Florida and Arizona—both states with large numbers of elderly voters concerned about the government shutdown and the possible loss of Social Security, Medicare, and other federal programs (Map 2-20). Dole's margins in the Plains and Interior West were substantially larger than those of

Map 2-20 *Electoral Vote for President, 1996*

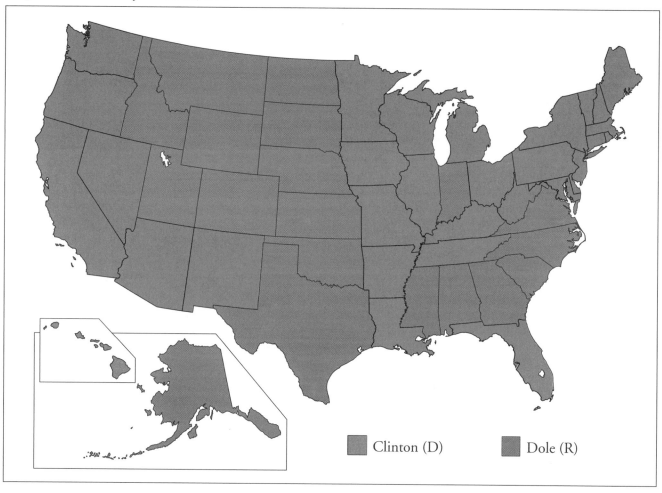

Clinton (D) Dole (R)

Bush in 1992, in part because of Perot's weaker candidacy (Map 2-19). In general, the Democrats improved in the cities and did worse in rural areas—a trend that would be magnified dramatically four years later.

Election of 2000

The presidential election of 2000 was the closest in more than 100 years. Not until five weeks after election day did Americans know for certain that Gov. George W. Bush of Texas would be the next president. When the ballots were counted in the electoral college, Bush defeated his Democratic opponent, Vice President Al Gore, by a margin of 271–266 (Map 2-22). (One Democratic elector from the District of Columbia declined to vote in protest of the District's lack of congressional representation).

The House of Representatives had impeached President Bill Clinton at the end of 1998 for perjury and obstruction of justice, charges that grew out of Clinton's extramarital affairs and his attempt to conceal them. The Senate failed to convict him, and he remained in office with high popularity ratings. He strongly supported Vice President Al Gore for the Democratic nomination. Gore beat back a challenge in the primary election from former senator Bill Bradley of New Jersey and was nominated by acclamation. Gore selected Sen. Joseph Lieberman of Connecticut as his running mate, the first Jewish candidate to run as a major party nominee for national office.

Despite peace, prosperity, a strong economy, and a popular incumbent, several prominent Republicans competed for their party's nomination. Governor Bush, the son of former president George Bush, was the early favorite. His chief challenger was Sen. John McCain of Arizona, who won the first-in-the-nation New Hampshire primary. Bush defeated McCain in the critical South Carolina primary, and McCain withdrew from the race two days after Super Tuesday. Bush chose Richard Cheney, a former representative from

Map 2-21 *Popular Vote for President, by County, 2000*

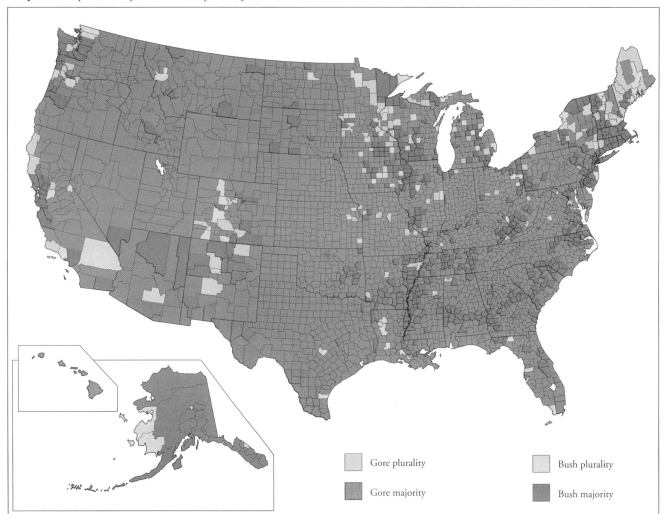

Gore plurality

Gore majority

Bush plurality

Bush majority

Wyoming and secretary of defense in his father's administration, as his running mate. Consumer activist Ralph Nader ran as the nominee of the Green Party, and conservative commentator Pat Buchanan, who had tried for the Republican nomination in the two previous elections, ran as the Reform Party's candidate.

The campaign was closely contested, with public opinion polls showing Bush and Gore within a few percentage points of each other throughout the fall. On election day, predictions of a close race were borne out. Gore bested Bush in the popular vote by about 500,000 votes, but Bush won an electoral college majority when the U.S. Supreme Court in effect awarded him Florida's twenty-five electoral votes. Bush won a popular vote plurality in Florida by less than 1,000 votes. Litigation over the ballot count in Florida delayed the certification of Florida's electoral votes for more than a month after the election. Nader received nearly

100,000 votes in Florida, leading observers to speculate that Gore might have won Florida, and the election, had Nader not run as a third party candidate.

The county-by-county results of the 2000 election confirmed a recent trend showing that urban areas had become more Democratic and rural areas more Republican. Bush carried nearly 2,500 counties across the United States (Map 2-21). Gore's large margins in populous urban centers such as Boston, Chicago, New York, San Francisco, and Washington gave him a popular vote plurality. Like Clinton in 1992 and 1996, Gore carried much of New England along with many counties in the manufacturing regions of Michigan, Ohio, and Pennsylvania and much of the upper Mississippi River valley. Outside the Northeast and Midwest, most of Gore's counties were those with sizable minority populations or large cities. Bush swept most of the South, the Great Plains, and the Rocky Mountain states. Outer

Map 2-22 *Electoral Vote for President, 2000*

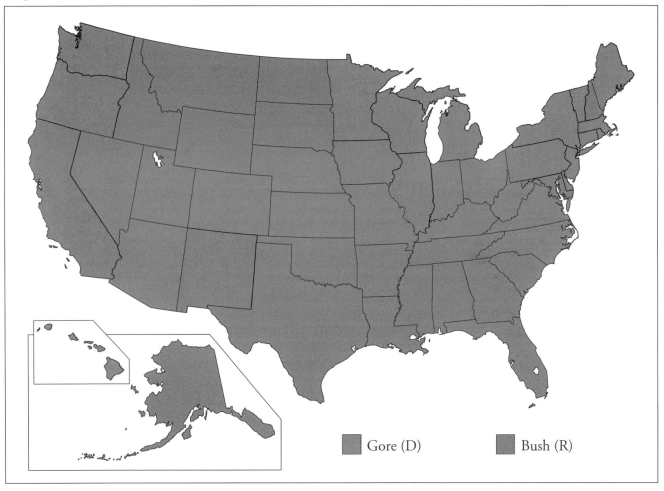

Gore (D)   Bush (R)

suburban counties around Atlanta, Memphis, and New Orleans, for example, proved critical to his margins of victory in their respective states.

Campaign Appearances, 1988–2000

In U.S. presidential elections, both major parties invest considerable amounts of money, time, and energy conducting their campaigns. Because the electoral college system makes American politics inherently geographical, presidential candidates and their campaign staffs pay careful attention to their geographic distribution of campaign resources.

Personal appearances by major party presidential and vice-presidential candidates are often important to a campaign's efforts to mobilize its supporters and sway undecided voters. A candidate's appearance allows voters to see the candidate in person. More critical to the success of a campaign is that candidate appearances generate considerable amounts of local newspaper, television, and radio coverage,

enabling the campaign to get its message out to even larger numbers of voters without buying media ads.

The unofficial presidential campaign is a lengthy process, with years of preparation necessary to secure a major party presidential nomination. Once the nominations are made, however, the traditional kickoff of the fall campaign is Labor Day, the first Monday in September. During the two months between Labor Day and the election, campaigns are at their height of activity, and the public begins to pay closer attention. Campaign appearances are especially critical, and the managers of both parties carefully schedule their candidates' appearances to achieve the maximize impact. As we saw with respect to the 1960 presidential election (Maps 2-1 and 2-2), Richard Nixon's promise to campaign in all fifty states was a mistake that might have cost him the election. Maps representing campaign appearances of major party candidates can therefore be valuable indicators of the geographical thinking underlying the strategies of each campaign.

Generally speaking, candidates appear most frequently

in the states that are believed to be crucial to the outcome in the electoral college. For this reason, both parties tend to target closely contested states. States that are believed to favor one side or the other strongly tend to be avoided; neither side wants to invest campaign resources where the outcome is assumed to be a foregone conclusion.

Because of the dynamics of the electoral college, moreover, candidate appearances tend to be concentrated in populous states. Victory in a large state can win or lose the election for a candidate, while victory in a small one may make no difference. In 2000, for example, the outcome in the disputed state of Florida determined the outcome of the election. Several less populous states, including Iowa, New Mexico, Oregon, and Wisconsin, were nearly as closely contested. Although Vice President Al Gore eventually won all of these states, losing Florida cost him the election.

A final consideration involves the location of media markets. Campaign appearances in a physically small state like New Jersey, for example, may be carried on television not only in New Jersey but also in its larger neighbors, New

York and Pennsylvania. States in which media markets extend into other states may have a disproportionate number of campaign appearances, especially if the neighboring states are large or competitive. Maps 2-23 through 2-30 depict the number of campaign appearances by the major party Democratic and Republican presidential candidates for the 1988 through 2000 elections between Labor Day and election day.

1988

Map 2-23 shows how many campaign appearances the Democratic nominee, Michael Dukakis of Massachusetts, made in the 1988 general election campaign. The map shows that the Democratic campaign targeted the Northeast and Middle West, although this effort proved unsuccessful (Maps 2-15 and 2-16). In addition to his home state and Texas, the home of running mate Lloyd Bentsen, Dukakis appeared at least five times in California, in the large midwestern industrial states of Illinois, Michigan, Missouri, and Ohio, as well as in Connecticut, New York, and

Map 2-23 *Democratic Campaign Stops, 1988*

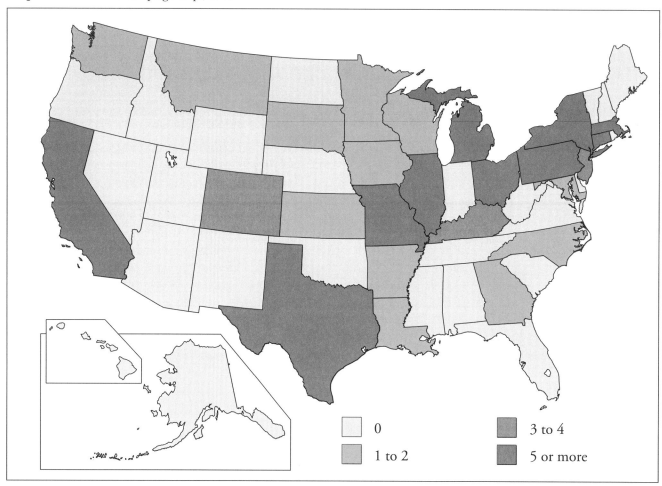

Pennsylvania. Among these eight large states, only New York ended up in the Dukakis column.

The Democratic nominee spent very little time in the South, the Plains states, or the Rocky Mountain states. The decision to ignore the South may have been surprising because since 1924 no candidate has won the presidency without significant numbers of electoral votes in the South. Dukakis lost the entire South to his Republican opponent, George Bush, but whether he could have won any southern states with more campaign appearances is uncertain. The decision not to focus on the Plains and Rocky Mountain states is less surprising, given the long history of Republican support in this region. Dukakis managed to carry Oregon despite not campaigning there.

Map 2-24 shows the campaign appearances of Republican George Bush of Texas during the 1988 campaign. The Republicans concentrated on large states, including California, Illinois, Michigan, Missouri, New Jersey, Ohio, and Texas, and won the electoral voters of all these states. Bush did not campaign as much in New York, but undoubtedly his appearances in New Jersey were covered by New York

media. Like the Democrats, the Republicans concentrated their nominees' appearances in states that, if won, could add up to a victory in the electoral college.

The Republican nominee did not appear at all in several safely Democratic states including Iowa, Massachusetts, Minnesota, and West Virginia. Nor did Bush campaign in smaller, safely Republican states, including Idaho, Kansas, and Wyoming. Perhaps in response to the Democrats' decision not to focus on the South, Bush made no appearances in Alabama, Florida, Louisiana, or Mississippi, all of which he won in the electoral college. That neither Bush nor Dukakis campaigned in Florida may be surprising given the state's size and pivotal status in electoral competition.

1992

Campaign appearances by Democratic nominee Bill Clinton of Arkansas are shown in Map 2-25. The Clinton campaign emphasized three areas: California, the industrial states of the Middle West, and the South. Clinton appeared at least five times in Arkansas, California, Florida, Georgia, Michigan, Missouri, New Jersey, North Carolina, Ohio, and

Map 2-24 *Republican Campaign Stops, 1988*

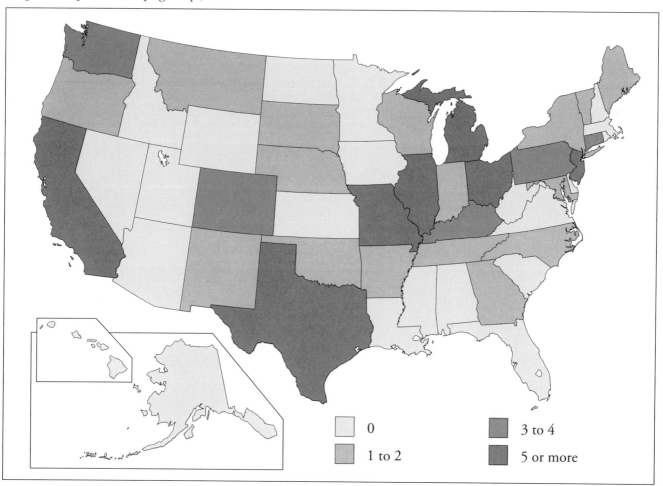

Map 2-25 *Democratic Campaign Stops, 1992*

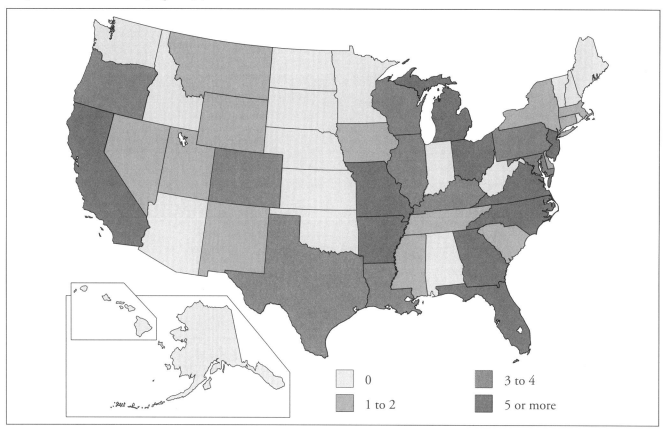

	0		3 to 4
	1 to 2		5 or more

Map 2-26 *Republican Campaign Stops, 1992*

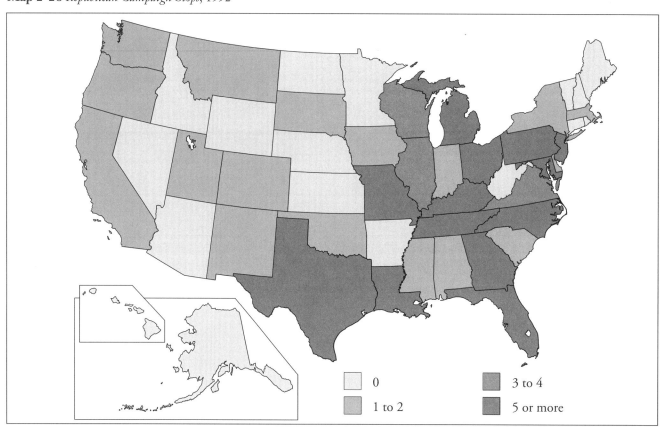

	0		3 to 4
	1 to 2		5 or more

Virginia. On election day, the Democrats lost Florida, North Carolina, and Virginia but won the others. Clinton's decision to campaign extensively in the South stands in significant contrast to the 1988 Democratic campaign (Map 2-23), which essentially wrote off the South.

The Clinton campaign scheduled no campaign appearances in the heavily Republican Plains states. He did not visit the small, safe Democratic states of Maine, New Hampshire, Vermont, and West Virginia. Nor did Clinton visit Vice President Dan Quayle's heavily Republican home state of Indiana. In the South, the Clinton campaign ignored some of the smaller and more reliably Republican states, including Alabama, Mississippi, and South Carolina.

Map 2-26 shows campaign appearances by President George Bush in his unsuccessful 1992 reelection campaign. The Bush campaign, like the Clinton campaign, concentrated on the South and the industrial Midwest. Bush appeared at least five times in Florida, Kentucky, Mississippi, North Carolina, and Texas, all of which the Republicans won. He also appeared frequently in Georgia, Louisiana, and Tennessee in an unsuccessful effort to carry these states. Outside the South, Bush focused on Maryland, Michigan, New Jersey, Ohio, and Pennsylvania, but the Bush-Quayle ticket lost all of these states to Clinton and Gore.

As is the case with other maps, where Bush did not appear is as significant as where he appeared most frequently. Bush did not visit several safely Democratic states such as Maine or West Virginia or Clinton's home state of Arkansas. Nor did he appear in Kansas, Nebraska, or North Dakota, states of the safely Republican Interior West. Indeed, campaign appearances by major party candidates in small-population states that are strongly oriented to either party are few and far between.

1996
Map 2-27 shows appearances by President Bill Clinton in his successful reelection campaign in 1996. Compared to previous Democratic campaigns, the 1996 campaign was more national in scope but especially emphasized the Sun Belt. Clinton appeared five or more times in California, Florida, Ohio, and Texas, winning all but Texas. He also emphasized the Southwest, with three or four appearances each in Arizona and New Mexico, which the Democrats won, and Colorado, which they lost. Clinton's strategy was to challenge the conventional Republican control of the Interior West, but he had only partial success. Democrats also emphasized Pennsylvania and the midwestern industrial states of Illinois, Michigan, Missouri, and Ohio. Nearly all of the states visited three or more times by Clinton or Gore went Democratic on election day.

The Clinton campaign declined to send its candidate to more than a dozen states, perhaps reasoning that the electoral votes of the states where he did appear were more than enough to win a majority in the electoral college. Several of the states where Clinton made no appearances were safe Democratic bastions, including Hawaii, Maryland, and Vermont. Many others, including Alaska, Kansas, Mississippi, Nebraska, Oklahoma, and South Carolina, were safely Republican.

Map 2-28 illustrates the campaign appearances of the 1996 Republican nominee, Sen. Bob Dole of Kansas. Dole, like Clinton, emphasized the Sun Belt and the Southwest. He appeared five or more times in California, Florida, Illinois, Louisiana, Michigan, Missouri, New Jersey, Ohio, and Tennessee, but Dole and running mate Jack Kemp ultimately lost all of these states. Dole also appeared several times in normally Republican bastions, including Nebraska and South Dakota and his native Kansas. Dole spent much more time in the Sun Belt than he did in the North. He did not appear in northern New England, the Pacific Northwest, Arkansas, or the Carolinas. The Republicans won North Carolina and South Carolina, but they lost the others to the Democrats.

2000
Map 2-29 illustrates campaign appearances by Vice President Al Gore in his close but unsuccessful race for the presidency in 2000. The Gore strategy was quite concentrated geographically, focusing on the Northeast, the South, and the Pacific Coast. Gore appeared at least five times in California, Florida, Iowa, Michigan, Missouri, Ohio, Pennsylvania, Tennessee, and Wisconsin. The popular vote was close in all of these states, and Gore's razor-thin loss in Florida cost him the election. The Democratic nominee also emphasized other southern states, as well as the Pacific Northwest and the northeastern industrial states.

Map 2-29 also shows that Gore did not campaign in a large number of safely Republican states. He did not visit the Plains or the Interior West, with the exception of New Mexico, which was the only state in the region he carried. Gore also declined to appear in heavily Republican Alabama, Indiana, and South Carolina. Perhaps reasoning that Sen. Joseph Lieberman's presence on the ticket would ensure the electoral votes of Connecticut, the Democratic nominee did not campaign there.

Map 2-30 shows the campaign strategies of George W. Bush, the Republican candidate. Maps 2-29 and 2-30 are remarkably similar, showing that both campaigns were competing for the same places. Bush appeared five or more times in the three largest Sun Belt states—California, Florida, and Texas. He also emphasized Illinois, Iowa,

Map 2-27 *Democratic Campaign Stops, 1996*

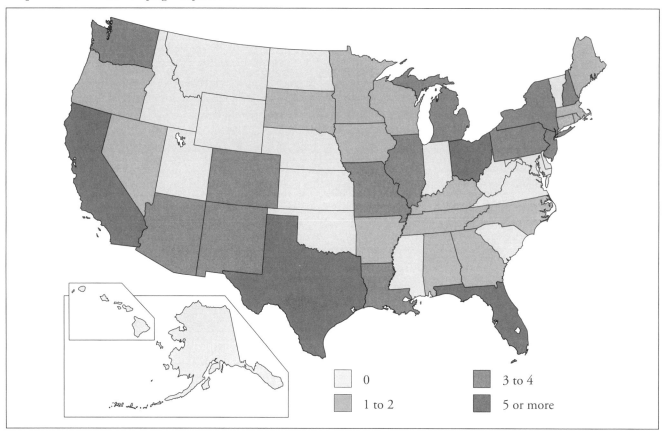

	0		3 to 4
	1 to 2		5 or more

Map 2-28 *Republican Campaign Stops, 1996*

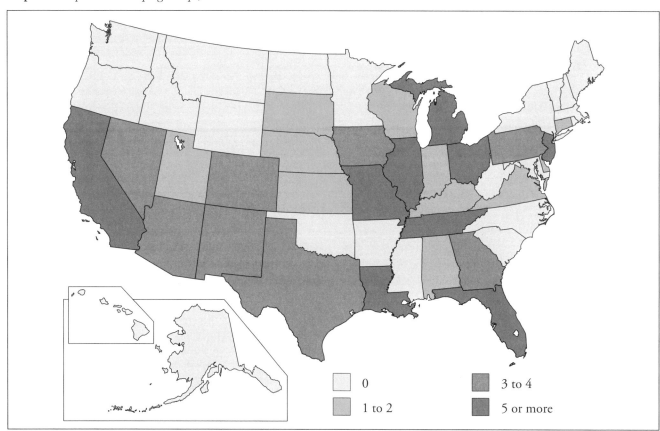

	0		3 to 4
	1 to 2		5 or more

Map 2-29 *Democratic Campaign Stops, 2000*

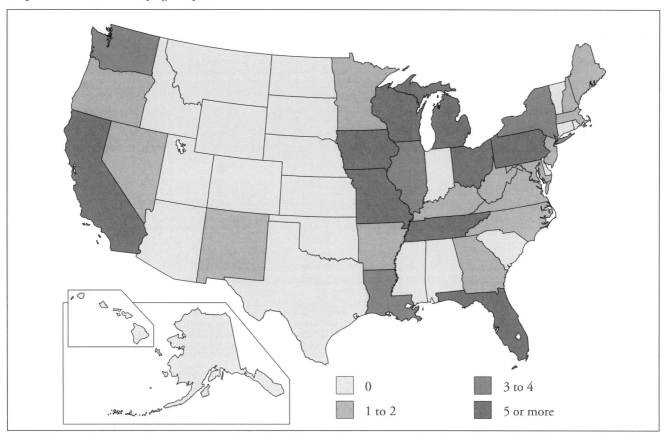

☐ 0	☐ 3 to 4
☐ 1 to 2	☐ 5 or more

Map 2-30 *Republican Campaign Stops, 2000*

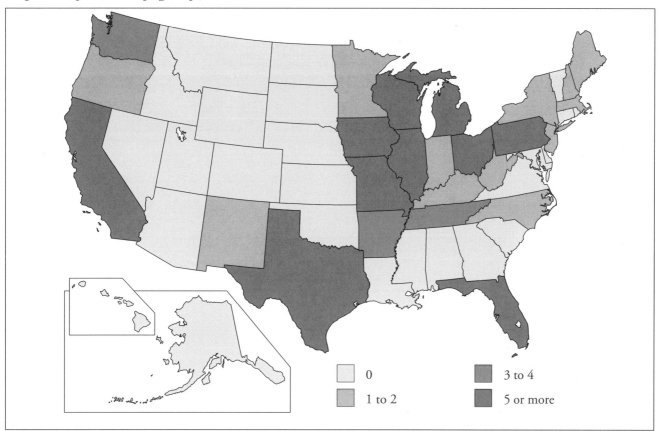

☐ 0	☐ 3 to 4
☐ 1 to 2	☐ 5 or more

Michigan, Missouri, Ohio, Pennsylvania, and Wisconsin. These states, as we have seen, were crucial to the outcome of the election. Bush also took his campaign to Gore's home state of Tennessee and President Clinton's native Arkansas, including a visit to both states on the day before the election. Bush's narrow victory in these two states proved critical to his success in the electoral college. Bush, like Gore, essentially ignored the Plains and Interior West. In the South, he focused on the more competitive states and did not campaign in the safely Republican Alabama, Mississippi, and South Carolina.

Voter Turnout

Maps 2-31, 2-32, and 2-33 show voter turnout by state in the elections of 1960, 1980, and 2000, respectively. Voter turnout is the percentage of people eligible to vote who actually cast ballots in a given election. Thus, in 1960 the voter turnout was the percentage of citizens aged twenty-one and over who voted. Ratification of the Twenty-sixth Amendment in 1971 gave eighteen-year-olds the right to vote, and, therefore, the 1980 and 2000 maps represent the percentage of citizens aged eighteen and over who voted.

Because younger people are generally less likely to vote than older persons, the long-term effect of the Twenty-sixth Amendment has been to reduce voter turnout slightly. This effect may be offset, however, by the fact that the percentage of elderly in the United States population is increasing (see Map 1-10).

The level of voter turnout in 1960, which was the closest election of the twentieth century, shows a clear north-south gradient. With the exception of New York, voter turnout was higher than 70 percent in every northern state from New England to the Pacific Northwest. In contrast, less than 40 percent of eligible voters in Alabama, Georgia, Mississippi, South Carolina, and Virginia cast ballots.

The difference between high voter turnout in the North and low turnout in the South has several causes. The political culture of the North, including New England, the Upper Middle West, and the Pacific Northwest, emphasizes the view that political participation, including voting in elections, is a civic responsibility (see Map 6-1). Minnesota, North Dakota, and Utah recorded the highest rates of voter turnout of any of the fifty states in 1960. In contrast, the political culture of the South discourages voter participation by people who are not part of society's elite. The most blatant application of this philosophy was passage of "Jim

Map 2-31 *Voter Turnout, 1960*

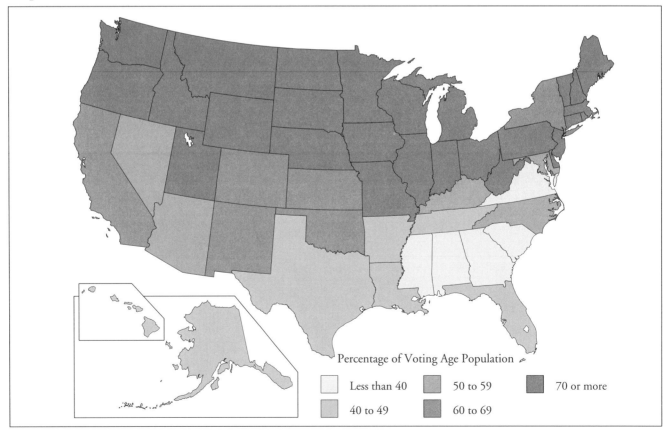

Map 2-32 *Voter Turnout, 1980*

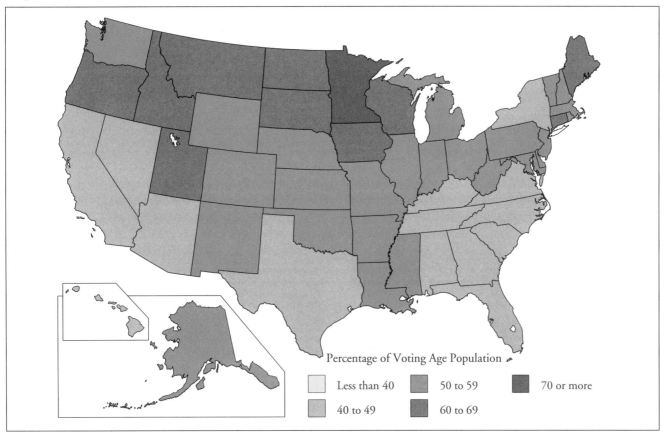

Percentage of Voting Age Population

- Less than 40
- 40 to 49
- 50 to 59
- 60 to 69
- 70 or more

Map 2-33 *Voter Turnout, 2000*

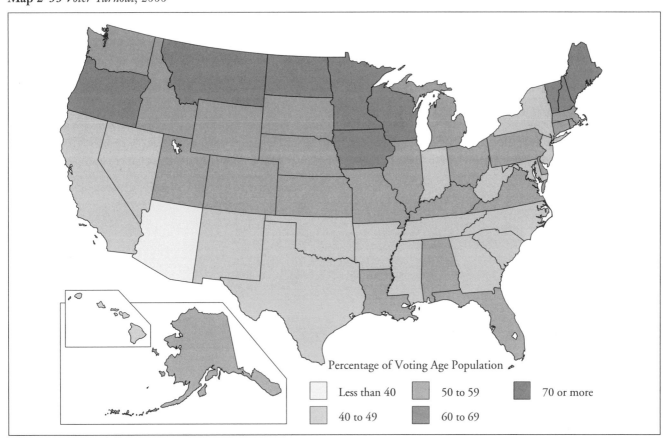

Percentage of Voting Age Population

- Less than 40
- 40 to 49
- 50 to 59
- 60 to 69
- 70 or more

Crow" laws, which made voting and political activity by African Americans difficult, if not impossible, especially in the Deep South. African Americans who tried to exercise their Fifteenth Amendment right to vote in the Deep South often met with harassment, intimidation, and in some cases violence. Note, however, that voter turnout rates were somewhat higher in Florida, which already had a large population of northern retirees, and in North Carolina, which lacked the large-scale plantation culture of neighboring Virginia and South Carolina but had a substantial number of industrial workers (Map 1-29).

In 1965 President Lyndon Johnson signed the Voting Rights Act into law. The act provided federal guarantees to the right to vote in those areas with a history of discrimination against the voting rights of African Americans and other minorities. During the latter half of the 1960s, voter registration among African Americans increased dramatically, and by 1970 voter turnout by blacks in the South was roughly equal to that of whites. Map 2-32 shows state-by-state voter turnout in 1980, some fifteen years after the enactment of the Voting Rights Act. The north-south pattern of 1960 remains evident, but the contrast between the North and South is less dramatic. In 1960 more than twenty states had turnout rates higher than 70 percent, but only Minnesota fell into this category in 1980. States in the Upper Middle West, the Northwest, and New England also had relatively high turnout rates, again reflecting the political culture of these regions. Declines in voter turnout in these areas can be attributed to several factors, including that the 1980 election was not as close and dramatic as that of 1960, the dampening effect of the Twenty-sixth Amendment, and perhaps an increased skepticism and cynicism on the part of the voting public in light of the cultural upheavals of the 1960s, the Vietnam War, and the Watergate scandal in the 1970s.

Five states had reported a less than 40 percent turnout in 1960, whereas in 1980 every state reported turnout rates higher than 40 percent. The number of states with less than 50 percent turnout increased considerably, however. These included many states in the South, as well as Arizona, California, Nevada, New York, and Texas. In general, by 1980 turnout in rural places exceeded turnout in urban places, in part accounting for low turnout in large states such as California, New York, and Texas.

Map 2-33 shows voter turnout rates in the 2000 election, which was the closest U.S. presidential election since 1876. The overall pattern of Map 2-33 is somewhat similar to that of Maps 2-31 (1960) and 2-32 (1980). Even though pollsters and journalists anticipated and predicted a very close election, turnout throughout the country in 2000 was decidedly lower than in 1960. Only nine states reported turnout levels higher than 60 percent, and all of them—Iowa, Maine, Minnesota, Montana, New Hampshire, North Dakota, Oregon, Vermont, and Wisconsin—are nonurban, small-population states with the political culture of the North. Polls showed that the candidates were running neck and neck in several of these states, including Iowa, New Hampshire, Oregon, and Wisconsin, which may have encouraged relatively high turnout. Most of the southern half of the country reported turnout of less than 50 percent, and Arizona reported a turnout rate of less than 40 percent. Low turnout rates in the Sun Belt reflect not only the region's association with southern political culture but also the concentration of young adults who decline to participate in the electoral process.

Notes

1. Theodore H. White, *The Making of the President, 1960* (Boston: Houghton Mifflin, 1961).

2. Ibid.

3. Theodore H. White, *The Making of the President, 1968* (Boston: Houghton Mifflin, 1969).

4. Theodore H. White, *The Making of the President, 1972* (Boston: Houghton Mifflin, 1973).

5. Fred M. Shelley and J. Clark Archer, "Some Geographical Aspects of the 1992 American Presidential Election," *Political Geography* 13 (1994): 137–159.

Chapter 3

Congress

The U.S. Congress is an inherently geographical institution. Geography manifests itself in the distribution of members, drawing of congressional district boundaries, regional aspects of political party support, and regional support for legislation as shown in roll call voting behavior. Chapter 3 explores the geography of Congress in maps and discusses the apportionment of seats in the House of Representatives, the party identification of senators and representatives, and the distribution of votes in Congress on issues of national importance.

As the U.S. population increased, the number of House members also grew from its original constitutional size of sixty-five. After the 1910 census, Congress set total House membership at 435, and it has remained fixed at this number ever since. The fixed size of the House means that after every census some states lose House seats and some states gain seats. Since 1960 population growth in the Sun Belt has increased this region's political power relative to the slower growing Northeast and Midwest. For example, in 1960 New York had forty-five seats in the House, and California had thirty. By 2000 California's apportionment had increased to fifty-four seats, and New York's declined to thirty.

The partisan makeup of Congress reflects the political composition of the nation in general and of particular sections, regions, and states. Indeed, almost every state has subregions that are strongly supportive of one party. Regional preferences in political affiliation and elections go back as far as the first congressional balloting in the 1790s. After the Civil War and Reconstruction, a strong sectional pattern of a Republican North and Democratic South developed in the United States. With the political realignment of the early 1930s, cities in the North became more Democratic. The period covered by this atlas, 1960–2000, encompasses the transition of U.S. electoral geography from the post–Civil War and Reconstruction pattern to a contemporary pattern of nationally competitive elections.

Most pieces of legislation in Congress have a greater impact on some areas of the country than on others. As the maps in Chapter 1 illustrate, the United States is a vast nation with significant differences in physical, economic, ethnic, and cultural composition. These differences become apparent in the regional support for and resistance to legislation, most obviously in final roll call voting behavior. Four recent roll call votes are mapped and discussed to demonstrate this geographic phenomenon.

Reapportionment of the U.S. House of Representatives

The U.S. Constitution directs that a census of population be taken every ten years to reallocate seats in the House of Representatives. The census also has a direct effect on presidential elections because the number of electoral college members from each state is equal to the numbers of its House members plus its two senators. In essence, political power in Congress and in presidential elections has been allocated on a population basis, consistently and systematically, since the first census in 1790.

Throughout American history, the populations of the states have grown at different rates because of variables in immigration, internal migration, and natural population growth. These differences cause some states and regions to gain in the reapportionment process and others to lose. Four major demographic and geographic trends have affected congressional reapportionment: first, the growth rate differences between the original coastal states versus the trans-Appalachian states associated with westward movement in the first fifty years of American history; second, the growth rate differences between free states and slave states in the decades before the Civil War; third, the rural to urban movement and the growth of cities and the industrial North, especially from 1870 to 1930; and, fourth, the population growth differences between the Sun Belt and Snow Belt in recent decades.[1]

This section covers the five reapportionments that followed censuses taken from 1960 through 2000. The census count is done during the first year of each decade—years ending in zero—and records the change in population since the previous census. Early in the following year the Census Bureau usually announces the reallocation of seats based on population shifts. Since the 1960s states have been required by law to ensure their citizens equal representation in state and local legislatures, as well as in Congress, which obliges states to redraw not only their congressional district boundaries but also the boundaries of all other legislative districts, based on the new population geography—even if the number of seats remains the same. The new congressional districts are first used in the House election in years ending in two and usually remain the same in the four subsequent elections.

Table 3-1 summarizes the seat shifts in Congress after each census from 1960 through 2000. In the last five censuses, eighty seats, nearly one-fifth of the House, were shifted between states and regions.

The maps in this section show the number of House seats allocated to each state based on census data from 1960 to 2000. Table 3-2 summarizes the fate of the states following each census. Sixteen states gained representatives during this period. All the states with a net gain are in the West and South. California, Florida, and Texas, which are the three major "growth poles" of the Sun Belt, account for fifty of the seventy-five, or two-thirds of the net seat transfer. California, Florida, and Texas are not only the demographic growth poles but also the political power growth poles of the late twentieth century. Twenty-six states lost House seats during this period, and twenty-three of them are in the

North, Northeast, or Great Plains. New York (-15) and Pennsylvania (-11) were the biggest losers, accounting for 35 percent of all lost seats.

The data in Table 3-2 show a shift in political power from the North and Northeast to the South and Southwest. In the text that accompanies Maps 3-1 through 3-5, each census and reapportionment is analyzed individually to give a more detailed decade-by-decade understanding of the demographic processes at work.

Map 3-1 illustrates the reallocation of seats in the House based on the 1960 census. California was by far the biggest winner, gaining eight additional House seats. This number represents the largest single gain during this period and one of the largest in American history. California's eight seats and Florida's increase of four account for more than half of all seats gained. Arizona and Texas, which were just beginning to experience rapid growth, each added one seat. Alaska and Hawaii entered the Union in 1959, and their seats are counted as a net gain.

The 1960 reapportionment map represents a transition period between historic demographic trends. Ohio and Michigan each gained one seat in 1960, reflecting, in part, the growth of the automobile industry in the post–World War II era and the 1950s. These gains represent the last phase of the movement of population from rural areas to the industrial urban North. New Jersey and Maryland also gained one seat each, in part because of the growth of suburbs at the expense of neighboring large cities in other states. New Jersey drew population from both New York City and Philadelphia. The loss of seats in New York and Pennsylvania was partly caused by this short but interstate movement of people between states. Maryland's gain can be attributed to the rapid growth of Washington, D.C., and the subsequent suburbanization across the District line. The seats added by Maryland, Michigan, New Jersey, and Ohio in 1960 were last seats gained by northern states, a development with enormous consequences for political power in the United States.

Sixteen states lost seats in this apportionment, the most in the 1960–2000 era. The biggest losers were the northeastern industrial states of Pennsylvania (-3), New York (-2), and Massachusetts (-2). The other losers included the midwestern agricultural states of Illinois, Iowa, Kansas, Minnesota, Missouri, and Nebraska. All of these states lost one seat each. Four southern states lost representation, mostly because of heavy out-migration by African Americans, especially from the Mississippi Delta region, where Arkansas, Louisiana, and Mississippi meet. Three of the four southern states that lost seats in the 1960–2000 period lost all or most of them in the 1960 apportionment. The Appalachian states of West Virginia and Kentucky also lost

Table 3-1 Transfer of House Seats by Decade, 1960–2000

	1960	1970	1980	1990	2000
States losing seats	16	9	10	13	10
States gaining seats	10	5	11	8	7
States with no change in seats	24	36	29	29	33
Net interstate shift in seats	21	11	17	19	12
Percentage of House shifted	4.8%	2.5%	3.9%	4.4%	2.8%

SOURCE: Kenneth C. Martis and Gregory Elmes, *The Historical Atlas of State Power in Congress, 1790–1990* (Washington, D.C.: Congressional Quarterly, 1993).

Table 3-2 Interstate Transfer of House Seats by Decade by State, 1960–2000

Census Year and Congress	1960 88th Congress	1970 93d Congress	1980 98th Congress	1990 103d Congress	2000 108th Congress	Seat Change 1960–2000
California	+8	+5	+2	+7	+1	+23
Florida	+4	+3	+4	+4	+2	+17
Texas	+1	+1	+3	+3	+2	+1
Arizona	+1	+1	+1	+1	+2	+6
Colorado	+1	+1	+1	+3		
Georgia				+1	+2	+3
Hawaii	+2					+2
Nevada			+1		+1	+2
Washington			+1	+1		+2
Alaska	+1					+1
Maryland	+1					+1
New Mexico			+1			+1
North Carolina	-1			+1	+1	+1
Oregon			+1			+1
Utah			+1			+1
Virginia				+1		+1
Tennessee		-1	+1			0
Connecticut					-1	-1
Louisiana				-1		-1
Maine	-1					-1
Minnesota	-1					-1
Montana				-1		-1
Nebraska	-1					-1
New Jersey	+1		-1	-1		-1
North Dakota		-1				-1
Oklahoma					-1	-1
South Dakota			-1			-1
Alabama	-1	-1				-2
Arkansas	-2					-2
Indiana			-1		-1	-2
Kansas	-1		-1			-2
Kentucky	-1			-1		-2
Mississippi	-1				-1	-2
Missouri	-1		-1			-2
Wisconsin		-1			-1	-2
Iowa	-1	-1		-1		-3
Michigan	+1		-1	-2	-1	-3
West Virginia	-1	-1		-1		-3
Massachusetts	-2		-1	-1		-4
Ohio	+1	-1	-2	-2	-1	-5
Illinois	-1		-2	-2	-1	-6
Pennsylvania	-3	-2	-2	-2	-2	-11
New York	-2	-2	-5	-3	-2	-15
Total United States	21	11	17	19	12	Net Transfer = 75

Sources: Data for 1960, 1970, and 1980 from Kenneth C. Martis, *The Historical Atlas of Political Parties in the United States Congress: 1789–1989* (New York: Macmillan, 1989). Data for 1990 and 2000 from Election Statistics, Office of the Clerk, United States House of Representatives, Washington, D.C., http://clerkweb.house.gov/elections/elections.htm.

Note: Forty-three of the fifty states lost or gained seats in the House of Representatives in one or more of the last five census reapportionments. Seven of the fifty states have had the same number of seats from 1960 through 2000; three states, Delaware, Vermont, and Wyoming have the required minimum of one seat; three states, Idaho, New Hampshire, and Rhode Island, held at two seats; and South Carolina held at six seats.

Map 3-1 *House of Representatives Decennial Apportionment Change, 1960 Census*

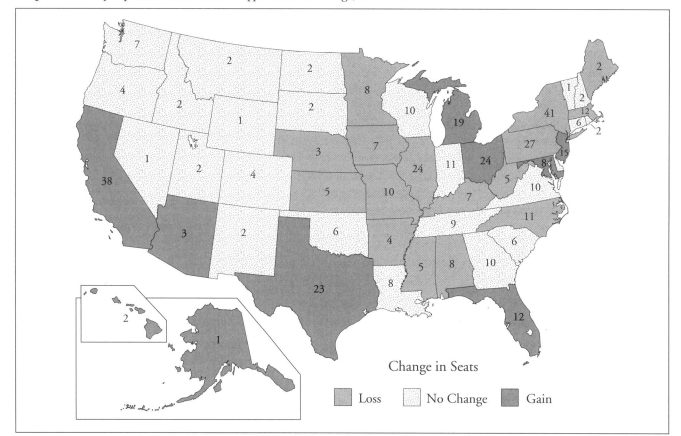

seats, in part because of mechanization in the coal mining industry.

The demographic maps and text in Chapter 1 illustrate and discuss the movement of population that helps explain the apportionment changes from 1960 to 2000. The 1960 apportionment map represents the transition between the final stages of northern industrial growth and southern decline and the beginning stages of northern industrial decline and southern growth. Four southern tier states—Arizona, California, Florida, and Texas—all gained seats in 1960, and they are the only four states that gained seats in all of the subsequent four reapportionments.

Map 3-2 illustrates the reallocation of seats in the House based on the 1970 census. Table 3-2 shows a total of eleven seats shifting from one state to another, the smallest net transfer during the 1960–2000 period. Five states gained seats, and nine states lost seats.

A cluster of four northeastern states lost seats: New York (-2), Pennsylvania (-2), Ohio (-1), and West Virginia (-1). The decline of the northeastern industrial economy began in the 1960s, and this decline is reflected in all the subsequent apportionment maps. Three agricultural midwestern

states, Iowa, North Dakota, and Wisconsin, each lost one seat. These losses reflected the out-migration from the agricultural Midwest and Great Plains. Two southern states, Alabama and Tennessee, each lost one seat. The South, especially the rural and African American South, continued to lose population, a trend that eventually began to reverse. This region lost only two more seats for the remainder of the 1960–2000 period. The big winners in 1970 were California (+5) and Florida (+3). Arizona, Colorado, and Texas also gained one seat each.

Map 3-3 illustrates the reallocation of seats in the House based on the 1980 census. The apportionment pattern shown in this map is the most regionally clustered of the 1960–2000 period, making this map symbolic of the larger trends and shifts of political power that occurred in the late twentieth century. All the seat losses were in the North and Northeast, and all the gains were in the South and Southwest. Table 3-2 shows a total of seventeen seats shifting from one state to another, with ten states losing seats and eleven gaining, which was the largest number of states increasing during this period.

The cluster of nine northern industrial states that lost

Map 3-2 *House of Representatives Decennial Apportionment Change, 1970 Census*

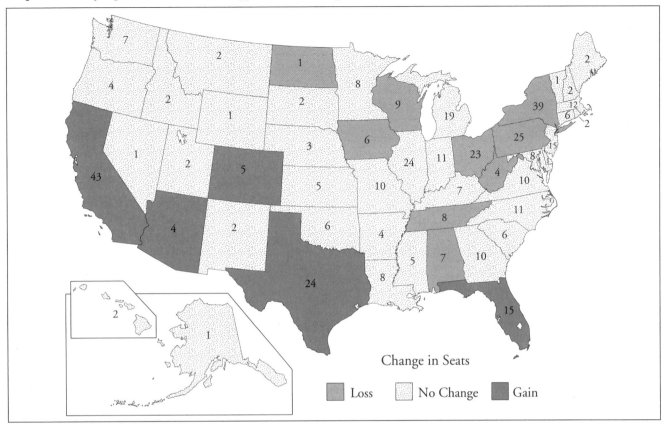

Map 3-3 *House of Representatives Decennial Apportionment Change, 1980 Census*

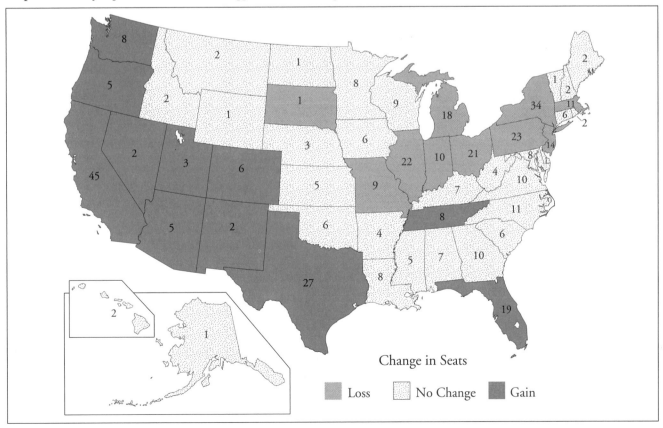

seats shows a nearly perfect outline of what geographers consider the American Manufacturing Belt. The decline of the 1960s was intensified in the 1970s in almost all large northern industrial cities. Precipitous population declines occurred in Buffalo, Cleveland, Detroit, and Pittsburgh. The biggest loser was New York: its decline of five seats was the largest single census loss of any state in the 1960–2000 period and one of the largest in U.S. history. Heavy rural out-migration in the midwestern states intensified the urban decline in states such as Indiana, Illinois, Michigan, Missouri, and Ohio. The loss in South Dakota also reflects agricultural population decline.

Florida led all gainers with four seats. Another southern state, Tennessee, regained the seat it lost in the previous census. The rest of the South was in a transition period in the 1970s: it stopped losing seats but did not register enough growth to make gains. The region with the most significant gains was the cluster of nine states in the Southwest and Pacific Coast, reflecting the postindustrial trend of American migration to high-amenity, environmentally pleasing coastal areas. The energy crisis of the 1970s, the subsequent oil boom, and the thriving cities of Houston and

Dallas-Ft. Worth account, in part, for making Texas, with three new seats, the biggest gainer in 1980.

Map 3-4 illustrates the reallocation of seats in the House based on the 1990 census. Table 3-2 shows a total of nineteen seats shifting from one state to another. Typically for this era, more states lost seats (13) than gained seats (8).

As in the 1980 census, the largest cluster of states losing seats after the 1990 census was in the northern American Manufacturing Belt. The economic and industrial restructuring of the early 1980s hit states such as New York (-3), and Illinois, Michigan, Ohio, and Pennsylvania (-2 seats each), especially hard. Appalachian coal mining areas of Kentucky and West Virginia lost population as the energy crisis eased in the 1980s. Continued agricultural out-migration is shown in the loss of one seat each by Iowa, Kansas, and Montana.

The growth pole states of California (+7), Florida (+4), and Texas (+3) account for fourteen of the nineteen seats transferred. California's population increase was partly due to heavy foreign immigration, especially from Mexico and Asia. Arizona and Washington each gained one seat. These changes are dramatic, but the gain of one seat each by the

Map 3-4 *House of Representatives Decennial Apportionment Change, 1990 Census*

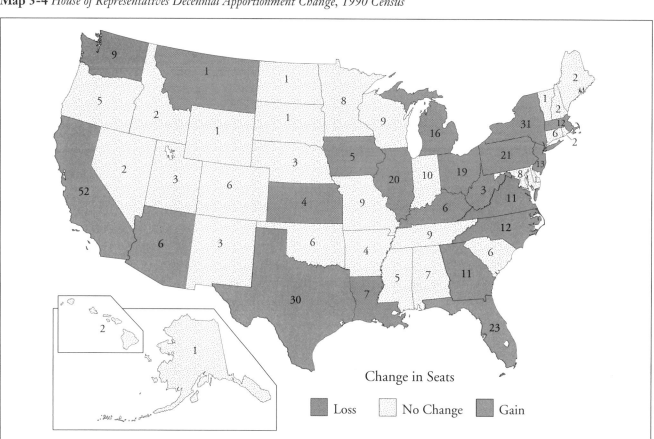

southern states of Georgia, North Carolina, and Virginia heralds a historic trend. Since the establishment of the 435-member House in 1912, at no time had three non–growth pole Deep South states gained seats. For the first two-thirds of the twentieth century, most of the Deep South was an economic backwater and, beginning in 1914, had experienced a substantial out-migration to northern industrial cities and to Florida, Texas, and the West. In the 1960s and 1970s, this trend slowed, and in the 1980s, reversed. Sprawling expansion in the Atlanta area aided Georgia's growth, and in North Carolina the same trend occurred in Charlotte and the Raleigh-Durham (Research Triangle) region. Virginia's increase came mainly from the explosive expansion of the Washington, D.C., suburbs in the northern part of the state. One southern state, Louisiana, lost population because of the easing of the energy crisis in the 1980s and the resulting decline in the oil industry. Most other southern states stabilized their population and began modest Sun Belt–type growth.

Map 3-5 illustrates the reallocation of seats in the House based on the 2000 census. Table 3-2 shows a total of twelve seats shifting from one state to another, with ten states losing seats and seven gaining.

Almost every state in the American Manufacturing Belt lost seats. New York and Pennsylvania lost two seats each, making them the two biggest decline areas in the 1960–2000 era. The shift of light and heavy manufacturing to southern states, Mexico, and overseas was one of the major economic and political phenomena of the late twentieth century. In addition, population in postindustrial society continued moving from the Snow Belt to the Sun Belt. Two states outside of the Snow Belt each lost one seat. In Oklahoma the decline in population was associated with losses in the agricultural and oil sectors, and in Mississippi the population loss stemmed primarily from out-migration from the Delta and other rural areas.

All the states that gained House members lie along the southern Sun Belt tier. This time, however, California gained only one seat, its smallest increase in 100 years. High housing costs, over-crowded freeways, and declining environmental conditions in recent years encouraged an interstate out-migration that was higher than in-migration. Only foreign immigration and a high internal birthrate kept California's population expanding. No state gained more than two seats. In the West, vigorous growth in Phoenix, Tucson, Las Vegas, and the Denver Front Range gave Arizona (+2),

Map 3-5 *House of Representatives Decennial Apportionment Change, 2000 Census*

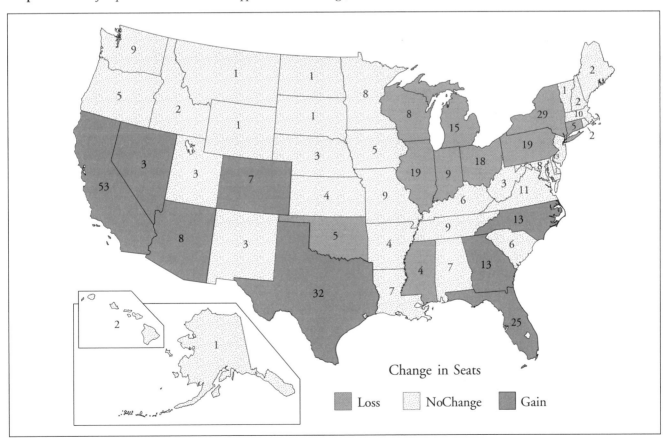

Nevada (+1), and Colorado (+1) gains. Texas and Florida gained two seats each, as did Georgia, because of the continuing expansion of the Atlanta metropolitan area. Another Deep South state, North Carolina, also gained a seat.

Throughout the 1960–2000 period the changes that occurred in the geography of the U.S. population caused the reallocation of seats in the House of Representatives to shift political power from the Northeast and Midwest to the South and West. The demographic maps and accompanying text in Chapter 1 deal with the population trends of the 1990s, but they also explain most of the apportionment changes from 1960 to 2000. These apportionment changes help shape not only the national political agenda but also most of the issues discussed in the atlas.

Partisan Affiliation of the U.S. Senate

The Constitution directs that each state, irrespective of population size, is to have two senators. Since the 1959 admission of Alaska and Hawaii, the forty-ninth and fiftieth states, the Senate has had 100 members. The Constitution divides the Senate into three classes or groups, and every two years one class, or one-third of the Senate, is elected. Because senators serve six-year terms, it sometimes takes more than one election to change the partisan majority of the Senate despite radical political changes in the nation. In contrast, the House can undergo sweeping changes in partisan numbers in a two-year period.

Senatorial elections can provide insight into the general political makeup of an individual state or a region. The political character of a state may favor one party, shift competitively between parties, or display divided affiliations. The competitive nature of state parties may change slowly over time or shift rapidly in response to radical changes in national elections and parties. Competitive or noncompetitive, almost all states have subregions that are strongly biased toward one party. For example, from 1874 to 1966 Tennessee consistently elected Democratic senators. Within Tennessee, however, the easternmost mountainous counties were heavily Republican, while the middle and western portions of the state were Democratic. Many senators are able to carve out long careers by virtue of incumbency, hard work, competence, and personal popularity, even though a good portion of their constituents belong to the opposite political party. Among the better-known "minority" senators, past and present, are Democrats George McGovern and Tom Daschle of South Dakota and Frank Church of Idaho, along with Republicans John Chafee of Rhode Island, Howard Baker of Tennessee, and Jacob Javits of New York. The maps in this section of the atlas illustrate partisan affiliation of the Senate

by state following the five elections in the census years from 1960 through 2000. These maps display important state and regional political party patterns within the Senate and give a better understanding of the overall political party membership data.

When the 87th Congress convened in 1961, the political party makeup of the Senate was sixty-five Democrats and thirty-five Republicans. Twenty-five states had two Democratic senators, ten had two Republicans, and fifteen had split delegations. The Democrats' majority in 1961 was the largest in all the election results discussed in this section and one of the largest of the 1961–2001 period. In 1960 Democratic senator John F. Kennedy of Massachusetts defeated Republican vice president Richard M. Nixon of California. National politics affects Senate races during a presidential election year by bringing out larger numbers of voters. In addition, the "coattail" effect can help elect a senator belonging to the party of the presidential candidate who seems likely to win the state.

The partisan makeup of the Senate in 1961 shown in Map 3-6 illustrates the regional structure set by the Civil War and Reconstruction. Each of the eleven states of the Old Confederacy had two Democratic senators and displayed a regional unity legendary in American politics. In fact, this region had, with few exceptions, uniformly elected Democratic senators since the post-Reconstruction period. This "Solid South" electoral behavior was still evident in the 87th Congress (1961–1963). If the Border States of Missouri, Oklahoma, and West Virginia are included, twenty-eight of the sixty-five Democratic senators came from this region. In the 87th Senate, ten states had two Republican senators, also a legacy of the Civil War and Reconstruction, which affected the regional makeup of political parties for at least 100 years.

Another political realignment occurred during the 1930s, when the Great Depression favored the Democrats and weakened the solid Republican hold on the North, especially in immigrant unionized industrial states and in the northern tier. Indeed, between 1932 and 1962 the Republican Party controlled the Senate for only four years.

In 1960, two pockets of Republicanism give further evidence of the general post–Civil War pattern. In the Midwest and Great Plains, the neighboring states of Iowa, South Dakota, Nebraska, and Kansas each had two Republican senators. In New England and the Northeast, the adjoining states of Vermont, New Hampshire, and New York also elected all Republicans. Three Border States—Delaware, Maryland, and Kentucky—each sent two Republicans to the Senate, showing the unpredictable, competitive, and changing nature of this region. For the most part, however, the Republican Senate members of the 87th Congress came primarily from the Northeast and Midwest.

Map 3-6 *Party Affiliation in the Senate, 1961*

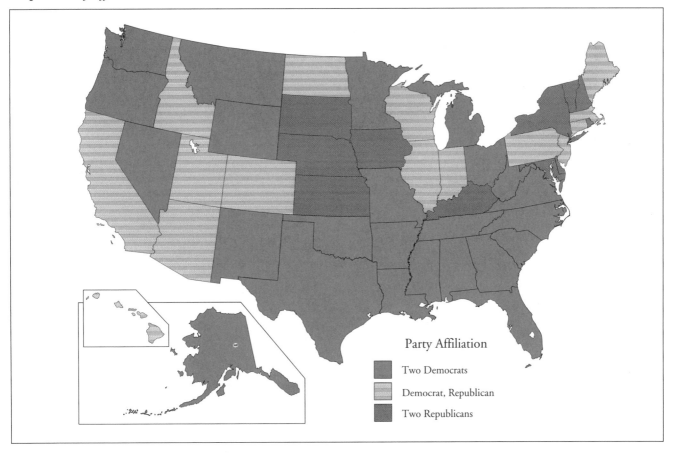

Party Affiliation

- Two Democrats
- Democrat, Republican
- Two Republicans

When the 92d Congress convened in 1971, the political party makeup of the Senate was fifty-four Democrats, forty-four Republicans, one conservative (from New York), and one independent (from Virginia). Seventeen states had two Democratic senators, twelve had two Republicans, and nineteen had split delegations. The Democratic majority had waned considerably from its nearly two-thirds in 1961. Even though the 1970 election was a midterm election, the Democrats lost seats in the Senate during Republican president Richard Nixon's first term.

Map 3-7 shows the regional structure of the partisan makeup of the 92d Senate. Most significant is that the Solid South shows signs of becoming less homogeneous, as displayed in Map 3-6. Counted among the Republican gains of the 1960s were the historic elections of senators from the South. The 1960s were a tumultuous time for the social, economic, and political character of the South. The civil rights movement was in full swing, and the beginnings of a New South economy could be detected. In 1961 the first Republican senator was elected from the Deep South in the twentieth century. Texas chose Republican John Tower to replace Lyndon Johnson, who had been elected vice presi-

dent. This election was a sign that, as a growth pole state, Texas had experienced significant migration from other regions.

The 1964 presidential election was historic in its change of U.S. geographic voting patterns. Conservative Republican senator Barry Goldwater of Arizona ran against moderate—and pro–civil rights—Democratic president Lyndon Johnson from Texas. As Maps 2-3 and 2-4 illustrate, the heart of the Deep South went for a Republican candidate, in part because conservative southern voters recognized Goldwater's nomination as a shift away from the "northeast Republican establishment," which they considered liberal.[2] Meanwhile, changes in the national Democratic Party in favor of civil rights and social legislation further alienated conservative southern whites.

The next crack in the once-Democratic Solid South came in the Senate during the 1964 election. Democratic senator Strom Thurmond of South Carolina, a conservative opponent of the civil right movement, announced in September that he was switching parties. In 1966 Thurmond was reelected to the Senate as a Republican. In 1968 Florida also elected a Republican. Florida was the southern state

Map 3-7 *Party Affiliation in the Senate, 1971*

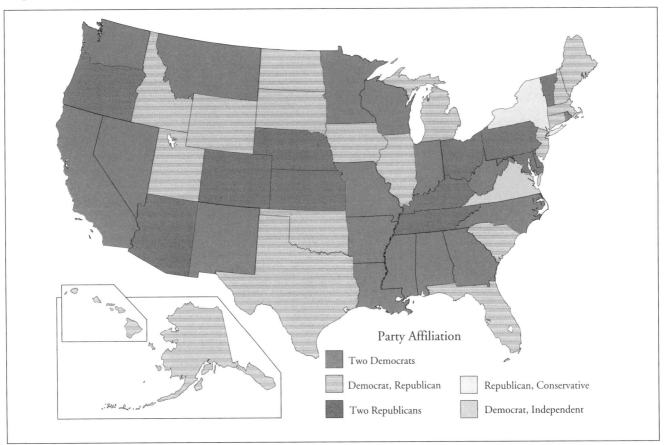

Party Affiliation

- Two Democrats
- Democrat, Republican
- Two Republicans
- Republican, Conservative
- Democrat, Independent

that changed the most in the 1950s and 1960s because of extensive northern migration. In the 1970 election, Tennessee—which always had a significant Republican presence—chose two Republican senators, making it the first of the eleven Confederate states to go entirely GOP.

Map 3-7 shows that the solid bloc of Democratic senators from the South was beginning to break up. Map 3-7 also shows that, for the most part, senatorial elections had become nationally competitive; that is, Democrats and Republicans were represented in every region. As the southern states also became more competitive, and greater numbers of Republicans were elected from this region, the historic Democratic hold on the Senate was threatened. In addition, as other regions also grow more conservative, the national Democratic Party became less competitive.

In the 1980 elections the Republicans won a majority in the U.S. Senate. When the 97th Congress convened in 1981, the political party makeup of the Senate was fifty-three Republicans, forty-six Democrats, and one independent (from Virginia). There was a twelve-seat swing in the Senate that year, the largest seat change in the 1960–2000 period. In the 1980 presidential election, conservative Republican Ronald Reagan of California ran against incumbent Democratic president Jimmy Carter of Georgia. Carter was in political trouble over high inflation rates and the hostage situation in Iran. As Maps 2-11 and 2-12 show, Reagan won in a landslide. He carried Republican candidates to victory on many levels.

Map 3-8 shows the geographic structure of the partisan makeup of the Senate in 1981. Eleven states had two Democratic senators, and fourteen had two Republicans. In just twenty years the South had gone from domination by one party to being almost completely competitive in senatorial elections. Only two Old South states, Arkansas and Louisiana, still had two Democratic senators, while another, North Carolina, elected two Republican senators. Reagan proved to be popular with white southern voters, changing the perception of the national Republican Party begun by Goldwater in 1964.

Map 3-8 also shows that senatorial elections were competitive nationwide during this period. No region is completely dominated by one party as was true in 1961 (Map 3-6). States with two Democratic senators and states with two Republican senators were found in all parts of the country.

Map 3-8 *Party Affiliation in the Senate, 1981*

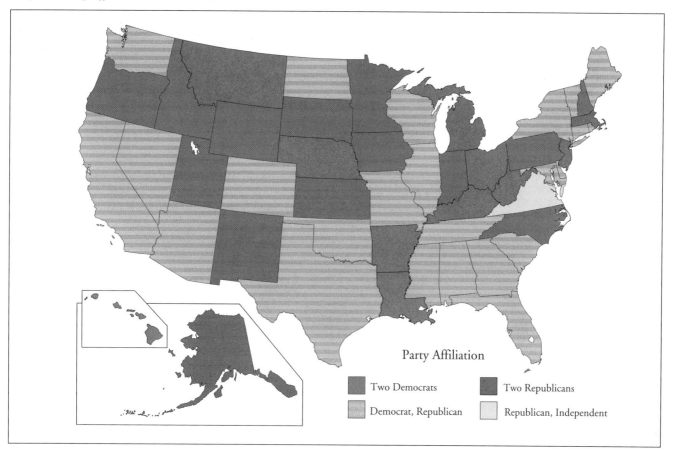

Party Affiliation

Two Democrats | Two Republicans

Democrat, Republican | Republican, Independent

Voting patterns in the Interior West indicate strong Republican growth in Idaho, Utah, and Wyoming, all of which had two Republican senators.

The Democrats regained the Senate majority by an eight-seat margin in the 1986 midterm elections. After the 1990 elections and when the 102d Congress convened in 1991, the political party makeup of the Senate was fifty-six Democrats and forty-four Republicans. Seventeen states had two Democratic senators, eleven had two Republicans, and twenty-two had split delegations.

Map 3-9 illustrates the spatial structure of the partisan makeup of the Senate for the 102d Congress. The continuation of nationally competitive elections is evident. The eleven states with two Republican senators were in all sections of the nation. The seventeen states with two Democratic senators were also found in all sections but were somewhat sparse in the West. Five southern states had two Democratic senators, which indicated a rebirth of the party in that region. In the North, states suffering economic decline tended to vote Democratic, in keeping with the party's stands on social issues, economic aid legislation, and trade policies. Vote results in Connecticut, Massachusetts,

Michigan, and West Virginia exemplify this northern Democratic trend.

When the 107th Congress convened in 2001, the political party makeup of the Senate was fifty-fifty, and it stayed that way until Sen. James Jeffords of Vermont declared himself an independent. The Republicans had gained back control of the Senate with a seven-seat swing in the historic 1994 congressional elections, which saw the House go Republican for the first time since 1952. Republicans held the Senate majority in 1996 and 1998. The 2000 Senate outcome mirrored the closeness of the presidential and House elections. The historic fifty-fifty split led to a power-sharing arrangement in Senate organization, but Vice President Richard Cheney gave the GOP a tie-breaking advantage in any strict party vote. That situation changed with Jeffords's dramatic announcement on May 24, 2001, which gave the Democrats a 50–49 advantage and control of Senate committees and the agenda.

Seventeen states had two Republican senators, and seventeen states had two Democrats. The remaining sixteen had split delegations. Map 3-10 shows the geographic pattern of the one-party and split delegations. The GOP del-

Map 3-9 *Party Affiliation in the Senate, 1991*

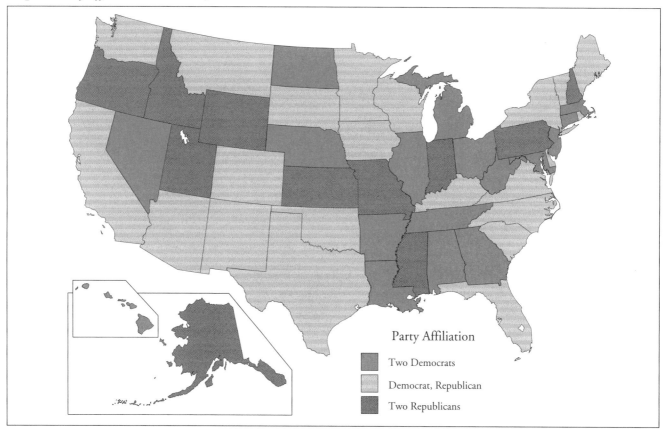

Map 3-10 *Party Affiliation in the Senate, 2001*

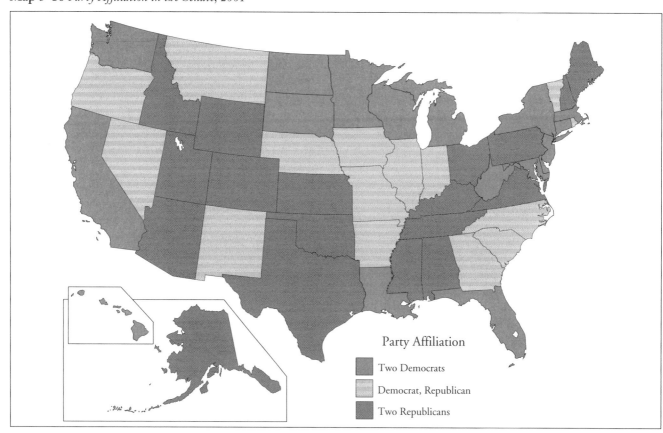

egations tended to be clustered in two regions. In the South, Alabama, Mississippi, Tennessee, Texas, and Virginia had two Republican senators—the exact opposite of the situation in 1960. Another large cluster of Republican senators was in the Interior West and southern Great Plains. Most of the states with two Democratic senators were in the North. On the Pacific Coast, California and Washington also elected two Democrats. Presidential voting trends discussed in Chapter 2 suggest the emergence of a national regional pattern of a Democratic North and Northeast and Pacific Coast versus a Republican South and Interior West. Recent elections show senatorial voting patterns following presidential patterns to a certain extent. It is possible that Map 3-10 shows the beginning of this pattern.

Party Affiliation in the U.S. House of Representatives

Maps 3-11 through 3-15 illustrate the party affiliation of the U.S. House of Representatives by state delegation for five selected elections from 1960 to 2000. The maps display state and regional patterns of House representation and give

a better understanding of the geographic structure of the overall political party membership data. Maps 3-16 (1983), 3-17 (1993), and 3-18 (2001) illustrate the partisan alignments in more detailed fashion by indicating the winning party in all 435 congressional districts.

When the 87th Congress convened in 1961, the political party makeup of the House was 263 Democrats and 174 Republicans. Alaska and Hawaii had been admitted as the forty-ninth and fiftieth states in 1959, and each was granted one seat in the House. These two additional seats were temporarily allocated for the 86th and 87th Congresses, bringing the total number of seats to 437. These Congresses were the only two since 1912 to have more than 435 members.

The 87th Congress had a strong Democratic majority, typical of the numbers from 1955 through 1993. The larger national picture influences House elections in a presidential election year. In 1960 Democratic senator John F. Kennedy of Massachusetts defeated Republican vice president Richard Nixon of California, and House races in some districts were affected. In the 87th House, state delegation size varied from forty-three in New York to the single member the Constitution provides for states with small populations, which at that time included Alaska, Delaware, Hawaii,

Map 3-11 *Party Affiliation in the House of Representatives, 1961*

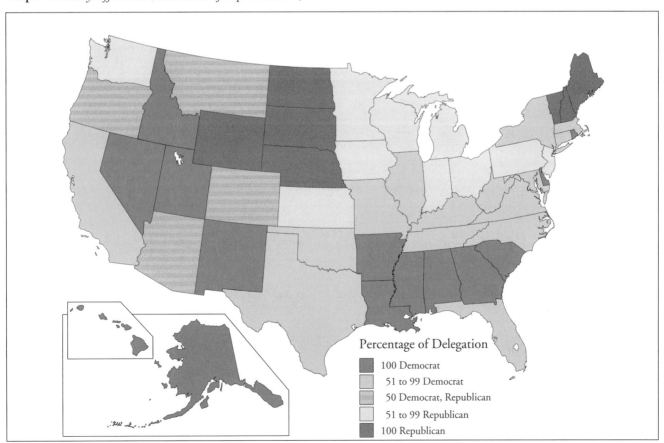

Percentage of Delegation

- 100 Democrat
- 51 to 99 Democrat
- 50 Democrat, Republican
- 51 to 99 Republican
- 100 Republican

Nevada, Vermont, and Wyoming. The partisan result of the statewide election of one House member indicates something about the political geography of that state and region, but we learn even more if the same party wins all the House seats in a state with numerous districts.

Map 3-11 shows a strong regional structure in the partisan makeup of the House. Fourteen states had 100 percent Democratic House delegations, and an additional fifteen had majority Democratic delegations. The heart of the 100 percent Democratic cluster was six states across the Deep South. As in the 1961 Senate map, Map 3-6, the 1961 House map displays a regional unity legendary in American politics. In fact, the South had—apart from a few exceptions—uniformly elected Democratic representatives since the post–Civil War Reconstruction period. This "Solid South" electoral behavior was still evident after the 1960 election. As Table 3-3 indicates, 93 percent of all Deep South seats were Democratic. Looking at the broader picture, all the states of the old Confederacy and all the Border States had a Democratic majority. Other areas of Democratic strength were in three states of the Interior West, Idaho, Nevada, and Utah, and four industrial Northeast states, Connecticut, Massachusetts, New York, and Rhode Island.

Seven states had a 100 percent Republican House delegation, and ten more had a majority Republican delegation. The 100 percent Republican delegations were in two clusters, one in the northern Great Plains states of Nebraska,

Table 3-3 Seats and Percentage Democratic in the U.S. House of Representatives, Southern States, 1960–2000

	1960 87th Congress	1970 92d Congress	1980 97th Congress	1990 102d Congress	2000 107th Congress
Alabama	9–0 100%	5–3 63%	4–3 57%	5–2 71%	2–5 29%
Arkansas	6–0 100%	3–1 75%	2–2 50%	3–1 75%	3–1 75%
Florida	7–1 88%	9–3 75%	11–4 73%	9–10 47%	8–15 35%
Georgia	10–0 100%	8–2 80%	9–1 90%	9–1 90%	3–8 27%
Louisiana	8–0 100%	8–0 100%	6–2 75%	4–4 50%	3–4 43%
Mississippi	6–0 100%	5–0 100%	3–2 60%	5–0 100%	3–2 60%
North Carolina	11–1 92%	7–4 64%	7–4 64%	7–4 64%	5–7 42%
South Carolina	6–0 100%	5–1 83%	2–4 33%	4–2 67%	2–4 33%
Tennessee	7–2 78%	5–4 56%	5–3 63%	6–3 67%	4–5 44%
Texas	21–1 95%	20–3 87%	19–5 83%	19–8 70%	17–13 57%
Virginia	8–2 80%	4–6 40%	1–9 20%	6–4 60%	4–6–1 36%
Total South Percentage Democratic	98–7 [105] 93%	79–27 [106] 75%	69–39 [108] 64%	77–39 [116] 66%	54–70–1 [125] 43%

Note: Numbers represent political parties in the following order: Democratic–Republican–independent.

North Dakota, and South Dakota and neighboring Wyoming. The other cluster was the northernmost New England states of Maine, New Hampshire, and Vermont. Almost all of the ten majority Republican states were those forming a band along the northern tier from the East Coast to the Midwest.

When the 92d Congress convened in 1971, the political party makeup of the House was 255 Democrats and 180 Republicans. The 1970 elections were midterm elections during President Nixon's first term. It is typical for the opposition party to gain seats in midterm elections, and in 1970 the Democrats picked up twelve. In the 92d House state delegations varied in size from forty-one in New York to the single delegates from the small-population states of Alaska, Delaware, Nevada, Vermont, and Wyoming.

Map 3-12 shows a less intense regional structure of House partisan makeup than Map 3-11. In 1971, ten states had 100 percent Democratic House delegations, and an additional nineteen had majority Democratic delegations. Only two Deep South states still had 100 percent Democratic delegations, but almost all southern and Border States still had Democratic majorities. The other pocket of Democratic strength was in the Northeast. Map 3-12 suggests that

the South and Northeast were the core of the House Democrats, along with the Pacific Coast states of California and Washington. Although northern and southern Democrats divided over many issues, they compromised in electing leaders, sharing power, and allocating budgets. The Democrats controlled the House continuously between 1955 and 1994. Speakers of the House during this period, in order of service, included Sam Rayburn (Texas), John McCormack (Massachusetts), Carl Albert (Oklahoma), Tip O'Neill (Massachusetts), Jim Wright (Texas), and Thomas Foley (Washington). Oscillation of control between the Southwest and the Northeast led many to identify this compromise as the "Austin-Boston" connection.

In 1971, five states had 100 percent Republican House delegations, and seven more had majority Republican delegations. These Republican states were located in all regions, but, with two states excepting, they were all in the northern tier in historically Republican areas. The two exceptions, Arizona and Virginia, are, however, telling. Since its admittance to the Union in 1912, Arizona had been a predominantly Democratic state, but in 1970 it elected Republicans to two of its three House seats. Northern migration and a changing state and national Republican

Map 3-12 *Party Affiliation in the House of Representatives, 1971*

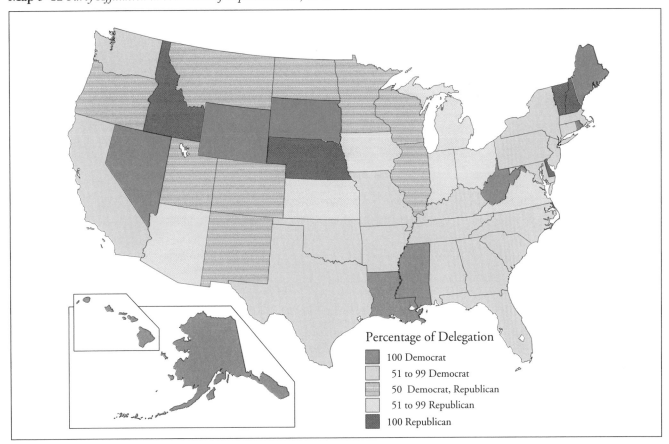

Percentage of Delegation

- 100 Democrat
- 51 to 99 Democrat
- 50 Democrat, Republican
- 51 to 99 Republican
- 100 Republican

Party were beginning to affect the electoral makeup of this Interior West state. Even more significant was Virginia. For the first time since the Civil War and Reconstruction, Virginia had a majority Republican House delegation of six to four. These Republicans were elected from northern Virginia districts close to suburban Washington, D.C., and from western Virginia mountain districts with some Republican heritage. Closest to the North and its strong urban and suburbanizing trends, this southern state was in the process of changing its electoral makeup.

When the 97th Congress convened in 1981, the political party makeup of the House was 242 Democrats, 192 Republicans, and one independent (from Pennsylvania). Despite losing thirty-three seats in 1980, the Democrats retained a majority typical of their margin from 1955 through 1993. The large loss of Democratic seats can be attributed, in part, to the sweeping presidential election victory of Republican Ronald Reagan over the incumbent Jimmy Carter (Maps 2-11 and 2-12). The size of state delegations in the House varied from forty-three in California to the single delegates from the states of Alaska, Delaware, North Dakota, Nevada, Vermont, and Wyoming. After the 1970 census, a historic demographic milestone was reached when California was allocated the largest House delegation, surpassing New York, which had held this position since 1810.

Map 3-13 shows a less intense regional structure of House partisan makeup than in previous decades. Three small states had 100 percent Democratic House delegations, and twenty-four others had majority Democratic delegations. As Table 3-3 shows, in 1980 no Deep South state had a 100 percent Democratic delegation, even though almost all southern and Border States still had Democratic majorities. The other pockets of Democratic strength were in the Northeast and Pacific Coast. The Republicans controlled nine states completely—two in New England, four in the Interior West, as well as Alaska, Delaware, New Mexico. The GOP controlled six other delegations—four in the Midwest and, significantly, Virginia and South Carolina in the South.

When the 102d Congress convened in 1991, the political party makeup of the House was 267 Democrats, 167 Republicans, and 1 independent (from Vermont). The 1990 elections took place in the midterm of the first and only term of Republican president George Bush. Typical of midterm elections, the party controlling the White House lost House seats, in this case, nine. In the 102d House, Cal-

Map 3-13 *Party Affiliation in the House of Representatives, 1981*

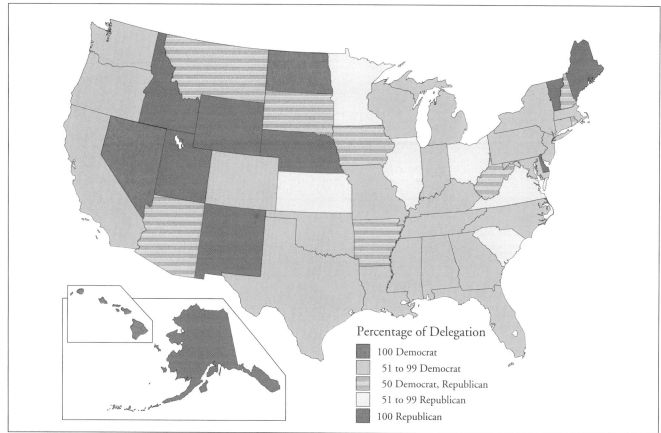

Percentage of Delegation

100 Democrat
51 to 99 Democrat
50 Democrat, Republican
51 to 99 Republican
100 Republican

Map 3-14 *Party Affiliation in the House of Representatives, 1991*

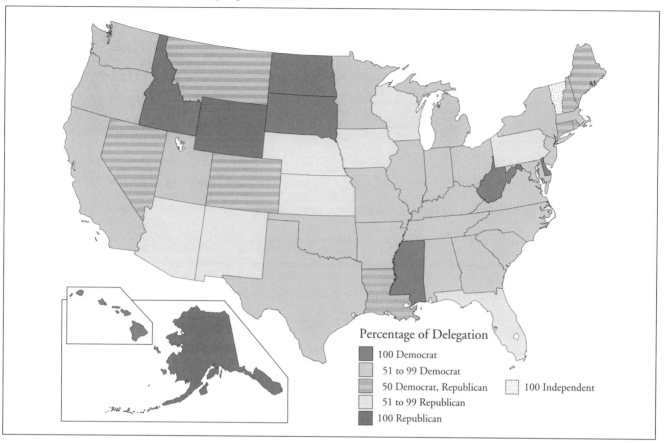

Percentage of Delegation

- 100 Democrat
- 51 to 99 Democrat
- 50 Democrat, Republican
- 51 to 99 Republican
- 100 Republican
- 100 Independent

ifornia had the largest delegation with forty-five members, and six states—Alaska, Delaware, North Dakota, South Dakota, Wyoming, and Vermont—had one representative each.

Map 3-14 shows the nationally competitive nature of congressional elections at the end of the twentieth century. Democrats controlled House delegations in seven states, and these states were located in all sections of the nation—Appalachia, northern Great Plains, South, and Interior West. All were either small or one-member delegations. The Democrats represented the majority in twenty-four states. Again, the southern and northern American Manufacturing Belt states formed two core areas. The Democrats were strong on the Pacific Coast but somewhat weak in the Interior West. The Republicans controlled only two states, the one-member delegations from conservative Wyoming and Alaska. The GOP had a majority in eight other states, with the largest grouping in the Midwest and central Great Plains.

The elections to the House of Representatives discussed in connection with Maps 3-11 through 3-14 show a dominant Democratic majority. The Democrats controlled the House in every session from 1955 to 1995, but that changed as a result of the 1994 midterm elections. The Republicans won a smashing historic victory in 1994, gaining fifty-three seats, which gave the party a 231–203 majority (with one independent from Vermont). The 1994 vote represented not only the usual midterm loss for the party controlling the White House but also the culmination of pro-GOP trends of suburbanizing, southernizing, and westernizing congressional seats. Elections to the House have always been affected by national trends, but inherently local and district issues and the quality of local candidates dominate them. Through the efforts of Rep. Newt Gingrich of Georgia and the GOP reform known as the Contract with America, the 1994 House elections were to a great extent "nationalized," and some observers suggest that this contributed to the magnitude of the swing. In subsequent elections in 1996, 1998, and 2000, Republicans retained their House majority, although with slightly smaller margins.

The closest presidential election in American history set the stage for the 2000 congressional elections, and the results reflect this closeness. The final count registered a 221–212 GOP edge on election night (with two independ-

Map 3-15 *Party Affiliation in the House of Representatives, 2001*

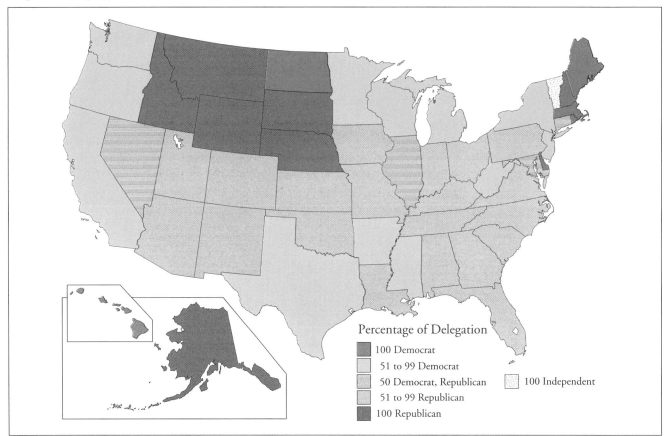

Percentage of Delegation

- 100 Democrat
- 51 to 99 Democrat
- 50 Democrat, Republican
- 51 to 99 Republican   100 Independent
- 100 Republican

ents, from Vermont and Virginia). Map 3-15 shows the historic nature of the changes in the House begun by the 1994 election. When the 107th Congress convened in 2001, the Democrats had a 100 percent control in only five state delegations and a majority in only twelve others; this was the smallest number in the period under consideration. The Republicans controlled eight delegations and were the majority in twenty others, the largest number in this period.

The change in the geographic nature of American politics shown in Map 3-15 may reveal even more about the present, and possibly the future, of parties and elections. As Table 3-3 shows, the Republicans controlled eight of the eleven state delegations in the Deep South. This pattern is almost a complete reversal of the patterns shown in Map 3-11. In 1961 the Democrats controlled 93 percent of Deep South seats, and by 2001 they controlled 43 percent, less than half. In addition, the Republicans controlled all or most of the House seats in the Interior West. Two of the fastest-growing regions, the South and Interior West, showed strong signs of trending toward the GOP. Furthermore, the GOP was still running strong in its traditional areas of strength in the Great Plains and rural and suburban Midwest. This new pattern could turn

out to be as powerful a regional coalition as the "Austin-Boston" connection was for the Democrats. Indeed, the new areas of GOP strength are reflected in the Republican House leadership, with Speaker Dennis Hastert coming from Illinois, and two representatives from Texas and one from Oklahoma in the other leadership positions.

The Democratic pattern in the 2001 House was also significant. The Democrats were dominant in only two areas. First, the states in the extreme northern tier became more dependably Democratic, although for decades they had been almost all solidly Republican, especially in rural areas. This change represents a regional switch similar to the Republican takeover of the South. Many of the states dominated by Democrats are declining areas, such as Massachusetts, Michigan, and New York. The reapportionment of House seats away from the North also means that areas where Democrats are strong are losing seats, especially in center city and urban areas. The other area of Democratic strength is the growing region of the Pacific Coast. Here seats are increasing, and, with progressive politics in Washington and Oregon as well as with new immigrant voters in California, the Democratic margin may be safe.

The redistricting process taking place in 2001 and 2002 will help determine if the GOP can continue its four-election run as the House majority party. Suburbanization and Sun Belt growth are changes in population geography that bode well for the GOP. In addition, the Republicans have the advantage of controlling more governorships and state legislature chambers (see Chapter 6) than at any time in recent history. The Republican ability to draw the new political maps of congressional district boundaries within the new population geography gives the party an edge not seen in recent decades.

Party Control of Congressional Districts, 1983, 1993, 2001

Maps 3-16, 3-17, and 3-18 present a view of House elections by showing the results in all 435 congressional districts in three different decades. These maps provide a more detailed look at the national congressional political geography and reveal intrastate differences as well as differences among urban, suburban, and rural areas.

When the 98th House convened in 1983, its political party makeup was 269 Democrats and 166 Republicans. The 1982 midterm elections took place during the first term of Republican president Ronald Reagan. The Democrats gained twenty-six seats, a typical result for the opposition party.

Six states—Alaska, Delaware, North Dakota, South Dakota, Vermont, and Wyoming—had only one representative each, and therefore the map shows the entire state in one color. In large states, such as Alaska and Wyoming, these are sizable areas of sparse population. The remaining forty-four states have two or more House seats.

Map 3-16 illustrates a nationally competitive House election. It shows that Democrats and Republicans were elected from all sections and regions, but a number of regional concentrations and other geographical patterns are also evident.

Map 3-16 *Political Party Control, House of Representatives, 98th Congress, First Session (1983)*

Party

Democratic (268) Republican (167)

A large area of the Southeast, from southern Virginia through Texas, was dominated by the Democrats. As Table 3-3 indicates, the South was approximately two-thirds Democratic in the early 1980s. Democrats were also strong in urban areas and central cities. The New York City and Los Angeles insets of Map 3-16 show that the core urban area is almost completely Democratic and the surrounding suburban and rural districts are almost all Republican. This core-periphery model is repeated in almost every sizable American city with large numbers of congressional districts, including Chicago, Cleveland, Detroit, and Philadelphia. In essence, by the middle of the twentieth century cities began to replace the "Solid South" as bastions of strength the Democrats could count on in every election.

Republicans also had some areas of regional strength. The rural parts of the northern states—upstate New York, upper New England, central Pennsylvania—and the agricultural areas of Illinois, Indiana, and Ohio were dominated by Republicans, a pattern that resulted from northern cohesion following the Civil War. Map 3-16 points out an emerging region of Republican strength in the Interior West. Pacific Coast districts in Washington, Oregon, and northern California voted Democratic, but from the Cascade and Sierra Nevada mountain ranges east to the Front Range of the Rockies, the geography, settlement pattern, and party preference changed to Republican. The Interior West, which was somewhat competitive in previous decades, was becoming more Republican.

At the start of the 103d Congress in 1993, the political party makeup of the House was 258 Democrats, 176 Republicans, and one independent (from Vermont). The 1992 elections coincided with the presidential election in which Democrat Bill Clinton defeated the incumbent, Republican George Bush (Maps 2-17 and 2-18). In spite of Clinton's victory, the Democrats lost ten seats in the House, a rare occurrence for the winning presidential party, and perhaps

Map 3-17 *Political Party Control, House of Representatives, 103d Congress, First Session (1993)*

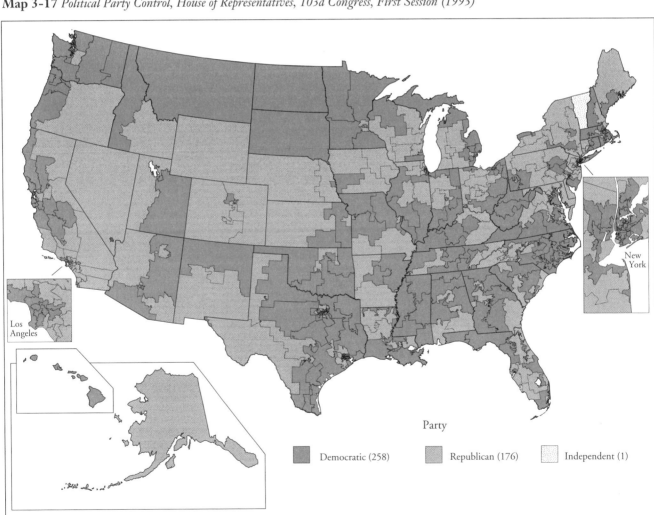

Party

Democratic (258)   Republican (176)   Independent (1)

a precursor of the historic change to come two years later.

Map 3-17 shows the geography of the 1992 congressional elections with the results in all 435 congressional districts. The party numbers are similar to those in 1983. Seven sparsely populated states—Alaska, Delaware, Montana, North Dakota, South Dakota, Vermont, and Wyoming—have one representative each and are depicted in one color. The remaining forty-three states have two or more House seats. Map 3-17 illustrates nationally competitive House elections similar to the 1982 elections and most of the same geographic patterns. The Democrats dominated a large area of the Southeast, from southern Virginia through central Texas, as Table 3-3 indicates. Urban areas and central cities remained places of Democratic strength. The Republicans also retained regional strength in many parts of the rural North and Interior West.

In the 2000 House elections the Republicans won 221 seats, the Democrats won 212, and two districts in Vermont

and Virginia were independent. In 1994 the Republicans had captured the House for the first time since the 1952 election by way of a fifty-three-seat swing. The 1994 election was an upset of historic proportions and is discussed in connection with Map 3-15. In spite of seat losses in 1996, 1998, and 2000, the incumbent election edge helped keep the Republicans the majority party in the House. In addition, reapportionment and redistricting advantages tend to favor the Republicans in 2002 and beyond.

Map 3-18 illustrates the geography of the 2001 House and the regional and sectional changes and gains made by the Republicans since 1994. The largest noticeable area of Republican strength is the Interior West. The map shows that this vast area has linked up with the Great Plains region, another traditional area of GOP strength. The Republicans continued to show strength in the rural Midwest and rural Pennsylvania and upstate New York. The South, however, is where the Republicans made their great-

Map 3-18 *Political Party Control, House of Representatives, 107th Congress, First Session (2001)*

Party

Democratic (212)   Republican (221)   Independent (2)

est gain, enabling them to win and retain control of the House. As Table 3-3 indicates, the Democrats became the congressional minority party in the South, a state of affairs that had not occurred for more than a century, since the end of Reconstruction. Once stalwart Democratic states like Georgia (73 percent Republican) and Alabama (71 percent Republican) led the way.

A casual look at Map 3-18 would indicate a very large Republican majority in the House, rather than a nine-seat margin. Map 2-21 of the 2000 presidential election also conveys this message. But much of the Republican strength in the House comes from sparsely populated areas, in which a congressional district may cover an entire state, such as Alaska. Much of House Democratic strength comes from densely populated urban congressional districts that appear very small on the map. The many districts depicted in the Los Angeles and New York City insets in Map 3-18 illustrate this phenomenon. In addition to the cities, Democrats were elected from areas such as Hispanic South Texas and African American minority-majority districts in the South. The districts hugging the Pacific Coast appeared again as a new unique region of Democratic electoral support.

The future electoral geography of the House will be determined by many variables, such as the national economy, international events, and scandals or misfortunes of a presidential administration. One important factor is the control over drawing new congressional districts for the 2002 elections and beyond. The 1994 GOP sweep occurred not only in the House but also in gubernatorial and state legislatures, many of which have carried forward to the post-2000 census redistricting period (see Chapter 6). These factors, along with the changing population geography and incumbency edge, favor the GOP in the near future.

Congressional Roll Call Votes

Throughout American history it has been evident that local, state, regional, and sectional concerns influence the success or failure of legislation in the U.S. Congress. The Framers undoubtedly knew they were constructing a system of government in which members of the House would be more concerned with issues closer to their constituents and members of the Senate would speak for their states and regions. Sectional and regional conflicts have been evident from the earliest years of the Republic and reached their most contentious point in the Civil War. A century and a half later, geographical and political differences still exist and manifest themselves in many ways: North versus South, East versus West, Interior West versus Coastal West, Sun Belt versus Snow Belt, agricultural regions versus nonagricultural

regions, public land states versus non–public land states, and rural versus urban. As a reflection of these conflicts, almost every conceivable regional roll call voting coalition has been put together in the course of congressional history.

The final vote to pass a bill is the culmination of a long legislative process. Why a member of Congress votes the way he or she does on hundreds of pieces of legislation has been studied intensively, and regional concerns are only one component. The final and most important decision-making variable may depend on the issue area, for example, foreign policy, agriculture, civil rights, social welfare, government management, or the environment. Most students of Congress point to constituency, party, and political ideology as the three keys to understanding and predicting the passage of legislation. Some say the constituency factor is the most important, and constituency issues, more often than not, are geographic. A member of the House from a cotton-growing district will usually support cotton subsidies in spite of possible party and ideological conflicts. Constituents from a small, northern, urban, industrial district, however, generally do not care about cotton subsidies, and that member can vote the ideological or party line.

Geographical aspects of roll call voting behavior have been studied for more than 100 years. The atlas offers four maps depicting roll call votes to demonstrate the geographical aspects of Congress and American politics. Maps 3-19 and 3-20 illustrate votes in the Senate, and Maps 2-21 and 2-22 illustrate two votes in the House, using all 435 congressional districts. These maps show the continuing importance of local, state, and regional differences in American politics that often override party and political ideology.

On December 19, 1998, the House of Representatives approved two of four articles of impeachment against President Clinton for "high crimes and misdemeanors" in connection with an extramarital affair and Clinton's attempt to hide it. Article I alleged that the president gave "false and misleading testimony" to a grand jury convened by the independent counsel, Kenneth Starr, about the nature of his relationship with a White House intern, Monica Lewinsky. Article II alleged that Clinton schemed to cover up not only the affair with Lewinsky but also evidence against him in a sexual harassment lawsuit by Paula Jones, a former Arkansas state employee.

As the Constitution directs, the Senate conducted the trial to determine guilt or innocence. When the second session of the 105th Congress began in January 1999, the Senate began trial preparations. The trial was presided over by the chief justice of the United States, William H. Rehnquist. On February 12, 1999, after twenty days of argument, the Senate acquitted Clinton of both charges on a roll call vote. Clinton's impeachment trial was the second in U.S. history.

Map 3-19 *Senate Vote to Convict or Acquit President Clinton on Impeachment Article II, February 12, 1999*

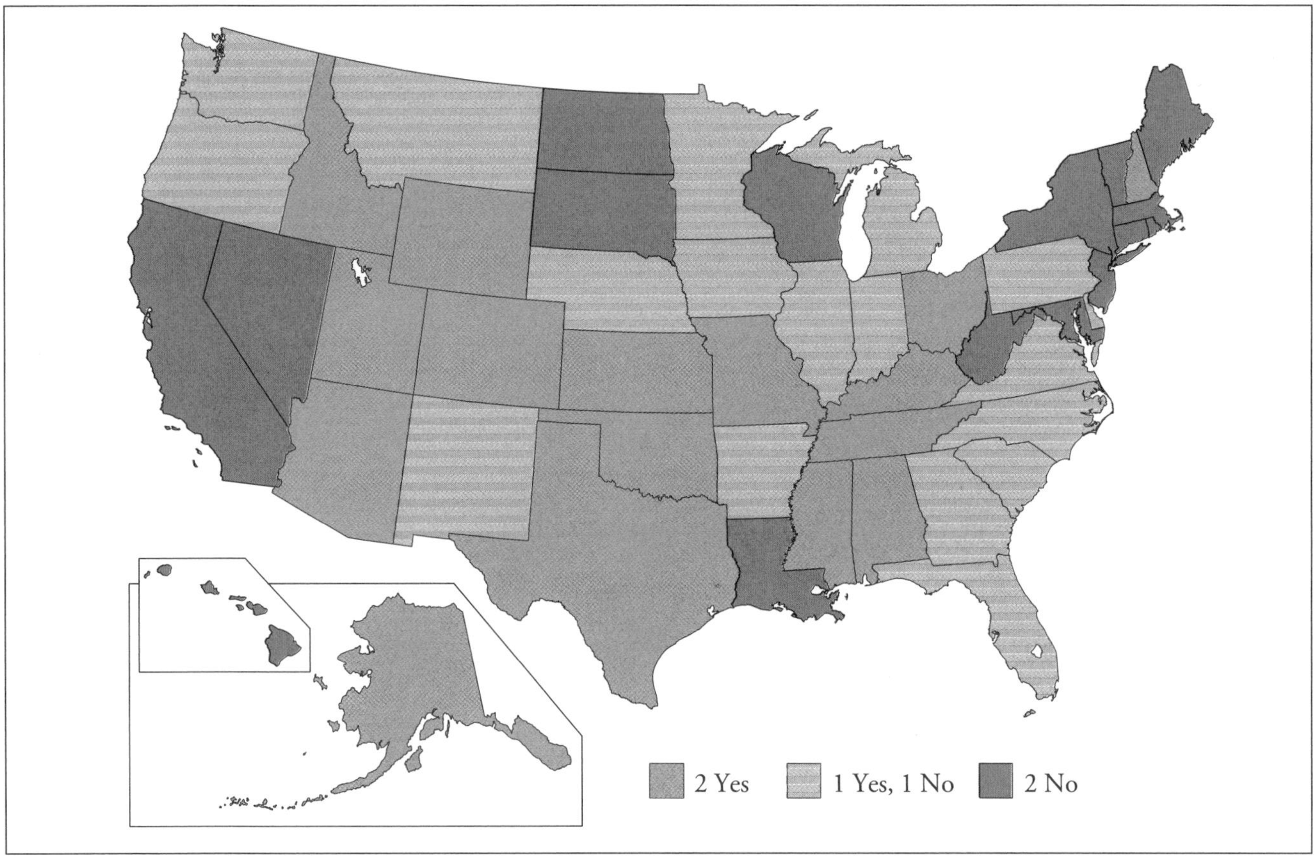

The first was conducted in 1868, when the Senate acquitted President Andrew Johnson by one vote.

The partisan makeup of the Senate at the time of Clinton's trial was fifty-five Republicans and forty-five Democrats. The Constitution states that a two-thirds vote of all the members present is needed to convict, or sixty-seven for the full Senate. At fifty-fifty, the vote on Article II was the closer of the two roll call votes, but far from the necessary two-thirds. All forty-five Democrats and five Republicans voted not guilty, and fifty Republicans voted guilty. In essence, this vote can be seen as highly partisan, with party affiliation the primary determinant. Also significant, however, were the geographic origins of the five Republican senators who voted to acquit: Susan Collins and Olympia Snowe of Maine, James Jeffords of Vermont, John Chafee of Rhode Island, and Arlen Specter of Pennsylvania. Public and constituency sentiment for impeachment was less fervent in the Northeast than in other regions. In addition, these senators were among the most ideologically moderate in the Republican Party and one, Jeffords, left the party to become an independent. As a partisan roll call map, Map 3-19 shows the core of Republicans favoring Clinton's conviction in the Interior West, southern Great Plains, and heart of the Deep South, and the least support for conviction in the Northeast.[3]

One of the keys to understanding congressional roll call voting behavior is that senators and representatives usually vote the interests of their constituencies, especially in matters that affect the economy of a state or district. If neighboring districts and states have similar interests and economies, large multistate voting blocs can be formed. An example of this phenomenon was the vote on the use of ethanol fuels, which was put before the Senate on August 3, 1994. On the surface the vote seemed to cross the three policy areas of agriculture, energy, and the environment. In the end, however, local economic interests won the day.

Ethanol is a liquid fuel derived from sugar and grain crops. In the United States, the grain most commonly used to make ethanol is corn. When added to regular petroleum gasoline, ethanol acts as an oxygenate allowing the fuel to burn more cleanly, which reduces pollution, namely carbon monoxide. Another alcohol fuel, methanol, also acts as an oxygenate, and in the United States it is derived most commonly from natural gas, a nonrenewable fossil fuel. The Clean Air Act of 1990 requires the production and sale of clean-burning oxygenated gasoline. The so-called reformu-

Map 3-20 *Senate Vote on Ethanol Mandate, August 3, 1994*

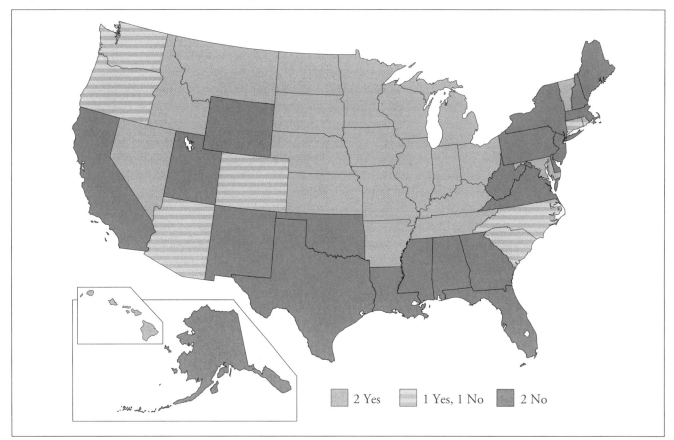

2 Yes   1 Yes, 1 No   2 No

lated gasoline (RFG) is mandated for summertime use in regions with the most heavily polluted air.

In December 1993 the Environmental Protection Agency (EPA) proposed a rule mandating that a large percentage of the RFG sold contain a renewable oxygenate—in other words, ethanol. The EPA ruling had the potential for increasing the demand and price of corn and decreasing the demand for and price of natural gas. In addition, the large oil companies were worried about the impact on their flexibility with respect to oil refining and gasoline production. The EPA's proposed rule, therefore, had enormous economic consequences, which set the stage for a battle between agricultural states on one side and petroleum and natural gas producing states and oil refining states on the other.

Almost immediately after the EPA ethanol proposal, a movement began in the Senate to block its implementation. The Democratic chairman of the Energy and Natural Resources Committee, J. Bennett Johnston of Louisiana, a leading petroleum, natural gas, and refining state, spearheaded the movement. Eventually Democratic senator Bill Bradley of New Jersey, another large oil refining state,

cosponsored with Johnston an amendment blocking the ethanol rule. Aligned on the other side were many senators from states with large agricultural sectors.

Map 3-20 illustrates the ethanol mandate vote, which was taken on August 3, 1994, as an amendment to an unrelated appropriations bill. The roll call vote was the closest possible, a fifty-fifty tie. Party and ideological considerations were generally put aside: the Republicans split 25–19 against the mandate, and the Democrats split 31–25 in favor of it. In forty-two states, both senators voted the same way.[4]

The map shows the large regional blocs that formed over this vote, clearly illustrating that geography, regional economy, and regional interests were the major factors. The core of support for the ethanol mandate was a bloc of states in the agricultural Midwest and Upper Great Plains. These states are not just agricultural; they are the center of U.S. corn production. In 1994 the top ten states in corn production were Iowa (1,930 million bushels), Illinois (1,786 million), Nebraska (1,154 million), Minnesota (916 million), Indiana (858 million), Ohio (487 million), Wisconsin (437 million), South Dakota (367 million), Kansas (305 million), and Missouri (274 million). In these states both senators, irrespective of party or ideology, voted in favor of the ethanol requirement.

The core of support to stop the ethanol mandate came from a bloc of states along the oil and gas producing Gulf Coast and farther west. In 1994, seven states produced more than $1 billion of crude petroleum, Texas ($8,849 billion), Alaska ($5,559 billion), California ($3,467 billion), Louisiana ($1,973 billion), Oklahoma ($1,395 billion), Wyoming ($1,087 billion), and New Mexico ($1,009 billion). In these states both senators, irrespective of party or ideology, voted against corn-produced ethanol. The senators from the refining and gasoline-consuming states in the Northeast also voted against the ethanol mandate. Johnston of Louisiana and Bradley of New Jersey formed an alliance of two regions with the same goal—to defeat the ethanol mandate. Large oil and gas and refining companies, such as Exxon and Mobil, lobbied against ethanol.

In his role as president of the Senate, the vice president of the United States casts tie-breaking votes. In this case, Vice President Al Gore voted in favor of renewable ethanol fuel, making the final tally 51–50 and killing the amendment proposed by two fellow Democrats. The ethanol mandate vote clearly shows that regional voting patterns on specific issues still exist in Congress. If the issue or policy in question is strong enough, regional considerations may override national, party, or ideological considerations.

One of the most important tariff and trade votes in the late twentieth century was the adoption of the North American Free Trade Act (NAFTA) on November 17, 1993. NAFTA not only irrevocably changed the labor and consumer market of the U.S. economy, but perhaps also set the stage for a larger Western Hemisphere trade agreement in the future. The Free Trade Area of the Americas (FTAA) was proposed by President George W. Bush and the leaders

Map 3-21 *District Vote on Implementation of North American Free Trade Agreement, November 17, 1993*

Vote

Yes (234)   No (200)   Not Voting (1)

of Canada, Mexico, and other Western Hemisphere countries at a summit meeting in April 2001.

Under NAFTA, the United States, Canada, and Mexico agreed to eventually eliminate all tariff and trade barriers among the three nations. At the time, the treaty created the largest trade bloc in the world. Previously, the United States and Canada had such an agreement, but NAFTA was more controversial. The inclusion of Mexico meant bringing in a developing nation. Critics of NAFTA pointed out that the Mexican labor wage rate was a fraction of the U.S. and Canadian rate and that tens of thousands of labor-intensive manufacturing jobs would move south of the border. Critics also pointed out that with Mexico's few (and poorly enforced) environmental regulations, U.S. and Canadian companies would find the cost of doing business there cheaper and therefore hasten their move south. Because of these issues, labor unions and environmental groups opposed NAFTA. A small number of conservatives also opposed the agreement, saying it reduced sovereignty, would deindustrialize America, and would hurt the total economy in the long run. Proponents argued that additional manufacturing jobs would be created in the United States and Canada because the Mexican market of 85 million consumers would be totally open. Proponents also pointed out that job loss was already occurring in the developing world, and, because the European Union and Japan and Asia were creating their own trade blocs, NAFTA was critical to the United States. With these arguments, large corporations and businesses generally supported the legislation.

Democratic president Bill Clinton was in favor of NAFTA, as were his two Republican predecessors. This stance put Clinton in conflict with a majority of his party at the time, especially in the House. Labor and environmental groups traditionally exert influence on like-minded Democratic House members, particularly on liberal members. Because business and corporate influence is traditionally strong with Republicans, and a majority believe in the general philosophy of the free market, most of the Republican members were predisposed to favor NAFTA. District, state, and regional economic issues, however, played a large role in the final passage of NAFTA, and these issues split both the Republican and Democratic vote in the end.

Map 3-21 illustrates the final implementation vote for NAFTA, which passed, 234–200. House Republicans favored the treaty, 132–43, and Democrats, including much of the leadership, opposed it, 156–102. (The one independent voted nay, and one Michigan representative did not vote.) Northern Democrats opposed the legislation by a wide margin, and many of the Republican opponents also came from this region.[5]

According to Map 3-21, the region of the nation feeling the most threatened by NAFTA was the northern American Manufacturing Belt. By 1993 the Snow Belt (or Rust Belt) was already twenty years into a decline, with jobs migrating south or to foreign countries. Labor unions and their liberal supporters began a high-profile effort over NAFTA, threatening electoral consequences for anyone who supported the legislation. As Map 3-21 illustrates, most of the NAFTA opposition came from the northeastern sector of the United States and along the northern tier. This opposition was most intense in cities, as illustrated in the urban insets of New York City and Los Angeles. Leadership against NAFTA came from representatives from declining northern cities such as Toledo, Pittsburgh, and the automobile-manufacturing region of Michigan.

States expecting the most gain from NAFTA were the four bordering Mexico: Arizona, California, New Mexico, and Texas. Much of new Mexican economic development is centered on or near the border, favorably affecting these states. Another positive side effect of NAFTA was to be a reduction in illegal Mexican immigration as the Mexican economy grows. This promise also helped gain the support of the border states and much of the Southwest. As Map 3-21 indicates, a core of NAFTA support and leadership came from the border region and neighboring states. Many agricultural districts in the Midwest and Great Plains also supported NAFTA because of the potential wheat and corn market opening in Mexico. Not everyone involved in agriculture were supporters, however; certain fruit and vegetable districts in Florida and California voted no in fear of competition from cheaper imports.

Democratic House support of NAFTA came from three sources. The first group was the majority of southern "New Democrats," who favored more moderate, business-oriented policies than the liberal party members. The second group consisted of Border State Democrats, exemplified by the cluster of Hispanic Democratic representatives from South Texas, who normally had a strong liberal voting record. The third group of NAFTA supporters was made up of many Democrats in western "new economy" districts, especially those producing computer hardware and software, who saw the opening of Mexico as an economic opportunity. Districts in California, mainly in the Silicon Valley, and in the Seattle, Washington, area, are examples.

NAFTA linked the U.S. economy irreversibly with Canada and Mexico. In addition, in the immediate post–cold war era, it established the United States as a world leader in advocating free trade and laid the groundwork not only for implementation of the World Trade Organization in 1995 but also for the proposal for a Free Trade Area of the Americas agreement early in the twenty-first century.

The Endangered Species Act, enacted in 1973, acknowl-

Map 3-22 *District Vote on Endangered Species Act Amendment, May 7, 1997*

Vote

Yes (227)   No (196)   Not Voting (12)

edges the scientific fact that biodiversity and a complex plant and animal community is important for long-term sustenance of life on Earth. The law calls for the identification and protection of all species threatened with extinction within U.S. borders. In addition to banning hunting of endangered species and other activities, the law recognizes that to protect animals and plants, a larger "critical habitat" must be identified, mapped, and sheltered. Habitat protection usually means the almost total prohibition of building and development on the land involved. Owners of land that is designated protected habitat, whether public or private, are effectively banned from changing or disturbing the land, and this is the most controversial aspect of the law.

Most legislation in Congress impacts some areas of the country more than others, and legislation to protect natural resources and the environment is a good example of this fact of political geography. In the United States most threatened and endangered species are found in deserts, mountains, and

tropical and subtropical areas. Moreover, endangered species are found in areas where human settlement is less dense or nonexistent and where the local habitat has not been disturbed by long-term settlement. Most of the endangered species in the United States, therefore, are found along the southern tier and in the West. The states with the highest number of protected species are Hawaii (312), California (275), Florida (100), Alabama (99), Tennessee (88), and Texas (81). The lowest number of endangered species are found in the Northeast and are virtually nonexistent in large metropolitan areas. The states with the lowest number of endangered species are Vermont (8), Rhode Island (9), North Dakota (9), Maine (10), Delaware (10), Connecticut (11), and New Hampshire (11).

Opponents of the law say the designation of critical habitat is, in essence, a federal expropriation of private property because landowners who have protected species discovered on their holdings may lose total development rights, significantly decreasing property values on the open market. Because many parts of the West are sparsely settled, have exotic or delicate habitats, but are rapidly growing, the Endangered Species Act has particularly impacted development in this region.

Since its passage in 1973, opponents of the Endangered Species Act have attempted to overturn it. Failing that, they have tried to make small incremental changes to erode the law's effectiveness in certain situations. After the Republicans took control of the House of Representatives in 1994, various bills were introduced to weaken the act. One measure in 1997 waived the Endangered Species Act for flood control projects. Sponsors of the bill from the West said this proposal was not an anti-environmental bill but a protection of humans bill. When the legislation came before the House, an amendment was introduced to alter the legislation in a way that upheld the Endangered Species Act. The amendment was introduced by a moderate Republican, Sherwood Boehlert of New York's Twenty-third District. On May 7, 1997, Boehlert's amendment passed, 227–196. The Republican vote was 169–54 against, and the Democratic vote was 172–27 in favor. The few Democrats voting against the amendment were from the South and West. But it was the fifty-four moderate Republicans, mostly from the Northeast and North, who, by voting for the bill, created regional turmoil in the 105th Congress. Western Republicans claimed the eastern Republicans had "sold them out" on an issue of great importance to their region. Western Republicans threatened that they were "not going to be there" with votes on issues important to eastern Republicans. In fact, the westerners insisted that House Speaker Newt Gingrich strip Boehlert of all committee power with respect to environmental issues.[6]

Map 3-22 illustrates the vote on the Endangered Species Act Amendment and shows that large areas of the Interior West, Great Plains, and South voted in favor of altering it. Although Alaska has few threatened species, it is conservative, Republican, and in favor of development and protection of private property, as is most of the Interior West. At first glance, Map 3-22 seems to indicate an overwhelming vote to alter the act, but that impression is incorrect. Many votes for the Endangered Species Act came from smaller, more heavily populated districts in the North and Northeast, especially from urban areas. The New York City metropolitan area inset shows almost complete unity in favor of the law, and many of the moderate Republican votes came from suburban districts in Connecticut, New Jersey, and New York. The Los Angeles inset also shows this urban, pro-environment pattern, even though Los Angeles is a western city. Most of the Pacific Coast representatives also voted in favor of the act. These westerners come from an active, Democratic, pro-environment part of the country. Hawaii is the state with the most endangered species, but its two representatives voted to save the act because they were liberal Democrats who recognized the value of exotic plants and animals to the state's tourist industry.

Most policy areas have their "day in the sun," a period in which they are seen as important and legislation can be passed. There were two such eras for natural resources and the environment: the great "conservation era" from the 1890s to 1910 and the "environmental movement" from 1962 to 1976. The Endangered Species Act, an example of legislation from the latter period, shows how regional interests can create tremendous tension among lawmakers and sow the seeds for future disputes.

Political Ideology Roll Call Vote Ratings

In the U.S. Congress, political ideology often supersedes political party affiliation in the support or rejection of legislation. This support or rejection is manifested at many different stages, such as co-sponsoring a bill, backing in committee meetings, pressuring the leadership to move or stop legislation before it reaches the floor, and final roll call voting. Roll call voting is the ultimate determinant of support and the one most easily tracked by interest groups and the public at large. To increase their leverage at election time, many special interest groups rate members of Congress with respect to their votes on legislation. Some of the most widely known ratings come from labor, business, and environmental organizations, but the earliest rating of representatives and senators came from general liberal and conservative organizations seeking to promote their political ideologies. One of the first of these was Americans for Democratic Action (ADA), a liberal organization founded in 1947. A counterpoint to ADA for many years was Americans for Constitutional Action (ACA), a conservative organization. The practice of both organizations was to rate members of Congress over the course of one calendar year, that is, one session, on a wide variety of issues they selected as symbolic of important ideological questions of the day. Some of these issues were civil rights in the 1960s, the Vietnam War in the late 1960s and early 1970s, environmental protection and women's issues in the 1970s and 1980s, and abortion and the military budget in the 1990s. Because ADA and ACA ratings are very close in describing the political ideology of representatives and senators over the years—liberals are liberals, no matter who is applying the label, and the same is true for conservatives—the atlas used the ADA ratings currently available.[7]

Americans for Democratic Action used twenty roll call votes in 1999 to determine the political ideology ratings of the 100 Senate members. An ADA rating of 100 percent means a senator is very liberal and 0 percent means very conservative. Box 3-1 gives the general issue areas of the roll call votes used. Using the votes selected, the general liberal stance is to: support abortion rights, restrict gun sales, reduce tax cuts to allow establishment of a Medicare prescription drug benefit program, place no restrictions on the District of Columbia budget, support the confirmation of President Clinton's nomination of Ronnie L. White of Missouri to the U.S. district court bench, pay the prevailing wage rate on all federal projects, support campaign finance reform, and increase the minimum wage. The general conservative stance is to: vote guilty on the impeachment of President Clinton, restrict or eliminate abortion, oppose gun control, reduce taxes across the board, impose restrictions on the District of Columbia budget from federal funds, oppose White's nomination, permit employers to not pay the prevailing wage rate on federal projects in disaster areas, oppose an increase of the minimum wage, and not impose restrictions on campaign contributions, advertising, or speech.

Map 3-23 illustrates the political ideology rating by state for the 106th Senate. Each state's rating is the average of the combined score for both senators. ADA scores of 0–19 equal conservative, 20–49, moderately conservative, 50–79, moderately liberal, and 80–100, liberal. In states with senators from different parties, or senators from the same party with different ideologies, the average score can place the state in one of the moderate categories.

Although liberal and conservative senators are found in all sections and regions, some broad clustering and regional differences can be seen. Twelve states have liberal ratings for both senators. The largest cluster of liberal senators is in the Northeast, centered on Connecticut, Massachusetts, New Jersey, and New York. The western states of California, Nevada, Oregon, and Washington are liberal or moderately liberal. The only liberal state located in the South is Louisiana. Four other southern states' senators are ranked moderately liberal—Arkansas, and three states with sizable in-migration, Florida, Georgia, and Virginia. The remaining states with liberal senators are located in the North.

Sixteen states were rated conservative. Conservative clusters are found in the Interior West (five states) and in the southern Great Plains (three states). Another conservative cluster is in the heart of Dixie: Alabama and Mississippi, linked with Kentucky, Missouri, and Tennessee. Only two conservative states are found in the North: Ohio and New Hampshire.

Region is important in understanding party and ideology in the United States. Within the Republican Party, senators from the Interior West and South tend to be the most conservative, while Republicans from the North tend to be more

moderate. Within the Democratic Party, senators from the Northeast and California tend to be the most liberal, and those from other regions must modify their stance in certain issue areas to be elected and reelected. Knowing the political party of a member of Congress is important to understanding the individual. However, understanding the region, political ideology, and issue area with respect to his or her state adds new dimensions to round out the picture.

Americans for Democratic Action used twenty roll call votes in 1999 to determine the political ideology ratings of the 435 House members. An ADA ranking of 100 percent means the representative is very liberal and 0 percent means very conservative. Box 3-2 gives the general issue areas of the roll call votes used. Using the votes selected, the general liberal stance is to: support abortion rights, restrict gun sales, support import quotas, support enlargement of environmental and conservation funding, favor full voting representation for the District of Columbia in Congress, favor full funding of the United Nations, increase support for AIDS, continue foreign aid, including family planning, favor campaign finance reform, favor a patients' bill of rights, including the

---

Box 3-1 *Roll Call Votes Used to Determine Senators' Political Ideology Scores by Americans for Democratic Action, 1999*

1. Impeachment of President Clinton/Article II
2. Fiscal 2000 budget resolution
3. Financial services
4. Gun show checks
5. Welfare report
6. Managed care revisions
7. Tax cuts
8. Medicare prescription drug benefits
9. Tax reconciliation
10. Fiscal 2000 District of Columbia appropriations
11. Teacher hiring plan
12. Ronnie L. White judicial nomination
13. Foreign aid
14. Closing tax "loopholes"
15. Prevailing wage requirement
16. Nuclear test ban treaty
17. Campaign finance revisions
18. Abortion
19. Late-term abortion ban
20. Minimum wage increase

SOURCE: Americans for Democratic Action, Washington, D.C. Navigate to: http://www.adaction.org/.

Map 3-23 *Americans for Democratic Action Rating of Votes by Senators, 106th Congress, First Session*

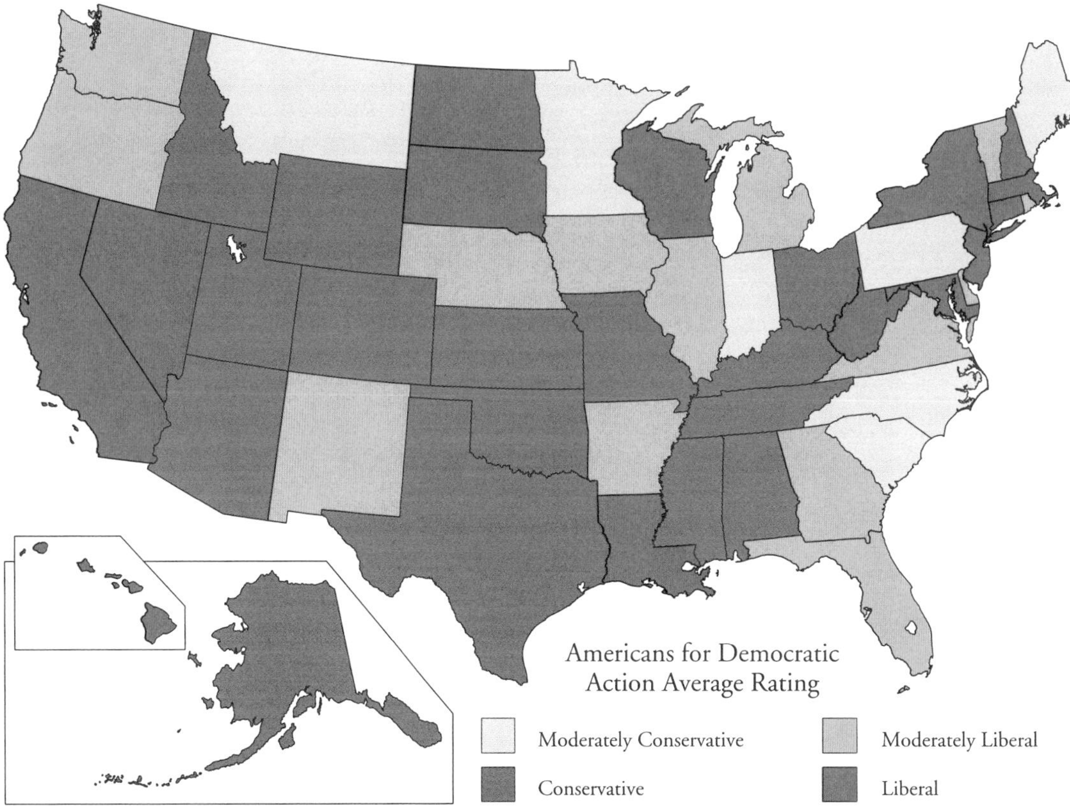

Americans for Democratic
Action Average Rating

Moderately Conservative   Moderately Liberal

Conservative   Liberal

Box 3-2 *Roll Call Votes Used to Determine Representatives' Political Ideology Scores by Americans for Democratic Action, House of Representatives 1999*

1. Steel imports
2. Local government census review
3. Tax limitation constitutional amendment
4. Gun shows/three-day background
5. Abortion assistance for minors
6. Financial services overhaul
7. Fiscal 2000 Interior appropriations/conservation fund
8. Religious expression
9. New teachers and training program
10. Tax cut package

11. District of Columbia representation
12. Abortion
13. School of the Americas
14. United Nations payment
15. Housing for AIDS patients
16. Shays-Meehan campaign finance overhaul
17. Juvenile justice
18. Foreign aid
19. Managed care "Patients' Bill of Rights"
20. Early grade school vouchers

SOURCE: Americans for Democratic Action, 1625 K Street N.W., Suite 210, Washington, D.C. 20006 http://www.adaction.org/.

right to sue HMOs, and oppose school vouchers for private schools. The general conservative stance is to: restrict or eliminate abortion, oppose gun control, favor unrestricted free trade, leave environmental funding and standards at current or reduced levels, oppose statehood and voting representation for the District of Columbia, support United Nations funding only with organizational reform, remove family planning from foreign aid, support school vouchers, and not restrict campaign contributions, advertising, or speech.

Map 3-24 illustrates the political ideology rating by congressional district for the 106th House. Each of the 435 congressional districts is rated and colored depending upon the 1999 score of the representative, and, therefore, this map presents a more detailed ideological map than Map 3-23. ADA scores of 0–19 equal conservative, 20–49 moderately conservative, 50–79 moderately liberal, and 80–100 liberal.

Although liberal and conservative representatives are found in all sections and regions, some definite spatial patterns are detectable. By far the most extensive region of ideological uniformity is the Interior West, which, especially since 1994, has elected mostly conservative Republican legislators to the House. Another conservative region is the Great Plains stretching from South Dakota to Texas. Conservatives are also found throughout the South. In the North, two clusters of conservatives are found in rural central Pennsylvania and rural Midwest agricultural districts stretching from Ohio through Indiana and Illinois. All these districts had Republican representatives who were in the majority in the 106th Congress.

Liberal clusters are somewhat smaller. New England has a large concentration of liberal and moderate liberal representatives. Hispanic-dominated districts tend to be liberal, such as the cluster in South Texas and the single districts in northern New Mexico and southern Arizona in the Interior

Map 3-24 *Americans for Democratic Action Rating of Votes by House Members, 106th Congress, First Session*

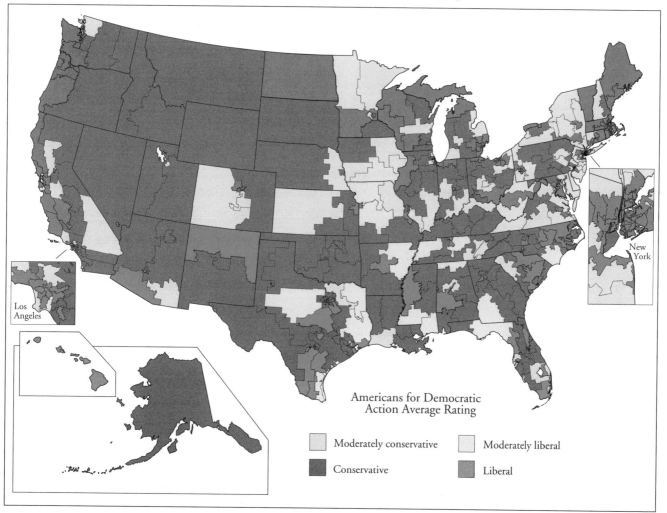

Americans for Democratic Action Average Rating

Moderately conservative
Conservative
Moderately liberal
Liberal

West. The Pacific Coast is a liberal region, electing mostly Democrats, as opposed to the inland, more conservative Republican areas. Liberal representatives are scattered throughout the South, many of them in African American minority-majority districts.

Map 3-24 does not adequately illustrate many liberal districts because they are small, densely populated urban areas. The New York City and Los Angeles insets give strong evidence of the urban nature of liberal representatives. In these two cities, almost every urban representative is liberal. The same is true in other cities with numerous districts, such as Chicago, Detroit, Philadelphia, and Pittsburgh. Urban districts with strong minority or union labor presence are among the most liberal in the United States. This urban liberal phenomenon is present in almost all regions, including the "islands" of liberalism in the generally conservative Interior West, illustrated by the cities of El Paso, Denver, and Phoenix.

Conclusion

In the 1960–2000 period profound changes occurred in the geographical makeup of Congress, among them a significant sectional switch in House membership from the North and Northeast to the South and Southwest. Since 1960 the pattern of North-South electoral competition has changed to a nationally competitive pattern. It must be noted, however, that the electoral maps also indicate that new areas of partisan strength and new regions of solid electoral support may be emerging in this period. In addition, the maps in this chapter demonstrate that, in spite of Democrats and Republicans being elected from all regions, sectional and regional coalitions in congressional roll call voting behavior can override national concerns or the dictates of political party leaders or personal political ideology. Chapter 3 demonstrates that understanding the geographical aspects of Congress can improve understanding of the members' political behavior.

Notes

1. For a more complete history of regional reapportionment changes, see Kenneth C. Martis and Gregory Elmes, *The Historical Atlas of State Power in Congress, 1790–1990* (Washington, D.C.: Congressional Quarterly, 1993).

2. Kevin P. Phillips, *The Emerging Republican Majority* (Garden City, N.Y.: Anchor, 1970), 32–33. For details on the changes in the regional geography of parties and elections on the congressional level, see the three-election sequence of 1960, 1962, and 1964 in Kenneth C. Martis, *The Historical Atlas of Political Parties in the United States Congress: 1789–1989* (New York: Macmillan, 1989), 215–219.

3. For additional information and the roll call vote of individual senators to convict or acquit, see *Congressional Quarterly Almanac, 1999* (Washington, D.C.: CQ Press, 2000), 13/6–13/22.

4. For additional information and the ethanol roll call vote of individual senators, see Congressional Quarterly Almanac, 1994 (Washington, D.C.: Congressional Quarterly, 1995), 25/C-26/C and 53/C.

5. For additional information and the NAFTA roll call vote of individual representatives, see *Congressional Quarterly Almanac, 1993* (Washington, D.C.: Congressional Quarterly, 1994), 43/C and 48-49/C.

6. For additional information and the endangered species roll call vote of individual representatives, see *Congressional Quarterly Almanac, 1997* (Washington, D.C.: Congressional Quarterly, 1998), C/40 and C/48-49; Gerald E. Webster and Christopher Meretti, "The Impact of Place and Ethnicity upon Congressional Support for Free Trade Extensions in the Americas," *Southwestern Geographer* 2 (1998): 40–56.

7. Americans for Democratic Action, Washington, D.C. http://adaaction.org/.

Chapter 4

Executive Branch

The executive branch of the U.S. government is responsible for administering the many federal programs and initiatives throughout the country. The maps in this chapter illustrate some of the geographic aspects of the executive branch's organization. To ensure that federal programs are effective in reaching citizens, the administrative functions of the federal government are decentralized. In addition to their headquarters in Washington, federal agencies maintain regional offices that are responsible for the administration of federal programs within designated areas. The locations of regional offices and the division of territory into administrative regions varies from one agency to another, as the maps in this chapter show.

The most frequently used regional framework is that used by the Bureau of the Census. This framework divides the country into four main regions and further subdivides it into nine census divisions. Much of the data obtained by the bureau, not only for the decennial Census of Population and Housing but also for many other census activities, are reported in terms of these regions and divisions. Other federal agencies, notably the Federal Reserve System and the Environmental Protection Agency, divide the country into different regions.

The administrative structure of the federal government is headed by the members of the president's cabinet, each of whom is responsible for administering a major department. The home states of cabinet officers over the past forty years form interesting geographic patterns. Although the map (Map 4-4) does not show which cabinet officers come from which states, presidents tend to select secretaries of state and treasury from large urban financial centers, secretaries of agriculture from the agricultural Midwest, and secretaries of the interior from the western United States. The geographical backgrounds of the president's cabinet members can reassure the public that the appointees are familiar with the goals and policies of the various departments.

Several maps in this chapter deal with the distribution of federal tax revenues and federal outlays. Taxes are collected by the federal government, and these revenues are spent on a wide variety of federal programs. As the maps show, some areas of the country receive more revenue than they provide in taxes, while others receive less than they pay out. The largest federal programs, including Social Security, agriculture, and defense, tend to have strong effects on the distribution of outlays relative to taxes collected. States with large numbers of elderly people, large numbers of farmers, or high per capita defense expenditures are among those that take in more federal money than they generate in taxes.

The chapter also examines the distribution of federal lands. The federal government owns vast quantities of land, especially in the western third of the United States. In some states more than half the land surface is federally owned. Many residents of the western states argue that federal land ownership has restricted their development opportunities.

Federal Divisions and Cabinet Secretaries' Home States

Map 4-1 shows how the Census Bureau divides the United States into divisions, which are subdivided into regions. In addition to counting population for the purposes of determining how seats in the House of Representatives are to be allocated, the Census Bureau makes periodic assessments of manufacturing, trade and commerce, agriculture, and mining. From these censuses, the bureau reports vast quantities of information about the rapidly changing American population and its social and economic activities. Much of this information is enumerated and reported geographically. Some information is reported at a geographical scale as small as a city block, while other data are reported by census tract, incorporated municipality, county, or state.

The census reports much of its information about the United States at a divisional and regional level. The fifty states are aggregated into four divisions: Northeast, Midwest, South, and West. Each of these divisions includes two or three regions. The Northeast division is made up of New England and the Middle Atlantic regions; the Midwest

Map 4-1 *Census Bureau Divisions, Regions, and Offices*

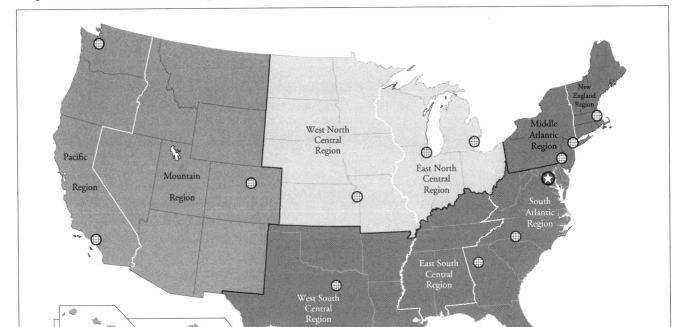

includes the East North Central and West North Central regions; the South contains the South Atlantic, East South Central, and West South Central regions; and the West includes the Mountain and Pacific regions. Each region, except East South Central, has at least one regional office. The East South Central regional office is in Atlanta, which is in the South Atlantic region.

Any partition of the country for tabulating and reporting information is bound to be controversial. The four divisions represent Americans' general perceptions of the basic geographic areas of their country, but it could be argued that some places within individual divisions might fit better in others. For example, Baltimore and Washington, D.C., are in the South division and the South Atlantic region, although throughout the twentieth century the economies of these cities have been closer to the Middle Atlantic and New England regions than to the rest of the South division. A wide variety of people, places, and economies can be found in every division: people in Ashtabula, Ohio, are in the same division as those in North Platte, Nebraska, as are the residents of El Paso, Texas, and Arlington, Virginia.

Some of the regional boundaries actually divide metropolitan areas, notably Cincinnati, Memphis, New York, and St. Louis. Nevertheless, the Census Bureau's boundaries have formed the basic units of reporting large-scale data for many years and will undoubtedly continue to be used in the years ahead. In several maps throughout this atlas, data are presented using these divisional boundaries.

Map 4-2 shows the twelve Federal Reserve districts and the locations of district and branch banks. The Federal Reserve System is the central bank of the United States. The system was established in 1913 to oversee the stability and growth of the U.S. economy. Its principal concern is monetary policy, which it controls in three ways: by establishing and enforcing reserve requirements, setting the prime lending rate at which depository banks may borrow from the Federal Reserve, and overseeing the purchase and sale of federal government securities.

The Federal Reserve's board of governors oversees monetary policy at a national level and at the system's twelve district banks. Members of the board of governors are appointed by the president for fourteen-year terms, subject

Map 4-2 *Federal Reserve Districts*

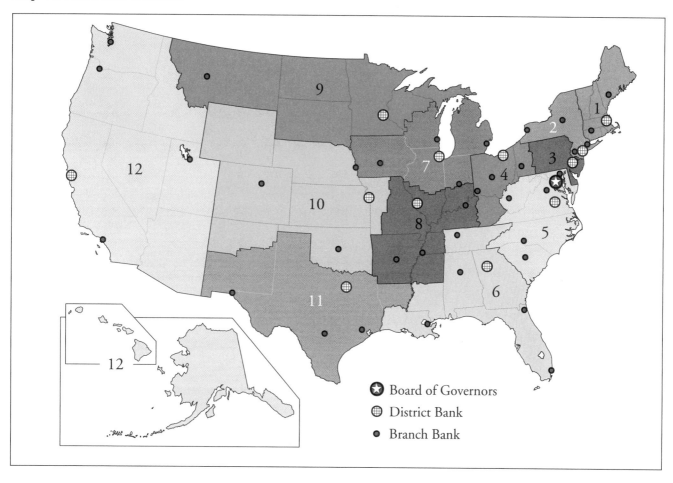

to confirmation by the Senate. Many of the operations of the Federal Reserve are decentralized, and the system's twelve district banks are responsible for carrying out various functions at the local level, as well as for ensuring the circulation of currency throughout their districts.

The district banks are located in Boston, New York, Philadelphia, Cleveland, Richmond, Atlanta, Chicago, St. Louis, Minneapolis, Kansas City, Dallas, and San Francisco. Each district bank has at least one branch bank. In District 6, for example, branch banks are found in Birmingham, Jacksonville, Miami, Nashville, and New Orleans.

Many states are divided by Federal Reserve districts, in contrast to Environmental Protection Agency regions (Map 4-3) and the federal judiciary circuits (Map 5-1). Indeed, the headquarters banks for the Eighth District and Tenth District are both in Missouri. The division of territory into Federal Reserve districts was intended to reflect patterns of economic activity and interaction, especially as they existed in the early twentieth century. For example, southwestern Connecticut, which is closely linked economically with New York City, is in the Second District, while the rest of the

state is in the First. Similarly, the Upper Peninsula of Michigan is in the Ninth District, reflecting this region's historic and contemporary economic ties with the upper Middle West through Lake Superior. The rest of Michigan is in the Seventh District, which also includes parts of Wisconsin, Illinois, and Indiana, and all of Iowa.

Map 4-3 shows how the Environmental Protection Agency (EPA) divides the United States into administrative regions. The EPA was established as an independent agency of the federal government in 1970. Its purpose is to administer federal environmental policies. The president appoints the EPA director, subject to the advice and consent of the Senate. In 2001 President George W. Bush elevated the position of EPA director to cabinet rank.

Prior to 1970 the functions now performed by the EPA were carried out by a number of federal agencies, including some under the auspices of the old Department of Health, Education, and Welfare, and others associated with the Department of the Interior. The EPA's responsibilities include preservation of the environment, alleviation of air and water pollution, and prevention of other types of pol-

Map 4-3 *Environmental Protection Agency Regions*

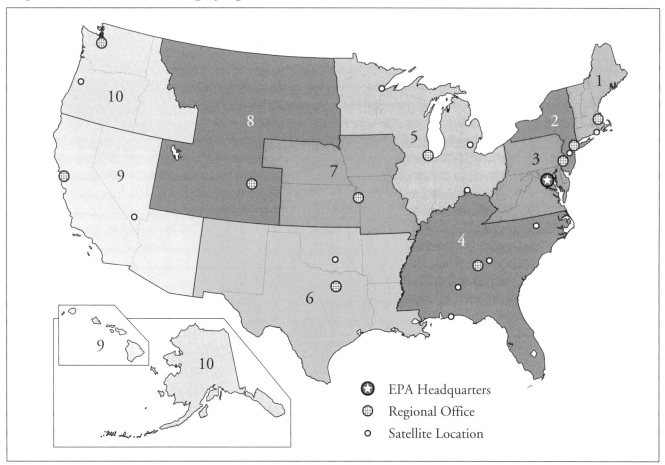

lution, including pesticides, radiation, toxic chemicals, and noise.

Many EPA activities involve monitoring environmental quality in the states and localities. The EPA collaborates with state and local governments and agencies to determine appropriate pollution standards and promote their enforcement. It promotes scientific research on pollution control, including radiation and hazardous waste disposal. It maintains the Superfund program, which provides assistance for cleaning up toxic waste sites. The EPA has about 18,000 employees, about a third of them in Washington and the rest in the regional offices.

Map 4-3 shows the ten EPA regions, each headed by a regional office. The regions consist of two to eight states, depending on the intensity of EPA activity. Regions with a small number of states tend to be densely populated urban areas or sprawling rural areas, both of which have relatively high levels of environmental protection activity. Region 2, which contains New York and New Jersey, is the smallest. This region, however, has more Superfund sites than any other in the country.

The president's cabinet is made up of the heads of the federal government's departments and some agencies. The Constitution does not specifically mandate the formation of a cabinet, but since the days of George Washington, the major executive officers of the federal government have served as advisers to the president. Cabinet officers are appointed by the president, subject to confirmation by the Senate.

The first cabinet consisted of the secretary of state, the secretary of the treasury, the secretary of war, and the attorney general, who headed the Justice Department. The War Department was merged with the Department of the Navy to become the Department of Defense shortly after World War II. These four positions, which are considered the most prestigious and influential, are sometimes referred to as the inner cabinet. Over the years, other administrative officers have been given cabinet rank. Today, in addition to the original four, the heads of the Departments of Agriculture, Commerce, Education, Energy, Health and Human Services, Housing and Urban Development, Interior, Labor, Transportation, and Veterans' Affairs hold cabinet rank, as

Map 4-4 *Cabinet Secretaries' Home States, 1961–2000*

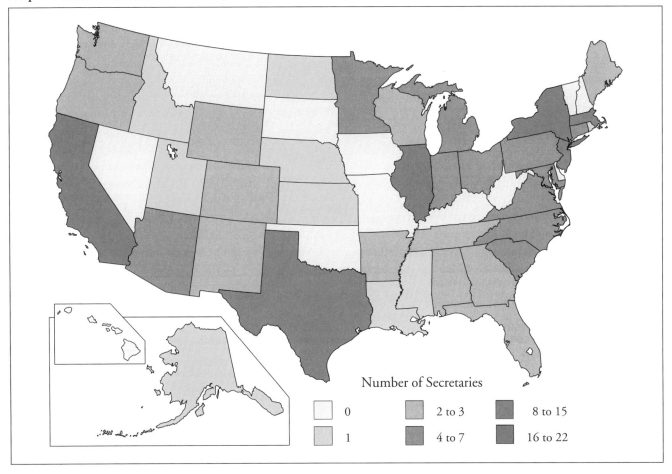

does the director of the Environmental Protection Agency.

Map 4-4 shows the home states of everyone appointed to cabinet-rank positions between January 1961 and the fall of 2000, or by Presidents John Kennedy, Lyndon Johnson, Richard Nixon, Gerald Ford, Jimmy Carter, Ronald Reagan, George Bush, and Bill Clinton. It does not include the cabinet officers appointed by President George W. Bush, who took office in January 2001. Generally speaking, the pattern shown in the map reflects the distribution of population, with larger and more urbanized states supplying larger numbers of cabinet officers. At least eight cabinet officers, or more than one per administration, came from California, Illinois, Massachusetts, New Jersey, New York, and Texas. In contrast, twelve states supplied no cabinet officers at all during the last four decades of the twentieth century. Most are small, but Missouri, which ranks as one of the twelve largest states in the country, supplied no cabinet members between 1960 and 2000. (In 2001 President Bush appointed former senator John Ashcroft of Missouri as attorney general.)

What the map does not show is a pattern of appoint-

ments to the different departments. The State and Treasury Departments, for example, generally have been headed by appointees from large cities, particularly in the Northeast. Of the secretaries of state who have served since 1961, three came from New York and two each came from California and the District of Columbia. Connecticut, Georgia, Maine, Michigan, and Texas each sent one. The secretaries of the Treasury during this period included three from New Jersey, three from Texas, two from Illinois, and two from New York. Connecticut, Indiana, Michigan, Rhode Island, and Virginia each supplied one. In 2001 President Bush followed the trend by appointing Colin Powell and Paul O'Neill, both from New York, to head the State and Treasury Departments, respectively.

The Department of Agriculture usually is headed by a secretary from the Midwest or another agricultural region. Since 1961 Illinois, Indiana, and Minnesota each supplied two secretaries of agriculture, and California, Kansas, Mississippi, Nebraska, and Virginia each supplied one. The secretary of the interior is often a westerner. Since 1961 two interior secretaries have come from Arizona. Alaska, California, Colorado, Idaho, Maryland, New Mexico, North Dakota, Oregon, and Wyoming each sent one. In 2001 Bush continued the trend by appointing Ann Veneman of California as secretary of agriculture and Gale Norton of Colorado as secretary of the interior. Since 1961 only one secretary of the interior and only one secretary of agriculture have come from the eastern United States.

Federal Outlays

Map 4-5 illustrates the redistribution of federal revenues during fiscal year 1989. (We exclude maps for 1969 and 1979 because the data for these years are not similar enough to 1989 and 1999 to be usable.) If federal outlays were equal to the taxes collected in each state, the ratio of expenditures to taxes would be 1 in each state. In fact, Map 4-5 shows a substantial variation in the ratio of federal expenditures to federal tax dollars. Twenty of the fifty states contributed more in taxes than they received in benefits, while the other thirty got back more in federal expenditures than they paid out in taxes.

In 1989, seven states—Alaska, Hawaii, Idaho, Mississippi, Montana, New Mexico, North Dakota, South

Dakota, and Utah—got back more than $1.40 for every dollar they contributed in taxes. These states are characterized by small populations and thriving agricultural sectors. Substantial numbers of elderly people live in most of them. For decades, young people have left Mississippi, North Dakota, and South Dakota in large numbers, leaving behind the elderly who are dependent on federal Social Security and Medicare payments. Many of these states had substantial numbers of defense contracts and military installations relative to their size—for example, Los Alamos and Sandia Laboratories and White Sands Air Force Base in New Mexico, several shipbuilding concerns with large Navy contracts, along with Keesler Air Force Base, on Mississippi's Gulf Coast, and the numerous Navy and Air Force units stationed in Alaska and Hawaii.

States that pay out higher amounts than they get back tend to be more populous, more urbanized, and wealthier. Most of the northeastern states fit into this category, as do California, Florida, Nevada, Oregon, and Texas. In 1989, eight states—Connecticut, Illinois, Michigan, Nevada, New Hampshire, New Jersey, New York, and Vermont—got back less than 89 cents for every dollar they paid. Many of these states have large metropolitan areas, such as Chicago,

Map 4-5 *Fiscal Expenditures per Dollar of Federal Taxes, FY 1989*

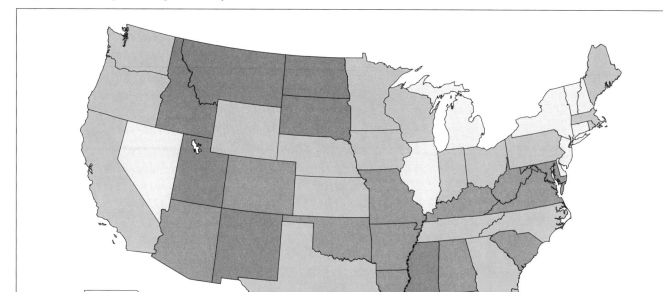

Dollars

0.89	1.00 to 1.19	1.40 or more
0.90 to 0.99	1.20 to 1.39	

Detroit, and New York, and, for the most part, they lack large per capita defense contracts, large agricultural populations relative to the size of the cities, or other major expenses that would increase their federal payments. Indeed, the Northeast in general contributed considerably more in federal taxes than it got back in federal revenues.

Map 4-6 depicts the ratio of federal tax expenditures to federal taxes collected in fiscal year 1999. As with Map 4-5, substantial variations between the states are apparent. In general, the pattern established in Map 4-5, in which larger, more urban states subsidized smaller, more rural states was maintained and reinforced during the 1990s.

In 1999, eleven states got back more than $1.40 for every dollar of federal taxes collected, including Alabama, Alaska, Hawaii, Mississippi, Montana, New Mexico, North Dakota, Oklahoma, South Dakota, Virginia, and West Virginia. Many of these states appeared in the same category in 1989. With the exception of Virginia, all are small population states that lack large metropolitan areas and have relatively high numbers of farmers and elderly people who benefit from individual subsidies. Despite the end of the cold war, military bases and defense contracting activities remain significant in most of these states.

In 1999, twelve states got back less than 89 cents for every dollar paid in federal taxes. With the exception of California and Nevada, all of these states were in the Northeast and Midwest, including Connecticut, Delaware, Illinois, Massachusetts, Michigan, Minnesota, New Jersey, New York, Rhode Island, and Wisconsin. Most of these states have major metropolitan areas or are on the fringes of them.

In the Midwest, the contrast between Iowa and its neighbors, Illinois, Minnesota, and Wisconsin, is instructive. Iowa has no major metropolitan area such as Chicago, Minneapolis-St. Paul, or Milwaukee and consequently has higher proportions of farmers and elderly residents than its neighbors. Each year Iowa takes in more federal dollars than it pays out, while the other three get back less than 89 cents for each tax dollar contributed. Ironically, most rural states—but not necessarily Iowa—that consistently benefit from federal expenditures have tended to support Republicans in recent presidential elections, even though the Republican platform generally calls for reductions in federal taxes and expenditures.

During the nineteenth and early twentieth centuries, defense expenditures as a percentage of overall federal outlays varied dramatically over time, going up sharply during

Map 4-6 *Fiscal Expenditures per Dollar of Federal Taxes, FY 1999*

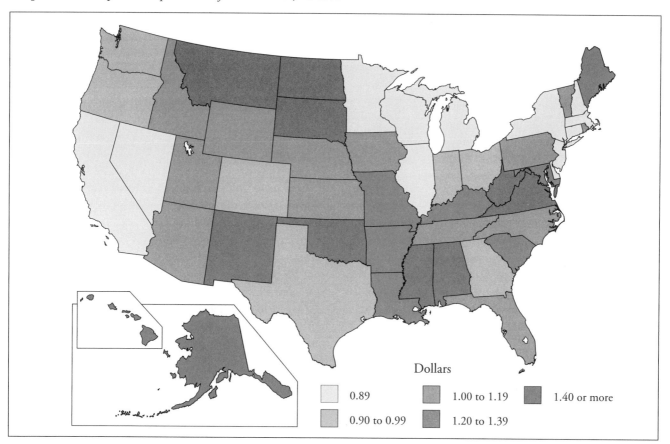

Dollars

0.89	1.00 to 1.19
0.90 to 0.99	1.20 to 1.39
	1.40 or more

Map 4-7 *Defense Outlays, by County, FY 1999*

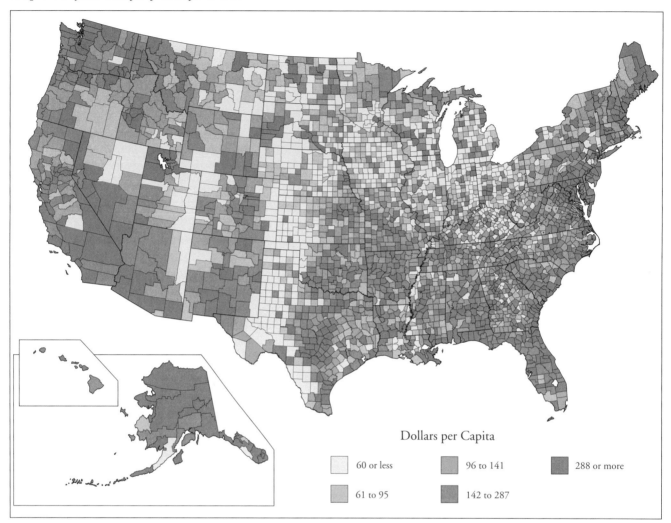

Dollars per Capita

60 or less

61 to 95

96 to 141

142 to 287

288 or more

wartime and dropping just as sharply in peacetime. Since World War II, however, defense expenditures as a percentage of federal outlays have been fairly constant, reflecting the U.S. policy of remaining a major world power. Defense expenditures continued at substantial levels during the 1990s, despite the collapse of communism in eastern Europe and the Soviet Union, which ended the cold war.

Defense expenditures since about 1950 may be fairly consistent, but where the money is spent varies widely. Map 4-7 shows per capita federal defense outlays by county in fiscal year 1999. The map shows dramatic differences between counties across the United States, and even between adjacent counties, demonstrating that many defense expenditures are highly concentrated geographically.

A considerable portion of the U.S. defense budget goes to the maintenance of military bases. These bases bring additional population to communities and afford opportunities for civilian employment, both on the base and in the provision of services to military and civilian personnel.[1] Not surprisingly, counties with large military bases show up with large per capita defense outlays. The counties with cities housing major military bases, such as Charleston, Honolulu, Norfolk, Pensacola, and San Antonio, can easily be identified. The greater Washington, D.C., metropolitan area stands out in particular as receiving high levels of defense outlays because of the location of the Pentagon in Arlington, Virginia.

Defense contracts represent another significant proportion of national defense outlays, and the map shows counties with major defense contractors as having high per capita defense outlays. Some of these areas, including southern California, Seattle, and St. Louis, are the homes of major corporations, such as Boeing, TRW, and McDonnell-Douglas, which have long-standing contracts to produce major weapons systems. (In 2001 Boeing moved its headquarters from Seattle to Chicago.)

Although most defense outlays are highly localized, broad regional patterns can be discerned from the map. In general, defense outlays tend to be concentrated along the Eastern seaboard, in the South, and in the West. This pattern reflects several historic trends, including the fact that both the Northeast and the South have generally been more supportive of foreign intervention than has the interior of the country.[2] The concentration of military personnel and installations in the South has been apparent since before the Civil War. Military training has been conducted there because of the climate, flat land, and other advantages. In addition, for much of the twentieth century, Democratic members of Congress from the South with high seniority status and defense committee chairmanships brought bases and other military posts to their home communities. The South also has long supplied a disproportionate percentage of officers and enlisted personnel to the service—a trend reinforced since the military draft was eliminated in the early 1970s.

Interior sections of the country, including the Midwest and Great Plains, tend to have relatively low per capita defense outlays. The relative absence of defense outlays in these regions may reinforce this region's historic isolationism and skepticism about active foreign involvement.[3]

The geographic distribution of nondefense outlays from the federal government by county, shown in Map 4-8, presents quite a different pattern from that associated with defense expenditures (Map 4-7). Across the country, the overall amount of revenue spent on nondefense programs far exceeds that spent on defense-related programs. Many of these expenditures are payments from the federal government to individuals. Among the largest such payments are outlays for Social Security, Medicare, veterans' pensions, federal welfare programs, farm subsidies, and payments to ranchers, suggesting that disproportionately large expenditures might be expected in areas characterized by elderly, rural, or impoverished populations.

Map 4-8 *Nondefense Outlays, by County, FY 1999*

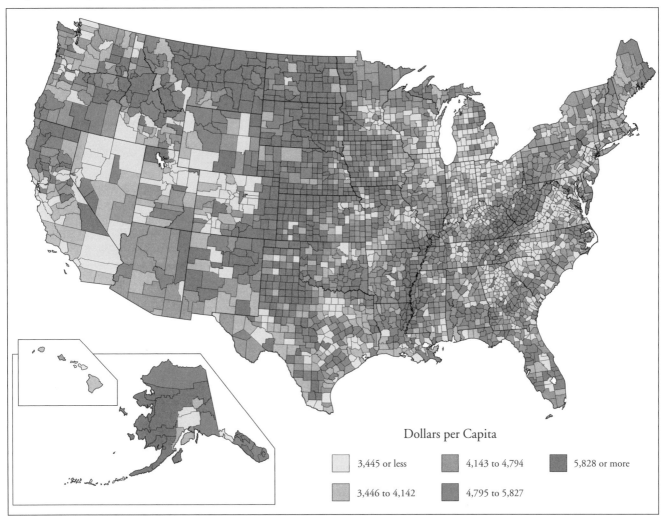

Dollars per Capita

3,445 or less

3,446 to 4,142

4,143 to 4,794

4,795 to 5,827

5,828 or more

This observation is borne out by Map 4-8. Several areas, including much of the heavily agricultural Great Plains, stand out as having relatively high per capita nondefense expenditures. Nearly all of western Kansas and western Nebraska, for example, fall into the maximum category. The rural counties in this region have not only a significant percentage of farmers and ranchers, but also, because of decades of out-migration by young people, they have a large percentage of elderly (compare with Map 1-10), who receive federal Social Security and Medicare benefits. The Mississippi Delta region of Arkansas, Louisiana, and Mississippi, the African American areas of Alabama and Georgia, and many counties in the central Appalachians from western Pennsylvania to Tennessee also have high per capita nondefense outlays.

The wealthier, more urban and suburban areas show relatively low nondefense outlays. This pattern is reminiscent of the ratio of outlays to taxes collected (Map 4-6). Much of Illinois, Ohio, Michigan, and Wisconsin, for example, report per capita nondefense outlays that are somewhat lower than the national average. Exceptions within these states are counties that are rural, slow growing, and low income, including many in western Illinois, southeastern Ohio on the margins of

Appalachia, and northern Wisconsin. Metropolitan areas, particularly suburban counties within metropolitan areas, also tend to receive relatively low per capita nondefense payments. Examples include the Atlanta, Chicago, Los Angeles, and Minneapolis-St. Paul metropolitan areas. In some cases, central city counties have somewhat larger per capita outlays than their suburbs, in part because of the concentration of federal offices and employment opportunities (such as the regional offices shown in Maps 4-1, 4-2, and 4-3) and in part because central cities also tend to have larger numbers of elderly and impoverished residents.

Federally Owned Land and Civilian Employment

Map 4-9 shows by state the percentage of land owned by the federal government. As of 1997 the federal government owned approximately 654 million acres, or 1.02 million square miles of land throughout the fifty states or 28.8 percent of the total land surface of the United States. Much of this federally owned land is in the western third of the coun-

Map 4-9 *Federally Owned Land, 1997*

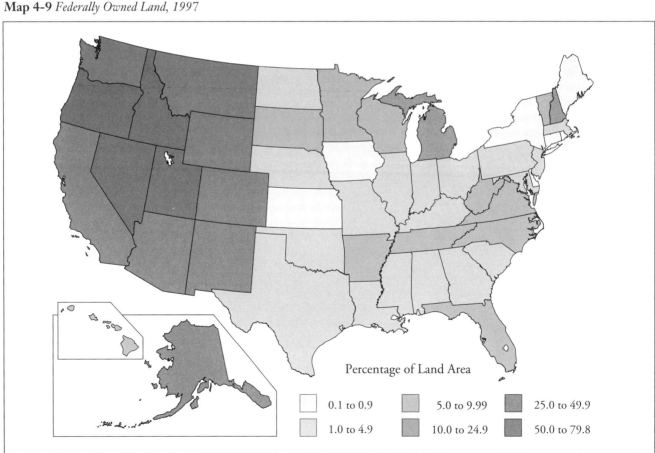

Percentage of Land Area

0.1 to 0.9	5.0 to 9.99	25.0 to 49.9
1.0 to 4.9	10.0 to 24.9	50.0 to 79.8

try, including Alaska. These lands are owned and administered by a variety of federal agencies, most of which report to the Department of the Interior. The National Park Service administers more than 83 million acres of federally owned land, much of it in large national parks. The country's largest national parks include Alaska's Denali, Glacier Bay, Katmai, Kobuk Valley, Lake Clark, and Wrangell-St. Elias, which together cover more than 20 million acres. Death Valley in California and Nevada, Grand Canyon in Arizona, and Yellowstone in Idaho, Montana, and Wyoming contain more than 1 million acres each. The Park Service also administers many smaller national areas, including historic sites, parks, battlefields, monuments, preserves, and memorials.

The National Forest Service and the Bureau of Reclamation are responsible for even larger quantities of land. National forests are found throughout the United States, and national grasslands, administered in similar fashion, are located in the Great Plains states. The Bureau of Reclamation administers large tracts of land in the western states. Much of this land is leased to farmers and ranchers who use it to run livestock. Smaller tracts are owned by other federal agencies, notably the U.S. Postal Service, which administers thousands of post offices across the country.

The percentage of federal land ranges from a high of 83 percent—a higher percentage than is shown in Map 4-9—in Nevada to less than 0.5 percent in Connecticut and New York. The map demonstrates that federal land ownership is concentrated west of the Rocky Mountains. East of the Rockies, the federal government owns more than 10 percent of the land in only two states: New Hampshire (13 percent) and Michigan (11 percent). In contrast, more than a quarter of the land in all of the states west of the Continental Divide (with the exception of Hawaii) is federally owned. After Nevada, the states with the highest percentages of federal land are Alaska (67 percent), Idaho (64 percent), and Utah (62 percent). The western states with the smallest percentages are Washington and Montana (28 percent each).

The concentration of federal land ownership in the West is a source of political controversy. During the 1980s many westerners argued that the federal government should transfer ownership to the states, local governments, or private landowners. This political movement, which was sponsored by several prominent Republican senators, was known as the "Sagebrush Rebellion." Despite their efforts, the government has not given up title to much land, and many west-

Map 4-10 *Federal Civilian Employment, 1998*

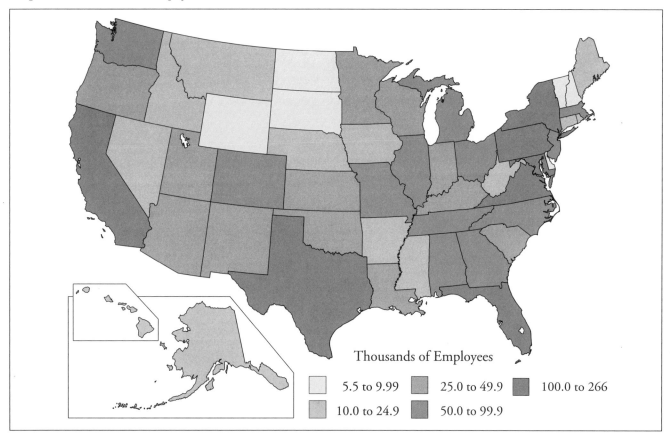

Thousands of Employees

5.5 to 9.99	25.0 to 49.9	100.0 to 266
10.0 to 24.9	50.0 to 99.9	

erners continue to oppose what they consider to be excessive federal land ownership.

A substantial proportion of the federal budget is used to pay the salaries and wages of the nearly 3 million employees of the federal government who live and work in all fifty states, the District of Columbia, and overseas. Map 4-10 shows the number of federal civilian employees by state in 1998, with data from the U.S. Office of Personnel Management. The data exclude active duty military personnel as well as some employees of agencies such as the Central Intelligence Agency, the National Security Agency, the Defense Intelligence Agency, and the National Imagery and Mapping Agency. They also do not include employees of the FBI and some other Department of Justice personnel by state.

As of December 31, 1998, the total of enumerated federal civilian personnel was 2,757,547 employees. The largest employers within the federal government were the U.S. Postal Service (985,565 employees), the Department of Defense (653,710 civilian workers), and the Veterans Administration (235,066 employees). All other included federal agencies totaled 883,206 civilian workers.

How are these employees distributed geographically? Not surprisingly, the highest numbers tend to be found in the largest states—California, Florida, New York, and Texas. The largest concentration of federal employees is found in Washington, D.C., and the neighboring states of Maryland and Virginia.

The distribution of federal employees in different agencies varies considerably. Postal service employees, for example, are scattered throughout the country, and, because every incorporated community has a post office, the distribution of postal employees closely mirrors the distribution of the population. Department of Defense employment is concentrated in areas near military bases and other installations. Federal defense-related employment, therefore, is concentrated along the coasts, in the Washington, D.C., area, and in the South. Other agencies have personnel distributed across various regional offices as well as in Washington.

Map 4-11 shows the distribution of federal employees on a per capita basis in 1998. For this map, the number of federal employees in each state was divided by the population, creating an index representing the contribution of the fed-

Map 4-11 *Federal Civilian Employees per 1,000 Population, 1998*

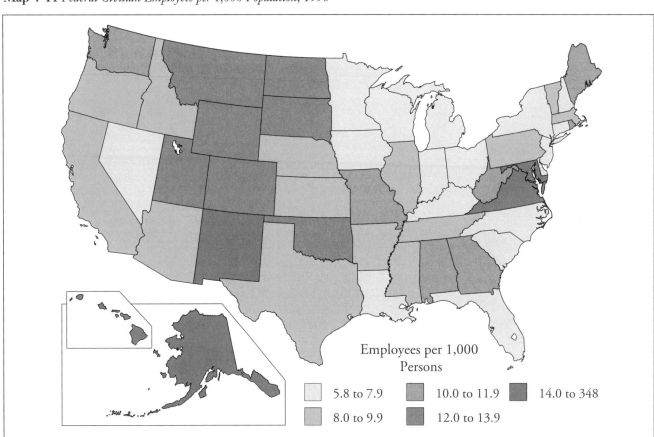

Employees per 1,000
Persons

5.8 to 7.9   10.0 to 11.9   14.0 to 348

8.0 to 9.9   12.0 to 13.9

eral government to each state's employment ba[...]he pattern shown in Map 4-11 differs dramatically from that of Map 4-10. In Map 4-10 the largest totals tend to be concentrated in the largest states. Map 4-11, in contrast, highlights those states in which a large proportion of employees work for the federal government.

In many areas, the federal government makes a substantial contribution to the local employment base. Not only does the government provide a substantial number of jobs for civilian employees, but also the presence of federal installations and agencies increases the demand for goods and services. Retail stores, physicians, teachers, and other service workers benefit.

The highest per capita employment figure was the District of Columbia, with more than 347 employees for every thousand persons. Within the fifty states, the highest ratios were found in Maryland (25.5 per 1,000), Alaska (23.3), Virginia (21.6), Hawaii (19.9), and New Mexico (14.9). Maryland and Virginia have high ratios because many federal employees work in Washington but reside in the suburbs. In addition, many federal agencies are headquartered in the Maryland and Virginia suburbs. The National Institute of Standards and Technology (formerly the Bureau of Standards) and the National Institutes of Health are located in Maryland, and the Pentagon, in which the Defense Department is headquartered, is located in Virginia. Alaska, Hawaii, and New Mexico show high ratios because these states have large numbers of federal offices and military bases relative to their size and do not have as many alternative sources of employment, such as private industry, as do larger, less-isolated states.

For similar reasons, the lowest ratios of federal employment to overall population are found in the Northeast. States such as Michigan, New Jersey, New York, and Ohio have large workforces in manufacturing and other private sector activities. With the exception of the Washington, D.C., area, ratios of federal employment to overall population tend to be higher in the West and in less-populated states. Note also the parallel between this map and Map 4-6. States with a relatively low ratio of federal outlays to federal taxes tend to have relatively few federal employees per capita.

Notes

1. Ann R. Markusen, *The Rise of the Gunbelt: The Military Remapping of Industrial America* (New York: Oxford University Press, 1991).

2. Peter Trubowitz, *Defining the National Interest: Conflict and Change in American Foreign Policy* (Chicago: University of Chicago Press, 1998).

3. Ibid.

Chapter 5

Judiciary

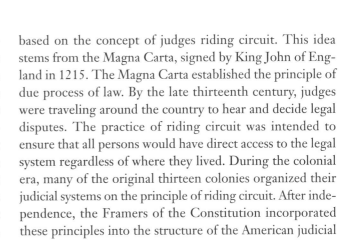

This chapter deals with spatial aspects of the American judicial system. Article III of the Constitution established the judicial system, including the Supreme Court and "such inferior Courts as the Congress may from time to time ordain and establish." Over the past two centuries, Congress has "ordained and established" a three-tiered judicial structure, which includes the U.S. Supreme Court, the circuit courts of appeals, and the district courts. The result is a highly geographical organization of the judiciary, as shown in Map 5-1. Geography plays no formal role in the selection of Supreme Court justices, but presidents often have been motivated by geographic considerations in their selections. The home states of recent Supreme Court members are shown in Map 5-2.

When a vacancy occurs on the Court, the president appoints a replacement, subject to majority confirmation by the Senate. Since 1960 the Senate has rejected three nominees: Clement F. Haynsworth Jr., G. Harrold Carswell, and Robert Bork. A fourth nominee, Clarence Thomas, was confirmed by a 52–48 vote, the narrowest margin in U.S. history. All of these appointments were highly controversial. Maps 5-3 through 5-6 show the geographic pattern of senators' votes on the Haynsworth, Carswell, Bork, and Thomas nominations, respectively.

The Supreme Court decides disputes that have been appealed from lower courts, as well as disputes between states. Most Supreme Court cases, therefore, originate in particular localities. Maps 5-7 through 5-9 illustrate the geographic origins of major Supreme Court cases in three issue areas: electoral districting, abortion rights and sex discrimination, and the environment. The pattern of case origin in these three important types of cases is quite different in each instance.

Even before the American Revolution, the American judicial system was organized along territorial lines. The three-tiered system of judicial organization shown in Map 5-1 is the product of more than two centuries of evolving judicial structure.

The spatial organization of the American judiciary is

based on the concept of judges riding circuit. This idea stems from the Magna Carta, signed by King John of England in 1215. The Magna Carta established the principle of due process of law. By the late thirteenth century, judges were traveling around the country to hear and decide legal disputes. The practice of riding circuit was intended to ensure that all persons would have direct access to the legal system regardless of where they lived. During the colonial era, many of the original thirteen colonies organized their judicial systems on the principle of riding circuit. After independence, the Framers of the Constitution incorporated these principles into the structure of the American judicial system.[1]

In keeping with Article III, Section I, Congress passed the Judiciary Act of 1789, which established the Supreme Court, three circuit courts, and thirteen district courts, one for each state. The first Supreme Court had only six justices, including the chief justice. The three circuits—Eastern, Southern, and Middle—were established on a geographical basis. Each of circuit courts was presided over by two Supreme Court justices and a district judge, and each of the thirteen district courts was presided over by a district judge. All of these judicial officers were required to ride circuit.[2]

In 1802 Congress increased the number of circuit courts to six and assigned one Supreme Court justice to each. As more states entered the Union, additional circuits were created. When the circuits were reorganized in 1867, several circuits included northern and southern states. As the country grew in areal extent and population, the tradition of having Supreme Court justices ride circuit became impractical. In 1891 Congress established an intermediate court between the district court and the Supreme Court. These appeals courts were known as circuit courts of appeals because the boundaries of their jurisdictions coincided with the circuit boundaries. By this time, Supreme Court justices had ceased to ride circuit, and the tradition of appointing Supreme Court justices from each circuit was abandoned. Contemporary justices still have jurisdiction over one or more of the federal circuits, usually located near the justice's

Map 5-1 *Organization of the Federal Judiciary*

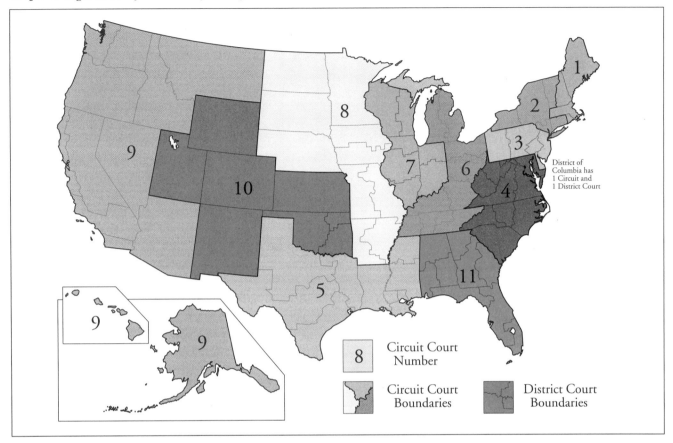

Circuit Court Number

Circuit Court Boundaries

District Court Boundaries

District of Columbia has 1 Circuit and 1 District Court

home region. The justices may issue injunctions, grant bail, or stay executions in these circuits.

As reorganized in the late nineteenth century, the circuits approached their modern configurations, but several new circuits have been created since then. As states west of the Mississippi River entered the Union, they were assigned to either the Eighth or Ninth Circuit. Because these large circuits were difficult to administer, the Tenth Circuit was created from the Eighth in 1928.[3] Since then, efforts have been made to divide the Ninth Circuit. In general, such proposals have been based on the idea that the Pacific Northwest should be separate from California, but so far Congress has not approved the idea. In 1980 the Eleventh Circuit, including Florida, Georgia, and Alabama, was created from the Fifth.[4]

Today, the federal judiciary consists of the Supreme Court, the eleven numbered circuit courts of appeals, a twelfth circuit based in the District of Columbia, a federal circuit (also in the District of Columbia but not shown on the map), and ninety-one district courts (including courts in Puerto Rico, which also does not appear on the map). With minor exceptions, such as Yellowstone National Park, the circuit court boundaries are the same as the states within the circuits. Larger states are divided geographically into two or more districts, as shown on the map. Each is named for its geographic position within the state; for example, the two districts of Arkansas are known as the Eastern District and Western District and are headquartered in Little Rock and Fort Smith, respectively.

Prior to the Civil War, geography was an explicit consideration when a president selected a nominee for the Supreme Court. Although geography is no longer given high priority, it remains a consideration in many presidential appointments to fill Court vacancies.

The Judiciary Act of 1789 established three circuit courts, the Eastern (New England), Middle, and Southern. Two Supreme Court justices were associated with each circuit. In his initial Court nominations, President George Washington selected justices who came from the circuits they would serve. The members of the first Court came from Massachusetts, New York, Pennsylvania, Virginia, North Carolina, and South Carolina. After the Judiciary Act was amended in 1802, one justice was assigned to each circuit. Until the Civil War, presidents usually filled vacancies

Map 5-2 *Home States of Supreme Court Justices, 1961–2000*

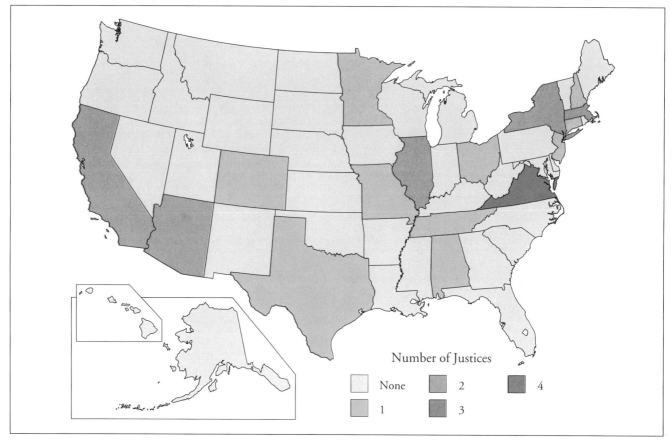

Number of Justices

None   2   4

1   3

with justices who came from one of the states in the circuit to which that justice would be assigned.[5]

During the Civil War, Abraham Lincoln abandoned the practice of explicit geographical representation on the Court. After a justice from Virginia died in 1860, and an Alabama justice resigned following his state's secession in 1861, Lincoln declined to fill the vacancies, fearing that qualified southerners would be unwilling to serve but not wishing to select northern justices whose terms of office would likely outlast the war. The judicial system was reformed in 1867, and presidents no longer automatically filled vacancies with a nominee from the same circuit. The tradition of selecting justices from certain regions of the country, however, continued for many years. For example, one seat was held by successive New Englanders for seventy-four years: Nathan Clifford of Maine (1858–1881), Horace Gray of Massachusetts (1881–1902), and Oliver Wendell Holmes of Massachusetts (1902–1932). Some contemporary presidents have tried to preserve geographical balance on the Court. In some cases, such as President Richard Nixon's unsuccessful nominations of Clement Haynsworth and G. Harrold Carswell (Maps 5-3 and 5-4), geography played a major role.

Since 1961 a total of twenty-four men and women have served on the Supreme Court. These justices represent seventeen states and the District of Columbia. The map may be somewhat deceptive because several justices actually lived and worked for much of their lives in states other than those from which they were appointed. For example, Virginia has been the home of four justices—more than any other state during this period, but only one of them, Lewis F. Powell Jr., was actually from Virginia. The other three (Warren E. Burger, Antonin Scalia, and Clarence Thomas) were members of the District of Columbia Circuit Court of Appeals and residents of Virginia when appointed to the Court. Burger was a native of Minnesota, Scalia was born in New York, and Thomas was born in Georgia. Likewise, William O. Douglas was born in Minnesota and lived for many years in Washington State, but was a Connecticut resident when appointed to the Court.

The map shows a relatively even distribution of Supreme Court justices across the United States, although the South and West tend to be underrepresented compared to the Northeast and Midwest. Large and medium-sized states tend to have more justices than smaller states, perhaps reflecting the greater influence that the legal communities of these states have on American jurisprudence. The Court in 2001 includes two justices each from Virginia and Arizona, along with one each from California, the District of Columbia, Illinois, Massachusetts, and New Hampshire.

Four Contentious Senate Confirmation Votes

When a vacancy occurs on the Supreme Court, the president nominates a successor, subject to Senate approval. Because of the enormous importance of the Court and its decisions on American life, proposed nominations are often highly controversial and highly politicized.

Since 1969, four Supreme Court nominations have been marked by particularly bitter controversy. The nominees were Clement F. Haynsworth Jr. in 1969, G. Harrold Carswell in 1970, Robert Bork in 1987, and Clarence Thomas in 1991. The first three failed to achieve majorities in the Senate, and Thomas was confirmed by a 52–48 majority, the closest confirmation vote in U.S. history. Maps 5-3 through 5-6 show how each state's senators voted on these nominees.

In the presidential campaign of 1968, Republican candidate Richard Nixon harshly criticized what he saw as the Supreme Court's activism, and he promised, if elected, to appoint conservative judges whose judicial philosophy was strict construction of the Constitution. Nixon's pledge was especially appealing to conservative white southerners, many of whom disapproved of judicial activism on civil rights and other matters.

Justice Abe Fortas resigned from the Supreme Court in May 1969, giving Nixon his first opportunity to select an associate justice.[6] On August 18 Nixon announced his selection of Judge Haynsworth, who came from South Carolina. President Dwight D. Eisenhower had appointed Haynsworth to the Court of Appeals for the Fourth Circuit (see Map 5-1) in 1957.

Haynsworth's nomination generated substantial controversy. Civil rights organizations and other critics pointed to Haynsworth's past opposition to racial integration. They cited opinions in which he expressed support for local resistance to school integration in Virginia. Some critics brought up a possible conflict of interest because in 1963 Haynsworth had participated in a Fourth Circuit case involving a subsidiary of another firm in which he had substantial financial interests. Critics charged that Haynsworth

Map 5-3 *Haynsworth Confirmation Vote, 1969*

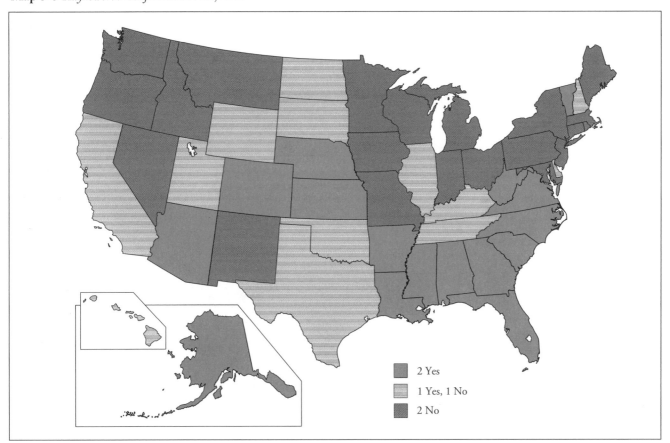

2 Yes

1 Yes, 1 No

2 No

should have recused himself from participating in that case. Both the civil rights record and the conflict of interest issues arose during confirmation hearings by the Senate Judiciary Committee and on the floor of the Senate.

On November 21, 1969, the Senate rejected the nomination, 55–45. Republicans favored the nomination, 26–17, while Democrats opposed it, 38–19. Both parties were deeply divided geographically. Only three of thirty-eight northern Democrats voted in favor of Haynsworth, while sixteen of the nineteen Democrats from the South supported the nomination. Only five southern senators were Republicans, and all five voted for Haynsworth. The map shows a solid block of support for the nomination in the South, and strong opposition elsewhere.

Following the defeat of Clement Haynsworth in the Senate (Map 5-3), an angry President Nixon charged Haynsworth's congressional critics with partisanship in rejecting his nomination. On January 19, 1970, Nixon announced his selection of G. Harrold Carswell of Florida to fill the vacancy, which had been created when Justice Abe Fortas resigned. A native of Georgia, Carswell had moved to Florida after an unsuccessful effort to win a seat in the Georgia legislature in 1948. President Dwight Eisenhower

had appointed him to the federal bench in 1958, and Nixon appointed him to the Fifth Circuit Court of Appeals in 1969.

Because of Haynsworth's rejection, the administration thoroughly investigated Carswell's financial records before submitting his nomination to the Senate. Civil rights activists, however, noted that Carswell had a long history of opposition to racial integration. In his 1948 legislative campaign, Carswell had given a speech in which he endorsed white supremacy. In 1956 he was a partner in a Tallahassee public golf course that was transferred to private ownership to avoid desegregation. Critics of his performance on the bench also pointed to a pattern of hostility to civil rights activists and their attorneys. Questions of Carswell's legal ability and professional competence also arose. Carswell's supporters charged that these accusations were motivated by political considerations.

The Senate voted on the Carswell nomination on April 8 and rejected it, 51–45, with four senators not voting. As with Haynsworth's nomination, the vote was more deeply divided along geographical than partisan lines. Republicans supported Carswell, 28–13, with all five southern Republicans in support of the nomination. Senate Democrats voted

Map 5-4 *Carswell Confirmation Vote, 1970*

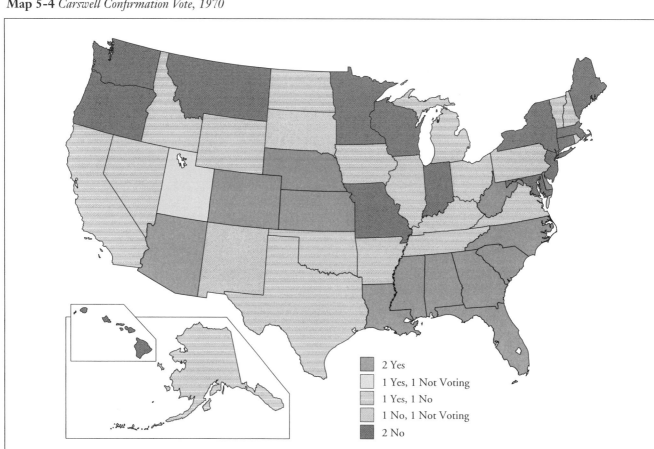

2 Yes

1 Yes, 1 Not Voting

1 Yes, 1 No

1 No, 1 Not Voting

2 No

38 to 17 against him, but southern Democrats supported Carswell 14 to 5, while northern Democrats overwhelmingly opposed him by a margin of 33 to 3. Map 5-4, like Map 5-3, shows solid support in the South and opposition in the North.

Following the Senate's rejection of Carswell, Nixon declared that no strict constructionist from the South could be confirmed. He then selected Harry Blackmun of Minnesota, who was confirmed unanimously and served on the Court for twenty-four years.

One of the bitterest controversies in recent American judicial history occurred when the Senate rejected the nomination of Robert Bork to be an associate justice of the Supreme Court. On June 26, 1987, Associate Justice Lewis F. Powell Jr. retired from the Court after fifteen years of service. Powell had often been a swing vote on a Court evenly divided between liberals and conservatives. On July 1, President Ronald Reagan announced the selection of Bork, who had served as solicitor general in the Nixon administration. In this post, Bork had fired Watergate prosecutor Archibald Cox after Bork's superiors in the Justice Department resigned rather than follow Nixon's orders. Bork subsequently became a law professor at Yale Univer-

sity. Reagan appointed Bork to the District of Columbia Circuit Court of Appeals in 1982. His supporters referred to him as a strict constructionist, while his opponents labeled him a conservative ideologue. Critics cited Bork's views on civil rights, sex discrimination, and the First Amendment as evidence of his conservative activism.

The Bork nomination sparked more than three months of rancorous partisan debate, part of which concerned the extent to which the Senate should consider questions of ideology rather than evaluating the nominee's competence. Neither side doubted Bork's competence and ability, but many Democrats argued that his record of conservative activism and ideology disqualified him for membership on the Court.

On October 23, 1987, the Senate rejected Bork, 58–42. Compared with the failed nominations of Clement Haynsworth in 1969 (Map 5-3) and G. Harrold Carswell in 1970 (Map 5-4), the Bork vote was more polarized on partisan grounds. Republicans supported him, 40–6, while Democrats opposed the nomination, 52–2. Bork's only Democratic supporters were from Oklahoma and South Carolina, while his six opponents in the Republican Party came from Connecticut, Oregon, Pennsylvania, Rhode

Map 5-5 *Bork Confirmation Vote, 1987*

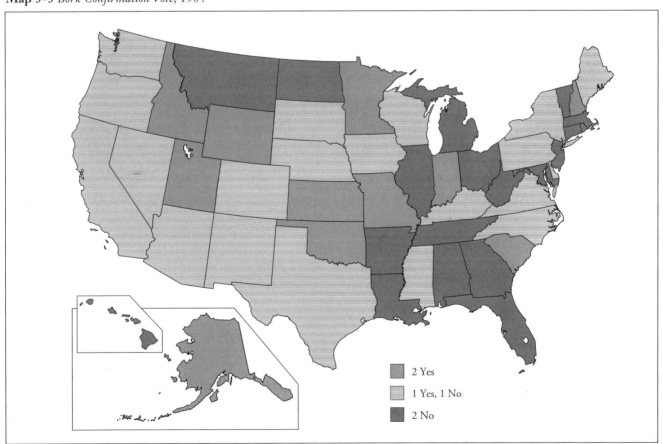

Map 5-6 *Thomas Confirmation Vote, 1991*

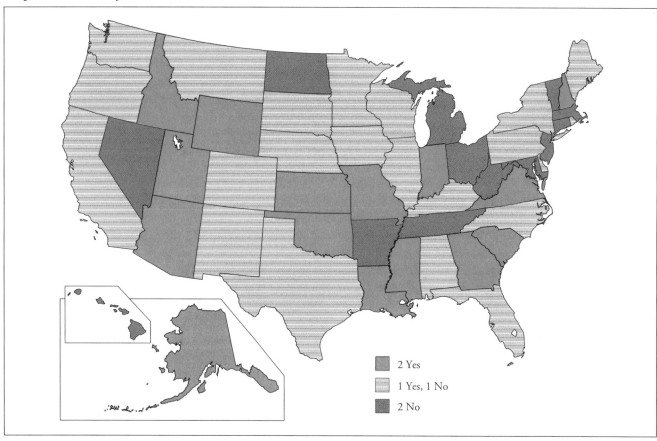

2 Yes

1 Yes, 1 No

2 No

Island, Vermont, and Virginia. To a large extent, Map 5-5 reflects how partisan the Senate was during the last years of Reagan's administration.

Map 5-6 shows how senators voted in 1991 on the nomination of Clarence Thomas to be an associate justice of the Supreme Court. The vote, 52–48, was the closest confirmation vote for any Court nominee.

Associate Justice Thurgood Marshall, the first African American to serve on the Court, announced his retirement from the Court at the end of the 1990–1991 term after twenty-three years of service. President George Bush selected Thomas, an African American with a solid conservative record, to fill the vacancy. Thomas had served as chair of the Equal Employment Opportunity Commission under President Ronald Reagan, and in 1990 Bush had appointed him to the District of Columbia Circuit Court of Appeals. Opposition arose among liberals who criticized Thomas's conservative views. Moreover, critics pointed out that Thomas had served on the bench for only a year and, therefore, his judicial experience was limited. Despite this criticism, Thomas's nomination appeared to be on the road to confirmation until a former employee accused him of sexual harassment. The allegations prompted some of

Thomas's supporters to reconsider their support for the nomination. In response to these allegations, the Senate Judiciary Committee held additional hearings to consider them.

The Senate voted on the nomination October 15. Map 5-6 shows that this vote was more partisan than geographical, although support by southern Democrats proved critical to the success of the nomination. The Republicans supported Thomas's nomination, 41–2, and the majority Democrats opposed it, 46–11. Eight of the eleven Democrats who voted for Thomas, who was born and raised in Georgia, came from the South. Because the national vote was so close, it was the support of these southern Democrats that proved critical to the success of the nomination.

State Origins of Major Supreme Court Cases

For more than 200 years, the Supreme Court has handed down decisions that have had far-reaching implications for American life. Although the impacts of the Court's decisions are felt across the country, most Supreme Court decisions are the result of litigation arising out of a particular dispute in a particular place. For example, *Brown v. Board of Education*, which desegregated public schools nationwide, arose from a dispute over segregated schools in Topeka, Kansas.

Geographic patterns of case origins differ considerably according to the issues involved. Maps 5-7, 5-8, and 5-9 deal with the geography of three types of Supreme Court cases that arose between 1960 and 2000. These include cases on apportionment and electoral districting, abortion and sex discrimination, and the environment.[7]

Map 5-7 shows the state origins of Supreme Court cases dealing with apportionment and electoral districting. Prior to the 1960s, many states permitted wide disparities in the populations of districts drawn to elect members of state legislatures and the U.S. House of Representatives. Such malapportionment was challenged in *Baker v. Carr*, a case in which plaintiffs pointed out that Tennessee's General Assembly districts had not been redrawn since 1900 and that, therefore, urban districts had several times as many residents as rural districts. In 1962 the Supreme Court ruled that Tennessee's malapportionment violated the equal protection clause of the Fourteenth Amendment to the Constitution because individual voters in large districts had less influence on the selection of their representatives than did

voters in smaller districts. The Court stated that this kind of question was a proper matter for federal courts to decide, and that malapportionment was unconstitutional. Following this decision, many other cases involving electoral districting were filed; in fact, *Baker v. Carr* initiated what has often been called the "reapportionment revolution." Within the next few years, the Court extended the basic principle of *Baker v. Carr* to city councils and other local governments and to congressional districts in *Wesberry v. Sanders* (1964). Because malapportioned districts were found in many of the states, legislatures throughout the country had to draw new district boundaries and the criteria for keeping the process fair attracted considerable attention.

The civil rights movement of the 1960s, which resulted in many far-reaching changes in American life, also affected the reapportionment revolution. Among the most fundamental changes were those associated with the passage and implementation of the Voting Rights Act of 1965. This law empowered the federal government to enforce the Fourteenth Amendment, which provides for equal protection under the laws. The act guaranteed federal enforcement of the right to vote to African Americans and other minority citizens. It also implied that districting patterns and systems

Map 5-7 *State Origins of Major Supreme Court Cases, Electoral Apportionment and Districting, 1960–2000*

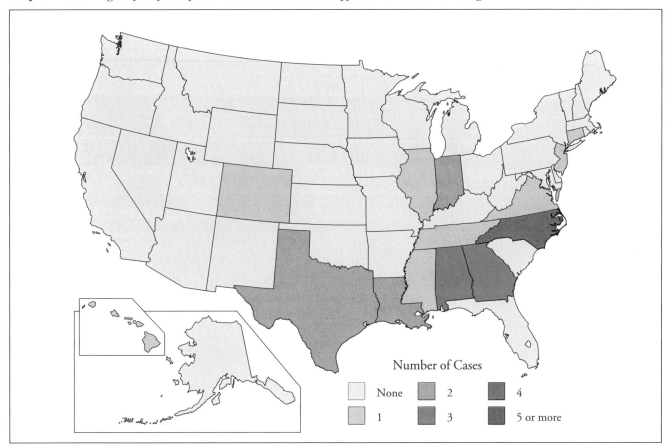

Number of Cases

None	2	4
1	3	5 or more

with built-in bias against minority voters were violations of the Constitution. Racial issues were closely associated with many of the districting cases decided by the Court after 1965.

Between 1960 and the late 1990s, the Supreme Court decided twenty-three important cases associated with apportionment and the delineation of electoral districts. Of these, seventeen or 74 percent originated in the South. Five of the seventeen originated prior to 1965, and only one of them dealt directly with racial issues. In contrast, all twelve southern cases that arose after 1965 pertained directly to racial issues. The combination of the reapportionment revolution and the civil rights movement created a legal framework based on interpretation of the Fourteenth Amendment, the Voting Rights Act, and the principle of equal apportionment as established in *Baker v. Carr*. Many of these southern cases arose in states and localities with long histories of racial discrimination, and the victims of discrimination used the federal court system for redress. Four cases originated in Georgia, three in Alabama, and three in North Carolina. Only six of the twenty-three racial discrimination cases arose in states outside of the South: Colorado, Connecticut, Hawaii, Indiana, and New Jersey.

Map 5-8 shows the states of origin for cases dealing with abortion and sex discrimination. Among the most controversial decisions of the late twentieth century was *Roe v. Wade*, which struck down state laws prohibiting abortion. *Roe v. Wade* originated in Texas and was decided in 1973. *Doe v. Bolton*, a companion case decided at the same time, originated in Georgia.

Before the decision in *Roe v. Wade*, numerous lawsuits challenged the constitutionality of laws that made abortion a crime throughout the United States. Six of these were appealed to the Court, which chose to hear and decide appeals from Texas and Georgia. The legal issues in *Roe v. Wade* and in *Doe v. Bolton* did not directly involve whether a woman had a constitutional right to an abortion, as was the case with disputes in the other four states. Rather, they dealt with procedures under which a woman seeking to have an abortion could be granted permission by the state. From a legal standpoint, therefore, the issues addressed in *Roe v. Wade* and in *Doe v. Bolton* were relatively uncontroversial, although the decision itself has been a source of major controversy ever since.

Map 5-8 *State Origins of Major Supreme Court Cases, Abortion Rights and Sex Discrimination, 1973–2000*

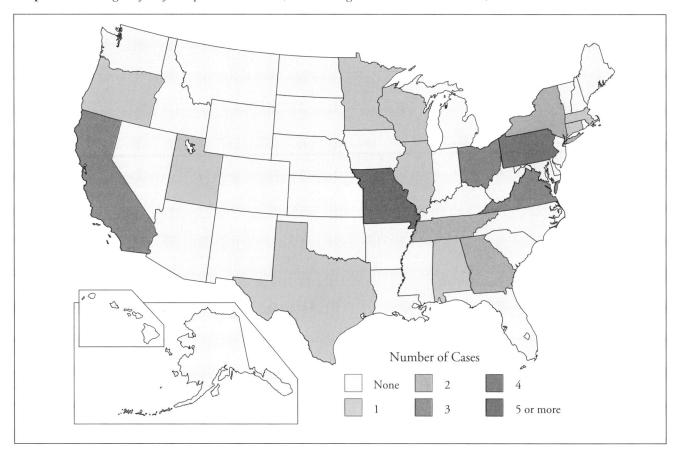

The Supreme Court has decided twenty abortion cases since *Roe v. Wade* was handed down in 1973. Of these, only two originated in the South. The remaining cases originated in the Northeast and West, with heavy concentrations in the Middle Atlantic states and in the Midwest. Five of the cases originated in Missouri, four in Pennsylvania, two in New York, and two in Ohio. These states have in common large populations, a considerable degree of cultural and political heterogeneity and diversity, and substantial numbers of Roman Catholics. It is in states with these characteristics that the abortion issue has been especially politicized since the early 1970s.

The issues of sex discrimination and sexual harassment in the workplace have also been addressed frequently by the Court since the early 1960s. Two examples of harassment cases are *Nashville Gas v. Sperry*, a Tennessee case from 1976, and *Washington County, Oregon v. Gunther*, an Oregon case from 1981. Fourteen cases dealing with such subjects originated from ten different states. Of these, six came from the South. Three originated in California, with the rest scattered among northern and other western states. Only two of the fourteen sex discrimination and harassment cases originated in the Northeast and Middle West, which were more frequent sources for abortion cases. In general, abortion cases tended to arise in urban areas, and those involving sex discrimination were more likely to originate in rural areas.

Map 5-9 shows the states of origin for Supreme Court cases dealing with the environment and environmental management. The pattern of origins of these cases was quite different from both the electoral districting cases portrayed in Map 5-7 and the abortion and sex discrimination cases shown in Map 5-8. Illustrating the importance of environmental issues to contemporary American life, the Court decided sixty-one major cases involving environmental issues in the period in question.

One difference between the environment cases and those involving electoral districting and women's rights is that not all environmental cases arise from disputes originating at specific locations. Rather, a significant number of cases involving the environment originated as challenges to laws or policies with nationwide applicability, rather from specific local challenges to these laws. Eleven of the sixty-one cases lacked geographical specificity. For example, *Ruck-*

Map 5-9 *State Origins of Major Supreme Court Cases, Environment, 1960–2000*

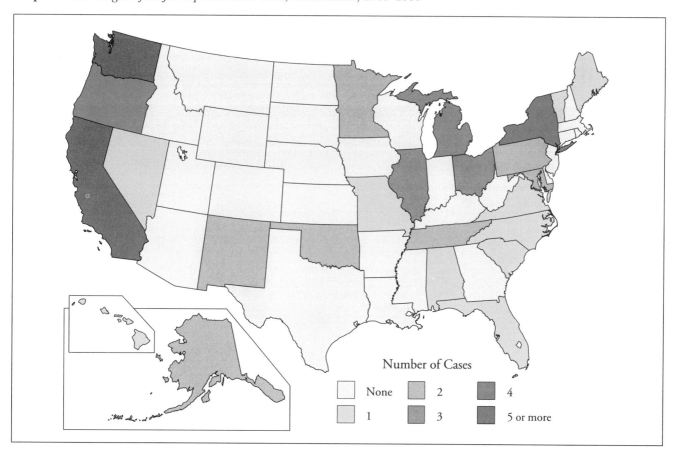

Number of Cases

None   2   4

1   3   5 or more

elshaus v. Sierra Club, a 1973 case, was a legal challenge to sulfur dioxide emission standards that were promulgated by the Environmental Protection Agency in the early 1970s that the Sierra Club believed were too weak to protect the environment adequately. Data from the remaining fifty cases, each of which is associated with a specific place of origin, is reflected in Map 5-9.

These fifty cases can be divided into three broad categories. The first category includes cases that involved issues such as the preservation of wilderness areas, protection of endangered species, and management of natural resources. A majority of these cases originated in the western United States. Some well-known examples include *Sierra Club v. Morton* (1972), which originated with a proposal by the Disney Corporation to develop a pristine natural area near Yosemite National Park in California into a ski resort, and *Alyeska Pipeline v. Wilderness Society* (1975), which concerned the environmental effects of the pipeline that had been built to transport oil from Alaska's North Slope to the Pacific Ocean in the 1970s.

A second and even larger category of cases involved more direct impacts of environmental policy on day-to-day activities. This category includes cases involving air pollution, water pollution, land development, and the generation and transport of hazardous wastes. A major difference between the two categories of cases is that cases in the first category deal with areas with substantial amounts of open space, while cases in the second arise in places of dense population. The majority of cases in the second category originated in the Northeast and Great Lakes states.

A third category of cases involves direct disputes between states and jurisdictions. In accordance with the Constitution, the federal judiciary is empowered to hear disputes between the states, and many such cases find their way to the Supreme Court. For example, the city of Philadelphia, Pennsylvania, sued the state of New Jersey over a New Jersey law that prohibited importing toxic chemicals into New Jersey. Another case in this category was *Milwaukee v. Illinois* (1981), in which Milwaukee authorities sued Illinois for allowing excessive pollution of Lake Michigan. Cases in this category were distributed fairly evenly across the country.[8]

Overall, the pattern of environmental disputes is associated with both dense populations and pristine areas, a pattern relatively consistent with Environmental Protection Agency regions (Map 4-3). Such cases are therefore concentrated in the Northeast and the West, with relatively few in the South.

Notes

1. Roscoe Pound, *Organization of Courts* (Boston: Little, Brown, 1940); Robert A. Carp and Ronald Stidham, *The Federal Courts*, 4th ed. (Washington, D.C.: CQ Press, 2001).

2. William A. Casto, *The Supreme Court in the Early Republic* (Columbia: University of South Carolina Press, 1995).

3. Arthur J. Stanley and Irma Russell, "The Political and Administrative History of the United States Court of Appeals for the Tenth Circuit," *Denver Law Review* 60 (1983): 119–146.

4. Erwin C. Surrency, *History of the Federal Courts* (New York: Oceana Publications, 1987).

5. Carp and Stidham, *Federal Courts;* Surrency, *History.*

6. Nixon had already selected Warren E. Burger to replace Earl Warren as chief justice. Bob Woodward and Scott S. Armstrong, *The Brethren* (New York: Simon and Schuster, 1979).

7. Stanley D. Brunn, Fred M. Shelley, Gerald R. Webster, and Wael M. Ahmed, "Place and Region in American Legal Culture: Origins of Landmark Supreme Court Cases," *Historical Geography* 28 (2000): 134–155.

8. Ibid.

Chapter 6

The Political Culture of States

The Tenth Amendment to the U.S. Constitution reserves all powers not specifically delegated to the federal government to the states or to the people. Each state, therefore, has considerable authority to establish its own policies with respect to policy and governance. Chapter 6 explores some of the geographic variations in state and local governance across the United States.

Many of the variations discussed in this chapter result from differences in political culture. Political scientist Daniel Elazar has postulated that three distinctive political cultures exist in the United States, which he associated with the North, the South, and the central part of the country. Each political culture is characterized by distinctive beliefs about the appropriate structure and scope of state and local governments, and these differences are evident in many of the maps in Chapter 6. The three political cultures (and subsequent mixtures of them) have led to variations in the procedures established for governing each state. They manifest themselves, for example, in the relative length of state constitutions, the length of terms for public officials, and whether citizens have initiative power.

Maps showing the distribution of party control of governorships and the upper and lower houses of state legislatures not only illustrate the influence of political culture, but also present an opportunity for comparisons with maps of presidential elections (Chapter 2) and congressional elections (Chapter 3). The maps show that the Republicans' dramatic gains in the South and the Democrats' increased strength in the North generally occurred first in presidential elections and later in state and local elections.

Among the responsibilities associated with state and local government are the collection of taxes and their disbursement for various public goods and services. Clear manifestations of the three political cultures can be seen in the maps that present state and local fiscal matters. The same is true of the final maps in the chapter, which show the distribution of elected officials, including women and minorities.

Political Culture Areas

Under the U.S. system of government, individual states have considerable autonomy in many areas of public policy. How that power is exercised within each state results, in part, from its political culture. Political culture refers to prevailing local attitudes about the nature and purpose of government and politics. These beliefs and attitudes vary widely from one state to another. In the 1960s political scientist Daniel Elazar postulated the existence of three major political cultures in the United States: the *moralistic* political culture of New England, the *traditionalistic* political culture of the South, and the *individualistic* political culture of the Middle Atlantic states.[1] Each originated in a specific area during colonial times, and each spread westward with the population holding it.

Moralistic political culture is based on the premise that the purpose of government and politics is to promote the common good. This view originated with the Puritan culture of colonial New England, which emphasized community self-sufficiency. Under moralistic political culture, political participation is regarded as a civic duty. Political parties are relatively weak, and voters and officeholders pride themselves on their independence. In 2001 the country's only independent senator (Jim Jeffords of Vermont), its only independent member of the House of Representatives (Bernard Sanders of Vermont), and its only two independent governors (Angus King of Maine and Jesse Ventura of Minnesota) come from purely moralistic states.

Traditionalistic political culture is based on the idea that the purpose of government and politics is to maintain the political and economic power of the landed elite. This political culture originated in the antebellum South, where a minority of the population controlled much of the region's land and resources and the majority of the population, slaves and small farmers, owned little or nothing. Political competition takes the form of rivalries between factions within parties, rather than competition between parties. Members of the elite are encouraged to be active politically, while those in the lower social classes are discouraged from political activity.

Individualistic political culture originated in the Middle Atlantic colonies, which were characterized by a central location, prosperity, and economic and cultural diversity. The individualistic political culture emphasizes the view that government and politics are a business and that political participation should result in private benefit. Individuals become active in politics to win office and use the power associated with the office to benefit themselves, people of their ethnic group or economic class, and their communities. Political parties are strong and well-organized, and vigorous two-party competition sets the tone for local and state politics.

Differences among the three political cultures are evident in the distribution of many variables associated with contemporary American government and politics, including those shown in other maps in this atlas. For example, levels of voter turnout tend to be highest under moralistic political culture and lowest under traditionalistic political culture (Maps 2-31 to 2-33). Under moralistic political culture, citizens are expected to vote; under traditionalistic political culture, participation by the masses is discouraged. Federal guarantees of the right to vote associated with passage of the Voting Rights Act of 1965 have reduced the extreme differences shown in Map 2-31, but significant differences in voter turnout remain.

Map 6-1, based on the research of Elazar and modified by the work of Fred Shelley, J. Clark Archer, Fiona Davidson, and Stanley Brunn, shows the contemporary distribution of the three political cultures.[2] In general, each of the three political cultures spread westward as, during the nineteenth century, migrants from the thirteen original colonies and their descendants moved from east to west roughly along the same latitudes. The moralistic political culture is associated not only with New England, but also with the Upper Midwest (Iowa, Minnesota, and Wisconsin) and with the Pacific Northwest. Traditionalistic political culture spread across the South as far west as New Mexico and Arizona, with individualistic political culture in the middle. In the late twentieth century, however, an increasingly mobile and urbanized United States polity has become more attuned to individualistic political culture, with the other two more associated with smaller states and rural areas within states. In addition, many states are a combination of two of the major political culture types. For example, Ohio and Iowa, located between the core areas of moralistic and individualistic political culture, show the influence of both political cultures.

Map 6-2 shows the variation in length of the fifty state

Map 6-1 *Political Culture Areas*

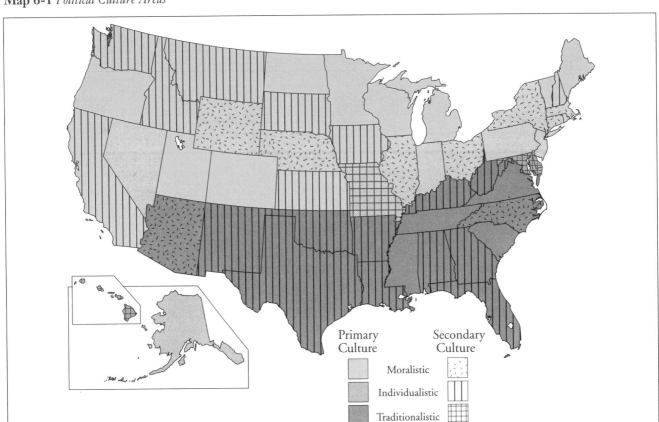

Primary Culture   Secondary Culture

Moralistic

Individualistic

Traditionalistic

Map 6-2 *Length of State Constitutions*

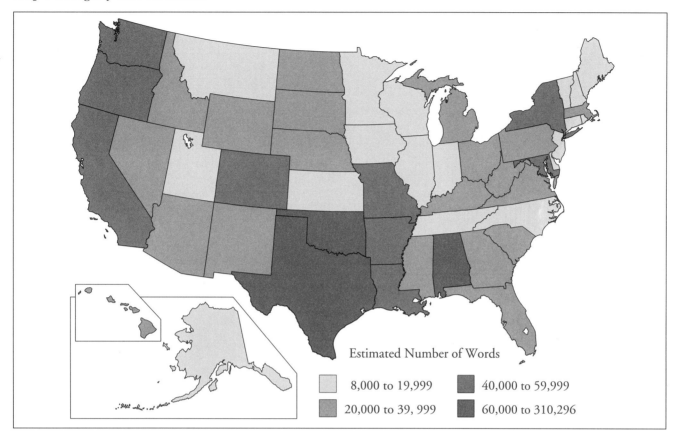

Estimated Number of Words

☐ 8,000 to 19,999   ■ 40,000 to 59,999

■ 20,000 to 39, 999   ■ 60,000 to 310,296

constitutions. Like the federal government, each state has a constitution that establishes and legitimates its system of government. The constitution specifies matters such as the length of term for the governor and other state officials and the duties and responsibilities of the governor, legislature, and judiciary.

The lengths of state constitutions present an opportunity to compare the states because the variations are significant. More than a third of the states have constitutions of less than 18,000 words. The longest state constitutions—those of Alabama, Oklahoma, and Texas—are each more than 40,000 words. In general, the length of the constitution is associated with the political culture underlying each state. Most of the states in the moralistic political culture region have fairly short constitutions, while the states with a traditionalist political culture have relatively long constitutions. The longer documents usually contain many detailed provisions that stipulate or limit the powers of state governments. Once in place, these constitutional provisions are difficult to alter because of the stringent constitutional amendment procedures that must be followed. Shorter constitutions tend to embody more generalized provisions, giving state legislatures greater flexibility to make changes to

their states' legal frameworks by enacting more easily altered statutes. The greater flexibility associated with shorter constitutions in moralistic states indicates that public participation is considered a civic duty, and therefore the public and its representatives are given considerable latitude in enacting policies that are seen as consistent with the common good. Longer state constitutions associated with traditionalistic political culture, on the other hand, may represent distrust of the masses of the population and may help to reinforce control by the elite.

State Governance

The governor of each state serves a fixed term established by law in that state. Map 6-3 illustrates the length of the governor's term for each state and whether the state imposes a limit on the number of terms a governor may serve. In most states, the governor serves a four-year term. The majority of states elect their governors in "off years," even-numbered years that are not presidential election years. Others elect governors in the same year the president is elected, and four—Kentucky, Mississippi, New Jersey, and

Map 6-3 *Gubernatorial Terms and Term Limits*

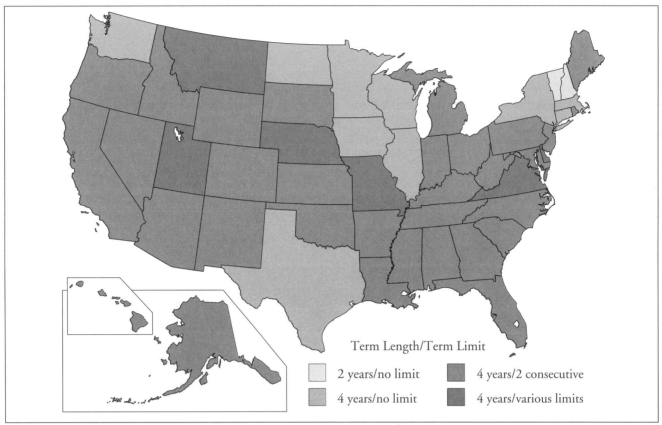

Term Length/Term Limit

- ☐ 2 years/no limit
- ☐ 4 years/no limit
- ☐ 4 years/2 consecutive
- ☐ 4 years/various limits

Virginia—elect their governors for four-year terms in odd-numbered years.

At one time, many governors served two-year terms, but that changed over the course of the twentieth century. Since 1960, for example, the states of Arkansas, Iowa, Michigan, and Texas, among others, have increased the term of the governor from two years to four. New Hampshire and Vermont are the only states that continue to elect governors for two-year terms.

States vary as to how many consecutive terms a governor may serve. Ten states, most of which are located in the North, allow their governors to serve an unlimited number of consecutive terms. The majority of states, however, limit their governors to two consecutive four-year terms. The other states have different limits. Virginia, for example, does not allow its governor to serve consecutive terms.

Map 6-4 shows the date of enactment of term limits for governors among the forty states that impose such limits (Map 6-3). Although most of the states have imposed their current term limits since 1950, the restrictions in New Jersey and Delaware have been in effect since the U.S. Constitution was drafted in 1787. As we saw in Map 6-3, ten states have no term limits.

During the early 1990s, several states enacted term limits for members of Congress, state officials, and other elected officials. By the mid-1990s, many western states had attempted to limit the number of terms that could be served by members of Congress. In *U.S. Term Limits v. Thornton* (1994), which originated in Arkansas, the Supreme Court declared that states could not impose term limits on federal offices. The Court's ruling did not apply to the election of state officials, however. Each state has considerable latitude to establish its own procedures for the election of its officials, provided that these procedures do not conflict with federal law.

The impact of the term-limit movement in the West is shown in Map 6-4. Most of the states in the Interior West enacted their current term limits beginning in 1990. Others, along with the Great Plains states of Kansas, Nebraska, Oklahoma, and South Dakota, did so in the 1980s. Many southern states also enacted their current term-limit laws in the 1970s or 1980s. In contrast to the western states, many had not allowed their governors to succeed themselves until that time. Most states in the Northeast and Midwest that limit the governor's terms did so prior to 1980.

Map 6-5 shows the length of state senate terms in each

Map 6-4 *Year of Enactment for Gubernatorial Term Limits*

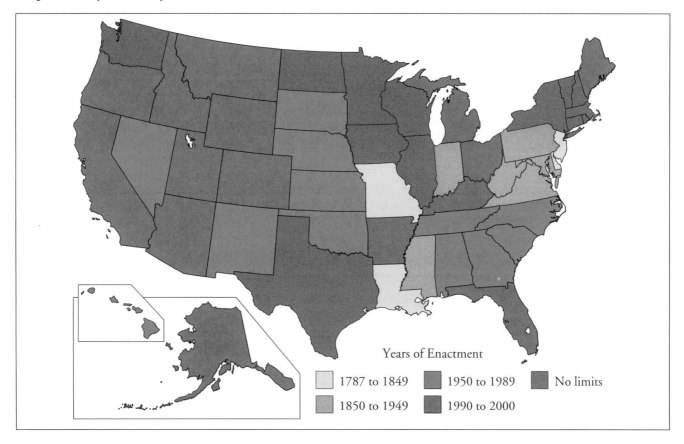

Years of Enactment

☐ 1787 to 1849	■ 1950 to 1989 ■ No limits
■ 1850 to 1949	■ 1990 to 2000

of the fifty states. The upper house of the legislature is called the senate in most states. Forty-nine states vest legislative power in a bicameral, or two-house, legislature. The exception is Nebraska, which has had a unicameral (one-house) legislature, known as the senate, since the 1930s. Twelve states elect senators for two-year terms. These include the six New England states and neighboring New York, along with Arizona, Georgia, Idaho, North Carolina, and South Dakota. The remaining thirty-eight elect their senators for four-year terms.

Term limits for senators are found in some two-year and four-year states. Arizona, Idaho, Maine, and South Dakota limit their state senators to four terms of two years. The remaining eight states that elect senators every two years do not limit the number of terms that can be served. Among the thirty-eight states with four-year state senate terms, most of the western states limit their senators to two or three terms. In the East and Midwest relatively few of the states have enacted term limits. This difference reflects the success of the term-limits movement of the mid-1990s in the West, and its relative lack of success in the eastern half of the country. The states that do not limit the number of terms that a governor can serve (Map 6-3) also do not limit

the terms of their senators. Across the country, states are more likely to limit the number of terms a governor may serve than to limit the terms of members of the state senate.

Map 6-6 shows the time frame in which states with term limits for state senators enacted them. The majority of the states with term limits enacted them between 1990 and 1994, when the term-limits movement reached its peak. Louisiana, Nebraska, and Nevada have done so since 1996. Massachusetts and Washington enacted term limits, which were later voided by legislative or judicial action. Map 6-6 reinforces the fact that term limits for elected officials are more commonplace in the western half of the country than in the East.

The judicial power in each of the fifty states, like that of the federal government, is vested in a state supreme court and other courts. Map 6-7 illustrates the procedures by which justices of the supreme court of each state are selected. Only twenty-seven states provide for gubernatorial appointment of supreme court justices; in the other states, the justices are elected.

In ten states the governor, subject to consent of one or both houses of the state legislature, uses a procedure analogous to that of the federal government to appoint state

Map 6-5 *State Senate Terms and Term Limits*

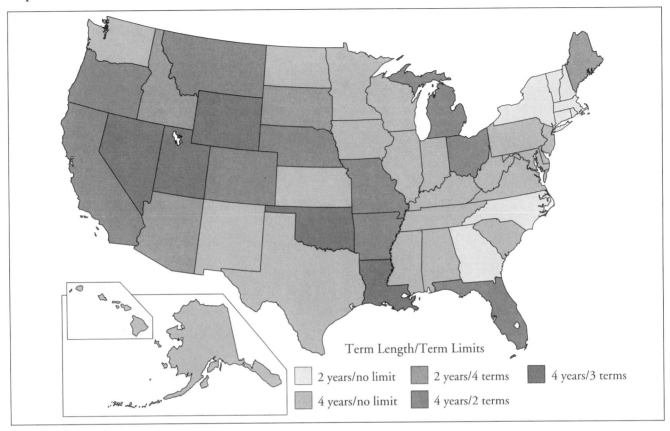

Term Length/Term Limits

2 years/no limit   2 years/4 terms   4 years/3 terms

4 years/no limit   4 years/2 terms

Map 6-6 *Years of Enactment for State Senate Term Limits*

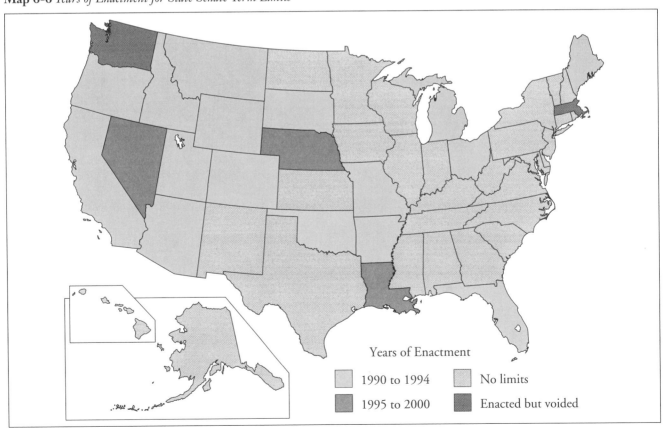

Years of Enactment

1990 to 1994   No limits

1995 to 2000   Enacted but voided

supreme court justices. These include the six New England states along with Hawaii, New Jersey, South Carolina, and Virginia.

In seventeen other states the governor appoints justices of the supreme court. Once appointed, however, the justices must face the voters in retention elections on a periodic basis. At times, retention elections can be highly politicized and bitter, as in 1986, when the voters of California ousted Chief Justice Rose Bird and two other justices on the grounds that they were allegedly soft on crime. Most of the states that follow this procedure are located west of the Mississippi River, although Florida, Indiana, Maryland, and Tennessee also use it.

The remaining twenty-three states elect their supreme court justices. In eight, justices run as members of political parties on partisan ballots. Because individual justices are seldom as well known to the public or as controversial as candidates for governor or other partisan offices, the fate of individual justices often depends on the outcome of other partisan elections. In a year in which a popular Republican nominee heads the ticket, the Republican candidates for supreme court seats would have an advantage, and the same would hold for Democrats. In the other fifteen states, justices run for office but are chosen on nonpartisan ballots.

States using this method are, for the most part, in the moralistic and traditionalistic political culture areas, where political parties tend to be weaker than in individualistic states (Map 6-1). They include the northern tier of states from Michigan to Washington but also include the Deep South states of Alabama, Georgia, and Mississippi.

The initiative is a device that enables voters to place constitutional amendments or legislative statutes on statewide ballots. Map 6-8 shows the states that currently provide for statewide initiatives.

During the early twentieth century, the Progressive movement swept the United States. Reformers advocated major changes in government procedures, including the use of the initiative. Typically, an initiative is placed on the ballot if signed by a specified number or percentage of the state's registered voters. If approved by a majority of the voters at a subsequent statewide election, the statute proposed in the initiative is enacted into law or the proposed amendment is added to the state's constitution, as the case may be.

A large majority of the states that permit statewide initiatives are located in the western United States. East of the Mississippi, only seven states provide for initiatives; west of the Mississippi, only seven states do not. Most western states provide initiatives for both the constitution and statutes, but

Map 6-7 *Selection of State Supreme Court Judges*

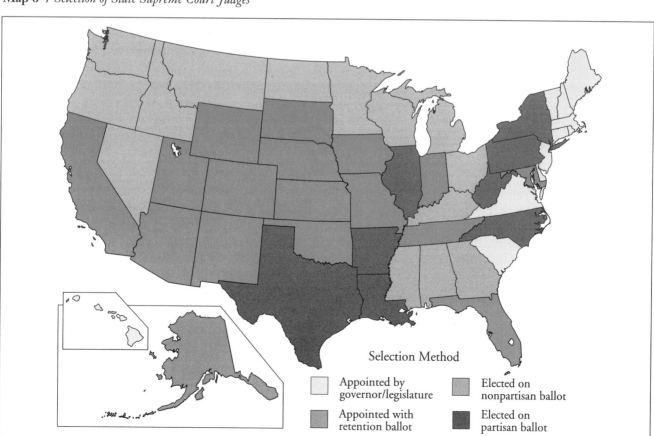

Selection Method

- Appointed by governor/legislature
- Appointed with retention ballot
- Elected on nonpartisan ballot
- Elected on partisan ballot

Map 6-8 *Amendment by Statewide Initiative*

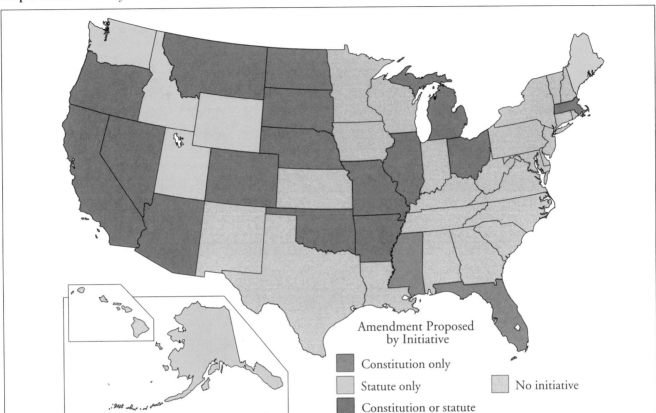

Amendment Proposed
by Initiative

Constitution only

Statute only

Constitution or statute

No initiative

several northwestern states, along with Maine and Alaska, permit the initiative only for statutes. Florida and Mississippi limit the use of initiatives to constitutional actions only.

Map 6-9 shows the states that permit recall of their officials and which officials are subject to recall. As with the use of the initiative, reformers in the Progressive movement also advocated procedures that enable the electorate to recall state officials. Under recall procedures, the voters are empowered to hold an election to determine whether a state official will be permitted to continue in office. A petition signed by a specified number or percentage of the state's registered voters initiates the recall. At a subsequent general election, the voters decide whether the official in question is to be recalled. If a majority supports the recall petition, the official is removed from office.

As with the initiative procedure (Map 6-8), the recall procedure is concentrated in the western United States. Only five eastern states provide for recall, but a majority of the western states do. Types of recall procedures vary considerably from state to state. Arizona, California, Georgia, Minnesota, Nevada, and Wisconsin allow all elected officials to be recalled. Several others, including Alaska, Colorado, Louisiana, and Washington, apply recall provisions to

elected executive or legislative officials but do not allow the recall of some or all judicial officers. North Dakota and Oregon allow recall of state officials but not members of Congress. Montana, New Jersey, and Rhode Island allow various combinations of state officials to be recalled.

Map 6-10 shows the states that permit the governor to exercise the line item veto. Under the system of checks and balances created by the U.S. Constitution, the chief executive has the right to veto legislation, and the legislature generally has the right to override a veto. At the federal level the president has the same right, and Congress also has the right to override. A two-thirds majority vote in each house of Congress is required to override a presidential veto. These strictures apply to entire pieces of legislation, normally so comprehensive that presidents are reluctant to exercise the veto. The line-item veto permits the chief executive to veto individual portions of legislation. Generally, the line-item veto is applied to spending bills. Executive officers holding the power of line-item veto can delete specific items without vetoing the entire budget bill.

Presidents have long advocated a law granting them the line-item veto. In 1996 Congress voted to grant the president line-item veto authority, but the power was short-lived.

Map 6-9 *Recall Provisions*

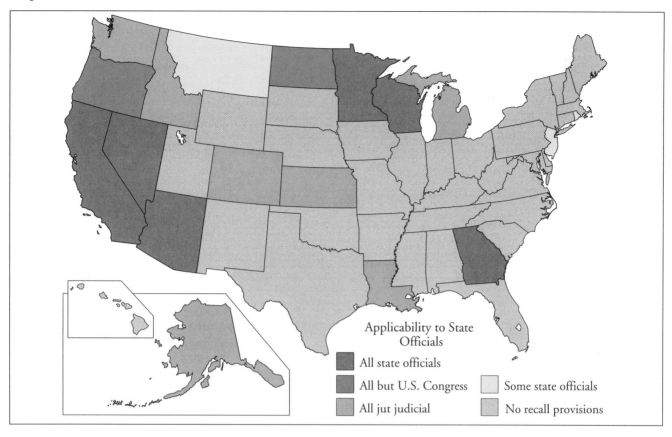

Applicability to State Officials

- All state officials
- All but U.S. Congress
- All jut judicial
- Some state officials
- No recall provisions

Map 6-10 *Gubernatorial Powers: Appropriations Item Veto*

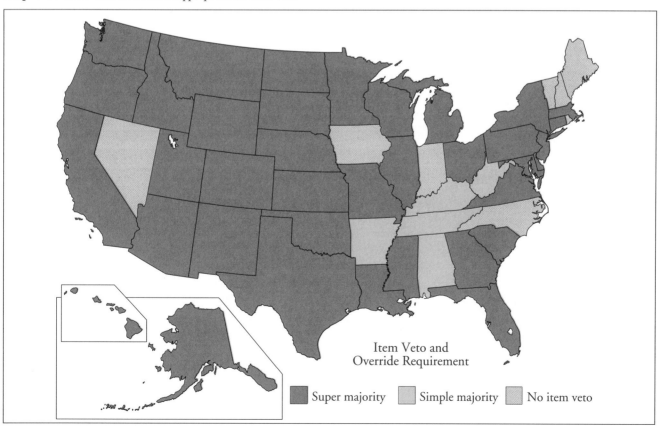

Item Veto and Override Requirement

- Super majority
- Simple majority
- No item veto

The Supreme Court struck down the line-item veto legislation in *Clinton v. City of New York* in 1998, saying that it violated Article I of the Constitution.

A majority of the states grant the line-item veto authority to their governors. As shown in Map 6-10, forty-two of the fifty states grant the governor authority to veto line items. The eight states that do not are Indiana, Iowa, Maine, New Hampshire, Nevada, North Carolina, Rhode Island, and Vermont. Of the remaining forty-two states, five allow the legislature to override the veto of a line item by simple majority vote. All are small, relatively rural southern states—Alabama, Arkansas, Kentucky, Tennessee, and West Virginia. Simple majority override of a line-item veto makes it difficult for the governor to impose his or her wishes on the legislature in the case of an individual budget item. The remaining thirty-seven states require more than 50 percent concurrence within their legislatures to override line-item vetoes.

Governors' Party Affiliations, 1961–2001

Maps 6-11 through 6-15 show the political party affiliations of the state governors from 1961 to 2001. The governor of each state heads the executive branch and is usually the most recognized, powerful, and influential political figure in each state. As we saw in Maps 6-3 through 6-6, the level of power and responsibility associated with the governor's chair varies from state to state. Regardless of the level of executive power, the governor is usually considered the leader of his or her political party within the state and may exert a good deal of influence over the party's activities. The governor's influence ranges from appointment of critical executive branch directors and selection of state judges to party organization on the county and state levels for presidential, senatorial, and even U.S. House elections. Governors also influence the redrawing of redistricting maps following the decennial census. Their importance in national politics has grown as well; four of the last five presidents (Carter of Georgia, Reagan of California, Clinton of Arkansas, and Bush of Texas) were governors of their states before moving to the White House.

Map 6-11 shows the party affiliations of state governors in 1961. Because governors serve terms of two to four years, the political party distribution of state governors in 1961 was the result of elections held in 1958, 1959, and 1960. The 1958 elections were off-year elections during the sec-

Map 6-11 *State Governor Party Affiliation, 1961*

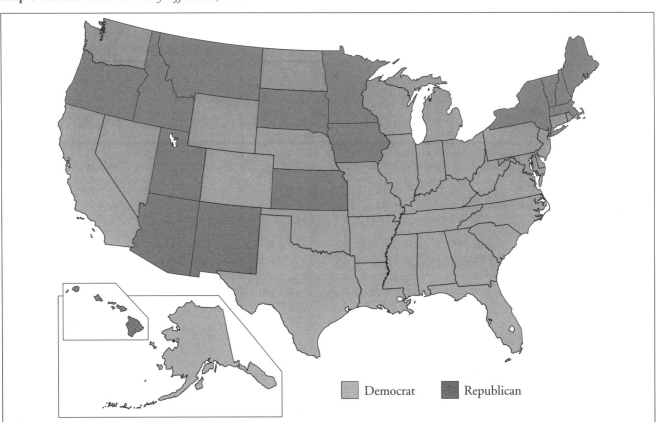

Democrat   Republican

ond term of Republican president Dwight D. Eisenhower. The president's party usually suffers losses in midterm elections, and the Republicans were at a further disadvantage because of a severe economic recession. The Democrats won twenty-five out of the thirty-three gubernatorial seats in 1958, including large states such as California, Michigan, Ohio, Pennsylvania, and Wisconsin where Republicans were strong. The larger national political picture tends to influence gubernatorial elections held in a presidential election year. In 1960 Democratic senator John F. Kennedy of Massachusetts defeated Republican vice president Richard M. Nixon of California (Maps 2-1 and 2-2), and the campaign affected governors' races in some states. After the 1958, 1959, and 1960 elections, the Democrats held a 34–16 edge in state executives, more than a two-thirds majority. This majority is the largest of the elections under consideration and one of the largest in the 1960–2000 period.

Map 6-11 illustrates the extent of the 1961 Democratic gubernatorial majority. Democrats controlled the South and the Border States, displaying a classic post–Civil War pattern. In addition to this traditional area of strength, Democrats held the governorships in all of the large Midwest industrial states, such as Illinois, Michigan, and Ohio, that were

suffering recession. Pockets of traditional northern Republican strength remained in New England and New York, the Upper Midwest, and several states in the Interior West. The Democratic control of governors in so many pivotal states, as well as California, Connecticut, and Pennsylvania, allowed them to exert strong influence over the post-1960 census congressional and state legislature redistricting. This control, in turn, helped to continue Democratic domination of the U.S. House of Representatives discussed in Chapter 3 and the state houses and state senates in the 1960s.

Map 6-12 shows the political party distribution of governors in 1971, resulting from elections in 1968, 1969, and 1970. The gubernatorial races in 1968 were simultaneous with the presidential election between former Republican vice president Richard Nixon and Democratic senator Hubert H. Humphrey of Minnesota (Maps 2-5 and 2-6). The Nixon victory and rising sentiment against the Vietnam War helped the Republicans in some state races. After the 1968, 1969, and 1970 elections, the Democrats held a 29–21 edge in state executives, a margin somewhat reduced from 1961.

Despite their continuing majority of governorships, in 1971 Democrats controlled only nine of the eleven in the

Map 6-12 *State Governor Party Affiliation, 1971*

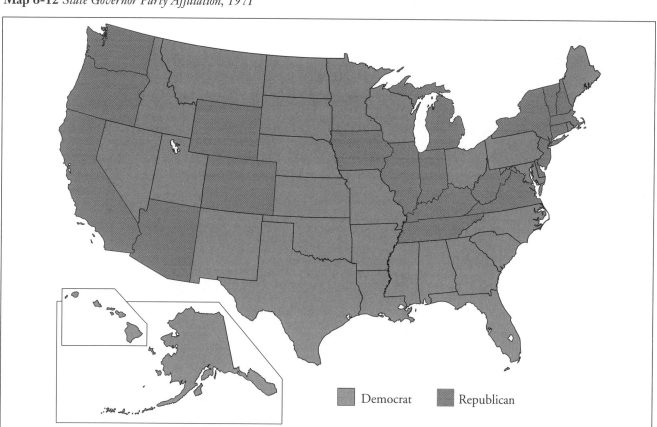

Democrat   Republican

Deep South. In 1969 Republican Linwood Holton had won a historic gubernatorial election in Virginia. Holton was the first Republican governor of Virginia and one of the few elected in the Deep South since the Civil War and Reconstruction. Between the 1940s and 1960s, many Republicans, some of whom worked for the Defense Department at the Pentagon or were on active duty in the armed forces, moved into northern Virginia's suburbs. Their support for Republican candidates for statewide office, coupled with traditional Republican support in the mountainous western part of the state, made the Old Dominion a competitive two-party state in state elections. In 1970 Tennessee elected a Republican governor, the first in more than fifty years. Arkansas had elected its first Republican governor, Winthrop Rockefeller, in 1966, but a Democrat, Dale Bumpers, defeated Rockefeller in his race for reelection in 1970. In this period the Democrats were competitive in the Great Plains and some Interior West states, and this strength contributed to their majority. Republicans continued to be represented in the Northeast and regained governorships in the Midwest and along the Pacific Coast.

Map 6-13 shows the political party distribution of governors in 1981, resulting from elections held in 1978, 1979,

and 1980. By 1981 the partisan control of governorships was almost even, with twenty-seven Democrats and twenty-three Republicans. This closeness reflects the changes in political parties, the growing unpopularity of President Jimmy Carter, and the landslide election of Ronald Reagan to the White House.

Democrats remained strong in the southeastern states, but two more Deep South states had Republican governors for the first time since Reconstruction. Texas elected its first Republican governor, William P. Clements, in 1978, and Louisiana elected David C. Treen in 1979. Democrats were competitive in the West and made inroads in New England, perhaps because the party was becoming recognized as more sympathetic than the Republican Party to the economies of declining regions. For example, in 1978 Democrat Hugh J. Gallen won in New Hampshire, where in the 100 years between 1875 and 1975 a Democrat had sat in the governor's chair for only ten years. Sixteen years earlier, the first Democratic governor since the 1850s was elected in Vermont. Although gubernatorial elections were becoming more nationally competitive, the traditional regional Republican hold on governors' chairs in the Midwest and Upper Midwest is still evident in Map 6-13.

Map 6-13 *State Governor Party Affiliation, 1981*

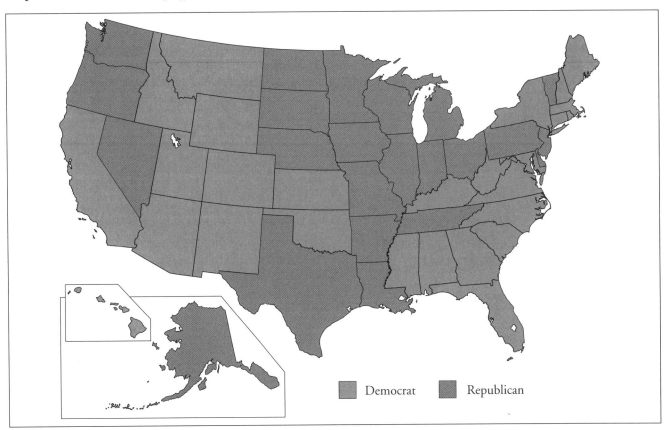

Map 6-14 shows the political party distribution of governors in 1991, resulting from elections in 1988, 1989, and 1990. The Democrats held a 27–21 edge in governors. This lead was similar to that seen after the political party realignment in the early 1930s. Elections to the House of Representatives and, to some extent, to the Senate, showed the same general Democratic dominant pattern. Democratic governors were found in all regions, including the Great Plains and West. Two states, Alaska and Connecticut, seated independent governors in 1991.

Map 6-14 shows that Republicans retained control in a majority of states in their traditional areas of strength in New England and the Midwest. First-time Republican governors in the South include Guy Hunt in Alabama, who had been elected in 1986 and reelected in 1990.

Map 6-15 shows the political party distribution of governors in 2001, resulting from elections in 1998, 1999, and 2000. The Republicans had twenty-nine governors, the Democrats had nineteen, and there were two independents, Angus King of Maine and Jesse Ventura of Minnesota. The Republicans' substantial numbers were the culmination of many demographic and political trends in the 1990s. In 1994 the Republicans had won the U.S. House of Repre-

sentatives for the first time since 1954. Similar Republican results occurred in senatorial and gubernatorial races, not only in 1994, but also in 1996, 1998, and 2000. At the turn of the century the Republicans held more governors' chairs than at any time in recent history, giving the party an important advantage in the congressional redistricting period in 2001 and 2002.

The most notable pattern in Map 6-15 is the cluster of states in the Interior West and Great Plains regions. The Interior West had become a "solid" Republican region on all levels of elections—presidential (Chapter 2), congressional (Chapter 3), and gubernatorial. The Great Plains region has been consistent in its support of Republican presidential candidates, and in recent times has given the edge to Republican governors. In 2001 Republicans controlled the governorship in three of the four most populous states, Florida, New York, and Texas.

As in presidential and congressional elections, the Democrats did well in the Pacific Coast states of California, Oregon, and Washington. In the South the Democrats controlled a line of states from North Carolina through Mississippi. Georgia has had only Democratic governors since the early 1870s, making it the last gubernatorial remnant of

Map 6-14 *State Governor Party Affiliation, 1991*

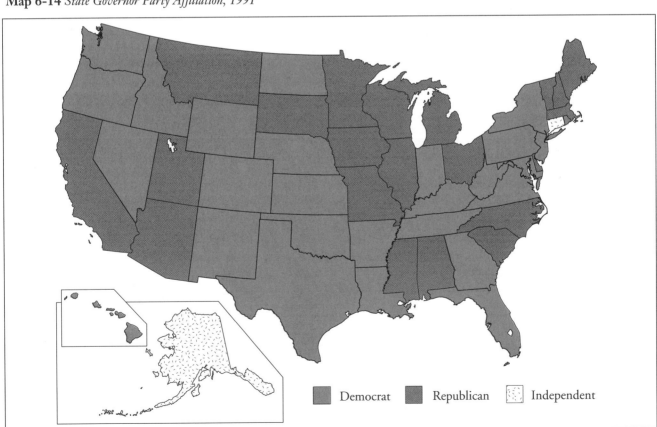

Democrat   Republican   Independent

Map 6-15 *State Governor Party Affiliation, 2001*

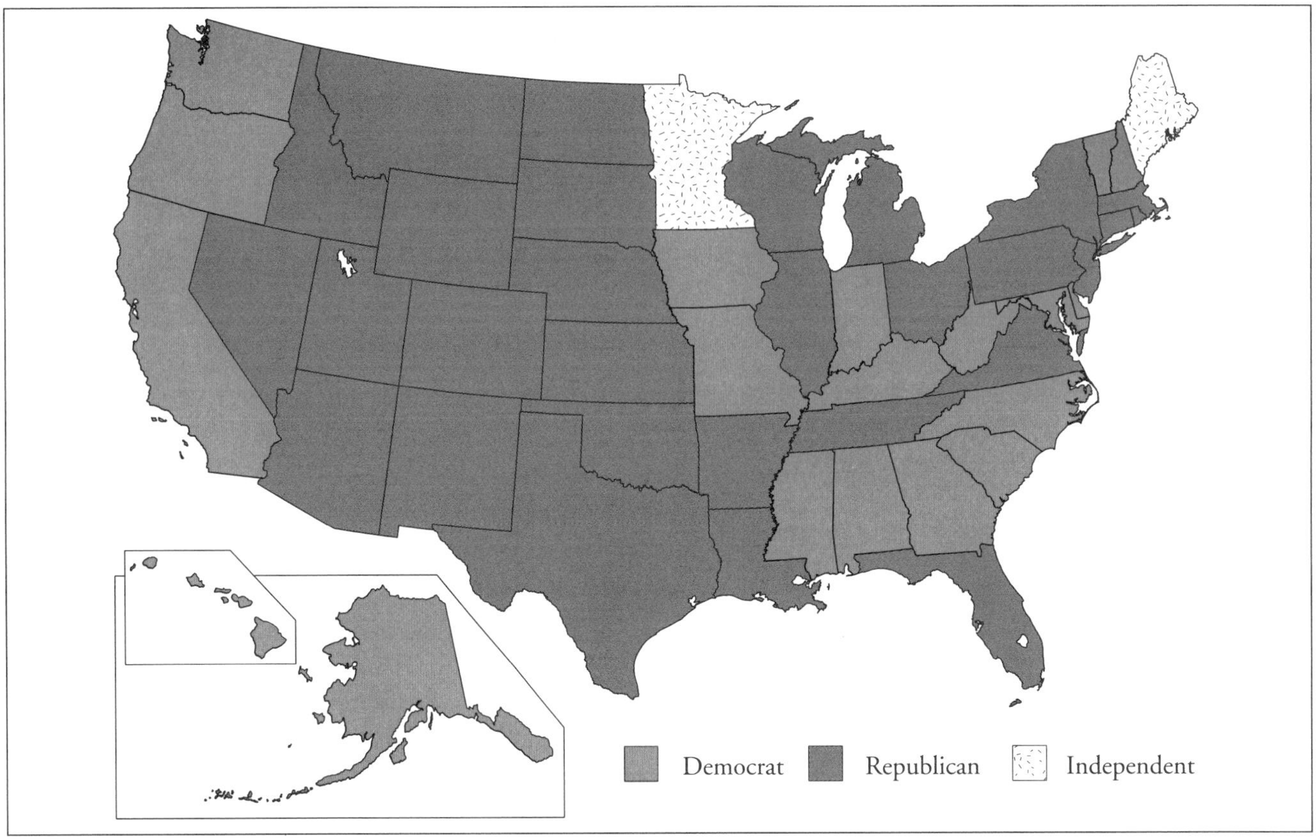

Democrat   Republican   Independent

the North-South pattern from the Civil War. Georgia aside, the traditional North-South cleavage has all but disappeared, but, if the Republicans continue to dominate the Interior West, a substantial East-West pattern may emerge in the twenty-first century as a new political and electoral geographical configuration.

State Senators' Party Affiliations, 1961–2001

The upper chamber of each state legislature is usually called the state senate (Map 6-5). For purposes of this atlas, this term is used to designate all state upper chambers. State senates range in size from Alaska's twenty members to Minnesota's sixty-seven members. Along with partisan control of the lower house of the legislature and the governor's chair, partisan control of the state senate is one of the critical points in the lawmaking process.

Maps 6-16 through 6-20 illustrate the political party affiliation of state senators from 1961 to 2001. The maps show six possible categories: 75 percent to 100 percent Republican, 75 percent to 100 percent Democrat, 51 percent to 74 percent Republican, 51 percent to 74 percent

Democratic, a 50 percent to 50 percent split, and nonpartisan. States with more than 75 percent control by one party are referred to as "dominant" for that party.

Map 6-16 shows the political party control of state senates in 1961. Democrats controlled thirty state senates and were dominant, with more than 75 percent of the seats, in nineteen of these. Republicans controlled seventeen state senates and were dominant in only three. Pennsylvania was evenly divided, and two states, Minnesota and Nebraska, were nonpartisan. (In 1934 Nebraska began placing candidates on a nonpartisan ballot as a reform measure.) The Great Depression political realignment in the early 1930s had made the Democratic Party the majority party in much of the United States, and the 1961 state senate map reflects this dominance. What is striking about Map 6-16, however, is the general electoral geography of the parties. Indeed, the 1961 state senate map shows one of the strongest regional patterns of all the maps in the atlas. All of the states in which the Democrats had more than 75 percent of the state senate lie in a continuous band, running south of the Mason-Dixon line through the Deep South, then west to California and the Pacific Coast. The pattern is a reflection of the southern tier post–Civil War

Map 6-16 *State Senate Party Affiliation, 1961*

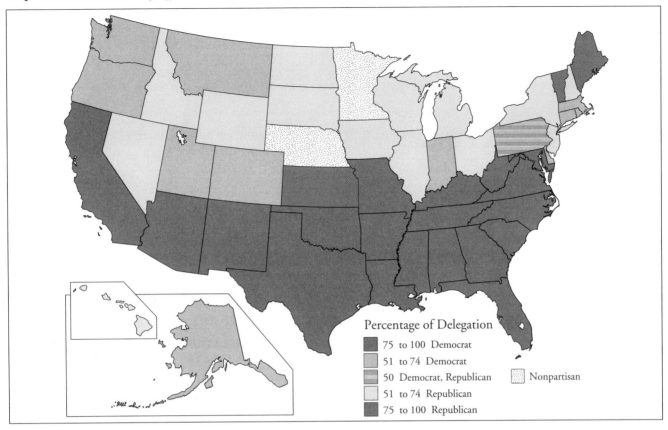

Percentage of Delegation

- 75 to 100 Democrat
- 51 to 74 Democrat
- 50 Democrat, Republican
- 51 to 74 Republican
- 75 to 100 Republican
- Nonpartisan

Reconstruction pattern, illustrated and discussed in Chapters 2 and 3.

As was pointed out in the discussion of Map 6-1, population geographers have demonstrated that much internal migration during the westward movement of the nineteenth century occurred east to west. In other words, migrants from New England and the Northeast moved directly west and over time settled the Midwest, the Upper Midwest, and the remaining northern tier. Migrants from the Southeast migrated west into Texas and even farther into New Mexico, Arizona, and southern California. Migrants take with them not only their possessions but also their "political baggage" of political parties and traditions. Map 6-16 may be one of the best illustrations of the remnants of this heritage in American political geography. By 2001, as illustrated in Maps 6-1 and 6-20, the traditionalistic southern tier had largely abandoned its support for Democrats, and Republicans had made major inroads into state legislatures throughout the South.

Republican strength in state senates in the early 1960s was found along the northern tier. Two of the three states that the Republicans dominated were in northern New England. Southern New England, however, had a strong

Democratic presence because of the area's patterns of industrialization and immigration. The two nonpartisan states, Minnesota and Nebraska, are northern states with a history of progressive and reform government, and both display the moralistic tradition of American political culture.

In 1971 the Democrats controlled twenty-seven states senates and dominated in thirteen. These numbers show a loss in both categories from 1961. The Republicans controlled eighteen states and dominated five, up slightly in both categories from a decade earlier. Three states were split 50 percent to 50 percent, and two were nonpartisan. Map 6-17 shows the striking national political geography of the political parties evident in Map 6-16. Democrats dominated in the Deep South and southern New England, and, as in 1961, the Republicans' greatest strength was along the northern tier.

Despite this continuity, Map 6-17 also shows the beginnings of political change. In the South, the Democrats were no longer the dominant party in Florida and Tennessee. Republicans had made sufficient inroads in these states to elect more than 25 percent of the members of the state senates. Florida was changing rapidly through northern migration. Tennessee experienced some migration from the

Map 6-17 *State Senate Party Affiliation, 1971*

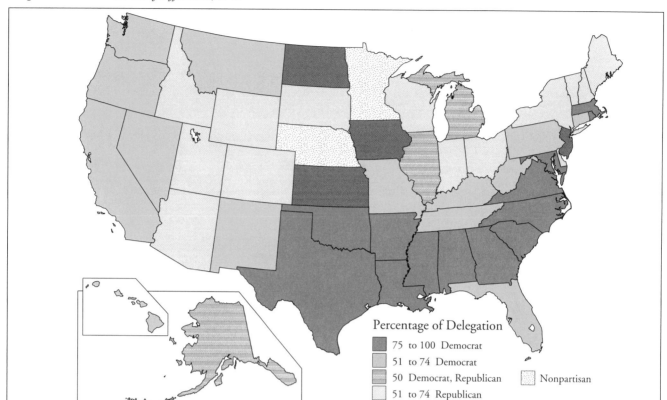

Percentage of Delegation

- 75 to 100 Democrat
- 51 to 74 Democrat
- 50 Democrat, Republican
- 51 to 74 Republican
- 75 to 100 Republican
- Nonpartisan

north, which, coupled with its historic Republican presence in the eastern mountains, made the GOP competitive in state elections. As we saw in Map 6-12, by 1970 both states had elected Republican governors.

The 1971 state senates also show change in the southwest, most radically in Arizona, which switched from a dominant Democrat state to a majority Republican. Demographic changes tilted the state closer to the GOP. In 1960 Arizona's population was quite small, so that even modest migration was able to change the political culture of the state. Many of the new arrivals were middle and upper class retirees from the North, especially from the Upper Midwest.

In 1981 the Democrats controlled more than 60 percent of state senates. Map 6-18 shows that Democrat domination continued in the South, even through this region gave Republican presidential candidate Ronald Reagan a smashing victory in 1980. Ticket-splitting had become commonplace in both the North and South, with many voters choosing one party on the national level and another on the state and local level.

Across the country, Democrats controlled thirty-one state senates, Republicans controlled eighteen, and Nebra-

ska remained nonpartisan. Republicans showed a majority in the Northeast, Upper Great Plains, and Interior West. In one Interior West state, Utah, more than 75 percent of the state senate was Republican. The changing nature of the two political parties, as demonstrated by Reagan's nomination and election, tilted the Interior West more toward the Republicans.

Map 6-18 also shows a change in Minnesota, which officially had a nonpartisan legislature from 1913 to 1973. In 1981 the Minnesota state senate was dominated by the Democrats. Since Minnesota reverted to a partisan legislature, Nebraska is the only state to have nonpartisan elections.

Map 6-19 illustrates that Democratic Party control of state senates continued into 1991. Thirty-two states favored the Democrats, while thirteen favored the Republicans. Four states were evenly divided, and one was nonpartisan. The GOP strength was clustered in two well-defined northern tier areas stretching from the Northeast to the Midwest and from the Interior West to the Central Great Plains. The two other states in which they were a majority also lie along the northern tier.

The Democrats retained control of the senates of six states in the core South with more than 75 percent of the

Map 6-18 *State Senate Party Affiliation, 1981*

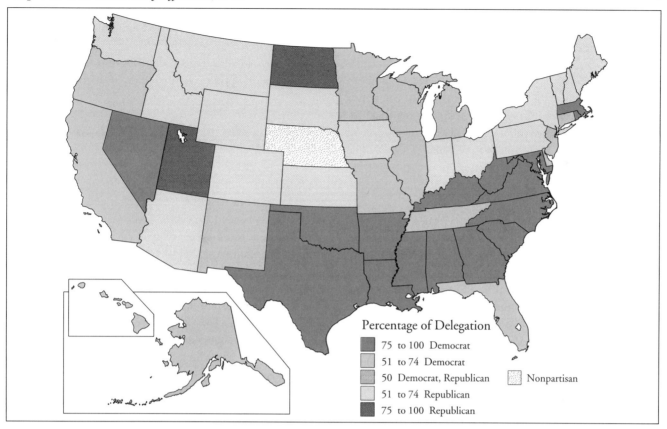

Percentage of Delegation

- 75 to 100 Democrat
- 51 to 74 Democrat
- 50 Democrat, Republican
- 51 to 74 Republican
- 75 to 100 Republican
- Nonpartisan

Map 6-19 *State Senate Party Affiliation, 1991*

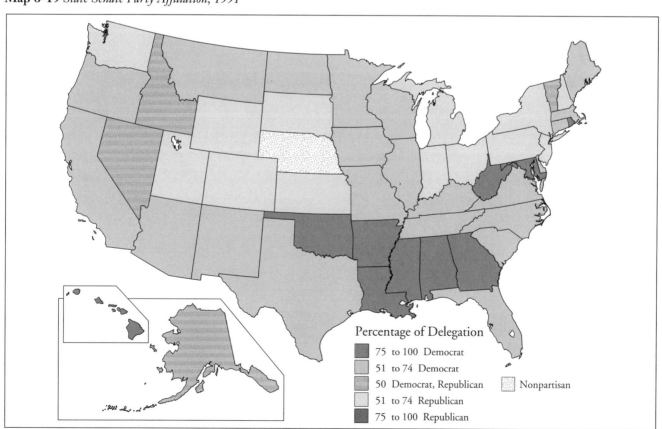

Percentage of Delegation

- 75 to 100 Democrat
- 51 to 74 Democrat
- 50 Democrat, Republican
- 51 to 74 Republican
- 75 to 100 Republican
- Nonpartisan

state senate. Compared to 1961, however, total control in the Deep South had eroded. In many southern states, Republicans had become a significant minority in the state senate. Outside of the South, the Democrats were represented in all regions.

Map 6-20 shows the party affiliations of state senates in 2001 and illustrates the changes in strength of the major political parties in the United States that began in 1994. The 1994 election is generally regarded as the beginning of a partisan political realignment of the American people. The 1994 election and subsequent elections may have made the Republican Party the majority party in the United States, and the dominance was apparent in the state legislatures.

In 2001 the GOP controlled twenty-four state senates, compared to twenty-two for the Democrats; three state senates were split 50 percent to 50 percent, and Nebraska continued to be nonpartisan. Map 6-20 shows that the Republican Party controlled most of the states along the northern tier of the nation. More significant, the party also held a majority in three large Deep South states, Florida, Texas, and Virginia, and South Carolina's senate was evenly divided. The 2001 map illustrates a monumental change from the 1961 map. The Democrats still controlled the core of the Deep South and had pockets of regional strength in New England, the Upper Midwest, and the Southwest. The GOP controlled the state senates in three of the four largest states, Florida, New York, and Texas. Republican strength was likely to continue because the party that controls the state senate enjoys an advantage in the congressional and legislative redistricting process following the decennial census.

State House Members' Party Affiliations, 1961–2001

Maps 6-21 through 6-25 illustrate the political party affiliations in state houses, the lower chamber and largest branch of state legislatures, 1961–2001. Some states give this chamber a different name; in Maryland, Virginia, and West Virginia, for example, it is known as the House of Delegates, and in California and Wisconsin it is the State Assembly. This atlas uses state house to identify all lower chambers of state legislatures. State house size ranges from Alaska's 40 members to Pennsylvania's 203 members and New Hampshire's gargantuan 400 members. In states with a large number of members, state house districts tend to be small and representatives tend to be long-time members of the local community and close to the people.

Map 6-20 *State Senate Party Affiliation, 2001*

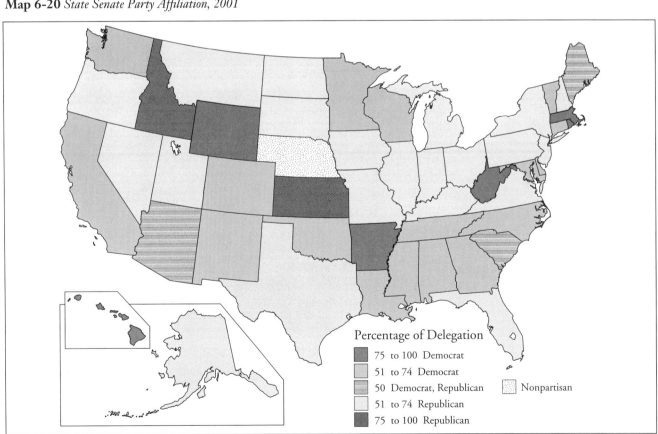

Percentage of Delegation

- 75 to 100 Democrat
- 51 to 74 Democrat
- 50 Democrat, Republican
- 51 to 74 Republican
- 75 to 100 Republican
- Nonpartisan

Partisan state house composition is divided into five categories: 75 percent to 100 percent Republican, 75 percent to 100 Democratic, 51 percent to 74 percent Republican, 51 percent to 74 percent Democratic, and a 50 percent–50 percent division. Nebraska, with its unicameral legislature, is excluded.

Map 6-21 shows the political party control of state houses in 1961. Democrats controlled thirty-one state houses and were dominant in sixteen, Republicans controlled seventeen and were dominant in only two, and one state, Minnesota, was nonpartisan. The pattern is quite similar to that of state senates illustrated in Map 6-16. Fifteen of the sixteen states in which the Democrats had more than 75 percent of the state house were in a group south of the Mason-Dixon line. This pattern reflects the post–Civil War Reconstruction pattern illustrated and discussed in Chapters 2 and 3. Republican strength in state houses in the early 1960s lay along the northern tier. Vermont and South Dakota were the only states in which Republicans dominated with more than 75 percent of the legislative seats.

Map 6-22 shows the political party control of state houses in 1971. In spite of having a Republican president, the United States in 1971 had Democratic majorities in the Senate, the House of Representatives, and many state legislatures, and was still a Democratic majority nation. The 92d Congress had large Democratic majorities in the Senate and House. On the state level the party controlled the majorities in state senates, as shown in map 6-17, and state houses. The margin in the state houses was 27–21, with Minnesota again nonpartisan.

Map 6-22 shows a clear geographical pattern of state house control. As in the 1961 map, the Democrats dominated the states south of the Mason Dixon line, from Maryland through Texas. The party also controlled the state houses of all the other southern states and the Border States. The Republicans continued to show strength along the northern tier. In addition, in the 1960s the GOP gained strength in the West, a region in which they controlled the majority of state houses for the rest of this period.

Map 6-23 shows the political party control of state houses in 1981, when the Democrats controlled thirty-two state houses compared to seventeen for the Republicans. The Watergate scandal of the early 1970s had a devastating effect on the Republican Party. The Democrats, already the majority party, had made gains in Congress, especially in 1974, but Watergate hurt the GOP in elections at every level, including for state legislatures and local officials. The Democrats' dominance occurred in spite of the over-

Map 6-21 *State House Party Affiliation, 1961*

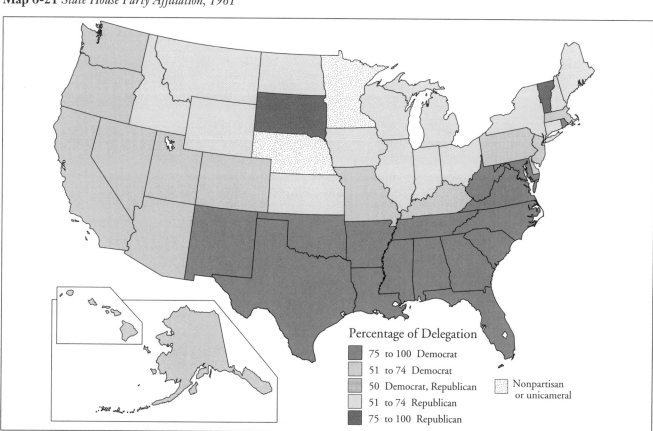

Percentage of Delegation

75 to 100 Democrat
51 to 74 Democrat
50 Democrat, Republican
51 to 74 Republican
75 to 100 Republican

Nonpartisan or unicameral

Map 6-22 *State House Party Affiliation, 1971*

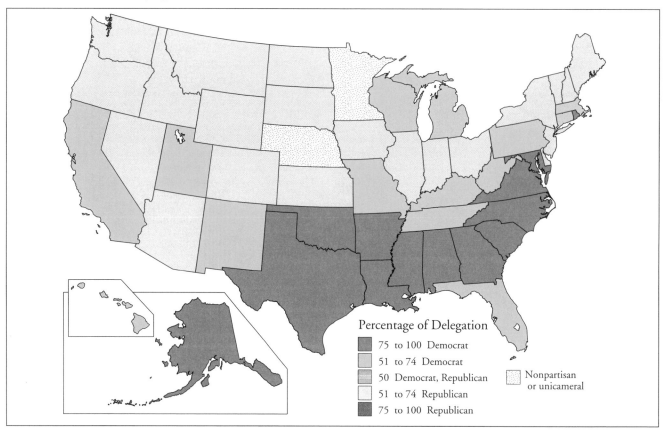

Percentage of Delegation

- 75 to 100 Democrat
- 51 to 74 Democrat
- 50 Democrat, Republican
- 51 to 74 Republican
- 75 to 100 Republican
- Nonpartisan or unicameral

Map 6-23 *State House Party Affiliation, 1981*

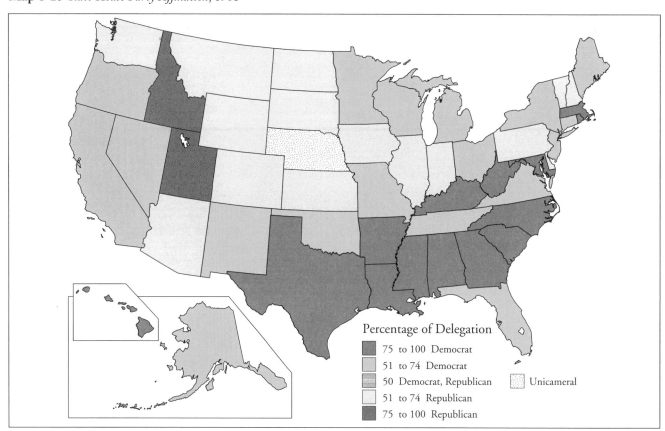

Percentage of Delegation

- 75 to 100 Democrat
- 51 to 74 Democrat
- 50 Democrat, Republican
- 51 to 74 Republican
- 75 to 100 Republican
- Unicameral

whelming 1980 presidential victory of Republican Ronald Reagan. Clearly, voters engaged in large-scale ticket splitting between national and state candidates.

The Democrats continued their iron grip in the Deep South. In addition, Watergate seemed to have helped them in Northeast and Midwest states. On the other hand, Republicans were strong in the Interior West and in their traditional area of strength in the northern Great Plains. The two states the Republicans overpoweringly controlled were Utah, with its Mormon majority (Map 1-19), and Idaho, both in the Interior West.

Map 6-24 shows the political party control of state houses in 1991, when Democratic control of state legislatures reached its peak. The Democrats controlled thirty-seven state houses versus twelve for the GOP. Map 6-24 shows national domination unequal to any other state house or state senate map. Although much reduced in percentages since 1961, the Democrats still controlled the entire South, including a six-state core region. The eastern half of the nation was Democratic, except for four states. The only large cluster of Republican states was in the West.

The Democrats also dominated the U.S. Congress in 1990 (Maps 3-9 and 3-14), but this period marks the end of the national domination by the Democratic Party, which had begun in the 1930s and had been especially evident since the 1950s. As mentioned in Chapter 3, beginning in the 1970s congressional elections had become more competitive across the country. State house and state senate elections, however, still showed strong regional patterns dating back to the post–Civil War and Reconstruction patterns. Although southern voting patterns have changed at the presidential and congressional level, state and local races still display a strong heritage.

Map 6-25 shows the political party control of state houses in 2001. In 2001 the Democrats and Republicans were a majority in twenty-four state houses each, and Washington State was evenly divided. These numbers are the highest for the Republicans and lowest for the Democrats in the five periods under review. As discussed above, since the political realignment of the 1930s, and especially since 1954, the Democrats have been considered the national majority party. The maps in Chapter 3 on Congress and in this chapter on governors, state senates, and state houses verify this majority. The 1994 election, however, was a milestone in U.S. electoral history. The Republicans not only regained the U.S. House for the first time in forty years, but also made significant gains in governorships and state legislatures. By pulling even with the Democrats in state houses, the GOP has demonstrated the great strides the party has taken toward possibly becoming the majority party.

Map 6-24 *State House Party Affiliation, 1991*

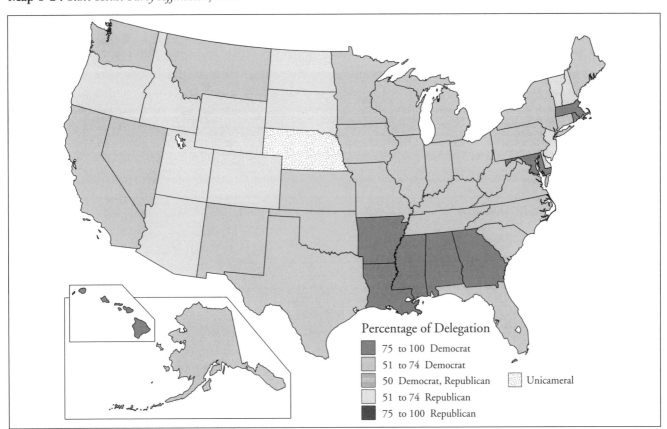

Map 6-25 *State House Party Affiliation, 2001*

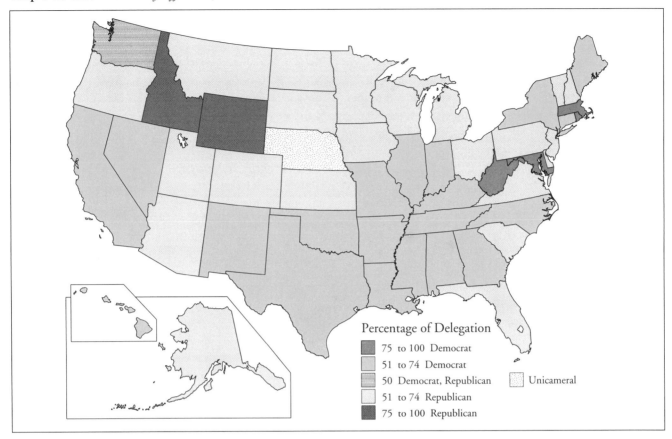

Percentage of Delegation

- 75 to 100 Democrat
- 51 to 74 Democrat
- 50 Democrat, Republican
- 51 to 74 Republican
- 75 to 100 Republican
- Unicameral

Republicans have made gains in state houses in the Coastal South states of Florida, South Carolina, and Virginia, all of which were dominated by the Democrats only a few decades ago. Republicans grew stronger in the Upper Midwest, Upper Great Plains, and Interior West. Democrats maintained strength in the same areas where they do well in presidential elections, the Northeast and Pacific Coast. The largest cluster of Democratic-dominated state houses, however, still is in the South. This pattern is in direct contrast to the 2000 congressional elections, which showed that the Democrats are now the minority party in the South (Map 3-15 and Table 3-3).

Political Culture and State Economics

One of the most important functions of each state's government is the collection of tax revenues and their disbursement to various individuals, agencies, and projects. States raise revenues from a variety of sources, including property taxes, sales taxes, income taxes, lotteries, and sales of services. In Chapter 4, the atlas looked at the distribution of federal outlays and the ratio between federal expenditures

and federal taxes. Maps 6-26 through 6-30 examine aspects of state government tax revenue collection, along with revenue sharing between federal and state governments.

Two factors affect the distribution of tax collections: the wealth of a state and its political culture. In states with a moralistic political culture, citizens believe the purpose of government and politics is to promote the common good. Voters tend to favor an activist government and are often willing to pay higher taxes to achieve higher levels of services. Most of the states with relatively high per capita tax collections are located in the northern part of the country, where the moralistic political culture is found. In addition, states such as Connecticut, Minnesota, New Jersey, and New York tend to have relatively high tax burdens because they have more sources of wealth to tax. Lower taxes and fewer government services characterize states in the traditionalistic political culture. Poorer states have fewer taxable revenue sources, and voters may be less willing to tax themselves at higher rates.

Naturally, there are exceptions to these general principles, and these exceptions often have interesting political implications. For example, New Hampshire is a low-tax state. In fact, it is the only state without a state income tax or sales tax. New Hampshire's revenues come from taxes on property, cigarettes, liquor, hotels and motels, and restaurants. In recent years, many people who work in the Boston area have moved to New Hampshire to escape the higher tax burdens in Massachusetts and elsewhere. These migrants have given the state's politics an increasingly conservative tilt, especially when compared to the rest of liberal New England (see Map 1-21). At the opposite end of the spectrum are people who prefer to combine higher taxes at home with the opportunity to work in a neighboring state where lower taxes attract business. For example, many people working in low-tax Sioux Falls, South Dakota, have chosen to live in neighboring Minnesota or Iowa, where higher taxes provide better schools and public services.

Map 6-26 illustrates the total amount of state taxes collected per capita in each state in 1999. The per capita tax burden varies considerably from state to state, ranging from less than $1,000 per person to nearly $3,000. In general, per capita tax revenues increase from south to north. Connecticut, Delaware, Hawaii, Massachusetts, Michigan, and Minnesota are the highest, with more than $2,399 each. The lowest category includes the four southern states of Alabama, Louisiana, Tennessee, and Texas, along with New Hampshire and South Dakota.

Map 6-27 shows per capita personal income tax collections for states in 1999. All but seven of the fifty states authorize the collection of income taxes. The seven exceptions are Alaska, Nevada, New Hampshire, South Dakota, Texas, Washington, and Wyoming.

Income taxes in the forty-three states that collect them ranged as high as $1,300 per capita per year. The highest per capita income taxes were collected in California, Connecticut, Massachusetts, Minnesota, New York, Oregon, and Wisconsin. These states are associated with moralistic political culture (see Map 6-1) as well as substantial per capita wealth. Income taxes were lower in many southern and western states, although some southern and Border States, such as Georgia, North Carolina, and Oklahoma, had higher per capita income taxes than might otherwise be expected.

Each year grants from the federal government are sent to state and local governments to supplement revenues raised locally through taxes and other collection procedures. Federal aid per capita in some states is nearly equal to the amount of revenues collected locally.

Map 6-28 shows the distribution of federal aid to state and local governments per capita in 1999. The amount of aid ranged from less than $800 per person per year to more than

Map 6-26 *Total State Tax Collections, 1999*

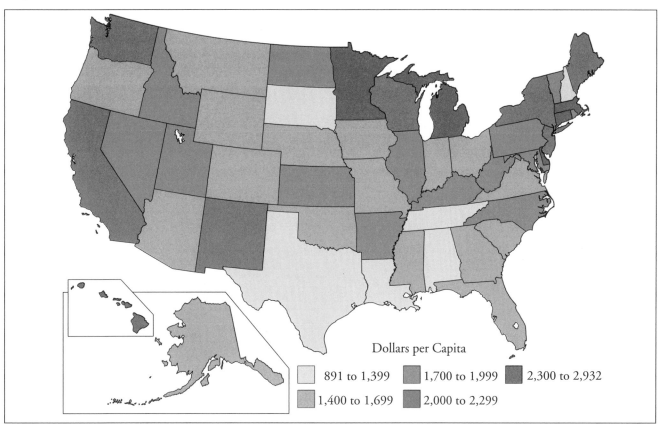

Dollars per Capita

891 to 1,399	1,700 to 1,999	2,300 to 2,932
1,400 to 1,699	2,000 to 2,299	

Map 6-27 *State Personal Income Tax Collections, 1999*

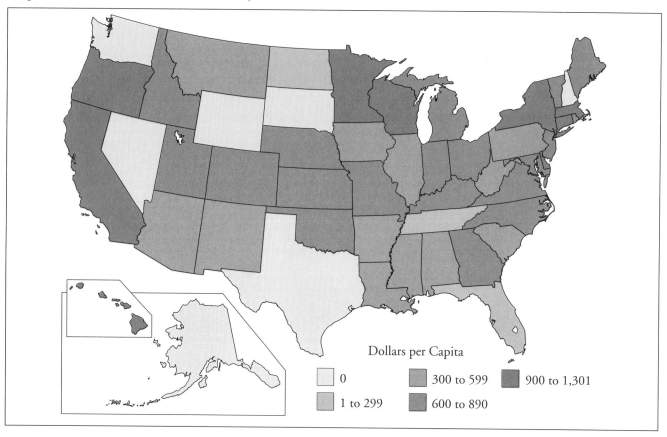

Dollars per Capita

0	300 to 599	900 to 1,301
1 to 299	600 to 890	

Map 6-28 *Federal Aid to State and Local Governments, 1999*

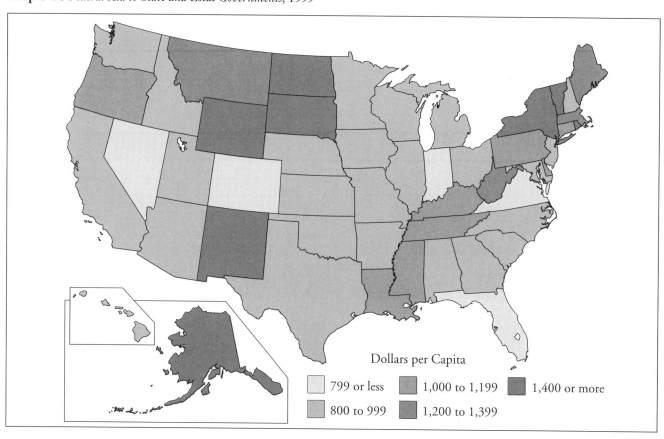

Dollars per Capita

799 or less	1,000 to 1,199	1,400 or more
800 to 999	1,200 to 1,399	

$1,500. The pattern of revenues reflected both the pattern of state taxes (Maps 6-26 and 6-27) and the ratio of federal tax dollars to federal revenues (Maps 4-5 and 4-6). The highest amounts of federal aid per capita went to several western states, along with New York and Vermont. Lower amounts went to states scattered across the country, including Colorado, Florida, Hawaii, Indiana, Nevada, and Virginia.

Map 6-29 shows the annual proceeds raised from state-administered lottery funds in 1998. New Hampshire in 1964 became the first U.S. state to authorize a state-run lottery to raise revenues. Today, thirty-seven of the fifty states sponsor lotteries, many of which were authorized by public initiatives and referenda (Map 6-7). In recent years, voters in Oklahoma and North Dakota turned down proposals to authorize their states to sponsor lotteries. The thirteen states that do not allow lotteries include several in the Upper South, along with Alaska, Hawaii, and some western states. Ironically, one of these states is Nevada, which has been a pioneer in legalized gambling since before World War II.

In the states that authorize lotteries, per capita revenues tended to be higher in the East and lower in the West. With the exception of Oregon and South Dakota, states in the western half of the country raised less than $25 per capita per year with their lotteries. The highest per capita lottery funds came from Delaware, Massachusetts, Oregon, Rhode Island, and South Dakota. States in New England, the Middle Atlantic states, and Great Lakes states, along with Florida, Georgia, and Texas also received fairly high levels of revenue from lottery proceeds.

The approximately 80,000 units of local government in the United States include more than 3,000 counties, many thousands of incorporated cities and towns, and numerous school districts and other units, such as flood control districts, conservation districts, and other special government districts. Local governments are created by the states, and laws within each state determine their authority, responsibility, and specific powers. Each unit of local government is empowered to collect taxes. Some of these revenues are raised through property taxes; sales taxes; hotel, motel, and restaurant surcharges; and user fees.

Tax revenues collected locally are supplemented by aid from the federal government and the states. In some states, nearly half of the revenues expended by local governments are raised through aid from the states in which they are located; in others, more than 80 percent of local revenues are raised locally.

Map 6-30 shows the distribution of state aid as a percentage of total local government revenue for 1996. States in which a high proportion of local revenues came from state aid

Map 6-29 *Proceeds from State-Administered Lottery Funds, 1998*

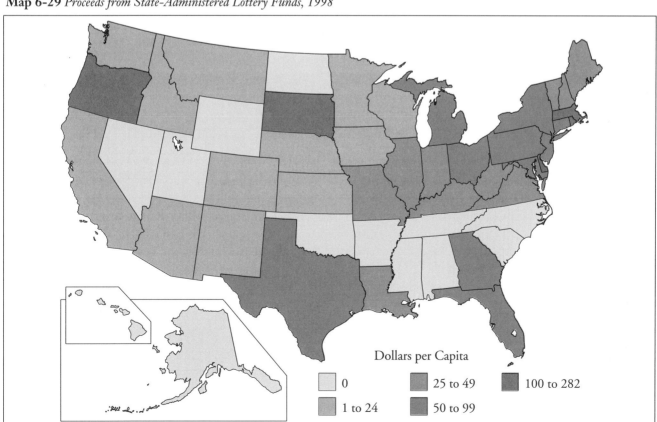

Dollars per Capita

0	
1 to 24	
25 to 49	
50 to 99	
100 to 282	

Map 6-30 *State Aid to Local Governments, 1996*

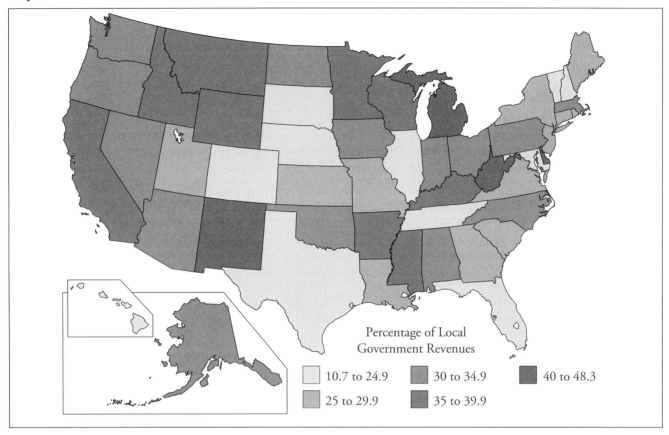

Percentage of Local
Government Revenues

10.7 to 24.9	30 to 34.9	40 to 48.3
25 to 29.9	35 to 39.9	

were scattered across the United States, but concentrated in the North and West. Most of the states west of the Rocky Mountains provided substantial amounts of aid to local governments. Relatively low percentages of state aid were found in the Southeast and the Northeast, especially in New England. Older states, with long established local governments, gave less state aid to local governments than younger states did. The exceptions to this general trend were found in Colorado, Hawaii, and Utah, where local governments relied more heavily on local revenues, and in Kentucky, Michigan, and West Virginia, where state aid levels were high.

Map 6-31 shows the salaries of governors of the fifty states for 2000. Each state pays its governor a salary, which varies from $60,000 to $170,000 per year. The amount of money paid to a governor has sometimes aroused political controversy. Advocates of high salaries point out that people qualified to be governor or to hold other state positions are also qualified to earn much larger salaries in the private sector and that an attractive salary encourages the best candidates to run for governor. Opponents argue that the salaries of state officials are substantially higher than average per capita incomes and that many governors are independently wealthy and not motivated to run

for public office because of financial considerations.

Ten states—California, Illinois, Maryland, Massachusetts, Michigan, Minnesota, New Jersey, New York, Pennsylvania, and Washington—paid the highest salaries, $120,000 per year or more. These states are relatively populous and wealthy, and each has one or more major metropolitan areas that would provide opportunities for talented people to earn large salaries outside of government. Smaller and more rural states that lack major metropolitan centers tended to pay their governors relatively low salaries. With the exception of the urbanized and wealthy Pacific Coast states, most of the western states paid low governor's salaries. The states in the East tended to pay higher salaries. In the South, the highest salaries were found in the most metropolitan states—Florida, Georgia, Texas, and Virginia. The best predictors of a governor's salary, therefore, are the wealth and metropolitan status of the state.

Local Elected Officials

The 80,000 units of local government in the United States are empowered to elect their legislative and, in many cases,

Map 6-31 *Governors' Salaries, 2000*

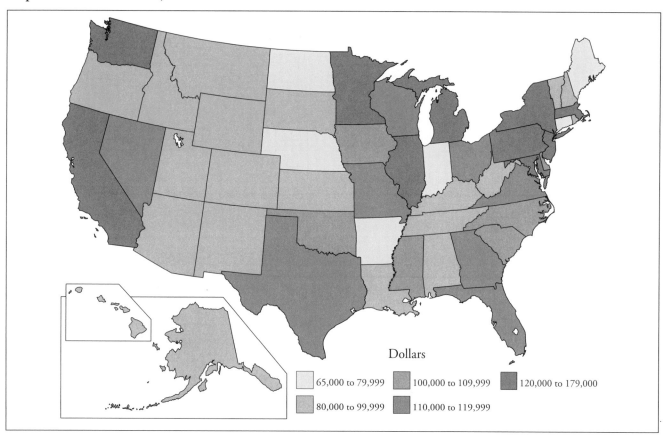

Dollars

☐ 65,000 to 79,999	☐ 100,000 to 109,999	■ 120,000 to 179,000
☐ 80,000 to 99,999	☐ 110,000 to 119,999	

executive officers. Today, approximately 500,000 Americans serve as elected local government officials—mayors, city and county council members, school board members, and the like.

Map 6-32 presents the ratio of elected officials to the overall population and shows an interesting comparison. Nationwide, there were roughly 18 elected officials per 10,000 population. On a state-by-state basis, however, this ratio varied from less than 10 to more than 200 per 10,000 population. The highest ratios of elected officials to overall population were found in the northern Great Plains and adjacent states, along with northern New England. Low ratios were concentrated in the South and along the Pacific Coast. This distribution reflects the intersection of political culture (Map 6-1) with urbanization. High numbers of elected officials are found in moralistic states, where the political culture emphasizes political participation as a civic duty. Ratios of elected officials to overall population are also considerably higher in rural states, where more local government units serve smaller numbers of people, than in urban states. In New England, for example, the ratios were higher in Maine, New Hampshire, and Vermont than in the more urbanized and heavily populated states of Connecti-

cut, Massachusetts, and Rhode Island. Highly urbanized Sun Belt states, such as California, Florida, and Texas, had particularly low ratios.

Minority and Female Elected Officials

Over the course of American history, participation in government has grown more diverse, in terms of both voting and holding office. When the U.S. Constitution was ratified, the franchise was limited for the most part to white men. Gradually, African Americans and other minorities and women were granted the right to vote and began to run for public office. Although some critics argue that a disproportionate number of white men continue to dominate public office in the United States, the number of minorities and women officeholders has increased dramatically in recent years and continues to rise.

Map 6-33 shows the number of African American elected public officials by state in 1998, as a ratio to the state population, expressed as the number per 1 million people. The highest ratio of African American elected officials was in the South, particularly in less urban areas. States in the North-

Map 6-32 *Local Elected Officials, 1992*

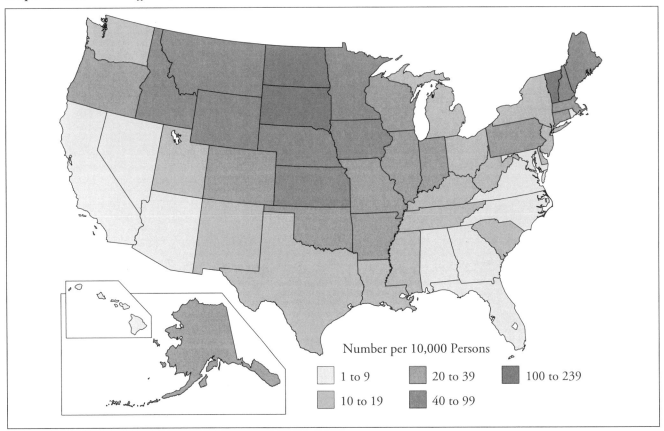

Number per 10,000 Persons

1 to 9	20 to 39	100 to 239
10 to 19	40 to 99	

Map 6-33 *Black Elected Officials, 1998*

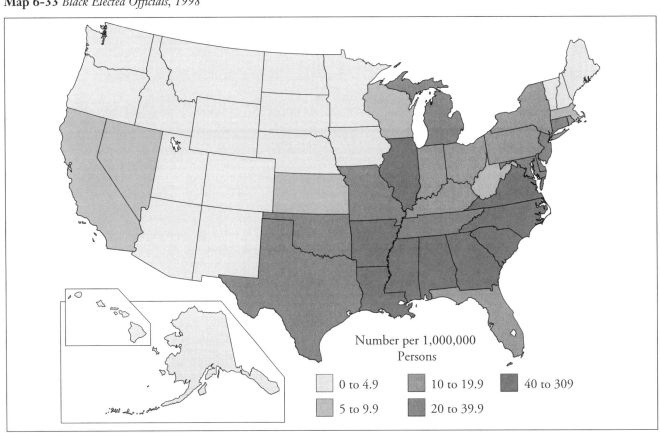

Number per 1,000,000 Persons

0 to 4.9	10 to 19.9	40 to 309
5 to 9.9	20 to 39.9	

east with substantial urban African American populations, including Connecticut, Illinois, Michigan, Missouri, and New Jersey, also had relatively high ratios. Low ratios were concentrated in the rural West, where African American populations are low (Map 1-12). To some extent, Map 6-33 also illustrates rural-urban differences. On a per capita basis, it was more likely that African Americans would serve in public office in less urban states with relatively high African American populations, for example, Alabama, Mississippi, and South Carolina. Large states, such as California, Florida, and New York, reported relatively few African American public officials despite their large African American populations.

Map 6-34 shows the ratio of Hispanic elected officials to the total population in 1994. The 2000 census showed a dramatic increase in the number of Americans of Hispanic descent in the United States, a trend that will no doubt also increase the numbers of Hispanic officeholders.

In contrast to Map 6-33, which shows a comparable ratio of African American elected officials, Map 6-34 shows a highly clustered distribution. Only five states—Arizona, Colorado, Illinois, New Mexico, and Texas—had more than forty Hispanic elected officials per 1 million population. Of these, all but Illinois have had large, nonurban populations

of Mexican and Spanish ancestry for many years. Map 1-13 shows that Hispanics, primarily of Mexican descent, made up a large majority of the population in much of South Texas, northern New Mexico, southern Colorado, and parts of Arizona. (Many Hispanics in northern New Mexico and southern Colorado refer to themselves as Spanish American rather than Mexican American because their ancestors moved to what is now the United States before Mexico became independent of Spain in the early nineteenth century.[3]) In such places, persons of Hispanic ancestry have served as county commissioners, city council members, mayors, and school board members for many years.

Most of the rest of the country had fewer than ten Hispanic elected officials per 1 million population. Despite large urban Hispanic populations in Florida, New Jersey, New York, and other states, relatively few Hispanics have been elected to public office in these states. In general, Hispanic success in achieving public office was concentrated in the states with long-established rural Mexican American communities. Fewer Hispanics from other ethnic backgrounds, including Cuban Americans and Puerto Ricans, have been elected to public office in states outside of the Southwest, with the notable exception of Illinois.

Before 1900 several states had granted women the right

Map 6-34 *Hispanic Elected Officials, 1994*

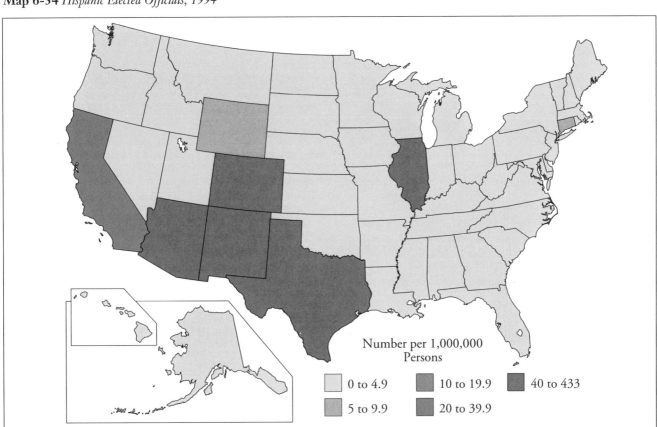

Number per 1,000,000 Persons

0 to 4.9	10 to 19.9	40 to 433
5 to 9.9	20 to 39.9	

Map 6-35 *Women in State Legislatures, 1999*

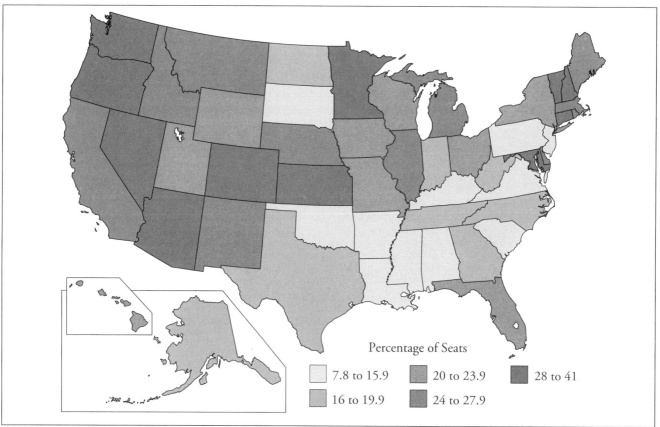

Percentage of Seats

7.8 to 15.9	20 to 23.9	28 to 41
16 to 19.9	24 to 27.9	

to vote, but women could not vote in all federal elections until the Nineteenth Amendment was ratified in 1919. Since that time, women have participated in the political process and have been elected to public office in increasing numbers. In 2001 more than 10 percent of members of Congress were women.

Perhaps a more significant indicator of the growing prominence of women in American public life is the percentage of women serving in state legislatures, as shown in Map 6-35. Nationwide, about 22 percent of state legislative seats were held by women in 1999. The percentage of seats held by women varied, however, from less than 10 percent in Alabama to more than 40 percent in Washington. Detailed analysis of the number of women in state legislatures by state is provided by Gerald Webster.[4]

The highest percentages of female legislators were found in the West. Wyoming was the first state to grant women the right to vote, and its nickname, the Equality State, stems from that historic decision. Colorado, Idaho, and Utah also granted women the right to vote before 1900. New England had a high percentage of women in its state legislatures. The lowest percentages were in the South, reflecting a long-standing historical trend. The South generally declined to

ratify the Nineteenth Amendment, which became part of the Constitution despite the region's opposition. With the exception of Maryland and Delaware, the percentages in the Middle Atlantic states were also low. This pattern may reflect the individualistic political culture, in which politics is regarded as a business and the opportunity to achieve private benefit.

Conclusion

In accordance with the U.S. Constitution, political power is shared explicitly between the federal government and the states. As a result, state governments have wide latitude to enact specific policies concerning government functions not specifically identified in the Constitution as belonging to the federal government. Even casual travelers across America can note the impact of federalism. Observable differences exist, for example, in alcoholic beverage sales, road quality, police presence, and traffic laws. Such variations demonstrate on a deeper theoretical level that each of the fifty states is an autonomous unit in many areas of governance. The states often act as experimental workshops for laws and practices that the national government eventually adopts. Now-standard laws, such as those abolishing slavery, granting women the right to vote, and protecting the environment, were established first at the state level. Many of the variations in state laws and practices can be traced to the historical political culture discussed at the beginning of the chapter in connection with Map 6-1. The clustering of states with common political cultures has given the United States broad regional political cultures, which, in spite of the homogenization of America in the 1960–2000 period, contribute to our understanding the political geography of this large and complex nation.

Notes

1. Daniel Elazar, *American Federalism: A View from the States*, 3d ed. (New York: Crowell, 1984).

2. Fred M. Shelley, J. Clark Archer, Fiona M. Davidson, and Stanley D. Brunn, *Discovering America's Political Geography* (New York: Guilford Press, 1996).

3. Richard L. Nostrand, *The Hispano Homeland* (Norman: University of Oklahoma Press, 1992).

4. Gerald R. Webster, "Women, Politics, Elections and Citizenship," *Journal of Geography* 99 (2000): 1–10.

Chapter 7

Foreign Policy

The maps in Chapter 7 depict various aspects of U.S. international relations and foreign policy. The topics covered include immigration and immigration policy, deployment of military forces, the distribution of foreign military and nonmilitary aid, and trade.

The United States has long been recognized as a nation of immigrants. For nearly four centuries, people from all over the world have chosen the United States, with its freedoms and opportunities, as their new home. Over the years, however, both the origins and destination areas of immigrants into the United States have undergone change. Today, the preponderance of immigrants come from Latin America and Asia, and a majority settle in the Sun Belt and in large cities, as shown in Maps 7-1 through 7-4.

The next section, Maps 7-5 through 7-11, shows military relationships and U.S. foreign aid. It includes maps of the North Atlantic Treaty Organization, the deployment of U.S. troops, the location of military installations, and recent terrorist incidents. Also included are maps showing the locations of both military and non-military foreign aid.

The final section of the chapter, maps 7-12 through 7-17, focuses on trade relationships between the United States and other countries. The maps show the origins and destinations of imports, the destinations of U.S. exports, and the location of American investment abroad as well as foreign investment in the United States.

Immigrant and Refugee Arrivals in the United States

Throughout its history, the United States has been one of the most favored destinations for international migrants. People anxious to escape poverty, ethnic violence, and religious and political persecution have long identified America as a place to make a new start. For many, the New World was associated with free or cheap farmland, plentiful jobs, and freedom of worship and political expression. Immigrant labor, in turn, proved critical to the emergence of the

United States as a major industrial power during the nineteenth and early twentieth centuries. Prior to the late nineteenth century, the majority of immigrants came from northern and western Europe. By 1890, however, eastern and southern Europe had eclipsed northwestern Europe in the number of immigrants coming to the United States.

After World War I, the United States took steps to limit immigration.[1] The Immigration and Naturalization Act of 1924 established immigration quotas for each country of origin. These quotas were determined on the basis of overall immigration levels dating back to 1790. The highest quotas were awarded to the United Kingdom, Ireland, and Germany because these countries had sent substantial numbers of immigrants to the United States as far back as the late eighteenth century. Countries such as Italy, Poland, and Russia, which did not begin sending large numbers of immigrants to the United States until the late nineteenth century, received smaller quotas. Quotas for non-European countries were very small.

In 1965 new immigration laws repealed national quotas, and immigration from less-developed countries, especially in Asia and Latin America, began to increase. Peace and prosperity in western Europe reduced the flow of European immigrants. Today, a large majority of immigrants into the United States come from Asia and Latin America, although immigration from the former Soviet Union has increased considerably since the collapse of the Soviet government in 1991.

Figure 7-1 is a set of bar graphs depicting immigrant origins from 1821 to 1998. During the nineteenth century, the majority of immigrants into the United States came from Europe. The highest number of immigrants, 8 million, arrived in the first decade of the twentieth century, and more than 95 percent of them were Europeans. The impact of the 1924 immigration act, along with the effects of the Great Depression and World War II, is seen in the relatively low immigration levels evident in the 1930s, 1940s, and 1950s, although European immigrants continued to outnumber those from other countries. During the 1960s immigrants from the Americas outnumbered those from Europe for the

Figure 7-1 *Immigration by Region of Origin, 1821–1998*

Millions of
Immigrants

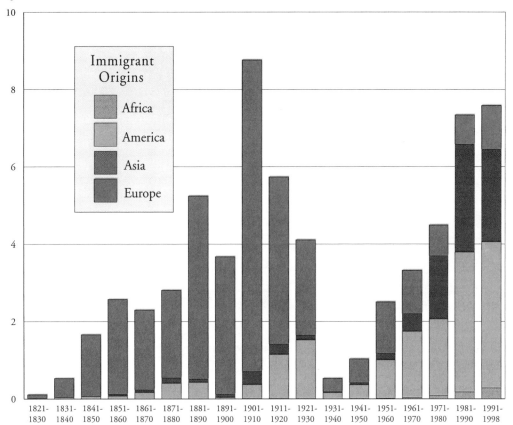

first time. This trend has continued ever since. A slight increase in European immigration in the 1990s may reflect movement from postcommunist Russia and eastern Europe, but Asia and Latin America continued to send the largest numbers of immigrants to the United States.

As we saw in Figure 7-1, the primary origin of immigrants to the United States has varied over the course of American history. Since 1965 the major source areas for immigrants have included Latin America and Asia. Traditional source regions in Europe declined in importance, in part because the prosperity of contemporary western Europe began to approach that of the United States.

Map 7-1 shows the number of legal immigrants admitted into the United States by country in 1998. Mexico was the leading origin of immigrants, followed by the Philippines. Other countries with more than 10,000 immigrants admitted in 1998 included the Latin American countries of Colombia and Peru, along with several Asian countries—China, India, Pakistan, and Vietnam. In addition, postcommunist Russia and eastern Europe, regions that once strongly discouraged emigration, began to send substantial

numbers of immigrants to the United States. Canada was an important, although often overlooked, source of immigration to the United States. Western Europe and Africa continued to send relatively few immigrants.

Where do new immigrants settle after being admitted to the United States? Immigrant destinations, like immigrant origins, have changed considerably over the past two hundred years (Figure 7-1 and Map 7-1). During the early nineteenth century, a majority of immigrants moved to rural areas, primarily in the Northeast and Middle West. After the Civil War, for example, thousands of Germans and Scandinavians obtained farmland through the Homestead Act and settled in the Dakotas, Iowa, Minnesota, Nebraska, and Wisconsin.[2]

When the frontier closed in the 1890s, immigrants began to settle in cities. New arrivals from Bohemia, Hungary, Italy, Poland, and Russia, as well as from other countries in eastern and southern Europe, provided industrial labor in large northeastern and midwestern cities such as Chicago, Cleveland, New York, and Pittsburgh. Many entered the United States through Ellis Island in New York Harbor, but

Map 7-1 *Immigrants Admitted, by Country of Birth, 1998*

Legend:

- 0 to 9
- 10 to 99
- 100 to 999
- 1,000 to 9,999
- 10,000 to 99,000
- 100,000 or more
- No data, or zero

Map 7-2 *Destination States of Immigrants Admitted, 1998*

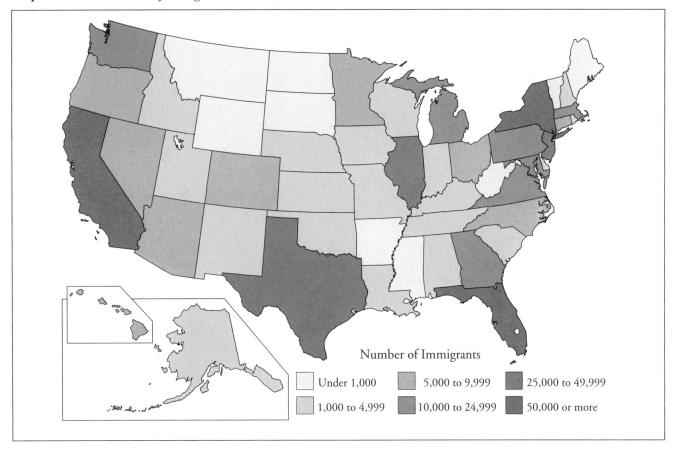

Number of Immigrants

Under 1,000	5,000 to 9,999	25,000 to 49,999
1,000 to 4,999	10,000 to 24,999	50,000 or more

Galveston, Texas, was also a major port of entry.[3] Industrial cities continued to draw the majority of immigrants until the reform of immigration law in the 1960s. Immigrants from Asia and Latin America were more likely to work in the service sector and to settle in the Sun Belt. Cities such as Dallas, Houston, Los Angeles, and Miami began to attract large immigrant populations, but many others continued to select large cosmopolitan cities such as Chicago, New York, and Washington, D.C. As in earlier times, today's immigrants choose their new homes on the basis of employment and professional opportunities. Many immigrants also join existing communities of people sharing the same national origin. For example, many emigrants from Arab countries have settled in the Detroit area, which has a large, long-established Arab American community.

Map 7-2 depicts the destination states of immigrants to the United States in 1998. Contemporary immigrants tended to be drawn to large metropolitan areas. The four states with the largest numbers of immigrants—California, Florida, New York, and Texas—were the country's four most populous states. Illinois and New Jersey each attracted more than 20,000 immigrants in 1998. Indeed, these six states were the destinations of more than 85 percent of the country's overall immigrant population. The 2000 census, however, showed a substantial increase in foreign-born persons in smaller, less urbanized states. Georgia, North Carolina, Oregon, and Washington each received more than 5,000 immigrants in 1998. The fewest immigrants were found in rural states with declining economies lacking in tertiary and quaternary sector employment. Arkansas, Maine, Mississippi, Montana, North Dakota, South Dakota, Vermont, West Virginia, and Wyoming each received less than 1,000 immigrants.

Among the reforms associated with the revised immigration law of 1965 was the ability to grant permanent resident status to individuals who could prove they were refugees from political or religious persecution. During the 1960s and 1970s this law allowed numerous refugees to emigrate from Cuba, Vietnam, eastern Europe, and other war-torn areas of the world.

By 1998 the cold war had been over for nearly a decade, but political and religious persecution continued in many parts of the world, causing thousands of refugees to seek permanent resident status in the United States each year.

Map 7-3 *Refugees Granted Permanent Resident Status, by Country of Birth, 1998*

5 to 9

10 to 99

100 to 999

1,000 to 9,999

10, 000 or more

No data, or zero

The distribution of these refugees by country of origin in 1998 is shown in Map 7-3. The largest numbers of refugees came from war-torn Burma and Somalia, along with Russia and the former Soviet republic of Ukraine. Smaller but substantial numbers of refugees arrived from Azerbaijan, Belarus, Ethiopia, Kazakhstan, and Sudan. Not surprisingly, refugee flows were highest from countries with recent histories of war and violence and from those lacking histories of stable democracy.

Map 7-3 examines the destination states of refugees granted permanent resident status in 1998. Although less than a tenth of legal immigrants are refugees, to a considerable extent, the pattern of immigrant settlement (Map 7-2) is similar to the pattern of refugee settlement. The largest numbers moved to the largest states, notably California, Florida, and New York. These three states alone accounted for more than half of all recent refugees. Others settled in Michigan, Minnesota, and Washington. These states attracted a larger number of refugees than might be expected, given the overall distribution of immigrants. Refugees may be choosing these states because of their relatively liberal political climate and the established communities of people from their countries of origin—for example, Arab Americans in Michigan and Southeast Asians in Minnesota.[4] The smallest numbers, as with immigrants in general, were found in small rural states with weak economies.

Military Relationships and U.S. Foreign Aid

In 1947 President Harry Truman responded to Soviet attempts to establish communist governments in Greece and Turkey by announcing the Truman Doctrine, which stated that the United States would actively oppose further Soviet expansion in Europe. The North Atlantic Treaty Organization (NATO) was established in 1949 as a military alliance in support of the Truman Doctrine. The NATO members agreed to defend one another in the event of a Soviet military invasion.[5] NATO was a cornerstone of American foreign policy during the cold war. Along with the Marshall Plan (see Map 7-10), NATO represented American efforts to contain Soviet influence in post–World War II Europe.

Map 7-4 *Destination States of Refugees Granted Permanent Resident Status, 1998*

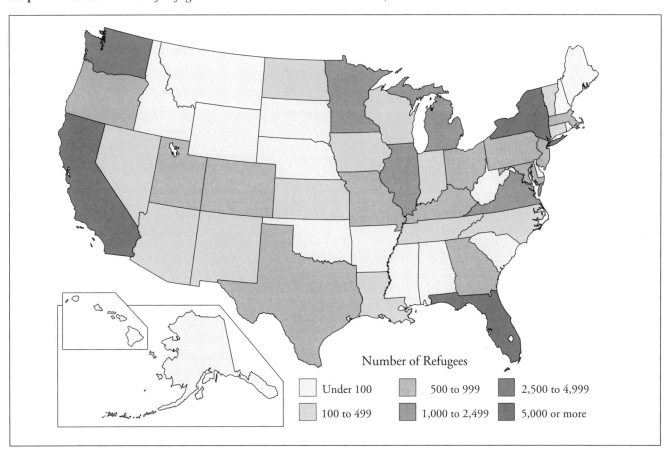

Number of Refugees

Under 100
100 to 499
500 to 999
1,000 to 2,499
2,500 to 4,999
5,000 or more

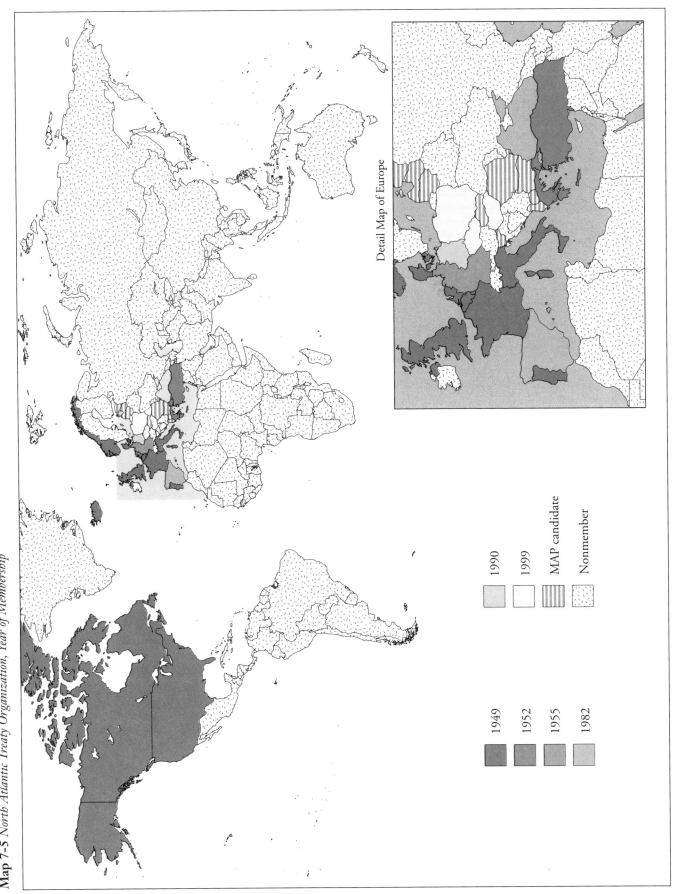

Map 7-5 *North Atlantic Treaty Organization, Year of Membership*

Detail Map of Europe

1949
1952
1955
1982

1990
1999
MAP candidate
Nonmember

Map 7-5 shows the membership of the North Atlantic Treaty Organization as it evolved over time. In 1949 the original members were the United States, Canada, and ten west European countries. Greece and Turkey, which were the focal points of the Truman Doctrine, joined in 1952, and West Germany was added in 1955. The membership of NATO remained stable until the late 1990s with two exceptions: France withdrew in the late 1960s, but later rejoined, and Spain joined in 1982. In 1997 the first east European members—Poland, the Czech Republic, and Hungary—were accepted.[6] Nine additional east European countries have applied for membership. These NATO Membership Action Plan candidates include the former Soviet republics of Estonia, Latvia, and Lithuania, the former Yugoslav republics of Montenegro and Slovenia, along with Albania, Bulgaria, Romania, and Slovakia.

As we saw in Chapter 4, the Defense Department is one of the federal government's largest employers, with military and civilian employees throughout the United States. Map 7-6 shows the deployment of Defense Department military and civilian personnel across the fifty states in 1999. Not surprisingly, the largest numbers of employees were found in the largest states. California and Texas each had more than 80,000 defense workers. Georgia, North Carolina, and Virginia, however, each had more defense employees than the much larger states of Illinois, Ohio, Michigan, and New York. Virginia is home to the Pentagon, the Defense Department's headquarters, and to a large naval base in Norfolk. Military installations in the other two states include Camp Lejeune in North Carolina and Fort Benning in Georgia. Other small states with large military bases and substantial numbers of Defense Department employees included Colorado, Hawaii, Oklahoma, and South Carolina.[7]

Smaller states tended to have relatively few Defense Department personnel, as might be expected. Several populous states, such as Massachusetts, Michigan, Tennessee, and Wisconsin, have relatively few because they lack active military bases.

Map 7-7 shows the distribution of U.S. active duty military personnel throughout the world in 1999. Since World War II thousands of Army, Navy, Air Force, and Marine Corps members have been on active duty on U.S. military bases, at sea, and in other operations in many different countries. Over time, the distribution of military person-

Map 7-6 *Military and Civilian Defense Department Personnel, 1999*

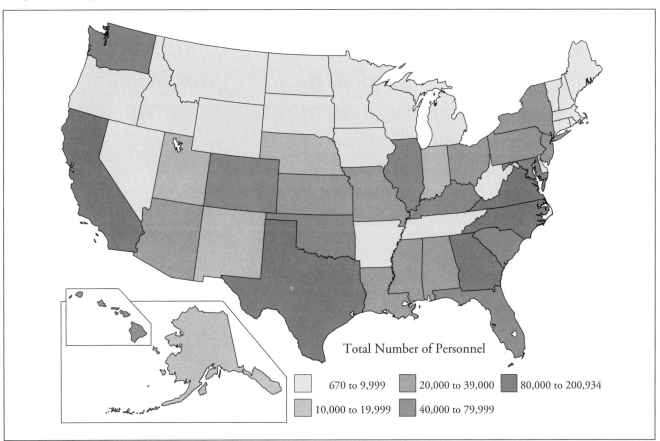

Map 7-7 *Active Duty U.S. Military Personnel, 1999*

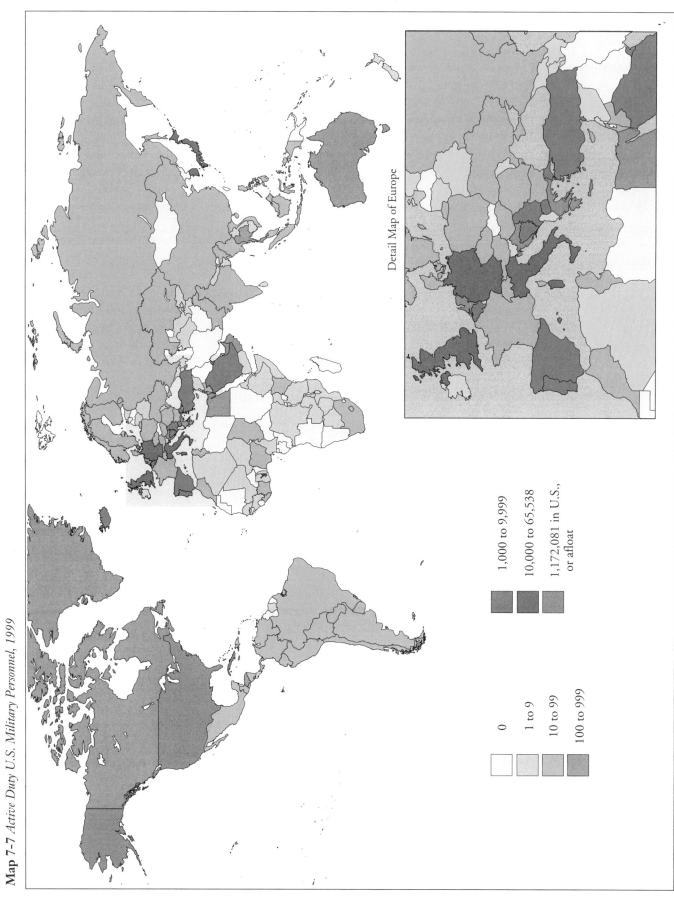

Detail Map of Europe

0

1 to 9

10 to 99

100 to 999

1,000 to 9,999

10,000 to 65,538

1,172,081 in U.S., or afloat

nel has changed. During the 1950s many American troops were stationed in Europe, Japan, and in Korea during the war there. In the 1960s the buildup to the war in Vietnam began, ending in 1975. Thousands of troops were deployed in the Middle East during the Persian Gulf War in 1991. By no means, however, did all of these troops live and work in war zones. Others have been stationed at military bases or on foreign soil throughout the world, participating in peacekeeping missions, training local military personnel, and protecting American embassies.

As Map 7-7 shows, in 1999 American military personnel were stationed in a majority of the world's countries. Europe, East Asia, and the Middle East had the largest U.S. military contingents. The United Kingdom, Germany, Italy, Japan, and South Korea each played host to more than 10,000 U.S. troops. Belgium, which is the headquarters of the North Atlantic Treaty Organization, had a substantial number of American military personnel, as did several countries along and near the Mediterranean, including Saudi Arabia, Spain, Turkey, and Yugoslavia. All of these countries have been important to U.S. foreign policy objectives for many years. Smaller numbers of troops are stationed throughout South America, Asia, and Africa. Only a few countries have no American military personnel at all. Most are countries that lack diplomatic or economic relationships with the United States, for example, Libya, Afghanistan, and Iraq.

Map 7-8 shows the transfer of U.S. arms abroad by country from 1994 to 1996. In addition to deploying troops around the world, the United States sells arms to foreign countries. During the cold war, the United States and the Soviet Union engaged in extensive military buildups, and many of the arms were transferred to other countries. Indeed, the Third World, as the less-developed countries were called, was a battleground of the cold war. Wars were especially prevalent in places identified by political geographer Saul Cohen as "shatterbelts."[8] These shatterbelts were characterized by ethnic diversity and conflict, along with strategic importance to both sides of the cold war. They included southeastern Europe, Southeast Asia, the Middle East, and southern Africa. Since the 1950s, millions of people have been killed in wars in Korea, Vietnam, the Middle East, Yugoslavia, Indonesia, Afghanistan, southern Africa, and many other less-developed areas.

Countries in these shatterbelts received large quantities of American aid. The end of the cold war, which eased tensions in some areas, resulted in increased instability in others, for example, the former Yugoslavia, which has been torn apart by civil war and ethnic conflict since 1991. In terms of arms transfers, the shatterbelts can still be identified. Among the largest purchasers and recipients of U.S. military equip-

ment during the 1990s were several countries in and near the Middle East, including Egypt, Israel, Saudi Arabia, and Turkey. The United States continued to contribute to the defense of Europe, with more than $1 billion in arms sales each to Finland, Greece, Italy, and Spain. Smaller but still substantial sales were made to other parts of Europe and to much of southern Asia. Not surprisingly, no arms were transferred to countries that did not have an American troop presence (Map 7-7).

Map 7-9 shows the distribution of U.S. foreign military aid by country between 1995 and 1997. The United States not only sells large quantities of arms but also provides billions of dollars in military assistance to other countries each year. The distribution of foreign military aid followed the distribution of arms sales (Map 7-8), although a relatively higher proportion of aid went to less-developed countries that otherwise could not afford to purchase weapons. As in Map 7-8, the distribution of U.S. foreign military aid by country followed the shatterbelts identified during the cold war.

Shatterbelts in the Middle East, southeastern Europe, and Southeast Asia can be identified clearly in Map 7-9. The largest quantities of U.S. foreign military aid went to several countries in the Middle East, with more than $100 million each going to Egypt, Israel, and Jordan. Greece and Turkey in southeastern Europe also received substantial quantities of U.S. military aid. In contrast, little has gone to Africa, South America, or mainland Asia.

Map 7-10 shows the distribution of U.S. foreign economic aid by country from 1995 to 1997. After World War II, the United States established the Marshall Plan, which provided American economic assistance to rebuild the economies of war-torn western Europe. The success of the Marshall Plan convinced U.S. policymakers of the wisdom of sending economic aid to troubled nations and less-developed countries. As with postwar western Europe, American economic aid was seen as a means of contributing to economic development and retarding the spread of communism. Even with the end of the cold war, U.S. economic aid to other countries remains substantial, and policymakers have argued that providing economic assistance to fledgling democracies strengthens their governments and prevents the re-emergence of dictatorships or communist governments.

With the end of the cold war, large quantities of economic aid began to go to the former Soviet Union. Russia and Ukraine were the main recipients. Other countries with substantial levels of American economic assistance are located in shatterbelt regions, including Angola, Egypt, Jordan, India, and Indonesia. With the collapse of apartheid, the now multiracial democracy of South Africa obtained large amounts of American aid to help it expand its economy.

Map 7-8 *U.S. Arms Transfers, 1994–1996*

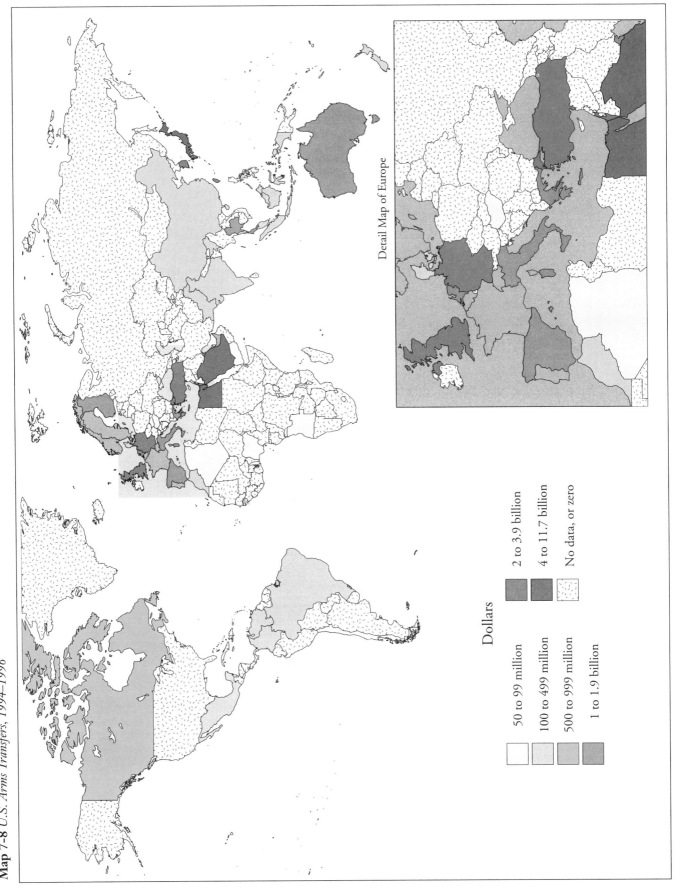

Detail Map of Europe

Dollars

☐	50 to 99 million
▨	100 to 499 million
▨	500 to 999 million
▨	1 to 1.9 billion
▨	2 to 3.9 billion
▨	4 to 11.7 billion
⋯	No data, or zero

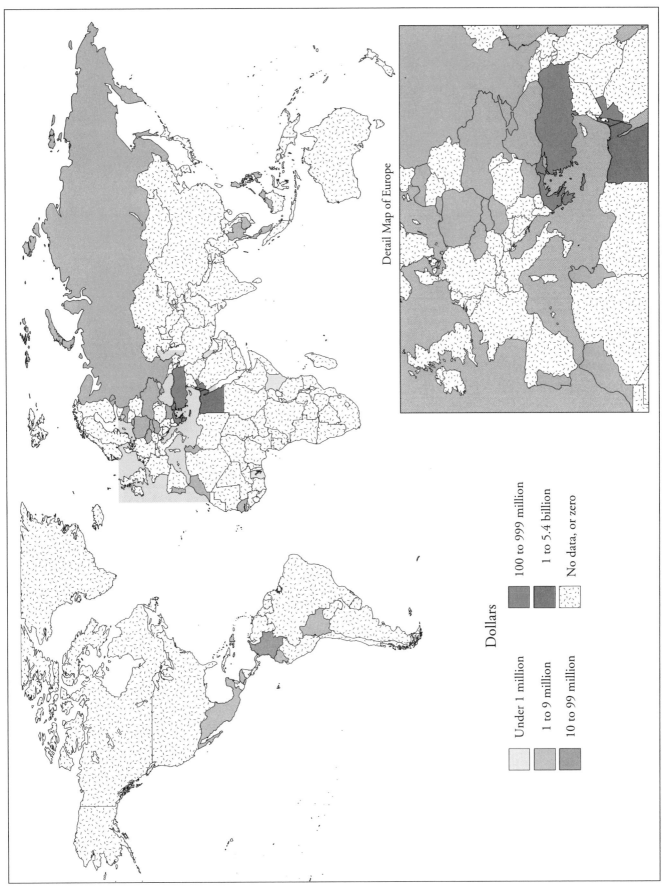

Dollars

Under 1 million

1 to 9 million

10 to 99 million

100 to 999 million

1 to 5.4 billion

No data, or zero

Detail Map of Europe

Map 7-9 *U.S. Foreign Military Aid, 1995–1997*

Map 7-10 *U.S. Foreign Economic Aid, 1995–1997*

Detail Map of Europe

Dollars

under 50 million

50 to 99 million

100 to 499 million

500 to 999 million

1 to 3.6 billion

No data, or zero

Map 7-11 shows the distribution of international terrorist incidents recorded by the Office of the Coordinator for Counterterrorism of the U.S. State Department from 1996 to 2000. Terrorism is the systematic use of violent acts against civilians to create a climate of fear in an attempt to pressure governments to take action the terrorists desire. Between 1996 and 2000 almost 1,700 acts of terrorism were recorded, an average of about 350 per year. About 40 percent of these acts were aimed directly against U.S. government civilian or military personnel, other American citizens, or American businesses in some part of the world. During the period, 67 Americans were killed and 591 were injured by terrorist actions. Prior to September 11, 2001, the worst in terms of American fatalities were the truck bombing of the Al Khubar apartment complex in Saudi Arabia in 1996, which killed nineteen Air Force personnel, and the attack against the USS *Cole* in the Yemeni port of Aden in 2000, which killed seventeen sailors. Other anti-American terrorist targets included oil pipelines in Colombia; American tourists in Egypt; an American Express office in Colombo, Sri Lanka; and U.S. embassies in Nairobi, Kenya, and Dar es Salaam, Tanzania. These embassy attacks killed more than 200 Kenyan and Tanzanian citizens in addition to several Americans.

Not surprisingly, the distribution of terrorist incidents in many ways reflects the pattern of wars and shatterbelts shown in Maps 7-7 and 7-8. Europe, the Middle East, South Asia, and Southeast Asia report the highest incidence of terrorist activity. In many European countries, terrorist activity was associated with efforts to promote independence or greater autonomy among minority populations within long-established countries, for example in Spain and France. Other countries with high levels of terrorism were those that have experienced ongoing civil war and/or nationalist movements within their borders, for example, Angola, India, Nigeria, and the Philippines. Terrorist activity was absent or minimal in developed countries with no ethnic tension or civil war, such as Australia, New Zealand, and the Scandinavian countries, but also absent in highly repressive states such as China and Iraq.

World Trade and Development

The remaining maps in this chapter deal with aspects of international trade and investment. Throughout the world, the volume of international trade increased dramatically over the course of the twentieth century and continues to grow. As the world's strongest political and economic power,

the United States has long played a pivotal role in international trade. Any visitor to a shopping mall or large department store can choose among hundreds of consumer goods made overseas, including electronics, computers, clothing, toys, and food. Numerous American-owned firms maintain production facilities abroad. For example, many Nike shoes are actually manufactured in Indonesia and Vietnam. Such products carry American manufacturers' labels but are actually imported from overseas. Overseas production by American firms is an example of foreign direct investment, which is also explored geographically in this section. Trade agreements, such as the North American Free Trade Agreement (NAFTA), have encouraged the expansion of international trade.

Map 7-12 shows the distribution of imports into the United States in 1999 in dollar values from each country. Several factors affect the distribution pattern of imports, including political and economic relationships between individual countries and the United States, the wealth and size of each country, and distance from the United States. The volume of trade between a given country and the United States is generally higher when the country in question is politically stable and has a long-standing trade relationship with the United States. Higher volumes of trade tend to exist between larger, wealthier countries. For example, trade between the United States and the United Kingdom exceeds trade between the United States and smaller or poorer countries such as Morocco or Portugal. Distance is a factor in determining trade volumes because the cost of shipping goes down as distance decreases and because intervening opportunities are less likely to affect trade flows between nearby countries. If the United States can import a particular agricultural product from Mexico, for example, it is unnecessary to import the same product from Southeast Asia at a higher cost.

Map 7-12 shows that the highest volumes of imports came from North America, Latin America, East Asia, and Europe. Canada and Mexico led the world in imports to the United States, followed by several European countries, Japan, China, and Brazil. Imports from Africa and parts of the Middle East are substantially lower and lacking entirely from countries such as Libya and Cuba, against which the United States maintains trade embargoes.

Map 7-13 shows the per capita value of nonagricultural exports by state of origin in 1999. Exports are valued at a minimum of $200 per capita in every state. In several states, however, exports are valued at more than $3,000 per capita. The highest values in exports are found in states along the coast, reflecting the historic economic ties between coastal regions and foreign countries. Note the high per capita

Map 7-11 *Terrorist Incidents, 1996–2000*

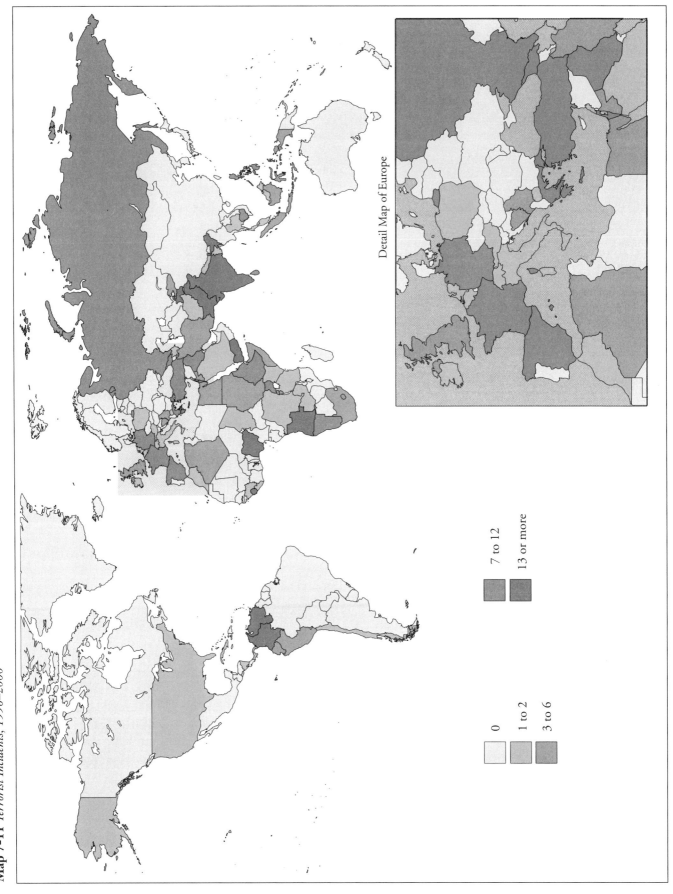

Detail Map of Europe

0

1 to 2

3 to 6

7 to 12

13 or more

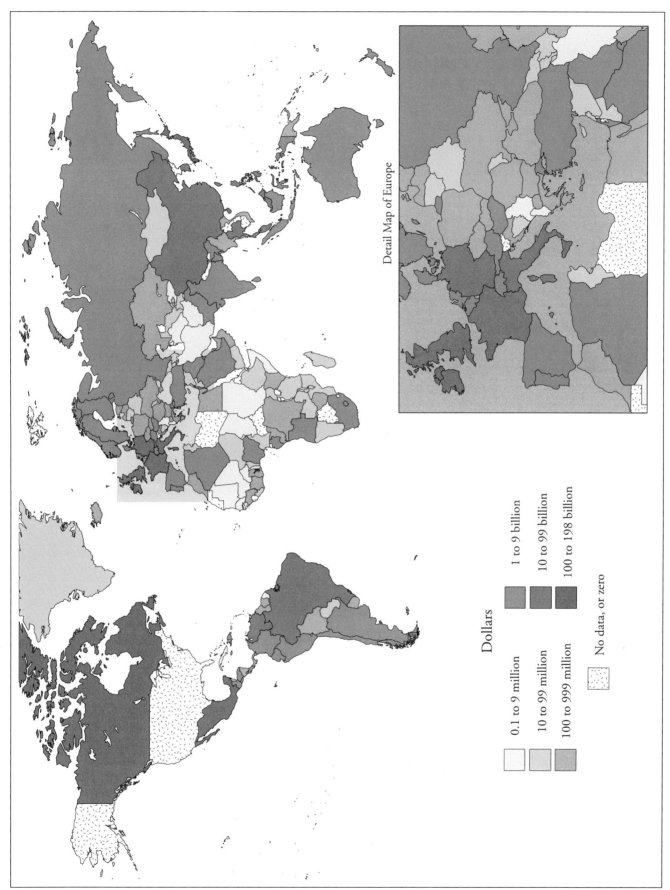

Dollars

	0.1 to 9 million		1 to 9 billion
	10 to 99 million		10 to 99 billion
	100 to 999 million		100 to 198 billion

No data, or zero

Detail Map of Europe

Map 7-12 *Imports by Country of Origin, 1999*

Map 7-13 *Nonagricultural Exports, 1999*

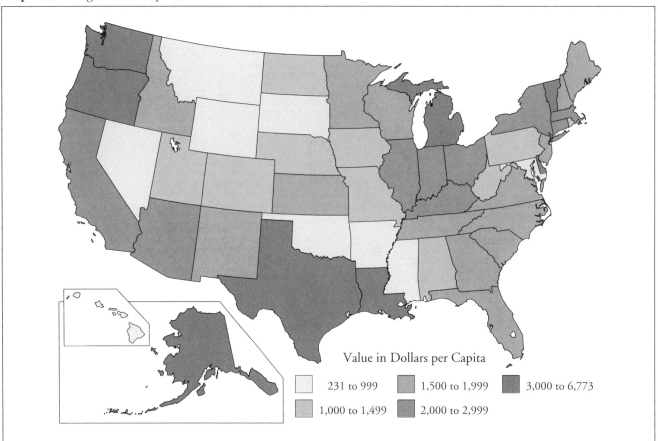

Value in Dollars per Capita

231 to 999 | 1,500 to 1,999 | 3,000 to 6,773
1,000 to 1,499 | 2,000 to 2,999

exports in Alaska, Louisiana, and Texas, states that export petroleum and petroleum products. States of the traditional industrial heartland of the United States, including Kentucky, Illinois, Indiana, Michigan, and Ohio, also rank high in per capita exports. High-cost durable goods, such as automobiles and other heavy machinery and equipment, account for much of these high values.

The lowest values are associated with primarily agricultural states, including much of the Great Plains. These states rank high, however, in exports of agricultural products per capita (Map 7-14). The economies of states such as Hawaii, Maryland, and Nevada are strongly oriented to the service sector, including tourism. These states also contributed relatively little export value per capita.

Historically, states in the Northeast and the South have had stronger trade and export linkages than states in the Midwest and West. This distinction is explained in part by the historical isolationism of the Midwest compared to the Northeast and the South, with their histories of foreign trade.[9] The isolationism of the central portions of the United States has begun to diminish, in part because eco-

nomic leaders in this region, as well as in other parts of the United States, have become actively involved in promoting foreign trade. States throughout the country have set up offices to promote the export of their states' agricultural and industrial products.

Map 7-14 displays the per capita dollar value of U.S. agricultural exports by state of origin for 1999. The highest values were in the agricultural heartland—Iowa, Kansas, Nebraska, North Dakota, and South Dakota, states that also had the highest percentage of the population engaged in agriculture. Arkansas, Idaho, and Minnesota also ranked high. Although California and Texas led the country in agricultural output, the per capita value of their exports was modest because of the large urban populations of these states. Moreover, a considerable proportion of the agricultural production of these states was in crops grown for domestic consumption rather than export.

As might be expected, nonagricultural states or those in which the agricultural sector is small compared to the value of industry and other activities have relatively low per capita agricultural exports. Examples include the New England states and Michigan, New York, and Ohio, with their well-developed industrial sectors, along with states such as Alaska, Arizona, and Nevada, where agricultural output is limited.

Map 7-15 shows the volume of exports, agricultural and nonagricultural, by country of destination for 1999. The pattern of exports from the United States was related to the pattern of imports, as shown in Map 7-12. North America, South America, and Europe were the leading consumers. Canada imported more U.S. goods than any other country. Many west European countries, including France, Germany, Italy, the Netherlands, and the United Kingdom, along with Brazil, China, Mexico, and Japan, each accounted for more than $10 billion in American exports. In general, the pattern of exports can be explained in terms of the importing country's history of trade relationships with the United States and its wealth, size, and distance from the United States. Smaller values were associated with small, poor, and distant countries and with those such as Libya and Iraq, which had a history of political and economic antagonism with the United States.

Another impact of globalization is the growing level of transnational investment. American corporations invest in production facilities overseas, while at the same time foreign business concerns invest in the United States. Toyota, Michelin, Samsung, and Mercedes-Benz are but a few of the well-known foreign firms that have invested in production facilities in the United States.

Map 7-16 depicts the distribution of foreign direct investment in the United States in 1997, in terms of the dollar value of investment in each state. The highest levels of foreign direct investment were in the largest states, including California, New York, and Texas, but substantial levels of foreign investment were also found in many smaller states, notably in the Southeast. Relatively small states, such as Kentucky, Louisiana, and South Carolina, each accounted for more than $16 billion of foreign direct investment. In fact, direct investment became an issue during the 1996 campaign for the Republican Party's presidential nomination. Sen. Bob Dole of Kansas, a supporter of free trade, stressed its importance to local economies in the critical South Carolina primary against his major opponent, jour-

Map 7-14 *Agricultural Exports, 1999*

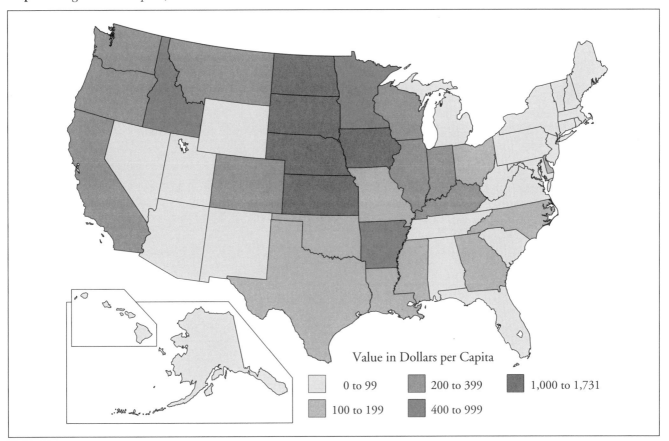

Map 7-15 *Exports by Country of Destination, 1999*

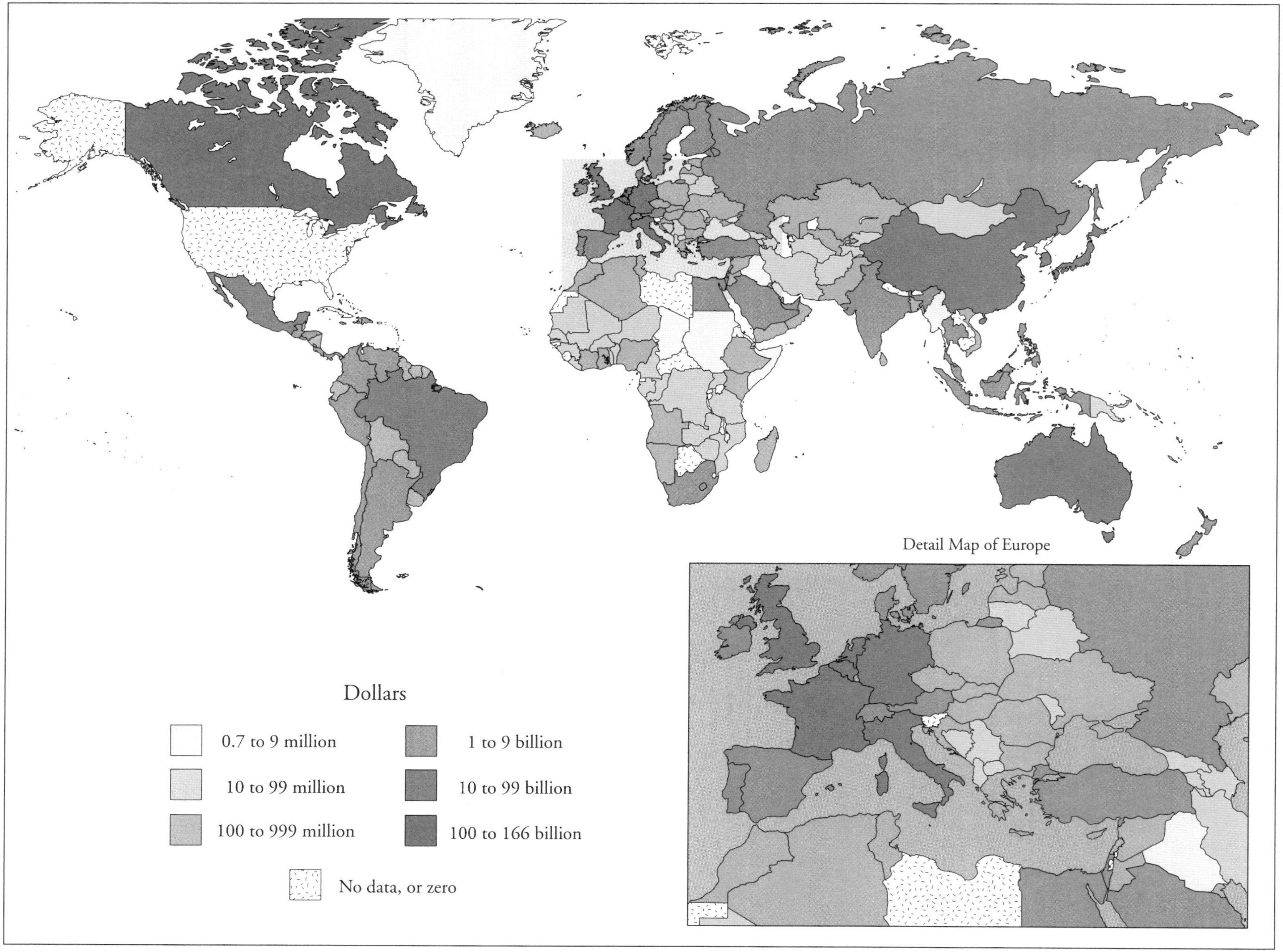

Detail Map of Europe

Dollars

☐ 0.7 to 9 million	☐ 1 to 9 billion
☐ 10 to 99 million	☐ 10 to 99 billion
☐ 100 to 999 million	☐ 100 to 166 billion

☐ No data, or zero

Map 7-16 *Distribution of Foreign Direct Investments, 1997*

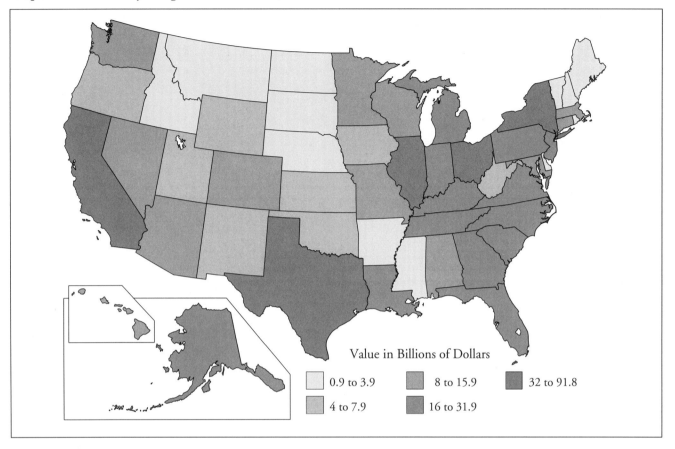

Value in Billions of Dollars

0.9 to 3.9	
4 to 7.9	
8 to 15.9	
16 to 31.9	
32 to 91.8	

nalist Patrick Buchanan, who advocated protectionist policies. In general, free trade encourages foreign direct investment, while protectionism or the absence of free trade tends to discourage it.

Relatively populous states, such as Massachusetts and Washington, reported modest levels of foreign direct investment, perhaps because of the high cost of labor in these northern states. The smallest levels of foreign direct investment were found in the Midwest and West. Many of these states had small labor forces, and their greater distances from the coasts increased the costs associated with shipping raw materials and finished products to and from production facilities.

Map 7-17 shows the distribution of U.S. direct investments abroad, by country, in 1998. For many years, U.S. business firms have invested heavily in production facilities overseas. Large American-owned corporations, such as General Motors, General Electric, Ford, and AT&T, maintain production facilities in numerous countries around the world. Foreign direct investment in less-developed countries is attractive to these companies because of access to for-

eign markets and because labor costs are lower than in the United States.

In general, Map 7-17 reflects the patterns of imports and exports into the United States (Maps 7-12 and 7-15), with the highest levels found in the Americas and in western Europe. Canada, the Netherlands, and the United Kingdom each reported more than $50 billion in foreign direct investment. Brazil, France, Germany, Japan, and Mexico also ranked high. Each of these countries has a large population and considerable economic growth potential. Smaller values were associated with less-developed countries. For example, there was little U.S. direct investment in Africa, with the exception of Egypt, Nigeria, and South Africa. Similarly, the Middle East and southern Asia also reported relatively little U.S. direct investment. Although country-specific data are lacking, U.S. investment in eastern Europe and the former Soviet Union, although increasing, was still modest in scale. In 1998 U.S. foreign direct investment in eastern Europe, including former USSR countries, totaled nearly $8 billion, or about the same as U.S. foreign direct investment in either Norway or Chile.

Map 7-17 *Direct Investments Abroad, by Country, 1998*

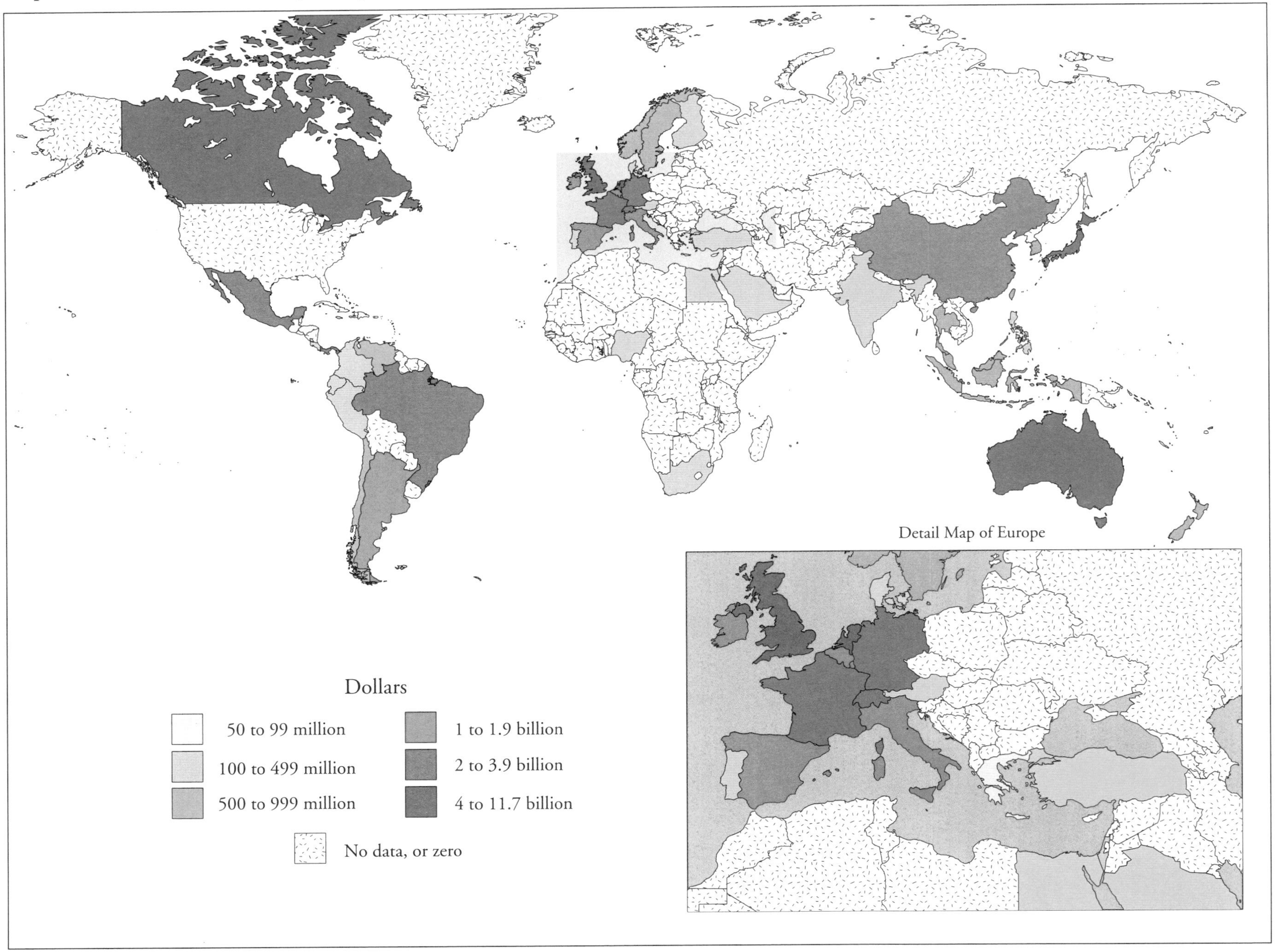

Detail Map of Europe

Dollars

	50 to 99 million		1 to 1.9 billion
	100 to 499 million		2 to 3.9 billion
	500 to 999 million		4 to 11.7 billion

No data, or zero

Notes

1. Michael C. LeMay, *From Open Door to Dutch Door: An Analysis of U.S. Immigration Policy since 1820* (New York: Praeger, 1987).

2. Robert C. Ostergren, *A Community Transplanted: The Trans-Atlantic Experience of a Swedish Immigrant Settlement in the Upper Middle West* (Madison: University of Wisconsin Press, 1988).

3. Susan W. Hardwick, *Mythic Galveston* (Baltimore: Johns Hopkins University Press, 2001).

4. Ines M. Miyares, *The Hmong Refugee Experience in the United States: Crossing the River* (New York: Garland, 1998).

5. Lawrence S. Kaplan, *The United States and NATO: The Formative Years* (Lexington: University of Kentucky Press, 1984).

6. Andrew A. Michta, ed., *America's New Allies: Poland, Hungary and the Czech Republic in NATO* (Seattle: University of Washington Press, 1998).

7. Ann R. Markusen, *The Rise of the Gunbelt: The Military Remapping of Industrial America* (New York: Oxford, 1991).

8. Saul B. Cohen, *Geography and Politics in a World Divided* (New York: Random House, 1963).

9. Peter Trubowitz, *Defining the National Interest: Conflict and Change in American Foreign Policy* (Chicago: University of Chicago Press, 1998).

Chapter 8

Social and Economic Policy

The Declaration of Independence states that the "pursuit of happiness" is an inalienable human right. The pursuit of happiness means many things, among them, the solace of worship, the blessings of health, the beauty of the natural world, the creature comforts associated with material wealth, and the appreciation of artistic, musical, and literary genius. Together, these aspects of domestic life in the United States describe Americans' quality of life, the subject of the maps in this chapter and elsewhere in the atlas.

The first section of Chapter 8 is devoted to the federal government's provision of Social Security benefits and economic assistance to those in need. The first map shows the distribution of poverty. To alleviate poverty, the federal government provides many different types of assistance to people who, for various reasons, are unable to generate income on their own. People who have lost their jobs are entitled to unemployment compensation, and farmers often rely on agricultural assistance payments to protect them from the effects of market forces beyond their control. Maps 8-2 through 8-5, respectively, show the distribution of such benefits.

The next section deals with health issues. Maps 8-6 through 8-10 show the distribution of death rates along with rates of death from specific causes including heart disease, stroke, and cancer. Maps 8-11 through 8-13 examine reproduction and reproductive rights. Map 8-11 shows the distribution of legal abortion—a subject of great controversy since *Roe v. Wade* (1973). Next are maps showing the distribution of births associated with low birth rates and teenage pregnancy rates and three maps depicting the distributions of health care coverage, physicians, and Medicare payments.

Most Americans consider education critical to the pursuit of happiness. Because the Constitution does not specifically mention education, states have wide latitude in organizing, providing, and financing education. The differences between states in per capita education expenditures, public school teachers' salaries, rates of high school and college graduation, and per capita books and serials in public libraries are shown in Maps 8-17 through 8-20. Protection from crime is also closely linked to the quality of life, as shown in Maps 8-21 through 8-25. Here we examine crime rates per state, incarcerations, executions, and gun control laws.

The final group of maps is devoted to issues of environmental quality, environmental management, and environmental protection. The maps examine three important areas of federal environmental protection—acid rain, the use of agricultural chemicals, and Superfund sites. Also included are measures of land development along with the distribution of endangered plant and animal species.

Poverty Rates and Economic Assistance

Map 8-1 shows the average percentage of each state's population that fell below poverty-level income from 1997 to 1999. Despite the economic boom of the 1990s, and despite decades of federal and state programs to maintain and enhance personal income, millions of people living in the United States remain impoverished, as defined on the basis of annual income. In 1999 the U.S. Census Bureau defined the poverty level as an income of $16,895 per year for a family of four. On average, from 1997 to 1999, nearly 13 percent of U.S. residents, or roughly one in eight, was classified below the poverty level.

Poverty-level percentages among the states ranged from less than 8 percent to more than 20 percent. In general, the distribution of poverty parallels the distribution of income, and states lacking extreme variability in income levels reported relatively modest poverty levels. States such as Indiana, Iowa, and Vermont, for example, do not have large concentrations of wealth, and had relatively few impoverished people, while states such as California and New York have high per capita incomes and reported considerably higher percentages of poor people than the wealthier rural states.

For the most part, states with low poverty rates were found in the northeastern part of the United States. States

Map 8-1 *Poverty Rates, 1997–1999*

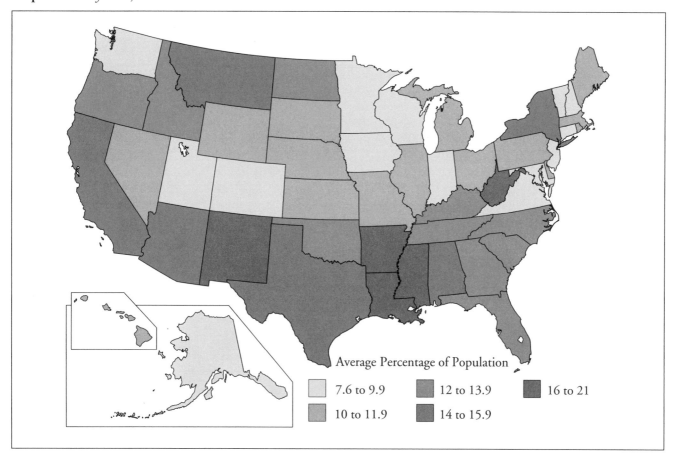

Average Percentage of Population

7.6 to 9.9	12 to 13.9	16 to 21
10 to 11.9	14 to 15.9	

with high incomes and substantial suburban populations, including Connecticut, Maryland, New Hampshire, New Jersey, and Virginia, as well as Colorado, had low rates of poverty. High poverty rates tended to be characteristic of the Southeast, particularly in those states that lack major urban centers with wealthy suburban clusters. Arkansas, Louisiana, and Mississippi had the highest poverty rates in the South. Other states with high poverty rates included Montana, New Mexico, and West Virginia. These states, like the poorest southern states, have relatively modest urban populations and high proportions of their rural residents living below the poverty level.

Map 8-2 shows the distribution of Social Security payments by state in 1999. The figures mapped are the sum of three Social Security programs—retirement insurance payments, survivors insurance payments, and disability insurance payments. The total of these payments received by residents of a state are divided by the state's population to obtain a per capita figure. The per capita figures varied from less than $700 to nearly $2,000 per year.

The Social Security program was established in the 1930s as part of President Franklin Roosevelt's New Deal.

Social Security is intended to provide federal assistance to retirees and disabled workers and survivors benefits for spouses and minor children. The program is funded by contributions made by workers and their employers during their working years.[1]

Social Security has become a political issue of considerable importance because, over the years, the percentage of Americans who rely on it and other income maintenance programs has grown. The increased number of Social Security recipients resulted not only from longer life expectancy but also from the expansion of coverage to include farmers and other self-employed people once excluded because they were not wage earners. Americans are living longer, which increases the average length of time that a typical recipient receives Social Security payments. In addition, the larger number of retirees means that the percentage of Americans who work is growing smaller. Fewer workers are therefore available to contribute from their paychecks into Social Security funds that support retirees. This situation is expected to reach a crisis point when the huge baby boom generation, born between 1946 and 1964, begins to retire in large numbers beginning around 2010.

Map 8-2 *Social Security Benefits, 1999*

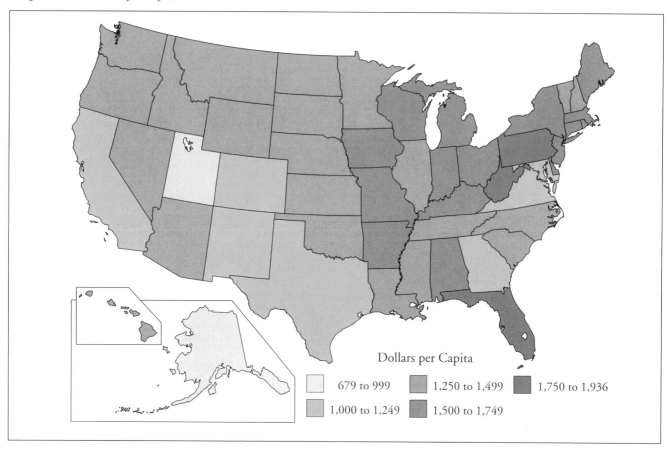

Dollars per Capita

679 to 999	1,250 to 1,499	1,750 to 1,936
1,000 to 1,249	1,500 to 1,749	

Utah and Alaska, two states with relatively few elderly people, reported less than $1,000 Social Security payments per capita each year. Utah's average age is low because Mormons, the predominant group, tend to have high birth rates (Maps 1-6 and 1-10). Alaska's rigorous climate is difficult for elderly people, many of whom return to the "lower forty-eight." Naturally, states with large numbers of elderly have high Social Security per capita payments. Some states, such as Florida, attract large numbers of retirees; others, such as Pennsylvania and West Virginia, have experienced relatively little in-migration, leaving them with high percentages of the elderly (Map 1-11). Still other states, such as Arkansas, combine modest overall growth rates with more rapid growth among retirees. In general, Social Security payments per capita were higher in the North than in the more rapidly growing Sun Belt. California, Colorado, Georgia, and Texas attract large numbers of new residents, many of whom are in their twenties and thirties and therefore not receiving Social Security payments. States with comparatively youthful populations, therefore, have low Social Security payments per capita.

Map 8-3 shows the distribution of welfare payments by

state in 1999. The values shown in Map 8-3 are the sum of payments distributed under the Supplemental Security Income (SSI), Temporary Assistance to Needy Families (TANF), and Food Stamps programs divided by the 1999 population of each state. The TANF and Food Stamps programs include both federal outlays and state matching funds. Not surprisingly, the patterns of this map are similar to those of Map 8-1, the poverty rate map. For example, welfare payments per capita in Louisiana, Mississippi, and New York, all of which have substantial percentages of impoverished people, were around $300 per capita. States such as Colorado, Indiana, Iowa, New Hampshire, and Utah, with low poverty rates, also had correspondingly low welfare payments per capita.

The purpose of welfare programs is to provide income assistance to people who are unable to work because of disability or other reasons. Over the years, critics have charged that welfare rolls have been crowded with people who were able to work but chose to live on welfare. In fact, only a small minority of welfare recipients are actually able to work.[2] Nevertheless, during the 1990s the federal government undertook a comprehensive reform of welfare pro-

Map 8-3 *Welfare Expenditures, 1999*

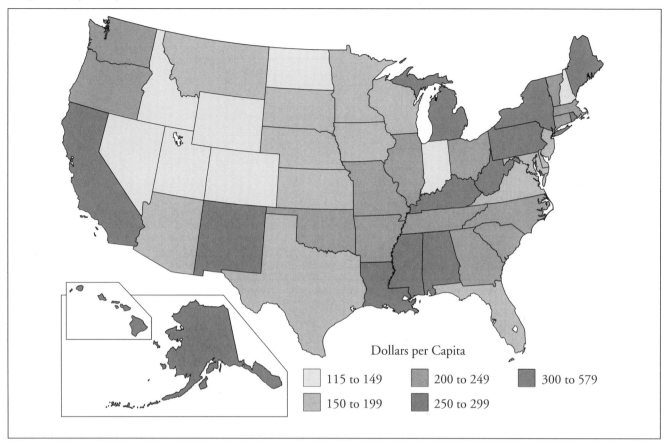

Dollars per Capita

115 to 149   200 to 249   300 to 579

150 to 199   250 to 299

grams, reducing welfare lists considerably. As a result of these reforms, the number of families receiving welfare payments fell by about 46 percent nationally from 1993 to 1998, although these changes varied considerably from state to state.

Map 8-4 shows the geographical distribution of payments from the Unemployment Compensation Trust Fund by state in 1999. Unemployment compensation is income assistance provided by the federal government in collaboration with state governments. Workers who are laid off, lose their jobs because their companies go bankrupt, or otherwise find themselves unemployed because of circumstances beyond their control can apply for unemployment compensation, which provides an income cushion while they seek new employment.

The map shows that in 1999 per capita unemployment compensation outlays ranged from less than $20 to nearly $200. Because the distribution of unemployment compensation was tied to the local rates of unemployment, the lowest levels of payments were found in states with low unemployment rates. These included rapidly growing states with numerous new jobs, such as Arizona and New Hampshire,

as well as states with fewer new job opportunities but relatively little recent population growth, such as Nebraska and South Dakota. The highest levels of unemployment compensation were found in several northeastern states, Alaska, and Nevada. In Connecticut, Massachusetts, New Jersey, and Pennsylvania, generous unemployment compensation policies coupled with corporate mergers and industrial restructuring contributed to higher payments. Because levels of unemployment compensation to individuals are tied to their working incomes, high-income states such as these experienced relatively high levels of compensation per unemployed person. Alaska and Nevada have resource-oriented economies that are highly volatile, and these states tend to experience relatively high levels of job turnover, which increases eligibility for unemployment compensation.

Map 8-5 shows the distribution of agricultural assistance to farmers across the country measured in dollars per capita in 1999. The federal government has provided extensive financial assistance to farmers since the1930s. For the most part, large-scale farm subsidies began with the New Deal, especially the Agricultural Adjustment Act. Aid to farmers includes price supports paid to protect them from the

Map 8-4 *Unemployment Compensation, 1999*

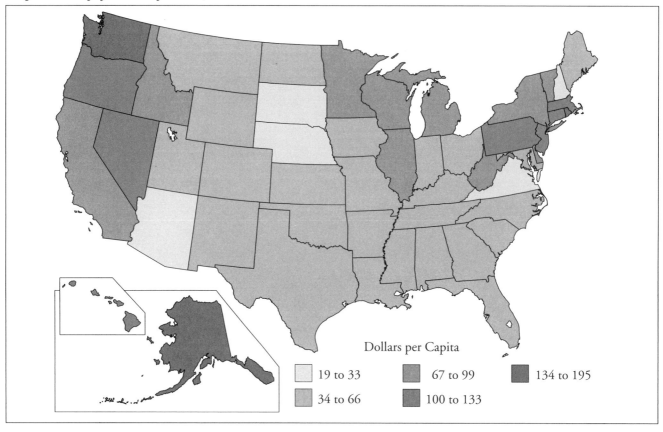

Map 8-5 *Agricultural Assistance, 1999*

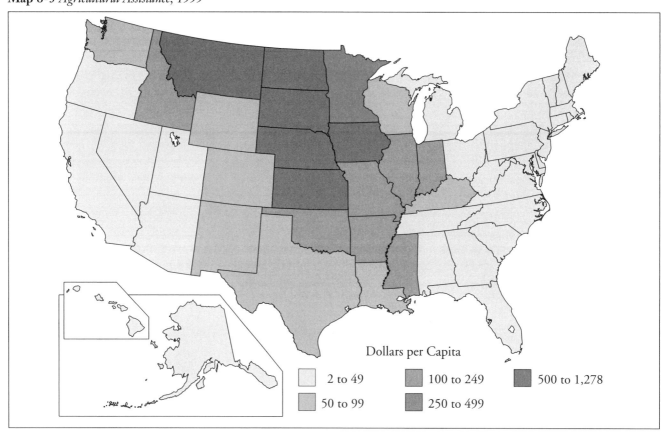

vagaries of international markets for agricultural products, along with assistance to farmers whose crops are damaged or lost because of storms, floods, and droughts.[3]

As the number of farmers in the United States continues to decline, many people question the value of continuing price supports, especially when some of the subsidies go to tobacco production, even though the government is attempting to discourage its use. Despite these concerns, each year the federal government pays out millions of dollars to farmers. The highest per capita agricultural assistance—more than $500 per person—was found in the states with the highest percentages of farm population and where wheat and corn are produced in large volumes. These states included the Plains states of Kansas, Nebraska, North Dakota, and South Dakota, along with neighboring Iowa and Montana. Agricultural states such as Illinois, Minnesota, and Wisconsin, which also have major metropolitan areas, reported lower per capita agricultural subsidies. Agricultural assistance payments were lowest in highly urbanized states, such as those along the Atlantic seaboard, and in states with relatively little commercial agriculture, such as Alaska, Hawaii, New Mexico, and West Virginia.

Causes of Death

With lower birth rates and longer life expectancy, the average age of the U.S. population continues to rise and, with it, greater numbers of deaths from diseases associated with aging. Today, the leading causes of death in the United States are cancer, heart disease, and stroke. Death rates by state for these diseases are shown in Maps 8-6 through 8-8, respectively. Two additional maps in this section deal with death rates by firearms and motor vehicle accidents.

Map 8-6 shows the distribution of cancer death rates by state in 1998. For several reasons, interpreting this map is problematic. Despite intensive research, much remains to be learned about causes of cancer. Risk factors include smoking, along with exposure to various carcinogens. Studies of environmental health have documented that cancer rates tend to increase in areas associated with various polluting industries such as the petrochemical industry, but the causal mechanisms linking this exposure to cancer are not certain. Moreover, death rates from cancer by state may be skewed because many elderly people move before or after being diagnosed with the disease, and the death rate is based on where patients died, not where they lived during most of

Map 8-6 *Cancer Death Rate, 1998*

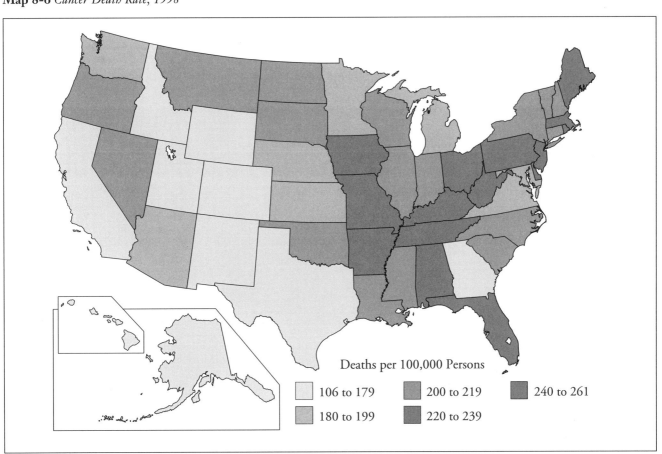

Deaths per 100,000 Persons

106 to 179   200 to 219   240 to 261
180 to 199   220 to 239

their adult lives. States that attract large numbers of elderly retirees may therefore have large populations of cancer patients. In addition, people diagnosed with cancer often move to other states either to seek treatment or to be near relatives or other caregivers.

These circumstances suggest that cancer death rates should be highest in areas with substantial numbers of elderly people and in areas with polluting industries and other economic activities associated with carcinogens. To a considerable extent, these expectations are reflected in Map 8-6. Florida's high death rate from cancer was likely associated with the state's high elderly population, and in West Virginia and Pennsylvania they were likely associated with these states' historic dependence on coal mining and steel production, as well as their high percentages of elderly people. Other slow-growing states with histories of dependence on industrial activity, including Delaware, Massachusetts, New Jersey, Ohio, and Rhode Island, also have high cancer death rates. The lowest death rates from cancer were found in rapidly growing states in the South and West, with their relatively small elderly populations. Alaska, California, Colorado, Georgia, Texas, and Utah have relatively young and

rapidly growing populations and cancer death rates well below the national average.

Map 8-7 shows the death rate by state in 1998 from cardiovascular, or heart, disease, the second leading cause of death in the contemporary United States. Medical researchers associate the likelihood of heart disease with a number of risk factors, including smoking, obesity, poor diet, lack of exercise, and stress. Because the risk of cardiovascular disease increases with age, states with older populations display a pattern of higher death rates on the map. As with Map 8-6, the fact that many people move to different states a relatively short time before their deaths should be taken into account in interpreting the map.

In general, high rates of heart disease deaths were associated with relatively elderly populations. Thus Florida, with its large population of elderly people, showed a high death rate from heart disease. Slow-growing states, such as Arkansas, Iowa, Mississippi, Nebraska, Oklahoma, Pennsylvania, and West Virginia, also have high elderly populations (Map 1-10), and these states reported high death rates from heart disease. The lowest death rates from heart disease were found in the states with high in-migration rates

Map 8-7 *Cardiovascular Disease Death Rate, 1998*

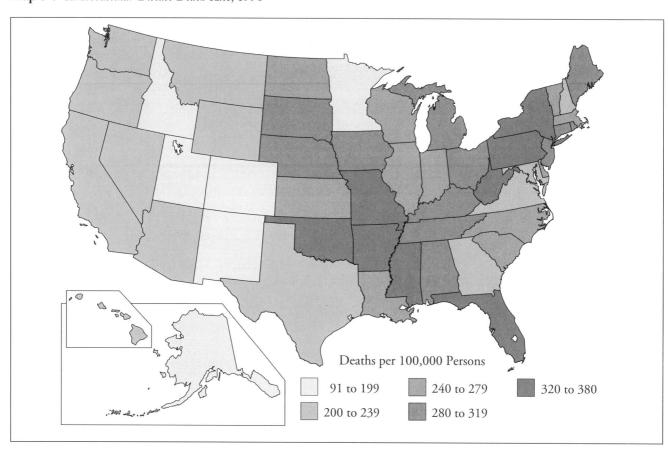

Deaths per 100,000 Persons

91 to 199 240 to 279 320 to 380
200 to 239 280 to 319

and therefore relatively high percentages of young people (Maps 1-9 and 1-11). Many of these states were in the South and West. Examples included Colorado, Georgia, Nevada, Oregon, Texas, Utah, and Washington.

Map 8-8 shows the death rates for cerebrovascular disease, or stroke, by state in 1998. Cerebrovascular disease, in which blood clots affect the functioning of the brain, is the third leading cause of death in the United States. Cerebrovascular disease risk factors are related to risk factors for heart disease (Map 8-7) and include smoking, obesity, lack of exercise, poor diet, and stress.

Because risk factors for stroke are similar to those for heart disease, and because cerebrovascular disease, like cardiovascular disease, is more likely to affect the elderly than the young, one might expect Maps 8-6 and 8-7 to display similar patterns. States with high elderly populations, such as Florida, Pennsylvania, and West Virginia, showed high rates of both cerebrovascular and cardiovascular disease deaths. The rates of death from stroke in these states, however, were actually lower than in several rural southern states, including Arkansas, North Carolina, South Carolina, and Tennessee. Iowa, North Dakota, and South Dakota, which have

high rural elderly populations, also reported high cerebrovascular disease death rates. Rates were lower in the West, and in particular in those states with rapid population growth, such as Alaska, Arizona, Colorado, Utah, and Texas.

Map 8-9 shows the distribution of firearm-related deaths by state in 1998. Although young people also die from cancer, heart disease, and stroke, a considerable percentage of deaths of people under the age of forty is caused by firearms or motor vehicle accidents. Fierce political arguments over efforts to restrict gun ownership have been raging for decades.[4] Proponents of gun control have pressed governments to mandate waiting periods to purchase weapons and for registration in an effort to keep guns out of the hands of criminals and the mentally ill. Opponents argue that the Second Amendment to the Constitution guarantees the right to keep and bear arms. The popularity of hunting and target shooting in many areas makes efforts to reduce gun ownership difficult to achieve politically, especially outside urban areas.

Generally speaking, death rates associated with firearm-related violence are highest in the South, the West, and in rural areas. Alabama, Alaska, Arizona, Louisiana, and Mis-

Map 8-8 *Cerebrovascular Disease Death Rate, 1998*

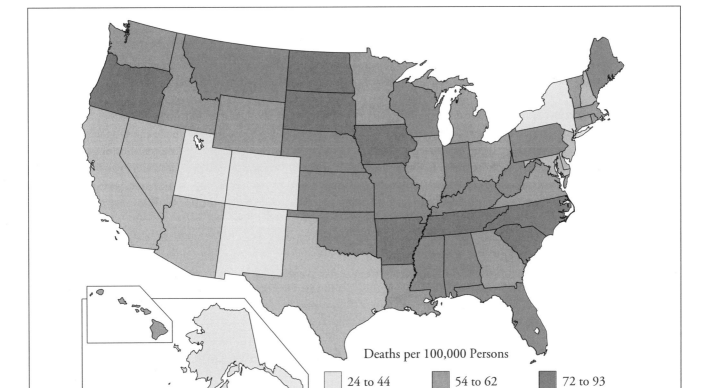

Deaths per 100,000 Persons

24 to 44	54 to 62	72 to 93
45 to 53	63 to 71	

Map 8-9 *Firearm Injury Death Rate, 1998*

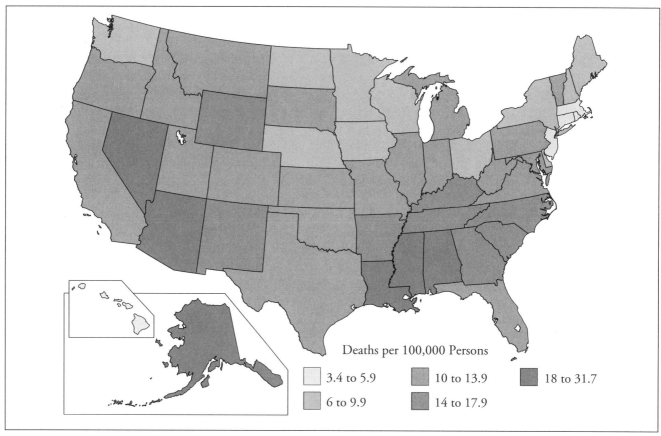

Deaths per 100,000 Persons

3.4 to 5.9	10 to 13.9	18 to 31.7
6 to 9.9	14 to 17.9	

sissippi all report death rates from firearms higher than 18 per 100,000 persons. Death rates from firearms tend to be lower in the Northeast and in the upper Middle West and Great Plains. The lowest rates in the country are found in Connecticut, Hawaii, Massachusetts, New Jersey, and Rhode Island. These states have relatively little rural space for hunting and shooting and low rates of gun possession. Other New England states, along with Iowa, Minnesota, Washington, and Wisconsin, also have low firearm-related death rates.

Map 8-10 shows the distribution of motor vehicle accident deaths per capita in 1998. Motor vehicle accidents are a leading cause of death and injury in the contemporary United States, especially among children and young adults. The publication of Ralph Nader's *Unsafe at Any Speed* in the 1960s called attention to the dangers associated with automobile manufacturing, and since that time foreign and domestic carmakers have been obliged to make cars safer.[5] Efforts to reduce alcohol-impaired driving and improve the quality of highways have also brought down the number of accidents relative to the overall number of miles driven. Nevertheless, motor vehicle accidents continue to claim thousands of lives each year.

In general, motor vehicle accident death rates are lower in the Northeast than in the South and the West. The lowest rates are found in Massachusetts, New Jersey, New York, and Rhode Island, states that limit maximum speeds to 55 miles per hour. Most states outside the northeastern corridor permit speed limits of 65 miles per hour or higher. The highest rates are found in the less urbanized states in the South and West, for example, Alabama, Arkansas, Mississippi, South Carolina, and Wyoming. Motor vehicle accident death rates are inversely associated with population density, perhaps because accidents that occur in rural areas while drivers are traveling at high rates of speed are more likely to be fatal. In urban areas, more collisions occur, but a lower percentage of collisions prove fatal because drivers in traffic are typically traveling at lower rates of speed.

Access to Health Care

Map 8-11 shows the abortion rate by state in 1996. The rate is calculated as a ratio between the number of legal abortions reported and the number of women in the prime

Map 8-10 *Motor Vehicle Injury Death Rate, 1998*

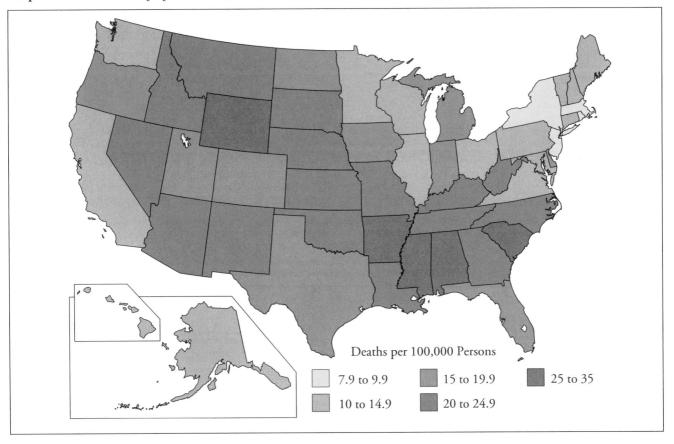

Deaths per 100,000 Persons

7.9 to 9.9 | 15 to 19.9 | 25 to 35
10 to 14.9 | 20 to 24.9

reproductive years, ages fifteen to forty-four, in the overall population.

In January 1973 the Supreme Court ruled in *Roe v. Wade* that states could not ban abortion. This decision established the principle that restricting abortion rights impinged on a pregnant woman's right to privacy. Ever since the *Roe v. Wade* decision was handed down, legal abortion has been a matter of considerable political controversy. Legislative statutes passed in many states in efforts to restrict abortion access have been appealed to and judged by the U.S. Supreme Court (see Map 5-7).

In interpreting Map 8-11, one must keep in mind that women seeking abortions sometimes travel across state lines to receive treatment. Therefore, the abortion rates shown on the map do not necessarily reflect the home states of women seeking to terminate pregnancies. Rates of abortion tended to be highest in large, highly urbanized states. California, Illinois, Maryland, Massachusetts, Michigan, New Jersey, and New York reported high abortion rates. The rates were lower in less urbanized states, especially in the South, Middle West, and Interior West. For example, rates of less than 10 abortions per 1,000 women of reproductive

age were reported from Iowa, Kentucky, Mississippi, Missouri, North Dakota, South Dakota, West Virginia, and Wyoming.

Map 8-12 shows the distribution of low birth weight infants, defined as less than 5.5 pounds, by state in 1998. Low birth weights are associated with health problems during childhood because small and premature babies are more prone to infection and more likely to suffer from various other diseases and complications. The distribution of low birth weights, therefore, can be seen not only as a general measure of the health of newborn infants but also as an indicator of overall public health.

Map 8-12 shows that in several states, including the rural southern states of Alabama, Arkansas, Mississippi, South Carolina, and Tennessee, more than 9 percent of all newborn infants had low birth weights. Note the correlation between high rates of poverty, as shown on Map 8-1, and high percentages of babies born with low birth rates, an indication of the relationship between poverty and poor nutrition and medical services.

New England and the upper Middle West had the lowest rates of low birth weight babies. Maine, Minnesota, New

Map 8-11 *Abortion Rate, 1996*

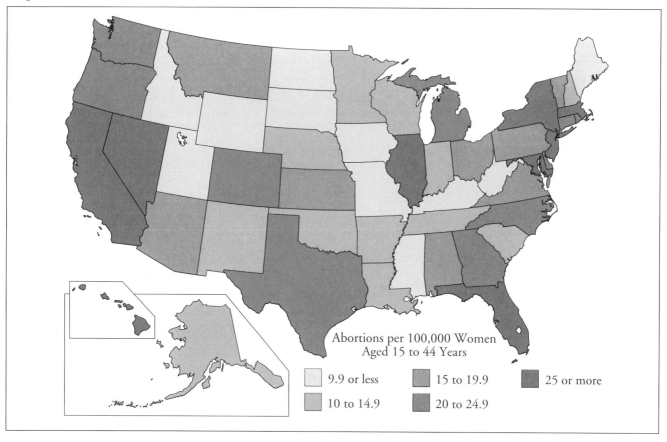

Abortions per 100,000 Women
Aged 15 to 44 Years

9.9 or less   15 to 19.9   25 or more

10 to 14.9   20 to 24.9

Map 8-12 *Low Birth Weight Infants, 1998*

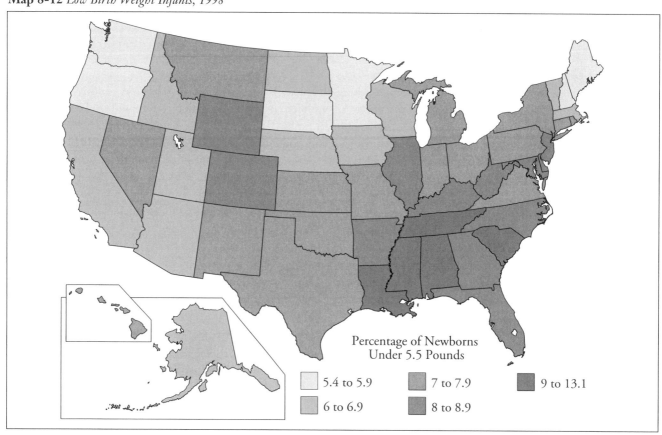

Percentage of Newborns
Under 5.5 Pounds

5.4 to 5.9   7 to 7.9   9 to 13.1

6 to 6.9   8 to 8.9

Hampshire, Oregon, South Dakota, and Washington reported rates of less than 6 percent. Neighbors of these states also had relatively low rates. The low proportions of low birth weight infants in these states is an indicator of the high quality of prenatal maternal care in these areas.

Map 8-13 displays the rate of births to teenage women by state in 1998. The teenage birth rate is a ratio of the number of births to women ages fifteen to nineteen to the overall number of women of the same ages in the population. Compared to older women, pregnant teenagers are less likely to have access to high quality prenatal care and are more likely than older women to give birth to infants with health problems or who need extended medical care.

Nationally, the teenage birthrate in 1998 was 51.1 per 1,000 women, an 18 percent decline from 1991. Among states, the 1998 rates ranged from about 24 per 1,000 to more than 86 per 1,000. The highest rates of teenage births in 1998 were in the Sun Belt, including Alabama, Arizona, Arkansas, Georgia, Louisiana, Mississippi, New Mexico, Nevada, and Texas. Rates declined consistently in a south to north pattern. The lowest rates, less than 35 per 1,000, were in the New England or northeastern states of Maine, Massachusetts, New Hampshire, New Jersey, and Vermont, and in the Upper Midwest states of Minnesota, North Dakota, and Wisconsin.

Map 8-14 shows the distribution of medical doctors engaged in patient care by state in 1998, based on the number of patient care physicians per 10,000 persons. Access to primary medical care is essential to maintaining public health. The lack of primary care is an issue of political and social importance, especially in inner cities, minority-dominated communities, and in isolated rural areas without sufficient numbers of medical doctors. In response, some states have established programs that give tuition assistance to medical students who agree to practice in underserved areas for specified lengths of time.

The map shows, with some exceptions, that states with high proportions of doctors tended to be the states in which the populations have relatively few health-related problems (Maps 8-6 through 8-13). High concentrations of physicians are found in several northeastern states, including Connecticut, Maryland, Massachusetts, New Jersey, and New York. In these states, levels of income and wealth are high (Map 1-24), and the population can afford a high level of service.

Small, rural states, such as Idaho, Iowa, Hawaii, Mississippi, Nevada, Oklahoma, and Wyoming, reported the low-

Map 8-13 *Teenage Birth Rate, 1998*

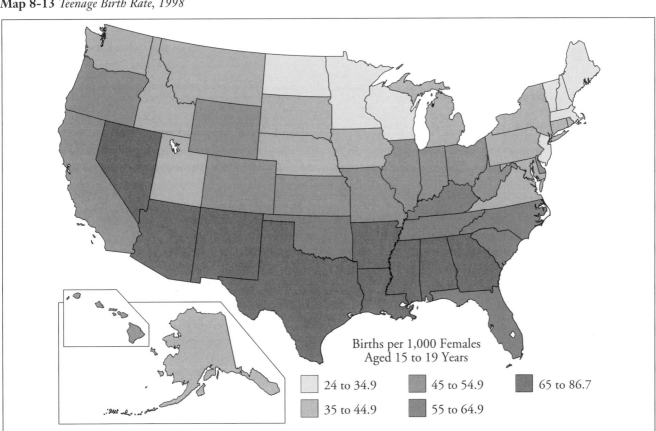

Births per 1,000 Females
Aged 15 to 19 Years

24 to 34.9   45 to 54.9   65 to 86.7
35 to 44.9   55 to 64.9

Map 8-14 *Medical Doctors Engaged in Patient Care, 1998*

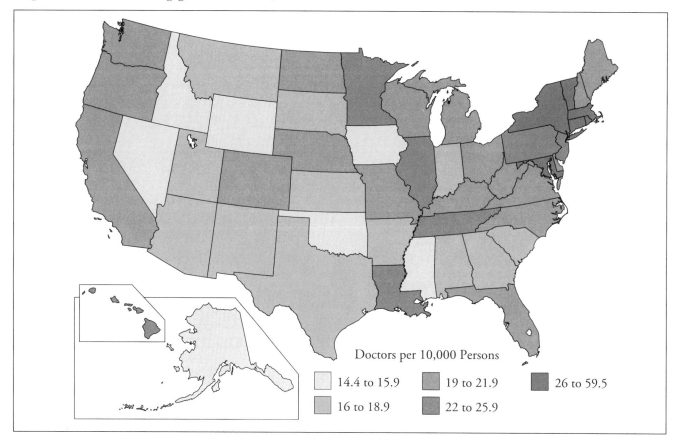

Doctors per 10,000 Persons

14.4 to 15.9   19 to 21.9   26 to 59.5
16 to 18.9   22 to 25.9

est ratios of physicians to the overall population. The problem of low access to medical care in rural areas is growing more acute as older physicians retire and few young ones are willing to replace them. Despite this consistent lack of access, however, the quality of health varied considerably among these states, as indicated in Maps 8-6 through 8-13. For example, Iowa had relatively low rates of teenage pregnancy, firearm deaths, and cancer deaths, while these rates were quite high in Mississippi and Oklahoma.

Map 8-15 shows the distribution of persons not covered by health care insurance by state in 1998. In 1994 President Bill Clinton attempted to nationalize health insurance coverage, but his proposal was defeated in Congress. Many Americans continue to advocate universal health care insurance. Opponents argue that such a system would be excessively bureaucratic and reduce choice and flexibility for patients and physicians.

The majority of Americans receive health care insurance through employers, private insurance companies, and Social Security, but millions still do not have basic coverage. The lack of insurance may discourage people from seeking prenatal care, preventive care for themselves and their children, or treatment when a disease or injury occurs.

The map shows that New England and the Northeast, including Pennsylvania and Ohio, had low rates of uninsured people. These states tend to have high incomes along with high levels of access to medical care (Maps 1-24 and 8-14). The Southwest states of Arizona, California, New Mexico, and Texas, reported high rates of noncoverage. All of these states have large immigrant populations (Maps 1-11 and 7-2), including illegal immigrants who are unlikely to seek or receive health care insurance. In general, higher rates of health insurance coverage tended to be associated with higher levels of income and wealth, and lower rates with lower levels of income.

Map 8-16 shows Medicare payments by state in 1999. President Lyndon Johnson signed the initial Medicare bill into law in 1965. The program provides federal assistance to elderly people, helping them to pay for medical care, prescriptions, and other health-related needs.

Medicare payments per capita were highest in states with large elderly populations. Florida led the country in Medicare payments per capita, followed by Pennsylvania and Massachusetts. Other states, including Alabama, Mississippi, and West Virginia, that experienced slow growth in recent years also had Medicare payment rates higher than

Map 8-15 *Lack of Health Care Coverage, 1998*

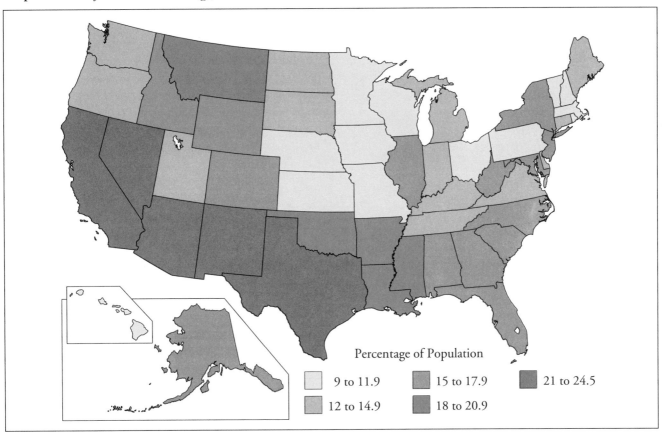

Percentage of Population

9 to 11.9   15 to 17.9   21 to 24.5
12 to 14.9   18 to 20.9

Map 8-16 *Medicare Expenditures, 1999*

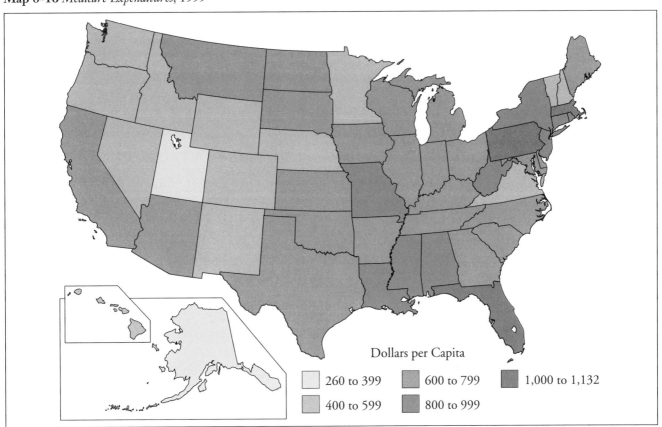

Dollars per Capita

260 to 399   600 to 799   1,000 to 1,132
400 to 599   800 to 999

the national average. The wealthy northeastern states of Connecticut, New Jersey, New York, and Rhode Island also had above-average rates, which may be associated with relatively expensive health care costs in these states. The lowest rates in the United States were found in Utah and Alaska. These states have young populations and so also have the lowest Social Security payment rates in the country (Maps 1-9 and 8-2).

Education

Maps 8-17 through 8-20 deal with aspects of contemporary American education and educational policy. One of the major controversies involving education is the question of whether spending more money on schools results in higher quality education. A related issue is who should pay the costs of public schools. Should they be financed mainly by revenues raised at the local level, state level, or federal level? At present, more than 90 percent of all of the costs associated with education are paid by state and local governments. One way to measure the performance of the nation's schools is to compare states' high school and college graduates.

Map 8-17 shows the percentages of total public school expenditures funded by revenues raised by local school districts or other units of local government within each state. These percentages varied from less than 1 percent in Hawaii, which has a single statewide school system, to more than 50 percent in several states with traditions of local responsibility for public education. The degree of local funding was highest in New England, particularly in New Hampshire, which has neither a state income tax nor a state sales tax. Fifty percent or more of all education funds are raised locally throughout New England and the Northeast.

Nonlocal funds tended to predominate in several southern and western states, in addition to Hawaii. Alabama, Alaska, North Carolina, Oklahoma, and Washington provided less than 25 percent of the funds for education. These states lack the long history of locally controlled public schools that characterizes New England and the Northeast. Indeed, overall geographical patterns of state government versus local government responsibilities for funding public education seem to strongly reflect geographical variations in political behavior and political culture across the United States (Maps 1-3 and 6-1).

Map 8-18 shows the overall per-pupil expenditure on public education in the 1997–1998 school year. The discus-

Map 8-17 *Local Funding of Public Schools, 1997–1998*

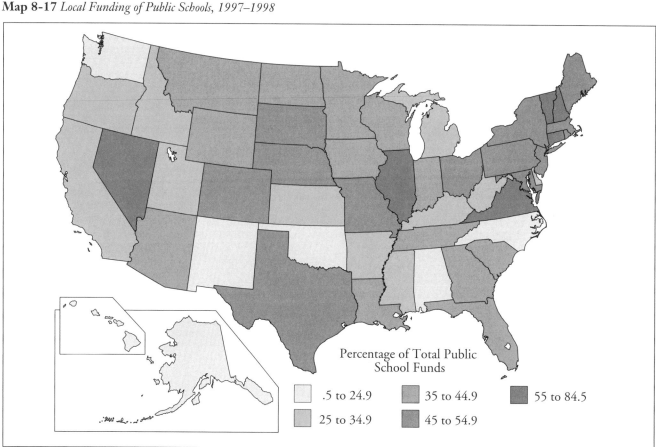

Percentage of Total Public School Funds

.5 to 24.9	35 to 44.9	55 to 84.5
25 to 34.9	45 to 54.9	

sion of Map 8-17 indicated that public schools in the United States are funded by a combination of local, state, and federal sources, with significant differences from one state to another in the amounts provided by each level of government. The amount of money spent on public school funding also varies significantly between the states.

Per-pupil expenditures in the 1997–1998 school year ranged from less than $5,000 to more than $10,000. The highest per-pupil expenditures were found in New England and the Northeast. These areas are characterized by high incomes (Map 1-24), a long history of support for public education, and high levels of educational attainment among adults (Map 8-22). Connecticut, Massachusetts, New Jersey, New York, and Rhode Island spent more than $8,000 per pupil per year on public education. In addition to these five northeastern states, Alaska also spends more than $8,000 per year per pupil. Alaska's expenditures are associated with petroleum production, which has generated a large revenue base for social services despite the state's small population. In addition, the high cost of labor, supplies, building materials, and transportation means that $8,000 in Alaska does not purchase as much as it would in most other states.

The lowest levels of expenditure were found in the South and West, especially in poor, rural states. Arkansas, Mississippi, and New Mexico spent less than $5,000 per pupil. Utah was an interesting anomaly; although Utah is a wealthy state and its heavily Mormon population prizes education, its per-pupil expenditures were low. The reason may be the state's high birth rate relative to other states. With much of the population residing in the highly urban and suburban Great Salt Lake Valley, Utah's schools are economically efficient, which drives down the per-pupil cost. Most Core South and southwestern states spent less than $6,000 per pupil for the 1997–1998 school year.

Map 8-19 shows the average salaries of public school teachers by state for the 1997–1998 school year. Teacher salaries were highest in several northeastern states, including Connecticut, New Jersey, New York, Pennsylvania, and Rhode Island, along with Alaska, California, and Michigan. Housing and other living costs are high in these states, especially in large metropolitan areas such as New York City, Los Angeles, and San Francisco. Other states with large metropolitan areas, including Illinois, Maryland, and Massachusetts, also paid teacher salaries well above the national average.

Map 8-18 *Expenditure per Public School Pupil, 1997–1998*

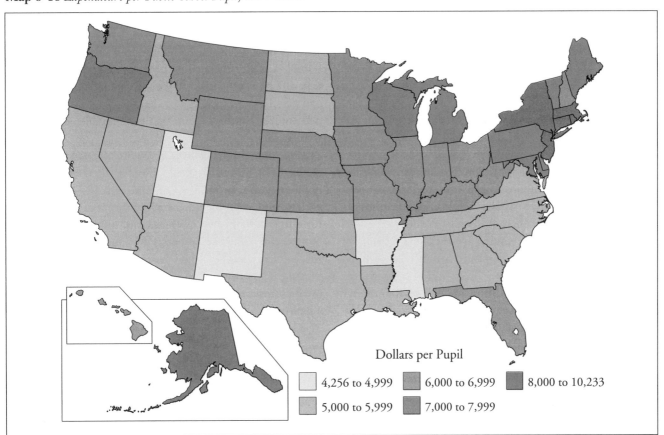

Dollars per Pupil

4,256 to 4,999   6,000 to 6,999   8,000 to 10,233
5,000 to 5,999   7,000 to 7,999

Map 8-19 *Teacher Salaries, 1997–1998*

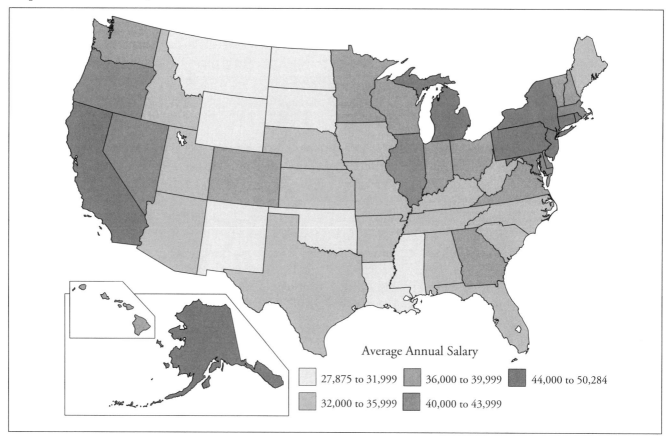

Average Annual Salary

27,875 to 31,999	
32,000 to 35,999	
36,000 to 39,999	
40,000 to 43,999	
44,000 to 50,284	

Teacher salaries were relatively low in places that pay less to support education, especially in the South and West. Rural states, which tend to have lower costs of living, paid teachers less than urban states. Salaries of less than $30,000 per year were reported in Louisiana, Mississippi, Montana, New Mexico, North Dakota, Oklahoma, South Dakota, and Wyoming.

Because compensation for teachers, administrators, and other public school employees constitutes a large proportion of the total public school expenditures, the amounts spent are a constant subject for political debate. Proponents of increased school funding argue that the salaries of American teachers have not kept up with those associated with alternative occupations. They link the quality of teacher to the quality of education and believe that higher salaries are needed to attract competent people to teaching. Opponents of increased funding argue that there is no relationship between teacher salaries and the quality of education. The question was raised anew because of the impending retirements of large numbers of teachers born during the baby boom of the 1940s and 1950s and the need to replace them.

Map 8-20 shows the rate of graduation from public high schools in the United States by state for the 1997–1998 school year. For each state, the public high school graduation rate represents the number of students who graduated expressed as a percentage of the number of students who had entered ninth grade in that state's public schools four years earlier.

Educational achievement is one measure of educational quality. The more successful school systems are those that graduate larger proportions of students. In contemporary society, high school graduation is a minimum requirement for entry into college, trade school, military service, and most occupations. High school dropouts find it difficult to succeed in today's information-oriented economy, and the income gap between high school graduates and those without diplomas continues to increase. Nevertheless, more than a quarter of all high school enrollees fail to graduate.

The map shows that several North Central states, including Iowa, Minnesota, Nebraska, North Dakota, and Utah graduated more than 80 percent of their high school students, while their neighbors were almost as successful. Utah ranked near the top in graduation rate despite its low levels of per-pupil educational funding (Map 8-18). Other northern and western states also reported high graduation rates.

Map 8-20 *Public High School Graduation Rate, 1997–1998*

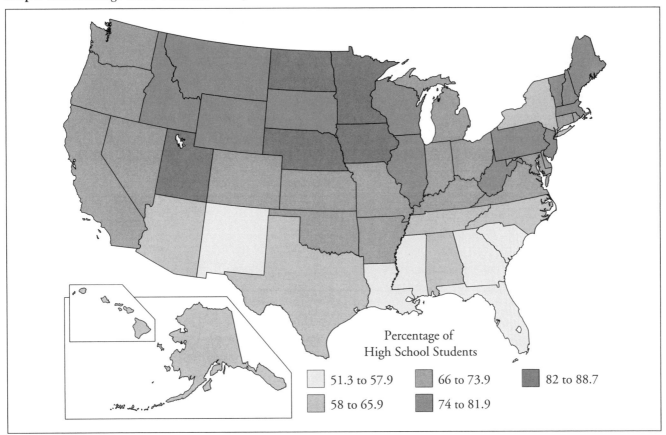

Percentage of
High School Students

51.3 to 57.9	66 to 73.9	82 to 88.7
58 to 65.9	74 to 81.9	

Graduation rates were lower in the South and in metropolitan areas. In Florida, Georgia, Louisiana, Mississippi, New Mexico, and South Carolina less than 60 percent of public school students graduated.

Map 8-21 shows the number of students enrolled in institutions of higher education per 1,000 population in each state in fall 1997. Since the mid-twentieth century, the number of high school graduates who have gone on to higher education has grown. Many attend traditional four-year colleges and universities, while others go to community colleges or to trade, vocational, and technical schools.

In general, the highest rates of higher education enrollment were found in the West and Northeast. Arizona, Colorado, Kansas, Nebraska, and Utah reported rates of higher education enrollment well above average, reflecting strong popular support for higher education in these rather rural states. Massachusetts and Rhode Island also had high rates, in part because of the reputations of the many colleges and universities located within them. The lowest rates of higher education enrollment were found throughout the South, especially in Arkansas, Florida, Georgia, and Kentucky. These low rates are due, in part, to in-migration of elderly people, but they also reflect the lower high school gradua-

tion rates characteristic of the South (see Map 8-20).

Map 8-22 depicts the percentage of adults aged twenty-five or older in each state who held four-year college degrees in 2000. To a considerable extent, the state-level residential patterns of college graduates parallel the geographical patterns of college enrollment rates. Many college graduates, however, move to other states after taking their degrees. States with strong educational systems but weak economies tend to export educated adults to other states. For example, thousands of new college graduates in Kansas and Nebraska leave these states each year to seek employment opportunities in Denver, Dallas-Fort Worth, Los Angeles, and other major metropolitan areas. By the same token, states with rapidly growing economies may not have especially large higher educational enrollment rates, but economic opportunities make them attractive as migration destinations to adult college graduates from states that offer fewer attractive jobs.

These trends are evident in Map 8-22. The highest percentage of college graduates were found in the Northeast, especially in those states with suburbs of large metropolitan areas, including Connecticut, Maryland, Massachusetts, New Jersey, and Virginia. Colorado and Minnesota, which have long histories of support for education, combined with large

Map 8-21 *Enrollment in Higher Education, Fall 1997*

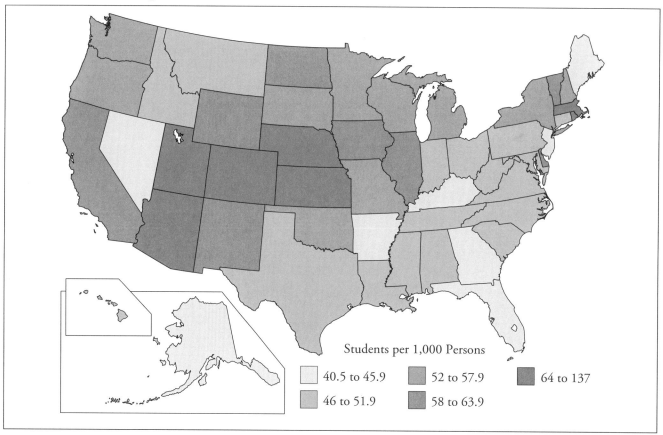

Students per 1,000 Persons

40.5 to 45.9   52 to 57.9   64 to 137

46 to 51.9   58 to 63.9

Map 8-22 *Adult College Graduates, 2000*

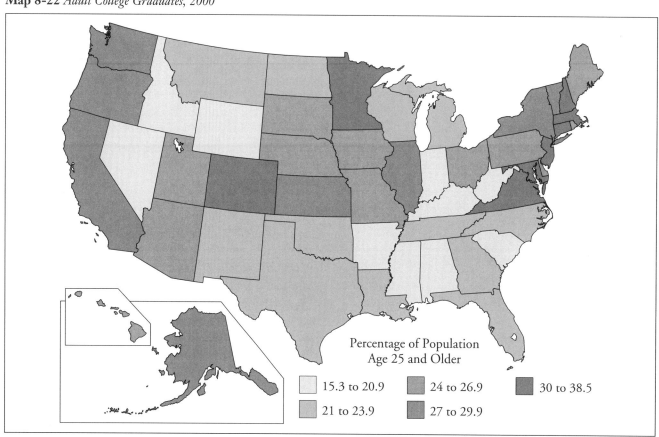

Percentage of Population
Age 25 and Older

15.3 to 20.9   24 to 26.9   30 to 38.5

21 to 23.9   27 to 29.9

and growing metropolitan centers in Minneapolis-St. Paul and Denver, respectively, also had high percentages of adult college graduates. The percentage of college-educated adults was somewhat lower in relatively rural states, such as Iowa and Nebraska, which export many young, college-educated adults to other states. The rates were lowest throughout the South and in Indiana, Kentucky, and West Virginia. These states have smaller cities and weaker economies than their neighbors and lose many of their college graduates to larger metropolitan centers in other states.

Access to Information and the Arts

A characteristic of contemporary American society is its growing dependence on information and the access to information. Books and magazines, newspapers, radio and television, and the Internet carry the information vital to American work, leisure, and educational life. In addition, the availability of art and public performances enhances the quality of life in small towns and major cities alike. Maps 8-23 through 8-26 display geographical distributions related to information availability and public funding of the arts.

Map-8-23 displays the number of books and serials, also known as periodicals, per capita in public libraries in each

state in 1997. The number of available books and periodicals varied from less than two to more than five per person. Availability was greatest in the Northeast and smallest in the South. Several southern states reported less than two library books and serial volumes per person. The highest number of available library resources was found in most of New England and Kansas, New York, South Dakota, and Wyoming. The north-south difference evident in Map 8-23 may be a reflection of differences in political culture. The moralistic political culture of the North stresses civil involvement, while the traditionalistic political culture in the South historically has discouraged civic participation and therefore places less emphasis on the written word and access to knowledge and information (Map 6-1).

Map 8-24 shows the distribution of households that had Internet access by state as of 1998. Internet availability no doubt has increased considerably since 1998, but the relative patterns shown on the map are unlikely to have changed. Internet access was highest in four widely separated, fairly small states: Alaska, New Hampshire, Utah, and Washington. All of these states are reasonably wealthy, and in each of these states Internet access may compensate for relatively long distances to major markets and large metropolitan areas. Elsewhere, Internet access was greatest in the Northeast corridor and in the West. It was least available

Map 8-23 *Public Library Books and Serials, 1997*

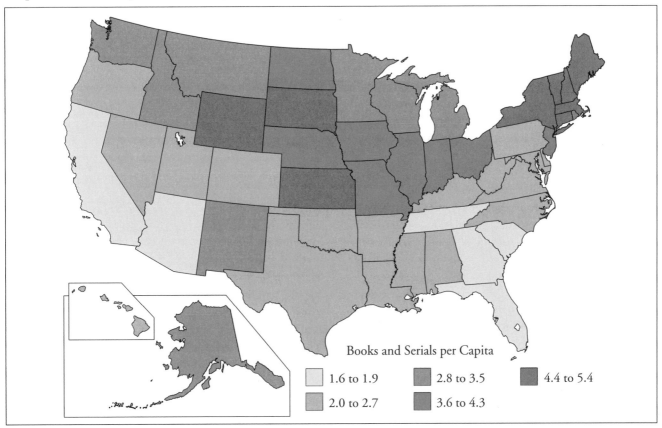

Books and Serials per Capita

1.6 to 1.9   2.8 to 3.5   4.4 to 5.4
2.0 to 2.7   3.6 to 4.3

Map 8-24 *Households with Internet Access, 1998*

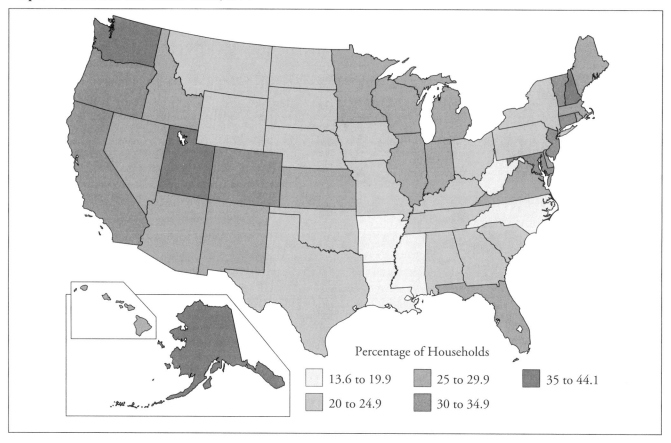

Percentage of Households

13.6 to 19.9	25 to 29.9	35 to 44.1
20 to 24.9	30 to 34.9	

in the South. Less than 20 percent of households in five states—Arkansas, Louisiana, Mississippi, North Carolina, and West Virginia—had Internet access in 1998. Perhaps it was significant that a president from Arkansas, Bill Clinton, strongly advocated universal access to the Internet in public schools throughout the United States. Clinton recognized that people who lack access to the Internet can be at a disadvantage in employment, housing, and many other aspects of modern life.

Map 8-25 depicts daily newspaper circulation by state in 1999. The information mapped is the number of newspapers sold each day per 1,000 population—a figure that ranged from 120 to more than 250. The highest circulation levels were in the Northeast, especially in urbanized states such as Massachusetts, New York, and Virginia. Circulation levels were also high in states in and near the Great Plains, including Colorado, Iowa, Nebraska, North Dakota, and South Dakota. Rates of newspaper circulation were lowest in the Southeast, especially in Alabama, Georgia, Mississippi, and Texas. The state of Maryland appears as an anomaly but may be explained on the basis of the fact that many Maryland residents read the *Washington Post*, published in Washington, D.C., as well as the Virginia-based *USA Today*

and New York's *New York Times* and *Wall Street Journal*.

Historically, most daily newspapers are oriented primarily to local coverage areas. Most local coverage areas focus on cities and their suburbs. Some newspapers, such as the *Des Moines Register*, Salt Lake City's *Deseret News*, and Little Rock's *Arkansas Democrat*, have essentially statewide circulation. In recent years, the circulation of national newspapers such as *USA Today* and the *Wall Street Journal* has grown considerably.

Map 8-26 shows the distribution of state funding to support the arts. The data represent the amount of state funding for the arts per 100 people. Values across the states ranged from a low of $14 to more than $150 per 100 of population—in other words, from fourteen cents to more than $1.50 per person per year. High levels of support tend to be found in states with or near large urban centers. Delaware, Florida, Hawaii, Maryland, Massachusetts, Michigan, Missouri, and New York spent more than $150 per 100 persons. These higher values may be explained by the relative wealth of these states and the large city populations that provide audiences for musical and theatrical performances and locations for viewing displays of art. Although Delaware has no large cities, its proximity to Philadelphia, Baltimore, and

Map 8-25 *Daily Newspaper Circulation, 1999*

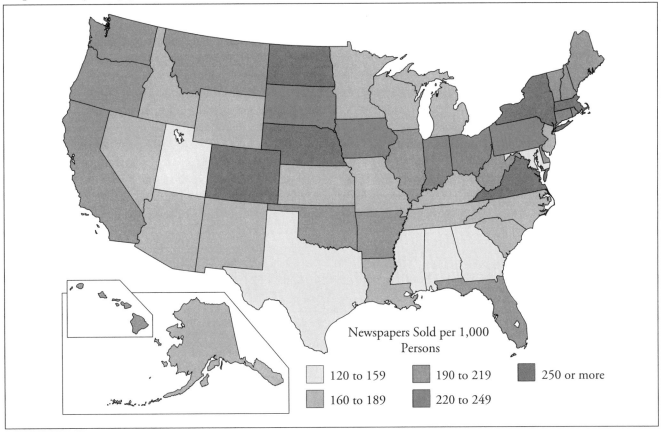

Newspapers Sold per 1,000
Persons

| | 120 to 159 | | 190 to 219 | | 250 or more |
| | 160 to 189 | | 220 to 249 | | |

Map 8-26 *State Funding for the Arts, 1997*

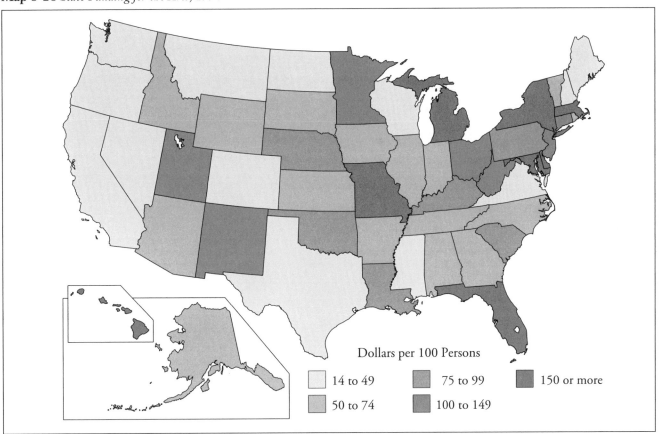

Dollars per 100 Persons

| | 14 to 49 | | 75 to 99 | | 150 or more |
| | 50 to 74 | | 100 to 149 | | |

Washington places it in close range of a very large urban population. Low values were found in many southern and western states, including the large states of California and Texas. Northern New England and the Plains states also did not support the arts as much as other states did.

The extent of federal, state, and local government support for artistic activity occasionally becomes an issue for debate. Proponents of public funding say it is essential to the maintenance of quality artistic expression—music, theater, and the visual arts. Opponents of public funding have argued that some artists' expressions are inconsistent with the basic values of contemporary society. On several occasions, conservatives in Congress have tried to eliminate or cut budgets for federal agencies, such as the National Endowment for the Arts and the National Endowment for the Humanities, that support artistic activity.

Crime and Law Enforcement

The control and prevention of criminal activity are vital functions of governments at all levels. The issue becomes political when police departments request more officers and

higher budgets. The efforts to prevent violent crime and property crime, prosecution and treatment of offenders, and capital punishment are also matters for political debates, some of which eventually come to the U.S. Supreme Court.

Map 8-27 shows the number of full-time police officers per 10,000 persons in the state populations in 1996. Police officers work for both state and local governments. Unlike many other maps in this atlas, no clear-cut pattern is evident. There is a modest tendency for the number of full-time police officers per 10,000 population to be greater toward the southern edge of the United States, but notable exceptions can be found throughout the country. Kentucky and West Virginia were the most southerly states in the lowest category of 17 or fewer full-time officers per 10,000 population, but much locational variation was found at the upper end of the scale. Several widely scattered states had more than 27 full-time officers per 10,000 population. Many were in the Northeast, even though northern New England, with its more rural population, had relatively few police officers. States in the South and West also varied widely, although the urban-rural differential characteristic of the Northeast is not applicable in these sections. For example, rural Wyoming and New Mexico had more offi-

Map 8-27 *Full-Time Police Officers, 1996*

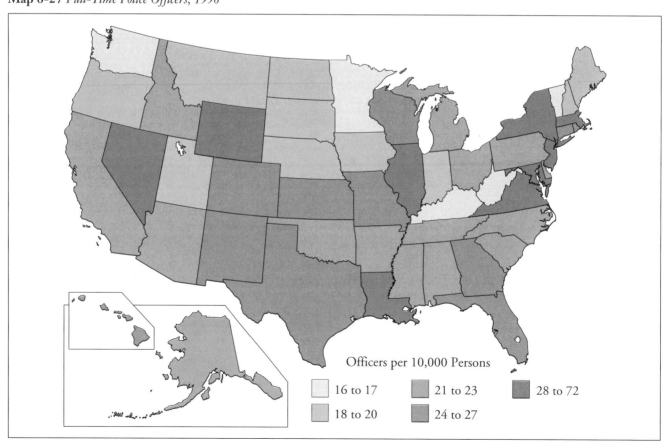

Officers per 10,000 Persons

16 to 17 21 to 23 28 to 72

18 to 20 24 to 27

cers per capita than did urbanized Arizona, California, and Washington.

Map 8-28 shows the state-by-state rates of violent crime for 1998. Violent crimes include murder, rape, assault and battery, and armed robbery. The rates are calculated as a ratio of the incidence of violent crimes to the overall population. This map shows the numbers of violent crimes known to law enforcement authorities per 10,000 population.

According to the map, rates of violent crime in 1998 ranged from 9 to 172 offenses per 10,000 population. Violent crime rates were highest in highly urbanized states and in the South. Among the localities with the highest rates of violent crime were the District of Columbia, Florida, Louisiana, Illinois, and Maryland. All have major metropolitan centers. Other large states with major metropolitan centers, such as California, Massachusetts, Michigan, and New York, also reported higher than average rates of violent crime. Rates of violent crime were considerably lower outside the South, especially in more rural states. The states in the Great Plains and Interior West generally had the lowest rates of violent crime in the country, and North Dakota and South Dakota had the lowest crime rates of any of the fifty states and the District of Columbia. The lowest rates in the eastern part of the country were found in the region's least urbanized states, including Kentucky, Maine, New Hampshire, Vermont, and West Virginia.

Map 8-29 shows the distribution of property crimes by state in 1998. These crimes are the theft of property without violence and include burglary, larceny, and automobile theft. As is the case with violent crime rates, property crime rates are calculated on the basis of number of offenses per 10,000 population. Rates of property crime generally far exceed rates of violent crime (Map 8-28). At the national level, the rate of property crime in 1998 was 405 per 10,000 population, about seven times the national violent crime rate of 57 per 10,000.

As the map indicates, the distribution of property crime is somewhat parallel to the distribution of violent crime shown in Map 8-28. The lowest rates of property crime, like violent crime, were found in North Dakota and South Dakota, but the lowest state-level number of property offenses (229 per 10,000 population) was much greater than the lowest state-level number of violent offenses (9 per 10,000) committed. The highest rates of property crime were in the South, notably Florida, Georgia, Louisiana, and South Carolina. In contrast to violent crime, however, property crime was less concentrated in major metropolitan areas.

Map 8-28 *Violent Crime Rate, 1998*

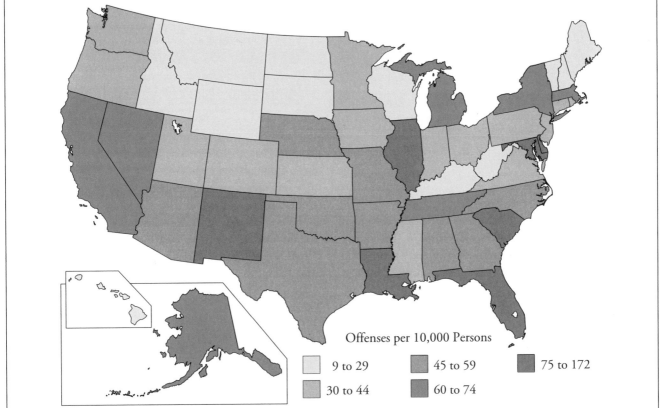

Map 8-29 *Property Crime Rate, 1998*

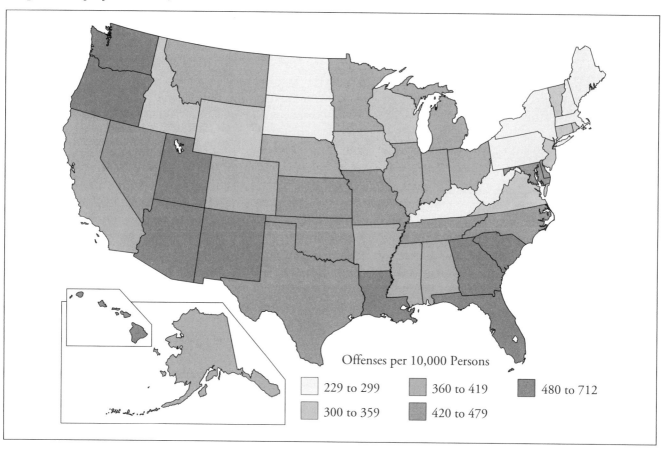

Offenses per 10,000 Persons

229 to 299	360 to 419	480 to 712
300 to 359	420 to 479	

Nonmetropolitan southern and Border states, including Kansas, North Carolina, Oklahoma, and Tennessee, reported property crime rates well above average. Property crime rates were low in most of the Northeast. Not only rural northern New England but also populous and metropolitan Massachusetts, New York, and Pennsylvania had low rates of property crime. In general, the distribution of property crime was differentiated more by region, while the distribution of violent crime was differentiated by region to an extent, but even more by metropolitan status.

Map 8-30 shows the rate of incarceration for prisoners in state and federal penitentiaries by state in 1998. The incarceration rate is defined as the number of inmates per 10,000 population. Today, more than half a million persons convicted of violent or property crimes in the United States are inmates in state or federal penitentiaries.[6] In some states, prison populations have increased to the point that state or federal courts have ordered the construction of new prison facilities to relieve overcrowding.

Not surprisingly, the rates of incarceration paralleled rates of violent and property crime (Maps 8-28 and 8-29). The highest rates of incarceration were in the South, which also had the highest crime rate. Some urbanized states out-

side the South, including California, Michigan, and Missouri, also had above averages rates of incarceration. The lowest rates of incarceration were associated with New England and the Upper Middle West, both of which reported crime rates well below the national average.

Map 8-31 shows expenditures for the police, courts, and prisons by state in 1996. The expenditures are measured in terms of dollars per capita per year. Justice system expenditures included personnel costs of police protection, administrative costs of criminal courts, and the costs of incarcerating convicted criminals. Keeping one person in prison runs to thousands of dollars per year for food, medical care, rehabilitation programs, salaries for wardens, guards, and other prison employees, and building and grounds maintenance.

Justice system expenditures do not always closely parallel crime rates (Maps 8-28 and 8-29) and prison populations (Map 8-30). The highest per capita justice system expenditures were indeed found in large urbanized states with significant crime rates, notably Florida, Maryland, New Jersey, and New York. Florida had a high incarceration rate, but New York and New Jersey did not (Map 8-30), so the high levels of justice system expenditures in these states only partly reflected large prison populations. Low per capita jus-

Map 8-30 *Incarceration Rate, 1999*

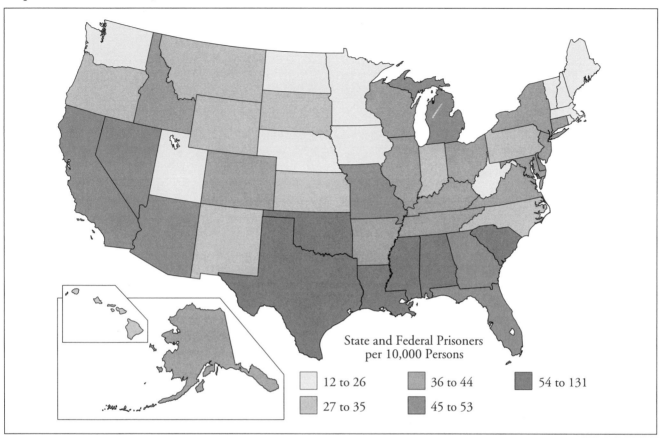

State and Federal Prisoners
per 10,000 Persons

12 to 26   36 to 44   54 to 131
27 to 35   45 to 53

Map 8-31 *Per Capita Justice System Expenditures, 1996*

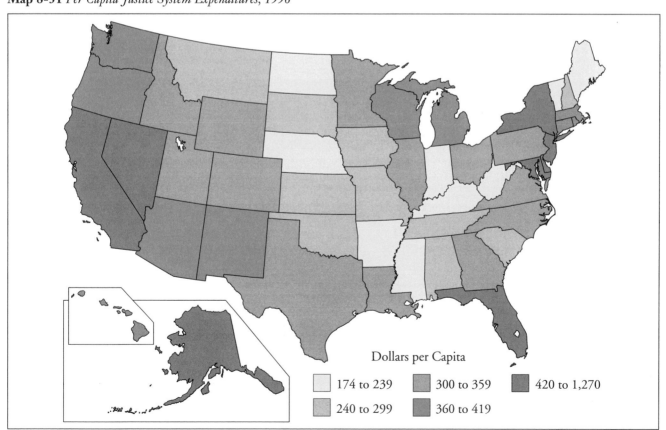

Dollars per Capita

174 to 239   300 to 359   420 to 1,270
240 to 299   360 to 419

tice system expenditures were generally found in rural states throughout the country. Some of these states, such as North Dakota and South Dakota, had low crime rates and low prison populations. In Mississippi and Arkansas, per capita justice system expenditures were low despite high crime rates and high rates of incarceration.

Map 8-32 shows the distribution of capital punishment methods in 1998. Twelve states and the District of Columbia did not impose a death penalty. Most of the states with no death penalty, with the exception of Hawaii, were in the North, especially in New England and the Upper Middle West. In the thirty-eight states that did impose a death penalty, lethal injection was the most common execution method. Some used lethal injection exclusively, and others combined injection with alternative methods, including electrocution and lethal gas. Electrocution, which is considered inhumane by many experts and members of the general public, was used exclusively in Alabama, Florida, Georgia, and Tennessee. A few states still retained the option of execution through hanging or firing squads.

During the 1960s, opponents of capital punishment argued that executions constituted cruel and unusual punishment in violation of the Eighth Amendment to the Con-

stitution. In addition, evidence that African Americans and Hispanics constituted a disproportionate number of death row inmates and those actually executed led many to conclude that capital sentences were handed down in a racially biased fashion, with convicted criminals more likely to be sentenced to death if they were members of minority groups.

These arguments persuaded the Supreme Court to ban executions for several years beginning in the early 1970s. In the late 1970s, states were given the option to reinstitute capital punishment, under guidelines intended to eliminate racial bias and to protect the constitutional rights of the condemned. The first legal execution under these revised laws took place in Utah in 1977. Recently, some states have begun to subject crime evidence to DNA tests to further reduce the probability of executing an innocent person. In Illinois, the discovery by a Northwestern University journalism professor and class that a man facing execution was in fact innocent persuaded that state's governor to impose a temporary moratorium on executions.

Since 1977 states have had the option to reinstitute capital punishment, and thirty-eight of the fifty states have done so. Map 8-33 shows the distribution of actual executions by

Map 8-32 *Methods of Capital Punishment, 1998*

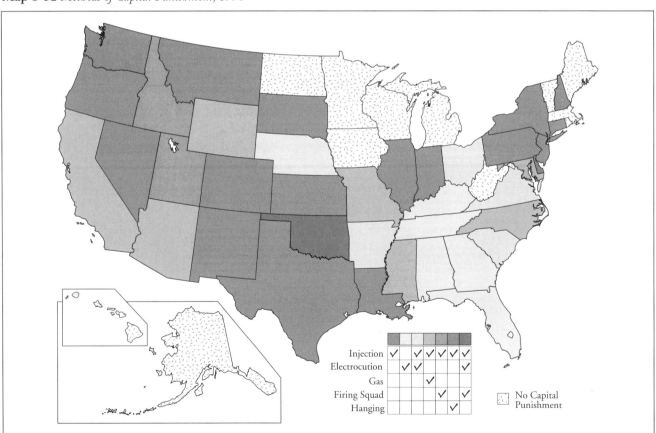

state between the reinstitution of capital punishment in 1977 and 2000.

Legal executions were most commonplace in the South. Texas was the only state in which more than 100 prisoners had been executed since 1977. Indeed, the high rate of capital punishment in Texas was an issue in the 2000 presidential campaign (Map 2-21). Opponents of the Republican candidate, Gov. George W. Bush of Texas, argued that his state's high number of executions, many of which occurred during his tenure as governor, represented an inappropriate approach to crime and punishment. Most of the other states with twenty-five or more executions were also in or near the South. These included Florida, Missouri, Oklahoma, and Virginia. Low numbers of executions took place in the North. Several northern states, including Connecticut, Kansas, New Jersey, and New York, have reinstituted capital punishment but have yet to execute any prisoners.

Environment

As early as the 1950s awareness of environmental degradation was becoming a political issue. It became more central to the public consciousness following the publication of seminal works such as Rachel Carson's *Silent Spring* in 1962 and Stewart Udall's *The Quiet Crisis* in 1963.[7] The first Earth Day, held in 1970, brought environmental quality to the political forefront. Measures of environmental quality as well as the impacts of various environmental policies and the effects of development are the subjects of Maps 8-34 through 8-43.

Map 8-34 shows the counties across the United States that were not in compliance with national air quality standards in January 2001, as measured by the Environmental Protection Agency. Severe nonattainment counties are those in which air quality was far below national air pollution standards. These counties, as might be expected, were in and near major industrial centers and large metropolitan areas, where heavy volumes of automobile traffic contributed to increased levels of air pollution. One such region is the Houston metropolitan area. In the 2000 presidential campaign, Democrats implied that the Republican candidate, Texas governor George Bush, would not be strong on environmental clean up, based on the failure to address Houston's low air quality. Other metropolitan areas listed in the severe nonattainment category included the major cities of

Map 8-33 *State Executions, 1977–2000*

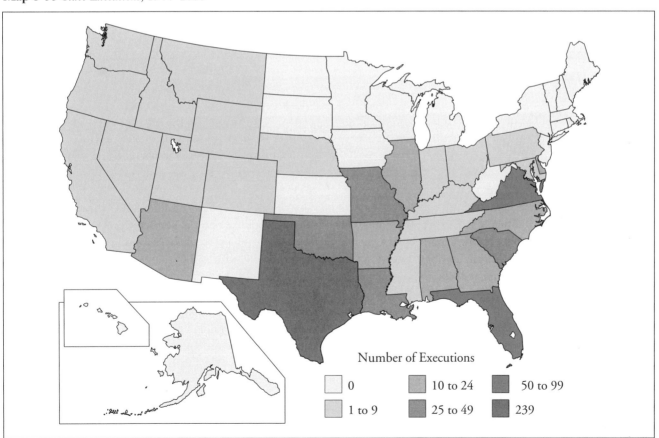

Number of Executions

0
1 to 9
10 to 24
25 to 49
50 to 99
239

Map 8-34 *Air Quality Nonattainment, January 2001*

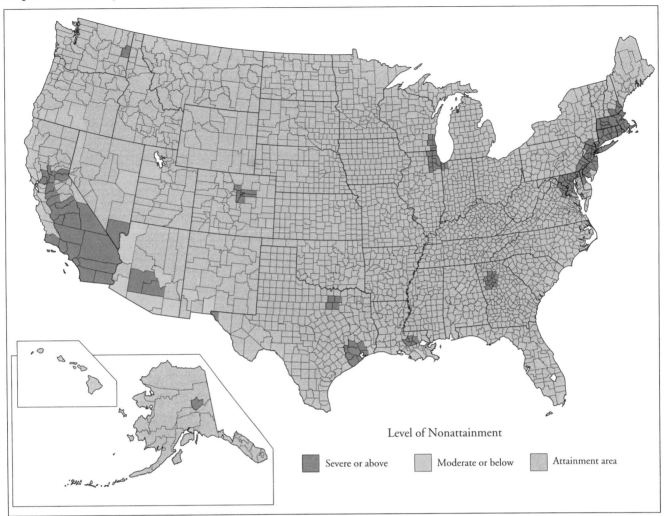

Level of Nonattainment

Severe or above   Moderate or below   Attainment area

the northeastern corridor, along with Atlanta, Chicago, Dallas-Fort Worth, Denver, Los Angeles, and Phoenix.

Surrounding these areas, and near other large cities and industrial complexes, were areas characterized by moderate to low levels of nonattainment. These included many of the nonmetropolitan counties of the Northeast, along with some of the country's smaller metropolitan centers, such as Birmingham, Buffalo, Pittsburgh, and Salt Lake City. In most rural and nonindustrialized counties, air quality attained national standards.

Map 8-35 shows the acidity of rain water across the United States in 1999. Acid rain is created when polluted air from industrial sites is discharged into the atmosphere through smokestacks and causes an increase in acidity in water vapor, which later falls to the Earth's surface in the form of rain or snow. Acid precipitation tends to be concentrated downwind from major industrial centers, not only in North America but also in other parts of the world. Acid

rain has been blamed for damaging rivers and lakes and causing deaths and diseases in plants, fish, and other animals in affected areas. Acidity is measured on the pH scale, which can range from a low of 0 to a high of 14. Pure acid has a pH value of 0, while a purely alkaline substance or base has a pH value of 14. Pure water is neither acid nor base, and therefore has a pH value of 7. Naturally occurring water is slightly acidic, with a pH value between 5 and 6.

Map 8-35 is an isopleth map, in which places with equal values on the variable being mapped—in this case, the pH level—are shaded similarly. The map shows that the measured pH value of rainfall in many areas of the country were acidic in 1999. In much of the northeastern and Great Lakes states, pH values of less than 4.3 indicated that the local rain water was more acidic than would occur naturally. This region includes areas in and downwind from the major industrial complexes of the Great Lakes states. With few exceptions, notably mining-oriented areas in Arizona and

Map 8-35 *Acidity of Rain Water, 1999*

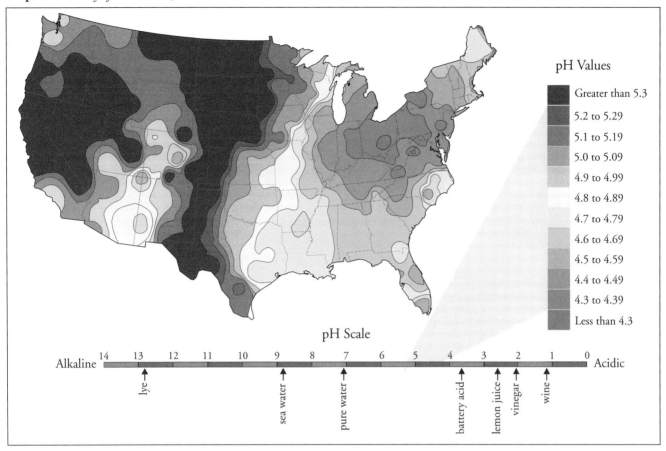

Utah, water in the West is more alkaline with pH values above 5. Acid precipitation is, therefore, a problem especially associated with the industrial Northeast.[8]

Map 8-36 shows the percentage of nonfederal developed land as of 1997. The growth of urban and suburban sprawl in the form of housing, commercial space, industry, and highways is reducing the availability of land for other purposes, including agriculture, recreation, and wildlife habitat preservation. Many would like stricter controls on land development to slow down sprawl, but developers continue to build new housing on the outskirts of metropolitan areas, and thousands of acres of farms, woodlots, and vacant lots are converted to housing and other urban uses every year.

As we saw in conjunction with Map 4-9, the federal government owns a considerable amount of land, especially in the western third of the country. Most federal lands are undeveloped, so the actual percentage of land that is developed in the West is less than appears on the map. Not surprisingly, Map 8-36 shows that the percentage of developed land is highest in the smaller, urbanized states of the Northeast, including Connecticut, Delaware, Maryland, Massachusetts, New Jersey, and Rhode Island, along with Florida. Larger northeastern states, including New York and Penn-

sylvania, have considerable amounts of developed land, but they also have large rural tracts, which reduces their percentages of developed land. The states in the Great Plains and the Interior West have very little developed land. Even though Colorado, Utah, Nevada, and Arizona are growing rapidly, much of their populations are concentrated in and near metropolitan centers such as Denver, Colorado Springs, Salt Lake City, Las Vegas, Reno, Phoenix, and Tucson. Maine is the only eastern state with relatively little developed land. Most of the northern half of Maine is owned by paper companies, and the land, which is largely uninhabited, is used primarily for logging.

Map 8-37 shows the per capita per day water use for 1995. The map indicates that per capita water use ranged from a low of 18 gallons per day (in Alaska, which has very little agricultural or industrial activity) to more than 4,000 gallons per day in many states. In addition to Alaska, low per capita water use was concentrated in the Northeast, especially in New England, Maryland, and New Jersey, and where water-intensive agriculture and industry are minimal. Water use increased from east to west, where conditions are drier and crops are irrigated. The highest values were in the Interior West, notably in Idaho, Montana, Nebraska, and

Map 8-36 *Nonfederal Developed Land, 1997*

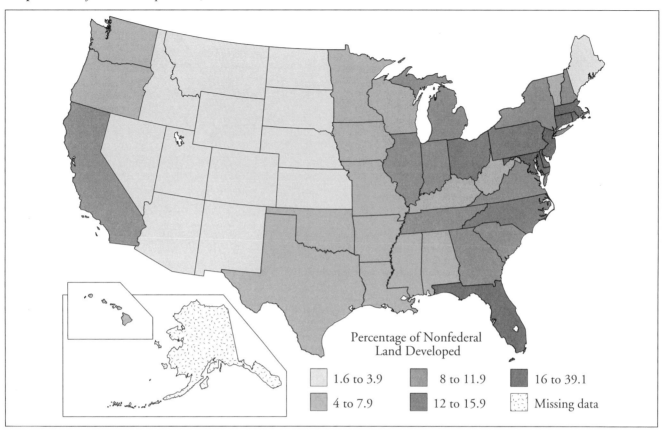

Percentage of Nonfederal
Land Developed

1.6 to 3.9	8 to 11.9	16 to 39.1
4 to 7.9	12 to 15.9	Missing data

Map 8-37 *Per Capita per Day Water Use, 1995*

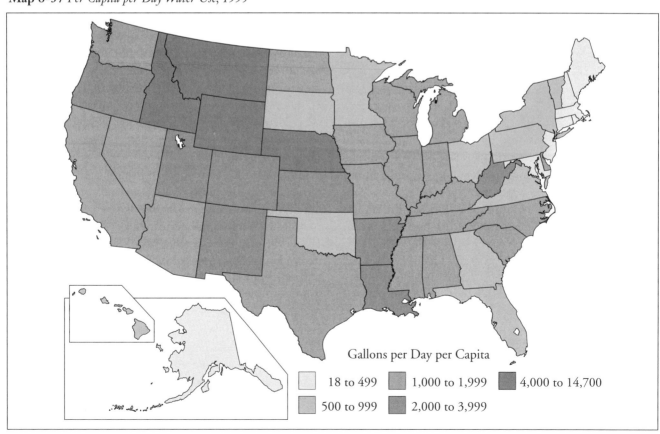

Gallons per Day per Capita

18 to 499	1,000 to 1,999	4,000 to 14,700
500 to 999	2,000 to 3,999	

Wyoming, where large quantities of water are used for crops. Water use in many cases is related inversely to water availability. In the Northeast, where water is generally plentiful, per capita water use is much less than in the West, much of which is arid.

Map 8-38 shows energy use, measured in British Thermal Units (BTUs) per capita per year, for 1997. The Northeast reported relatively low per capita energy use, particularly in New England, Maryland, and New York. For the most part, these states lack the heavy industry that is a major consumer of energy. Other states with low per capita energy use included Arizona, California, Florida, and Hawaii, where mild winters keep the demand for home-heating fuels low. Nevertheless, the highest levels of energy use, with a few exceptions, were in the South. Among the highest per capita consumers of energy were the major energy-producing states, Louisiana, Texas, and Wyoming, as well as Alaska, where energy tends to be relatively cheap. The cold climate of Alaska and Wyoming increased demand for home heating in these states. Elsewhere, states in the South, which has cheap energy and high demand for air conditioning, along with industrial states throughout the country, tended to consume the most energy per capita.

Map 8-39 shows the distribution of hazardous waste generated in each state in 1997, measured in terms of the number of pounds of hazardous waste produced per capita per year. In contemporary industrial society, the production of goods and services generates vast quantities of waste products. Many of these waste products, including chemicals, pollutants, and other toxic substances, are potentially hazardous. If untreated, hazardous waste can cause disease, result in major health hazards, and affect agriculture, development, and recreation.

The map shows that the quantity of hazardous waste produced varies from 2 pounds per person per year to more than 2,000. The highest levels of hazardous waste generation were in areas with high levels of industrial activity and energy production. Louisiana, Texas, and the Great Lakes industrial states, including Illinois, Indiana, Michigan, and Ohio, produced substantial quantities of hazardous waste. Hazardous waste generation was lower along much of the eastern seaboard and in the West. The light industry and service industries more characteristic of these areas did not generate nearly as much hazardous waste as was found in the heavy industry and energy-producing states.

Map 8-40 shows the number of hazardous waste sites, on a state-by-state basis as of 1999. The map identifies the total number of hazardous waste sites in each state placed on the National Priority List by the Environmental Protection Agency since the Superfund program was established in

Map 8-38 *Per Capita Energy Use, 1997*

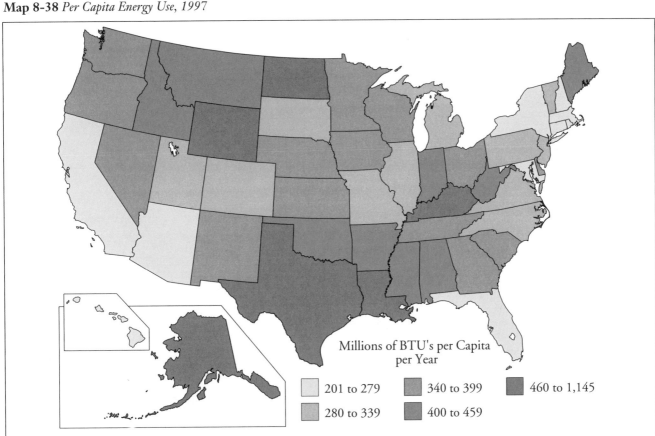

Millions of BTU's per Capita per Year

201 to 279   340 to 399   460 to 1,145

280 to 339   400 to 459

Map 8-39 *Per Capita Hazardous Waste Generation, 1997*

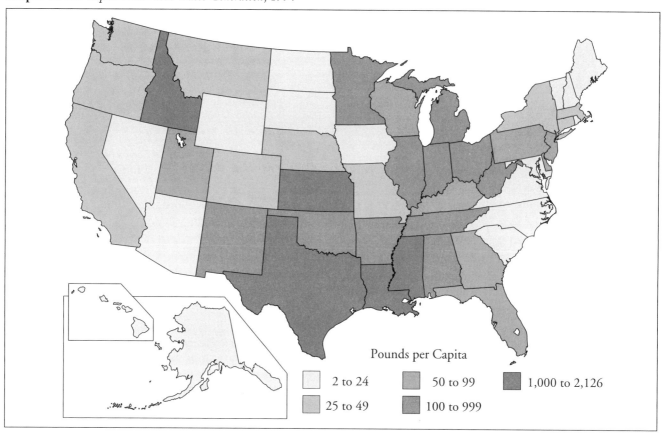

Pounds per Capita

2 to 24   50 to 99   1,000 to 2,126
25 to 49   100 to 999

Map 8-40 *Hazardous Waste Sites on National Priority List, 1999*

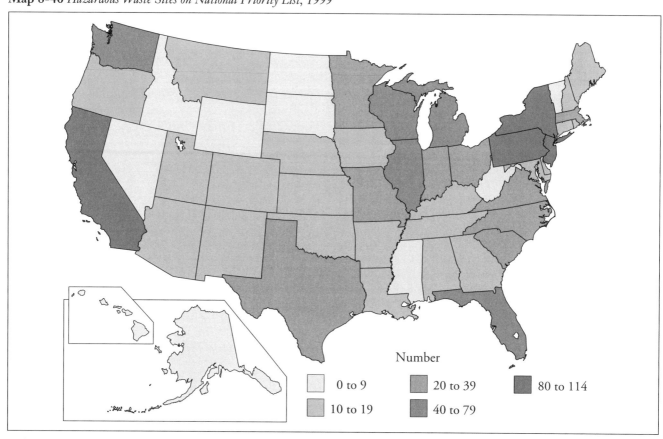

Number

0 to 9   20 to 39   80 to 114
10 to 19   40 to 79

1981.[9] Hazardous waste generation and disposal are not evenly distributed within states. Rather, hazardous wastes tend to be produced in specific places (for example, by industrial sites) and/or stored in specific locations. One function of the Environmental Protection Agency is to identify locations in which large quantities of hazardous waste have been disposed of or stored unsafely.

The lowest category represents states in which there were fewer than ten hazardous waste sites on the National Priority List. Alaska, Mississippi, and Vermont, and several states in the Interior West were in this category. States with more than eighty hazardous waste sites on the National Priority List included California, New Jersey, New York, and Pennsylvania. Other states with large industrial complexes and/or high populations, such as Florida, Illinois, Michigan, and Wisconsin, also had higher than average numbers of Priority List waste sites.

The distribution of hazardous waste sites is not necessarily consistent with the per capita production of hazardous waste itself (Map 8-39). This is true for several reasons. First, large, populous states, such as California, New York, and Pennsylvania, have many different industries, and therefore many different places where hazardous waste can be generated. In states such as Texas and Louisiana, a high volume of hazardous wastes may be generated by a relatively small number of producers. New Jersey and Illinois have larger numbers of hazardous waste producers, but each producer was responsible for a smaller volume of waste.

Map 8-41 shows the density of hazardous waste sites on the National Priority List for 1999. Density is determined by dividing the number of National Priority List hazardous waste sites in each state by that state's land area. This calculation yields the density of hazardous waste sites per 10,000 square miles in each state. The map was developed because Maps 8-39 and 8-40 reveal inconsistency: some states produced considerable volumes of hazardous waste at relatively few sites, while others had many sites but relatively little waste. This apparent inconsistency may be due in part to the fact that Map 8-40 shows the absolute number of sites.

Map 8-41 shows that the highest density of hazardous waste sites was in the Northeast and that density decreased consistently to the south and west. The states of Connecticut, Massachusetts, New Jersey, Pennsylvania, and Rhode Island each have more than 20 hazardous waste sites per 10,000 square miles. Other northeastern states, including Maryland, Michigan, and New York, also ranked well above average. Low density of hazardous waste sites on the National Priority List was characteristic of the entire western half of the country. With the exceptions of California

Map 8-41 *Density of Hazardous Waste Sites on the National Priority List, 1999*

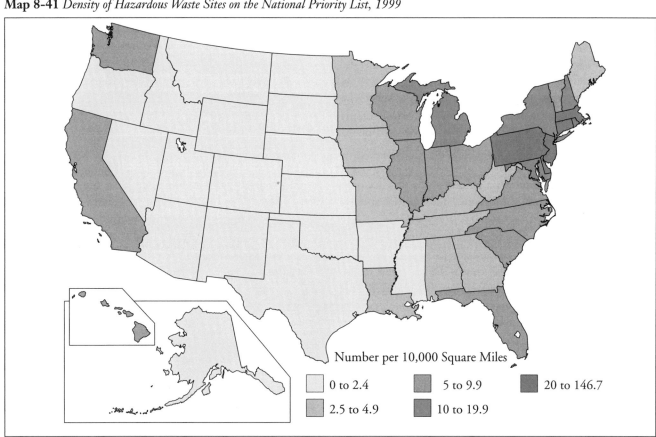

Map 8-42 *Threatened and Endangered Species, 2001*

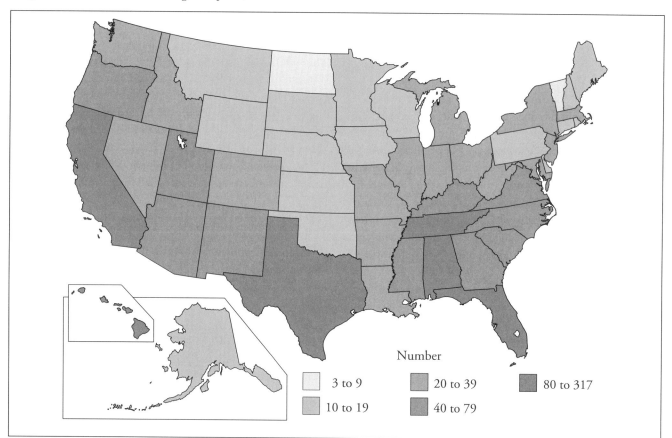

Number

3 to 9 20 to 39 80 to 317

10 to 19 40 to 79

and Hawaii, all of the states from the Great Plains westward reported less than 2.5 sites per 10,000 square miles, as did Arkansas and Mississippi.

Map 8-42 identifies the number of endangered species by state in 2001. Over the past several hundred years, numerous species of mammals, birds, reptiles, insects, and plants have become extinct. The passenger pigeon and Carolina parakeet became extinct during the twentieth century in the United States. The bison, trumpeter swan, and whooping crane reached the brink of extinction but survived and are growing in numbers.

Many other species face possible extinction because of habitat loss, competition from introduced species, environmental destruction, and other causes. In the early 1970s, Congress enacted the Endangered Species Act. This law authorized the Environmental Protection Agency to establish lists of threatened and endangered species and authorized the government to take steps to preserve these species.[10]

As shown in the map, Hawaii had by far the largest number of endangered species. Hawaii's isolated location gave rise to highly specialized flora and fauna that are found

nowhere else. These plants and animals have been unable to compete with introduced species and with environmental destruction associated with human activity. Outside of Hawaii, in general, the number of endangered species was parallel to the overall number of species in the state. Large states characterized by considerable biodiversity, such as California, Florida, and Texas, also had large numbers of endangered species. The number of endangered species tended to be high throughout the warm, humid, and biodiverse South. States located in desert environments also had many highly specialized species; therefore, Arizona, New Mexico, Oregon, and Utah all had above average numbers of endangered species. Fewer endangered species were found in the North, where levels of biodiversity are lower and the overall numbers of living species also are lower. For example, Vermont and North Dakota, which are characterized by relatively few species, had few endangered species.

Map 8-43 shows the density of threatened and endangered species in 2001, determined by dividing the number of threatened and endangered species in a state by that state's land area. Just as Map 8-41 looks at the density of hazardous waste sites to address apparent contradictions in

Map 8-43 *Density of Threatened and Endangered Species, 2001*

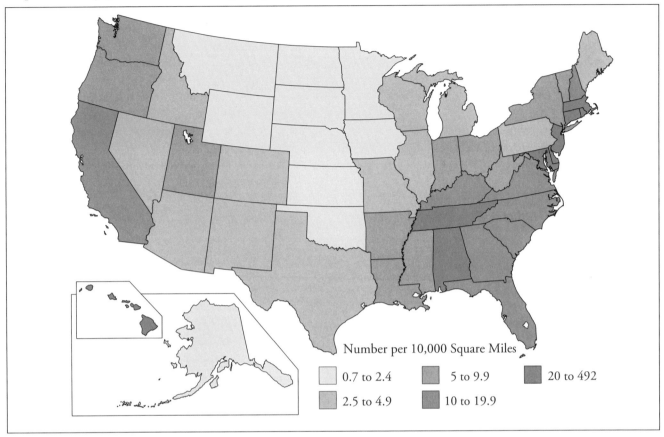

Number per 10,000 Square Miles

0.7 to 2.4	5 to 9.9	20 to 492
2.5 to 4.9	10 to 19.9	

the maps involving hazardous waste incidence, Map 8-43 augments the information in Map 8-42, which shows the number of endangered species in each state.

As might be expected, the highest density level was found in Hawaii, which has a highly specialized environment, with numerous endemic species of plants and animals, in a very small area. Indeed, Hawaii had nearly 500 threatened and endangered species per 10,000 square miles. Other states with more than 20 threatened and endangered species per 10,000 square miles included Alabama, California, and Tennessee. All of these states have substantial levels of biodiversity over fairly small areas. Most of the South and states along the Atlantic seaboard also had above average densities of threatened and endangered species. These states are characterized by substantial environmental variability and, especially in the Northeast, high human densities and high levels of development (Maps 1-3 and 8-36) that may affect the survival of various plants and animals. The Great Plains and other interior areas, which are characterized by low levels of biodiversity and fairly small human populations, had the lowest density of threatened and endangered species.

Conclusion

The maps in Chapter 8 represent just a few of the many indicators of various aspects of the quality of life in the United States. At the same time, individually and collectively, they reveal many interesting patterns. The states that consistently rank high on quality of life measures tend to be in and near the country's economic core in the Northeast and Middle West. The South and the Interior West, with long histories of dependence on the Northeast and Middle West, tend to lag behind in many aspects of quality of life. Will these differences continue to be evident in the years ahead, or will the Sun Belt continue its recent history of closing the gap with the North?

Notes

1. Sylvester J. Scheiber and John B. Shoven, *The Real Deal: The History and Future of Social Security* (New Haven: Yale University Press, 1999).

2. Richard L. Koon, *Welfare Reform: Helping the Least Fortunate Become Less Dependent* (New York: Garland, 1997).

3. Gilbert C. Fite, *American Farmers: The New Minority* (Bloomington: Indiana University Press, 1981).

4. Harry Henderson, *Gun Control* (New York: Facts on File, 2000).

5. Ralph Nader, *Unsafe at Any Speed* (New York: Grossman, 1965).

6. Kevin Johnson, "State Prison Populations Drop at End of 2000: Officials Attribute Decline to Fewer Violent Crimes in the Past Decade," *USA Today*, August 13, 2001, A7.

7. William D. Solecki and Fred M. Shelley, "The Environment as a Developing Political Issue in the 1950s," *Government and Policy* 14 (1996): 215–230; Stewart L. Udall, *The Quiet Crisis* (New York: Holt, Rinehart, and Winston, 1963); Rachel Carson, *Silent Spring* (Boston: Houghton Mifflin, 1962).

8. Gwyneth Perry Howells, *Acid Rain and Acid Waters*, 2d ed. (New York: Horwood, 1995).

9. U.S. Environmental Protection Agency, *Superfund 20-Year Report* (Washington, D.C.: U.S. Environmental Protection Agency, 2001), also available at www.epa.gov/superfund.

10. Robin W. Doughty, *Endangered Species* (Austin: University of Texas Press, 1989).

Map Sources

Introduction

Map IN-1 Original map of coastlines and other geographical features produced using program by Col. Scott A. Loomer, "Micro-CAM for Windows, Version 2.03," Geographic Sciences Laboratory, U.S. Military Academy, West Point, New York, January 27, 2000.

Map IN-2 Tom L. McKnight, *Regional Geography of the United States and Canada*, 2d ed. (Englewood Cliffs, N.J.: Prentice-Hall, 1997), 16; H. J. de Blij and Peter O. Muller, *Geography: Realms, Regions and Concepts*, 9th ed. (New York: Wiley, 2000), 157; and David L. Clawson and James S. Fisher, *World Regional Geography: A Developmental Approach*, 6th ed. (Englewood Cliffs, N.J.: Prentice-Hall, 1998), 94.

Map IN-3 J. Clark Archer and Peter J. Taylor, *Section and Party* (New York: Wiley, 1981), 103–109; J. Clark Archer and Fred M. Shelley, *American Electoral Mosaics* (Washington, D.C.: Association of American Geographers, 1986), 48–54; and Fred M. Shelley, J. Clark Archer, Fiona M. Davidson, and Stanley D. Brunn, *Political Geography of the United States* (New York: Guilford, 1996), 282–287.

Chapter 1

Map 1-1 Fred M. Shelley, J. Clark Archer, Fiona M. Davidson, and Stanley D. Brunn, *Political Geography of the United States* (New York: Guilford, 1996), 42; F. W. Hewes & H. Gannett, eds., *Scribner's Statistical Atlas of the United States* (New York: Scribner's, 1883), plates 12–17; H. U. Faulkner & T. Kepner, *America: Its History & People* (Washington, D.C.: U.S. Armed Forces Institute, War Dept. (Harper & Brothers, 1944); U.S. Geological Survey, *Maps of an Emerging Nation: The United States of America, 1775–1987* (Reston, Va.: U.S. Geological Survey, 1987).

Map 1-2 Council of State Governments, *The Book of the States, 1998–1999 Edition* (Lexington, Ky.: Council of State Governments, 1998), 448.

Map 1-3 U.S. Census Bureau, "Census 2000 Redistricting Data (Public Law 94-171 Summary File), Table QT-PL Race, Hispanic or Latino, and Age: 2000," downloaded March 2001 from http://factfinder.census.gov.

Map 1-4 U.S. Census, "Metropolitan Counties in Alphabetical Order, by State, with Metropolitan Area Title," downloaded October 4, 2000, from http//www.census.gov/population/estimates/metro-city/a99mfips.txt.

Map 1-5 U.S. Census Bureau, Table QT-PL.

Map 1-6 U.S. Census Bureau, "County Population Estimates for July 1, 1999; and Demographic Components of Change: April 1, 1990 to July 1, 1999 (includes revised April 1, 1990, Population Estimates Base) (CO-99-4)," Population Estimates Program, Internet release, March 9, 2000.

Map 1-7 Ibid.

Map 1-8 Ibid.

Map 1-9 U.S. Census Bureau, "USA Counties 1998 on CD-ROM," machine-readable data files issued May 1999.

Map 1-10 Ibid.

Map 1-11 U.S. Census Bureau, "County Population Estimates for July 1, 1999, and Demographic Components of Change: April 1, 1990 to July 1, 1999."

Maps 1-12–1-15 U.S. Census Bureau, Table QT-PL.

Map 1-16 "Churches and Church Membership in the United States, 1990," machine-readable data, Roper Center for Public Opinion Research, University of Connecticut; Martin B. Bradley, Norman M. Green Jr., Dale E. Jones, Mac Lynn, and Lou McNeil, "Churches and Church Membership in the United States, 1990: An Enumeration by Region, State and County, Based on Data Reported for 133 Church Groupings" (Atlanta, Ga.: Glenmary Research Center, 1992).

Maps 1-17–1-22 "Churches and Church Membership in the United States, 1990."

Map 1-23 U.S. Census Bureau, "Small Area Income and Poverty Estimates 1995 State and County FTP Files and Description," http://www.census.gov/housing/saipe/estmod/est95ALL.dat. Downloaded August 17, 2000.

Map 1-24 Ibid.

Maps 1-25–1-27 U.S. Census Bureau, "1990 Census of Population and Housing: Summary Tape File 3 on CD-ROM" (May 1992).

Chapter 2

Maps 2-1–2-20 Inter-University Consortium for Political and Social Research (ICPSR) data sets; Congressional Quarterly, *America Votes*, (Washington, D.C.: Congressional Quarterly, various years); U.S. Census Bureau, *Statistical Abstract of the United States* (Washington, D.C.: Government Printing Office, 2000); and *The World Almanac and Book of Facts 2001* (Mahwah, N.J.: World Almanac Books, various years), for votes; and Alaska Election Commission for Alaska election district boundaries.

Map 2-21 www.cnn.com; and secretaries of state sites for New England states and Alaska.

Map 2-22 National Archives and Records Administration, "2000 Presidential Election: Electoral Vote Results," http://www.nara.gov/fedreg/elctcoll/2000res.htm.

Maps 2-23–2-30 Daily issues of *USA Today*, Labor Day to election day, for 1988 election through 2000 election.

Maps 2-31 and 2-32 *America Votes*.

Map 2-33 www.census.gov, November 2, 2000, for voting age population; www.cnn.com, November 22, 2000, for presidential vote by state.

Chapter 3

Maps 3-1–3-4 U.S. Census Bureau, *Statistical Abstract of the United States* (Washington, D.C.: Government Printing Office, various years).

Map 3-5 http://www.census.gov/population/cen2000/tab01.txt.

Maps 3-6–3-9 Census Bureau, *Statistical Abstract*.

Map 3-10 www.cnn.com, November 22, 2000; and www.senate.gov, May 31, 2001.

Maps 3-11–3-14 Census Bureau, *Statistical Abstract*.

Map 3-15 www.cnn.com, November 22, 2000.

Map 3-16 *Congressional Quarterly Almanac, 98th Congress, 1st Session, 1983* (Washington, D.C.: Congressional Quarterly, 1984), 10–11.

Map 3-17 *Congressional Quarterly Almanac, 103rd Congress, 1st Session, 1993* (Washington, D.C.: Congressional Quarterly, 1994), 6–7.

Map 3-18 www.cnn.com, November–December, 2000.

Map 3-19 Ibid., 55-C.

Map 3-20 *CQ Weekly*, February 13, 1999, 409.

Map 3-21 *CQ Almanac, 1993*, 48-C–49-C.

Map 3-22 *Congressional Quarterly Almanac, 105th Congress, 1st Session, 1997* (Washington, D.C.: Congressional Quarterly, 1998), C-48–C-49.

Map 3-23 http://adaction.org, accessed November 3, 2000.

Map 3-24 Ibid.

Chapter 4

Map 4-1 Census divisions and regions, U.S. Census Bureau, *Statistical Abstract of the United States* (Washington, D.C.: Government Printing Office, 1999); Census Bureau offices, www.census.gov/main/www/m-img/orgchart.jpg, accessed January 10, 2001.

Map 4-2 http://www.federalreserve.gov/otherfrb.htm, accessed December 10, 2000.

Map 4-3 http://www.epa.gov/epahome/locate2.htm, accessed December 18, 2000.

Map 4-4 William A. McGeveran Jr., ed., *The World Almanac and Book of Facts 2001* (Mahwah, N.J.: World Almanac Books, 2001), 182–186.

Map 4-5 Tax Foundation, "Tax and Spending Policies Benefit Some States, Leave Others Footing the Bill," http://www.taxfoundation.org/pr-fedtaxspendingratio.html, released June 27, 2000, accessed September 28, 2000.

Map 4-6 Ibid.

Map 4-7 U.S. Bureau of Census, "Consolidated Federal Funds Report for Fiscal Year 1999," http://www.census.gov/govs/www/cffr99.html on May 11, 2000.

Map 4-8 Ibid.

Map 4-9 U.S. Census Bureau, *Statistical Abstract, 1999*, 240.

Map 4-10 U.S. Office of Personnel Management, "Biennial Report of Employment By Geographic Area, As of December 31, 1998" (Washington, D.C.: US Office of Personnel Management, September 1999), 9; http://www.opm.gov/feddata, accessed May 9, 2001.

Map 4-11 Ibid.

Chapter 5

Map 5-1 Federal Judicial Center, *Federal Courts and What They Do* (Washington, D.C.: Federal Judiciary Center, 1996), 3, 20; personal e-mail communication from Matt P. Sarago, Information Services Office, Federal Judicial Center, updating Florida counties and districts, January 11, 2001.

Map 5-2 Robert Famighetti, ed., *The World Almanac and Book of Facts* (Mahwah, N.J.: World Almanac Books, 1999), 91.

Map 5-3 Congressional Quarterly, *Almanac, 1969* (Washington, D.C.: Congressional Quarterly, 1970), 29-S.

Map 5-4 Ibid., 21-S.

Map 5-5 Congressional Quarterly, *Almanac, 1987* (Washington, D.C.: Congressional Quarterly, 1988), 60-S.

Map 5-6 Congressional Quarterly, *Almanac, 1991* (Washington, D.C.: Congressional Quarterly, 1992), 29-S.

Maps 5-7–5-9 Stanley D. Brunn, Fred M. Shelley, Gerald R. Webster, and Wael M. Ahmed, "Place and Region in American Legal Culture: State Origins of Landmark Supreme Court Cases," *Historical Geography* 28 (2000): 135–155.

Chapter 6

Map 6-1 Fred M. Shelley, J. Clark Archer, Fiona M. Davidson, and Stanley D. Brunn, *Political Geography of the United States* (New York: Guilford, 1996), 61, based on map in Daniel J. Elazar, *American Federalism: A View from the States*, 3d ed. (New York: Harper, 1984), 135–136.

Map 6-2 Fred J. Vickers, ed, *The Book of the States, 2000-2001 Edition*, vol. 33 (Lexington, Ky: Council of State Governments, 2000), 3.

Map 6-3 Ibid., 15–16.

Map 6-4 "State Gubernatorial Term Limits," http://www.ustermlimits.org/Current_Info/State_TL/gubernatorial.html, accessed May 18, 2001.

Map 6-5 Vickers, *Book of the States*, 70–71; National Conference of State Legislatures, "Term Limits for State Elected Officials," http://www.ncsl.org/programs/about/termintro.html, accessed May 16, 2001.

Map 6-6 National Conference of State Legislatures, "Term Limits," http://www.ncsl.org/programs/about/termintro.html, accessed May 16, 2001; "State Gubernatorial Term Limits," http://www.

ustermlimits.org/Current_Info/State_TL/gubernatorial.html, accessed May 18, 2001.

Map 6-7 Vickers, *Book of the States*, 137–139.

Map 6-8 Ibid., 233–237.

Map 6-9 Ibid., 248–249.

Map 6-10 Ibid., 20–21, 101–103.

Maps 6-11–6-14 U.S. Census Bureau, *Statistical Abstract of the United States* (Washington, D.C.: Government Printing Office, 1970, 1980, 1990).

Map 6-15 *National Journal*, "The 50 States at a Glance," November 11, 2000, 3606–8.

Maps 6-16–6-19 U.S. Census Bureau, *Statistical Abstract of the United States* (Washington, D.C.: Government Printing Office, 1960, 1970, 1980, 1990).

Map 6-20 Council of State Governments, http://www.statesnews.org/election2000/2000_statehouse_control.htm, accessed December 20, 2000.

Maps 6-21–6-24 U.S. Census Bureau, *Statistical Abstract of the United States* (Washington, D.C.: Government Printing Office, 1960, 1970, 1980, 1990).

Map 6-25 Council of State Governments, http://www.statesnews.org/election2000/2000_statehouse_control.htm, accessed December 20, 2000.

Map 6-26 U.S. Census Bureau, "State Government Tax Collections: 1999," http://www.census.gov/govs/statetax/99tax.txt, accessed December 23, 2000.

Map 6-27 Ibid.

Map 6-28 U.S. Census Bureau, *Statistical Abstract of the United States* (Washington, D.C.: Government Printing Office, 2000), 305.

Map 6-29 U.S. Census, "1998 State Government Finance Data: Income and Apportionment of State-Administered Lottery Funds, 1998," http://www.census.gov/govs/www/state98.html, accessed May 20, 2001.

Map 6-30 Census Bureau, *Statistical Abstract 2000*, 322.

Map 6-31 Council of State Governments, www.csg.org, accessed December 20, 2000.

Map 6-32 U.S. Census Bureau, "1992 Census of Governments, Vol. 1 Government Organization, No. 2 Popularly Elected Officials," June 1995, Table 3.

Map 6-33 Census Bureau, *Statistical Abstract 2000*, 288.

Map 6-34 Ibid.

Map 6-35 Ibid., 287.

Chapter 7

Figure 7-1 U.S. Immigration and Naturalization Service, *Statistical Yearbook of the Immigration and Naturalization Service, 1998* (Washington, D.C.: U.S. Government Printing Office, 2000), 20–22.

Map 7-1 Ibid., 24–28.

Map 7-2 Ibid., 71.

Map 7-3 Ibid., 98.

Map 7-4 Ibid., 118.

Map 7-5 North Atlantic Treaty Organization, *NATO Handbook: The Origins of the Alliance*, http://www.nato.int/docu/handbook/2001/hb0101.htm, accessed May 21, 2001.

Map 7-6 Department of Defense, Directorate for Information Operations and Reports, "Department of Defense Selected Man-

power Statistics, Fiscal Year 1999," http://web1.whs.osd.mil/mmid/mmidhome.htm, accessed May 22, 2001.

Map 7-7 Ibid.

Map 7-8 U.S. Census Bureau, *Statistical Abstract of the United States* (Washington, D.C.: Government Printing Office, 2000), 364.

Map 7-9 Ibid., 790.

Map 7-10 Ibid.

Map 7-11 Compiled from "Chronology of Significant Terrorist Incidents" in U.S. Department of State, "Patterns of Global Terrorism 1996" (April 1997); and subsequent annual issues published in April 1998, 1999, 2000, and 2001.

Map 7-12 Census Bureau, *Statistical Abstract 2000*, 794–797.

Map 7-13 Ibid., 793.

Map 7-14 Ibid.

Map 7-15 Ibid., 794–797.

Map 7-16 Ibid., 784.

Map 7-17 Bureau of Economic Analysis, "International Investment Data: U.S. Direct Investment Position Abroad on a Historical-Cost Basis, 1998, " updated June 29, 2000, http://www.bea.doc.gov/di/diapos_98.htm, accessed January 20, 2001.

Chapter 8

Map 8-1 Joseph Dalaker and Bernadette D. Proctor, "U.S. Census Bureau, Current Population Reports, Series P60-210, Poverty in the United States: 1999" (Washington, D.C.: Government Printing Office, September 2000), p xiii.

Map 8-2 U.S. Census Bureau, "Consolidated Federal Funds Report for Fiscal Year 1999," 2.

Map 8-3 Ibid., 2–3; Department of Health and Human Services, Administration for Children and Families, "Expenditures in the TANF Program in Fiscal Year 1999," http:/www.acf.dhhs.gov/programs/ofs/data/q499, accessed January 21, 2001.

Map 8-4 Census Bureau, "Consolidated Federal Funds Report," 3.

Map 8-5 Ibid.

Maps 8-6–8-10 Sherry L. Murphy, "Deaths: Final Data for 1998," National Center for Health Statistics: National Vital Statistics Reports, Vol. 48, No. 11, 83–86 (http://www.cdc.gov/nchs).

Map 8-11 William A. McGeveran Jr., *The World Almanac and Book of Facts 2001* (Mahwah, N.J.: World Almanac Books, 2001), 875.

Map 8-12 Stephanie J. Ventura, Joyce A. Martin, Sally C. Curtin, T. J. Mathews, and Melissa M. Park, "Births: Final Data for 1998," National Center for Health Statistics: National Vital Statistics Reports, Vol. 48, No. 3, 80 (http://www.cdc.gov/nchs).

Map 8-13 Ibid.

Map 8-14 A. P. MacKay, L. A. Fingerhut, and C. R. Duran, "Health, United States, 2000, with Adolescent Health Chartbook" (Hyattsville, Md.: National Center for Health Statistics, 2000), 304–305.

Map 8-15 Ibid., 365.

Map 8-16 Census Bureau, "Consolidated Federal Funds Report," 3.

Map 8-17 National Center for Education Statistics, *Digest of Education Statistics, 2000*, 176, http://nces.ed.gov/pubs2001/digest, accessed June 3, 2001.

Map 8-18 Ibid., 188.

Map 8-19 Ibid., 85.

Map 8-20 "Public High School Graduation Rates, 1997–1998," in *The World Almanac and Book of Facts 2001* (Mahwah, N.J.: World Almanac Books, 2001), 265.

Map 8-21 National Center for Education Statistics, *Digest of Education Statistics, 2000,* 220, http://nces.ed.gov/pubs2001/digest, accessed June 3, 2001.

Map 8-22 Eric C. Newburger and Andrea E. Curry, "Bureau of the Census: Current Population Reports, Series P20-536, Educational Attainment in the United States (Update)" (Washington, D.C.: Government Printing Office, March 2000), www.census.gov, accessed December 20, 2000.

Map 8-23 National Center for Education Statistics, *Digest of Education Statistics, 2000,* Table 422, http://nces.ed.gov/pubs2001/digest, accessed June 3, 2001.

Map 8-24 U.S. Census Bureau, *Statistical Abstract of the United States* (Washington, D.C.: Government Printing Office, 2000), 569.

Map 8-25 Ibid., 577.

Map 8-26 Ellen Meltzer, ed., *New Book of American Rankings,* rev. 3d ed. (New York: Facts on File, 1998), 212–213.

Map 8-27 Census Bureau, *Statistical Abstract 2000,* 214.

Map 8-28 Ibid., 202.

Map 8-29 Ibid., 204.

Map 8-30 Department of Justice, Bureau of Justice Statistics, "The Sourcebook of Criminal Justice Statistics, 1999," Table 6.27, www.albany.edu/sourcebook, accessed June 5, 2001.

Map 8-31 Ibid., Table 1.7.

Map 8-32 Borgna Brunner, ed., *The Time Almanac 2000* (Boston: Information Please, 1999), 877.

Map 8-33 Department of Justice, Bureau of Justice Statistics, "Prisoners Executed Under Civil Authority in the United States, by year, region, and jurisdiction, 1977–2000," http://www.ojp.usdoj.gov/bjs, accessed January 21, 2001.

Map 8-34 Environmental Protection Agency, "EPA Green Book: Currently Designated Nonattainment Areas for all Criteria Pollutants, Listed by State, County, then Pollutant, As of January 29, 2001," http://www.epa.gov/oar/oaqps/greenbk, accessed June 6, 2001.

Map 8-35 National Atmospheric Deposition Program, "1999 Annual Summary," 4, http://nadp.sws.uiuc.edu, accessed June 2, 2001.

Map 8-36 U.S. Department of Agriculture, Natural Resources Conservation Service, Resource Inventory Division, "Acreage and Percentage of Non-Federal Land Developed, table revised December 2000, http://www.nhq.nrcs.usda.gov/land, accessed June 2, 2001.

Map 8-37 Census Bureau, *Statistical Abstract, 2000,* 233.

Map 8-38 Department of Energy, Energy Information Administration, "State Energy Data Report, 1997," 9, http://www.eia.doe.gov/emeu/sedr, accessed May 16, 2001.

Map 8-39 Environmental Protection Agency, "Executive Summary: The National Biennial RCRA Hazardous Waste Report (Based on 1997 Data)" (EPA530-S-99-036, September 1999, http://www.epa.gov/epaoswer/hazwaste/data, accessed June 2, 2001.

Map 8-40 Census Bureau, *Statistical Abstract, 2000,* 240.

Map 8-41 Ibid., 240.

Map 8-42 U.S. Fish and Wildlife Service, "Threatened and Endangered Species System (TESS): Listings by State and Territory, Last Updated December 8, 2000," http://ecos.fws.gov/webpage_usa_lists.html, accessed June 2, 2001.

Map 8-43 Ibid.

Index

Note: Bold page number indicates map.